Saint Teresa of Jesus

SAINT TERESA OF JESUS

and other
Essays and Addresses

by

E. ALLISON PEERS

Gilmour Professor of Spanish
in the University of Liverpool

FABER AND FABER

24 Russell Square

London

First published in mcmliii
by Faber and Faber Limited
24 Russell Square, London, W.C.1.
Printed in Great Britain by
Western Printing Services Limited, Bristol

To

RAMÓN MENÉNDEZ PIDAL

in affectionate homage

Contents

Preface

In *Saint John of the Cross*, published in 1946, I collected a number of lectures and addresses given in English during my first twenty-five years at the University of Liverpool. This companion volume represents part of six years' subsequent activity. As most of my work during this latter period has been in Spanish mysticism, it will be found to be more homogeneous than its predecessor in subject, though the essays may well be more varied in type and style. Some of them, having been delivered as lectures, retain colloquialisms of form; others have been written solely for publication.

Of the three essays on Saint Teresa, the first was given as an address, on 15th October 1946, during the centenary celebrations of the Society of the Holy Child Jesus. Parts of the second have appeared in *Studies*, the *Church Times* and the Dominican review, *Cross and Crown*. The third, not previously published, is to be taken as a preliminary survey of a very wide field, in which I hope in due course to work in much greater detail.

The essay on 'The Historical Problem of Spanish Mysticism' is based upon an article published in the *Hispanic Review*; the two others have appeared in the *Bulletin of Hispanic Studies*; the pages on Lope de Vega were also published in the first volume (1950) of *Estudios dedicados a Menéndez Pidal* and those on Espinosa in *Homenaje al R. P. Félix Restrepo*.

To these pages on mystical literature I have added three lectures delivered during the Cervantes quatercentenary celebrations of 1947–8: the first was given in English, in the form here printed, at the University of Liverpool, the second, together with some material translated from the first, was delivered, in Spanish, at the University of Valencia; the third, under the title 'Aportación de los Hispanistas extranjeros al estudio de Cervantes', was read, in Spanish, before the international Asamblea Cervantina and published, in Spanish, in the Actas of that body (Madrid, 1948), and in the *Revista de Filología Española* (Madrid, 1948,) XXXII, 151–88. These are less specialized than the preceding essays and are to be taken as contributions to the quatercentenary offered by a lover of Cervantes rather than a Cervantist.

The last essay demands a word of explanation. For some time after the death of Dom Edmund Gurdon, in 1940, I had hoped to write a full-length biography of him, a project which was abandoned only because of the impossibility of obtaining necessary material. In the short sketch here given, however, I have been enabled to use letters kindly lent me by correspondents, and such was his devotion to Saint Teresa of Jesus and Saint John of the Cross that I think he would have liked to see it in a volume largely concerned with them.

E. A. P.

26th November 1951

PART I

Saint Teresa, Foundress
Saint Teresa in her Letters
Saint Teresa's Style: a Tentative Appraisal

Saint Teresa, Foundress[1]

[1]

The greatest woman in Spanish history, and one of the greatest in the annals of the world, Saint Teresa owes her pre-eminence less to her profundity than to her many-sidedness. First and foremost, she was a saint, and her sanctity, so attractive as well as so sublime, was recognized by her contemporaries during her own lifetime. She was also outstanding as a contemplative: the accounts of the Mystic Way which she has left us are based, not, like those of many other writers, upon reading, but upon her own experience. Yet, saint and mystic though she was, she never ceased to be human. There was nothing forbidding in her personality: if princes and prelates respected her, muleteers and peasants adored her. Nor was even her saintliness of the statuesque variety—the kind that makes one feel how hopeless it is to try to be good. Far from having had a flying start on perfection's ladder, she had begun, as her autobiography shows, right down at the bottom. And so, throughout her life and writings, she showed a particular concern for beginners: we can see her, in the *Way of Perfection* and the *Foundations*, musing over the problems they present—some of them perplexing, some merely interesting, some rather humorous. For Teresa was no 'frowning saint',[2] nor even a saint with a serene and

[1] A lecture given on Saint Teresa's Day (15 October), 1946, during the centenary celebrations of the Society of the Holy Child Jesus. The quotations from Saint Teresa's works in this and the next two essays will sometimes be found to differ slightly from the corresponding passages in my *Complete Works of Saint Teresa of Jesus* (London, Sheed and Ward, 1946, 3 vols.) and *Letters of Saint Teresa of Jesus* (London, Burns, Oates, 1951, 2 vols.), abbreviated *CWSTJ* and *LL* respectively. This is because the context has often had to be supplied in the translations, and in such cases I have made the versions afresh from the Spanish.
[2] *CWSTJ*, III, 351.

cryptic smile. Again and again she tells us how she enjoyed a good laugh. She would laugh at the devil when she had routed him; she would laugh when flatterers heaped praise on her; and she would laugh heartily to herself when people annoyed her,[1] 'for all the wrongs of this life seem to me so light that their weight cannot be felt'.[2]

Then, again, Saint Teresa had a transcendent personality. Had she been born to a throne, she would have been a greater queen even than Isabel the Catholic, with whom she had a good deal in common—which may have been one reason why she was thought so much of by Isabel's great-grandson, Philip II. And she was also a remarkable writer. Unlettered, untrained, inexperienced, she wrote nothing at all till she was nearly fifty; and thereafter she took up her pen only at odd moments and worked amid continual distractions; yet, notwithstanding those handicaps, she has won a place in Spanish literature which is quite her own. She is distinct and unique, as Cervantes, Lope de Vega and Calderón are distinct and unique. Even those for whom the wonderful spiritual experiences of which she wrote have no meaning are compelled to acknowledge that her writing is like the writing of no other Spaniard, and that Spanish prose would be very much the poorer had she confined her creative activities (as she sometimes felt would have been more seemly) to spinning.[3]

And even now I have not described every side of her. For, if the *Life*, the *Way of Perfection* and the *Interior Castle* present her as saint, as mystic, as a dominant personality and as a remarkable writer, that precious collection which she has left of over four hundred and fifty letters reveals a shrewd woman of affairs, with a great aptitude for business and a gift for handling both men and women with whom she was brought into contact and putting them exactly where she thought they would best fit. In this respect, again, unbelievers have had to pay her their tributes of admiration—and it is only fair to them to say that some of these have been very handsome ones.

Finally, we have Saint Teresa's fifth major work, the *Foundations* —and we have Saint Teresa the foundress, in whom all the other Teresas meet. Had she not been so practical, she would not have been so efficient a foundress. Had she been less of a personality she

[1] *Life*, XXXVI, XXXVII; *Relations*, II; *Conceptions*, II (*CWSTJ*, I, 251, 263, 315; II, 369).
[2] *Relations*, II (*CWSTJ*, I, 315).   [3] Cf. p. 81, below.

would have been a less successful foundress. Had she not been a born writer, the story of her foundations would have been known to comparatively few. Had she not been a saint, their influence would have been immensely less than it has been. And had she not been a contemplative—why, then, it is true, we should have had the *Letters* and the *Foundations*, but neither the *Way of Perfection* nor the *Interior Castle*, nor even the finest pages of the *Life*. And even in the *Letters* and the *Foundations* there are many passages which would never have been written. The more one reads about Saint Teresa, the more one realizes how perfectly, in her life, as in her writings, contemplation blended with action. She is a living refutation—and I say 'living' because, as Fray Luis de León wrote, after her death, she *does* live, in her daughters and in her books— of those mistaken, though well-meaning persons who picture actives as crawling about busily on the earth, like animated insects, and contemplatives as floating aloft, vaguely and complacently, in the clouds. I often wish there were some word in the English language which we could substitute for the word 'mysticism'; for, as long as it continues to be used, the non-instructed reader will associate it with mistiness; and there was never less mistiness anywhere than in those most practical, determined and clear-cut persons, the mystics, among whom none has those three qualities in more generous measure than Saint Teresa.

[II]

Altogether Saint Teresa made seventeen foundations for women within the space of exactly twenty years (1562–82), during just over four of which (1576–80) she was prevented from making any by strife within her Order. All these seventeen were houses for women. If we add to them the houses for men which were founded through her influence, and then read the history of the Discalced Reform during the ten or fifteen years immediately following her death, we begin to gain some idea of the extent of her achievement. And if we try to imagine the conditions under which most of her foundations were made—we who are accustomed to easy and rapid travel, to a sufficiency of food and to comfortable living—we shall realize that a foundress in the sixteenth century needed to possess the heroic virtues on a very large scale.

And Saint Teresa had to cope with other trials than sixteenth-century roads and inns—to which we shall shortly return—and those disconcerting seasonal alternations between semi-tropical heat and semi-Arctic cold which comprise Spanish weather. She had to face the fiercest, most determined, and sometimes most unreasoning opposition on the part of extremely important and influential people. Nor must we fall into the error of supposing all the opposition to have been perverse and ill-intentioned. Today, in a Spain of some 28,000,000 people, there are about 50,000 religious, and that number has not greatly varied for the last hundred years.[1] But at the end of the sixteenth century the total population of the country hardly exceeded 8,000,000,[2] and of monks alone there were 400,000: a census taken in 1570 showed that one-quarter of the entire population was clerical.[3] Small wonder if, in some of Spain's numerous cathedral cities, which were not particularly wealthy, attempts were made to set a limit on the number of new foundations, especially if they had no endowments or were unlikely to be able to subsist on those which they had. Beneath Saint Teresa's narrative of the foundation of her first convent, Saint Joseph's, Ávila—a narrative which so confidently and cheerfully attributes all the opposition with which she met to the devil—we can sometimes sense the genuine concern of people who in principle had the keenest sympathy with her projects, lest, in her zeal for making foundations 'in poverty', she might be imposing fresh burdens upon charitably disposed citizens who were already giving more to religious houses than they could well afford.

Saint Teresa, however, believed that there was a great future for houses founded without endowments—that is to say, founded in the spirit of poverty which had characterized the primitive Carmelite Rule. She might not be able to dig, but, as Cardinal Hinsley once said about a good cause for which he was pleading, to beg she was *not* ashamed. She had long wished, she tells us, 'that it were possible for a person in my state of life to go about begging for the love of God, without having . . . any possessions'.[4] Nobody, in those early days, agreed with her—not even her own confessor: there were so many penniless convents, they told her, in which spiritual life was at a low ebb. She knew the answer, however, to that. Certainly there were: she had seen such houses herself.

[1] Cf. my *Spain, the Church and the Orders* (London, 1939), p. 206.

[2] Cf. R. Trevor Davies, *The Golden Century of Spain* (London, 1937), p. 274.

[3] J. P. de Oliveira Martins, *A History of Iberian Civilization*, trans. A. F. G. Bell (Oxford, 1930), p. 241.

[4] *Life*, XXXV (*CWSTJ*, I, 242).

But 'their distraction was not due to their poverty: it was their poverty which resulted from their not being recollected. Distraction does not make people richer and God never fails those who serve Him.'[1] And then she carried the war into the enemy's own camp. She had seen some of those well-to-do houses, she said (indeed she had: had she not lived in one for a quarter of a century?). And she could assure her critics that 'the possession of revenue by a convent entailed a great many inconveniences: it was a cause of unrest and even distraction'.[2] Her opponents, of course, would not allow the matter to remain there:

'They put so many contrary arguments to me that I did not know what to do. . . . Sometimes they even convinced me; but, when I fell to prayer again and looked at Christ hanging poor and naked upon the Cross, I felt I could not bear to be rich. So I besought Him with tears to bring it to pass that I might become as poor as He'.[3]

That was the spirit in which the first of her foundations was made. She would plant; she would water (I use the figure of speech which she loved best); and she would trust God to give the increase. And give it He did. After nearly two years of argument and dissension, of intermittent lawsuits, of permissions granted and permissions revoked, of opposition from within the Order, from theologians, from the municipality, from the Bishop and the cathedral chapter, Saint Joseph's, Ávila was founded—a community of four nuns which was never to grow beyond a maximum of thirteen; and, says Saint Teresa, when the bell was hung, the statues of our Lady and Saint Joseph installed and the Blessed Sacrament reserved, 'it was like being in Heaven'.[4]

For five years she remained in that haven of holy poverty—years which, as she wrote long afterwards, 'were the most restful of my life'.[5] At Saint Joseph's, Ávila, there was none of the incessant conflict between the semi-worldly atmosphere of the fashionable Convent of the Incarnation and that other world which was within her and in which she made her home. 'Any unrest and any strife can be borne', she once wrote, 'if we find peace where we live.'[6] Undistracted as she now was, she could make much greater progress than before in mental prayer—and how remarkable was that

---

[1] *Life*, XXXV (*CWSTJ*, I, 242).   [2] Ibid., 243.   [3] Ibid.
[4] *Life*, XXXVI (*CWSTJ*, I, 250).   [5] *Foundations*, I (*CWSTJ*, III, 1).
[6] *Interior Castle*, IV, i (*CWSTJ*, II, 235).

progress we can estimate by comparing her first book, the *Life*, with the *Interior Castle*, written fifteen years later. She had time to write—and she completed her *Life* and wrote the whole of the *Way of Perfection*. And she had time to think; which brings us to the rest of the foundations, for one of the things she thought about most was the spiritual progress of Christ's children—and this she thought about until, as she tells us, it became 'the aim of all her desires'.[1] Soon she was projecting the establishment of more of these small foundations, where conditions were so favourable for spiritual growth. Profiting by the fortunate chance of a visit to Spain by the General of her Order, she obtained from him formal permission to found more houses, not only for women, but for men, together with safeguards against possible opposition.

'He was glad when he saw our way of life; for it gave him a picture, however imperfect, of our Order as it had been in its early days; and he was able to observe how we were keeping the Primitive Rule in all its strictness. . . . And being willing, as he was, that we should continue what we had begun, he gave me complete patents for the foundation of more houses, and also added censures, so that no Provincial should be able to stop me. . . . [Later, from] Valencia, . . . he sent me a licence for the foundation of two priories, as might have been expected of one who desired the strictest observance of the Rule in the Order. Lest there should be opposition, he sent the licence to the then Provincial, and also to his predecessor, whom it was extremely difficult to convince.'[2]

So, in 1567, there begins that long list of achievements, each attained only after the surmounting of many obstacles of the most diverse kinds. Teresa started her work near home—at Medina del Campo, some fifty miles from Ávila—and here, as there, she met with opposition, and on the same score. She and her companions had to go into their house at dead of night and spend the few hours before dawn in making the improvised chapel fit for the celebration of Mass on that same morning. And, when morning came, she discovered that the house was in such a tumble-down state as to be quite unfit for them to live in. So for a full two months they had to stay elsewhere until it could be repaired. This was an ill wind, however, which blew an amazing amount of good, for it was during those weeks of waiting that she made the acquaintance of her fellow-reformer, the 'little friar', Saint John of the Cross.

[1] *Life*, XL (*CWSTJ*, I, 298).   [2] *Foundations*, II (*CWSTJ*, III, 5–6, 7).

After these troubles came a period of calm, for the third foundation, at Malagón, near Ciudad Real, was sponsored by a wealthy patroness who for their first week offered the nuns the hospitality of her castle, and for the foundation ceremonies organized a grand procession. The fourth convent, at Valladolid, was also opened in the sunshine of popular favour, but here, as at Medina, there were practical difficulties: the house was a large one, near the river, and had an excellent garden, but it was so damp that all the nuns fell ill and they had to move.

Encouraged by the success which was beginning to attend her Reform, Saint Teresa made her next foundation in Spain's ecclesiastical capital, Toledo. Here she encountered, not opposition, but a singular lack of helpfulness: they had a house, but no furniture, no food and no fuel—'not so much', she records, 'as a piece of brushwood to broil a sardine on'.[1] However, as soon as it became known that they were there, so many gifts poured in upon them that they grew quite depressed, thinking that they must have said goodbye to holy poverty. They encountered the same type of difficulty at Salamanca. This was a university city, and their house had previously been occupied by students, who, as Teresa euphemistically put it, 'were not very careful people'. Besides being in bad condition, it was large, damp, and cold: Salamanca stands 2,600 feet above sea level; they were sleeping on straw, with a single blanket to cover them; and the month was November. A very different kind of trouble had met them, eighteen months previously, at Pastrana. Here, as at Malagón, they had a patroness, but she proved to be an extremely exacting and dictatorial one, and the vehemence of her temperamental whims was too much for even the tactfulness of Saint Teresa. In the end she had to do what she had never done either from ill-health or from privations—break up the community and transfer the nuns to another.

Before her career entered upon a new phase with the extension of the Reform to Andalusia, Teresa made two more foundations in the north—at Alba de Tormes (where, eleven years later, she was to die) and at Segovia. But these two foundations were separated from each other by a triennium during which she served as Prioress at her original Avilan convent of the Incarnation. After living for nine years in the invigorating atmosphere of the Reform she must have found it a sharper trial than any she had suffered as a foundress to have to return to a house where the nuns were addressed

[1] *Op. cit.*, XV (*CWSTJ*, III, 74).

collectively as 'ladies' and individually as 'madam', and allowed to leave the convent, to receive visitors, to accept presents and to give parties. What would have made it worse was that the convent had fallen upon evil days, and the 'ladies' had become so discontented that they were talking of asking to be freed from their vows. Only when she arrived there and found that some of them were prepared to keep her out by physical force did she realize what she had come to. Personally, I have never admired her more than when she stood before the High Altar at the Incarnation facing the hundred or so well-born malcontents whom she was to rule. It would be a good exercise in imagination to re-create her position and then to read the address which she made to the nuns at her first Chapter.[1] A masterpiece of holy tact, you will say at once; yes, but consider what humility, what courage, what self-mastery went to the making of it too! 'My ladies', she said, addressing them with the deference to which they were accustomed:

'Have no misgivings as to how I shall govern you; for, though I have thus far lived among and governed nuns who are Discalced, I know well, through the Lord's goodness, the way to govern those who are not. My desire is that we should all serve the Lord in quietness and do the little which our Rule and Constitutions command us for the love of that Lord to Whom we owe so much. I know well how very weak we are; but, if we cannot attain in deed, let us do so in desire. For the Lord is compassionate and will see to it that gradually our deeds become commensurate with our desires and intentions.'

Not until she had restored discipline to the house, and, with the help of Saint John of the Cross, who had come as its confessor, had instilled into it some of the spirit of the Reform, was she able to resume her life of wandering, and only after visiting a number of her Castilian foundations did she travel south. Castilians and Andalusians are proverbially antipathetic to each other and doubtless she counted herself fortunate in having to remain in Andalusia for no more than sixteen months. Her experiences there were not pleasant. After founding a convent at Beas de Segura, a picturesquely situated spot associated with two other great Carmelites, Saint John of the Cross and the Venerable Anne of Jesus, she made a long journey to Seville, where the physical trials which she had

[1] Reproduced in my *Mother of Carmel* (London, 1945), pp. 88–9.

to suffer on her travels reached their height. The damp, hot summers of Andalusia can be terribly oppressive; and, when the sun beat upon the covered carriages in which the nuns travelled, going into them, records Teresa, was 'like entering Purgatory'.[1] In the midst of these experiences the Mother Foundress developed a high fever, which was not improved by spending a night in the fields, as an alternative to a verminous inn, or by having to wait anxiously for some hours in the gathering darkness on the bank of a broad river because the ferryboat which was bringing her carriage across had lost its rope, and was proceeding downstream, carriage and all, with every indication that it would go on till it reached the sea.

And after all this, when Seville was reached and they were four hundred miles from home, the nuns found themselves faced with the same opposition as years before at Ávila and Medina. There was a house for them there, but the Archbishop refused to allow them to enter it. Holy tact was again called for, accompanied by a considerable measure of holy persistence. Weeks passed before the Archbishop was won over, and even then the nuns had a hard fight to get enough food. But in the end holy persistence overcame everything; and it is perhaps typical of the way in which Teresa's struggles always ended that for the foundation ceremonies at Seville there was not only a procession through the streets, but there were decorations, minstrels, and, at the end of the day, fireworks!

'So you see, daughters, these poor Discalced nuns were honoured by everybody, though a little earlier it had seemed as if, for all the water in the river, there would not be enough for them. The number of people who came was astounding.'[2]

These Sevilian experiences were followed by the four years' interval already alluded to; the persecution of the Reform by the unreformed friars who feared they might be incorporated in it; the abduction and imprisonment of Saint John of the Cross; and other events of this type which were to end with the partition of the Order. During these years Saint Teresa was ordered to remain in Castile and only narrowly escaped a second term as Prioress of the Incarnation. Turning her necessities into opportunities, however, she took up her pen again, and wrote a large part of the *Founda-*

---

[1] *Foundations*, XXIV (*CWSTJ*, III, 123).
[2] *Op. cit.*, XXV (*CWSTJ*, III, 133).

tions, together with the whole of her sublimest work, the *Interior Castle.*

The convent at Seville had been her eleventh foundation: in January 1576, while she was still there, a twelfth, at Caravaca, in the remote south-east, was founded in her absence. For the thirteenth, after visiting a number of her earlier foundations, she travelled southward again to Villanueva de la Jara, near the borders of La Mancha. Here, once more, the difficulties which she encountered were quite fresh ones. The nuns who were to live in the convent were not her own, as they had been everywhere else. They were a group of women who for some years had been an independent community and were now seeking incorporation with the Discalced Carmelites. The obstacles to their admission were these. First, it would be hard for independent recluses to accustom themselves to so new and so strict a Rule. Secondly, there was no neighbouring Discalced Carmelite house from which they could be discreetly guided. Thirdly, it was unlikely, in so small a place, that the population would be able to support them. The last obstacle was the first to be overcome, by an offer from the municipality at Villanueva to make itself responsible for their maintenance. The others crumbled before the good reports which Saint Teresa received of the postulants—and before her own faith. And when she arrived there, she realized that both the reports and the faith had been justified. These women were her true spiritual daughters, for 'however many difficulties and trials they might meet, with the Lord's help they would bear them all': 'the more I had to do with them, the more pleased I was I had come'.[1]

In March 1580, after spending a month with these new daughters—a month, we may be sure, that they would never forget—Saint Teresa left southern Spain for the last time. She was now sixty-five; and her health, never robust, was fast deteriorating. Of her four remaining foundations, one, at Granada, was made in her absence; the other three—Palencia, Soria and Burgos—came to birth amid constant struggles with illness and depression, as well as with the utmost hardships of travel. On one journey, she had to cope with the 'terrible heat' of a Castilian August: on another, with the bitter cold of a Castilian January. Anyone who, even to-day, has had experience of third-class roads in Spain will know how to interpret the simple statement that a certain 'road was very bad for carriages'. Others will gain some idea of what Spanish

[1] *Op. cit.,* XXVIII (*CWSTJ,* III, 164–5).

roads could be like from Saint Teresa's own descriptions. In one place, on the way from Soria to Ávila, 'the road was so bad that we often had to alight and the carriage went along steep precipices till it almost hung in the air . . .'.

'If we took guides, they would direct us as far as they knew the road to be good, and then, before we came to a bad part, they would leave us and say they now had some business to do elsewhere. Before reaching our inn, as we were not at all sure of the country, we had to endure a great deal of sun and often to risk the overturning of the carriage.'[1]

In another place, near Burgos, on the journey from Palencia, the roads were often flooded, and the men who accompanied the nuns 'had to go on ahead to find the best paths, and help to drag the carriages out of the marshes. . . . It was quite usual for the carriages to sink into the mud and the animals would then have to be taken out of one of them to drag out another.' And then they came to a ford over the river, their only means of crossing it, which was flooded.

'We could not find any way of going on, for there was water everywhere, and on either side it was very deep. . . . If the carriages heeled slightly, all would be lost. . . . When I saw that we were entering a world of water, with no sign of a path or a boat, even I was not without fear.'[2]

One hardly less vivid account of this journey to Burgos has been left us by the constant companion of Saint Teresa's last years, Ana de San Bartolomé:

'Once, when we going along a river bank, the mud was so thick that the carriages stuck in it and we had to get down. After escaping from this danger we were climbing a hill when we espied before our eyes another and a worse one. For the holy Mother saw the carriage in which her nuns were travelling about to overturn, and the hill we were climbing was so steep that even a large number of people could not have saved them by preventing the carriage from falling. But at the same moment one of the youths whom we had with us saw it and seized the wheel and saved the carriage from overturning.'[3]

---

[1] *Op. cit.*, XXX (*CWSTJ*, III, 183). [2] *Op. cit.*, XXXI (*CWSTJ*, III, 190).
[3] *CWSTJ*, Appendix, III, 354.

At another point 'the rivers were so swollen that the water had risen nearly two feet above the bridges'.

'The innkeeper . . . offered . . . to pilot us through the water; for, with the river in such a state and the bridges submerged, it was impossible to see the road. . . . The bridges were wooden ones, and so narrow that the carriage-wheels could hardly get on to them: if they had swerved only slightly, we should have fallen into the river.'[1]

Human nature, however, soon reacted cheerfully. The Father Provincial, who accompanied the party, was 'of such a placid temperament that nothing seemed to upset him'.[2] The Mother Foundress, we may be sure, gave no hint of her apprehensions. She 'cried out', records Ana, 'as gaily as could be': 'Come, now, my daughters! What better end would you have than to become martyrs here for love of Our Lord?" And then she said that she would go on first, and, if she were drowned, they must not proceed any farther, but return to the inn.'[3]

The nuns found her gay courage infectious. They were 'all quite happy', she reports; and, 'once the danger passed, they enjoyed talking about it. It is a great thing to suffer under obedience.'[4]

[III]

This brief outline of the history of Saint Teresa's foundations should convey some general idea of the nature of the manifold and varied difficulties which beset her. Let us now look at the journeys in greater detail.[5]

Perhaps the most unpleasant feature of them, especially to a person as fastidious about cleanliness as we know Saint Teresa to have been, was the indescribable state of the worst of the inns at which they could not always avoid staying. The bedrooms were often windowless, malodorous and verminous, while the beds, 'full of ups and downs', were as hard as if they had been stuffed with stones—and these, we must remark, were the criticisms of women quite content to sleep on a bed of straw spread on a bare

[1] *CWSTJ*, Appendix, III, 354. [2] *Foundations*, XXXI (*CWSTJ*, III, 190).
[3] *CWSTJ*, III, 354-5. [4] *Foundations*, XXXI (*CWSTJ*, III, 191).
[5] As many of the descriptions which follow are composite, the source of each detail in them is not quoted. Some of them will be found in *CWSTJ*, III, 338-68; most of the remainder in P. Silverio, *Obras de Santa Teresa de Jesús* (Burgos, 1915-24), II, 232-41, 291-369; V, vii-xxiv; VI, 147-50, 198-200, 234-7, 284-6.

stone floor. In a typical inn of the worst type, the Mother, when running a high temperature, was given a room in which (writes the Seville Prioress, María de San José) 'I think there had been pigs. The ceiling was so low that we could hardly stand upright, the sun came in on all sides and . . . the place was full of cobwebs and infested with vermin.'[1] That was in the south, but the centre and north had their trials too. The Mother 'would go for some days through rain and snow, without finding a village for leagues on end or having anything to keep off the wet, and at nightfall she would come to some inn where there was no fire, and no means of making one, and nothing to eat, and the sky was visible through the roof of her room, and the rain would come through into the room, and sometimes even their clothes would suffer'.[2]

On the famous journey to Burgos, when the innkeeper piloted the company through the water, the reason they had decided not to stay at the inn until the water subsided was apparently that the said innkeeper 'could not even make our holy Mother a bed'. Not that she always had a bed: on one occasion she had to sleep in a hermitage, 'where, between saying our prayers and lying down on the cold, hard flags of the church, we spent the night very happily, though with little comfort'. Perhaps they preferred such lodgings to inns where there was not only dirt but noise: 'the shouts and oaths of the people in the inn and the hubbub of the tambourines and dancing', to say nothing of violent quarrels often ending in free fights and lasting till nearly morning.[3] 'If we had not seen them', writes María de San José of an occasion when they were resting in their carriages near an inn, 'we could not have believed there were such dreadful people in Christendom.'

'Our ears could not endure the oaths and curses and the abominable things they were saying; and, when they had finished their meal, they became more violent still. . . . Finally, they drew their swords and began fighting.'

It may be added that Saint Teresa took this much less tragically than her companions, who, putting their heads inside the Mother's carriage, with the idea of getting in and taking refuge with her, found that 'although she had been very much upset when they

---

[1] P. Silverio, *op. cit.*, V, xiv. [2] *CWSTJ*, III, 346.
[3] P. Silverio, *op. cit.*, VI, 237, 239.

had begun blaspheming . . . by this time she was laughing heartily, which was a great consolation to us.'[1]

Another problem was food. They would take some with them when they left a convent—if the convent had any[2]—but at best, never knowing how long their journey would last, they were unable to take much, and not infrequently they eked it out so slowly that it went bad. 'There were many days', we read of the long journey to Seville, 'when we had nothing to eat but beans, bread and cherries, or things of that kind, and if ever we found our Mother an egg, that was a great thing.'[3] Salt fish was often to be had—María de San José refers feelingly to 'very salt sardines'[4]—but in the south the heat and the lack of water made this a last resort. They might start with 'a large wineskin full of water', but, once emptied, it was hard to replenish: water, in the small southern villages, was often more expensive than wine. The heat could be overpowering, and, as many of their routes led them across vast treeless plains, shade to rest in was eagerly sought, regardless of any minor inconvenience.

'We went under a bridge to have our siesta, so that we could get a little shade. There were some pigs there, but we drove them away and took their places; and so fierce was the sun that we thought ourselves very lucky to have it.'[5]

Saint Teresa's mode of transport depended, not so much upon what was fitting, as upon what was available. For long journeys she generally travelled in a mule-drawn vehicle—at best, in a sumptuous carriage such as that provided for her by the Princess of Éboli when she left Pastrana or in a conveyance providing good bourgeois comfort in which her brother Lorenzo took her from Seville to Toledo; at worst, in a covered cart. She preferred the carriage ('It was a much better idea than coming in covered carts')[6], though it sometimes led to rumours that she was 'a frivolous woman, who took fine ladies and gallants about with her when she travelled', and on occasion led to her being openly abused.[7] But she was a good rider and often travelled on muleback.

---

[1] *Op. cit.*, VI, 240.

[2] Readers of Saint Teresa will recall a revealing remark in the *Constitutions* (*CWSTJ*, III, 226–7): 'When there is anything to eat, dinner shall be taken at half-past eleven.'

[3] P. Silverio, *op. cit.*, VI, 238.   [4] *Op. cit.*, VI, 240.   [5] *Op. cit.*, VI, 234–5.

[6] *LL* 95.   [7] *LL* 95 (p. 242, n. 5); P. Silverio, *op. cit.*, V, viii, n. 1.

Gracián, who was less skilled in this art and so often fell off his mount that Teresa thought he would have to be tied on,[1] once remarked that she was 'as safe on a mule as in a carriage', and recalled how, when her beast once showed signs of bolting, she checked it 'without going to any womanly extremes'.[2]

None the less, even at best this travelling must have been a tiring business and not the least trying part would have been the uncertainty as to what they would find at their journey's end. There might be a house for a new foundation, or there might not. If there were, it might be in a tumble-down condition, as at Medina, or in an unhealthy situation, as at Valladolid, or large, cold and wholly unfurnished, as at Salamanca. Or workmen might still be busy there, in which case, as at Malagón in 1579, after a 'very trying' journey which made her feel 'as if there were not a bone in her body that was not aching', she would be 'the first each morning to take the brush and dustpan' and stay 'with the workmen every day from dawn to midnight'.[3] Sometimes, too, in places where nothing of the sort had ever been seen before, her little caravan was looked askance at, and even jeered at and insulted. But as she herself became better known, and the fame of her Reform travelled ahead of her, there were occasions when the kindly reception she received made up for all the trials of the way. Crowds would gather, even in the villages, to cheer her; mothers would bring their children to receive her blessing; prominent citizens would offer embarrassing hospitality. Once, so her chaplain Julián de Ávila reports, a horseback procession from the village of Beas, where she was particularly well known, came out to meet her, followed by the inhabitants in a body.[4] And there was the never-to-be-forgotten triumphal progress from La Roda to Villanueva de la Jara, the friars at La Roda coming out a long way to meet the nuns and infecting with their enthusiasm all who saw them:

'The holy Mother said that the sight had made her very happy, for it had reminded her of the desert saints of our Order. They all knelt down when they arrived and asked for her blessing, and then led her in procession to the church. A great many people came to see her while she was there, as the news of her arrival had spread throughout the surrounding villages.

'Thence we set out to Villanueva de la Jara, and a good while

---

[1] *LL* 81. [2] P. Silverio, *op. cit.*, V, xii.
[3] *CWSTJ*, III, 347, 348. [4] *Op. cit.*, III, xv.

before we arrived there a great many children came out very devoutly to meet the holy Mother. When they met her carriage, they knelt down and then went on in front of her, bareheaded, until they reached the church.'[1]

Opposed though she always was to meaningless ceremony and display, this simple and natural ebullience of popular feeling towards her Reform could not have failed to touch her deeply. And no doubt that was one of the things which her nuns, being human, most looked forward to. Another would have been the intimacy with the Mother which these journeys gave them, especially at recreation-time, when she would lay herself out, not only to edify them, but to distract them. After the discomforts of the day:

'Sometimes she would speak of the weightiest subjects; at other times she would say things for our entertainment; sometimes, again, she would make up verses, and very good ones, for at this she was most skilful. . . . Given though she was, therefore, to prayer, our spiritual intercourse with her was none the less friendly and beneficial both to the soul and to the body.'[2]

Todo se pasaba riendo, says María de San José of the verse-making sessions. 'We were laughing all the time.'[3]

These last experiences are among the lighter and brighter aspects of Saint Teresa's journeyings; and it is true to say that, as one reads of them, whether in her own writings or in those of her contemporaries, one gains a persistent impression of the deep spiritual joy which lay beneath all her experiences, pleasant or not, as well as of the mirth and the gaiety which continually found their way to the bubbling surface. The Mother who had such a horror of 'frowning saints' was not likely to indulge in frowning herself or to allow it in her daughters. Then there would be enjoyment coming from frequent contacts with new places, and, however indirectly, with new people; most of the nuns were young enough to like that. And there would be the beauties of the landscape, to see which they would be permitted from time to time to alight from their carriages, or, at any rate, to draw aside the canvas. Castile, stern and barren though it is, has a beauty quite its own, enhanced by the glory of the Castilian sun and the crystal-clear air: there can be few lovelier sights than the finest of Castilian mountain-landscapes in the early morning. And on those southern

[1] *Op. cit.*, III, 349–50. [2] *Op. cit.*, III, xii. [3] P. Silverio *op. cit.*, VI, 238.

journeys, too, there were the luxuriance of the Andalusian meadows and the lovely vistas of the Sierra Morena. There was one point in the journey from Beas to Seville where the party halted for the siesta on the banks of a little stream, in the shade of a wood, and Teresa, finding the beauty too much for her powers of conversation, went away by herself to mount the ladder that leads from Nature to God. 'We could hardly drag our holy Mother away from that piece of woodland,' reports one of the company, 'for all the various flowers and the thousands of singing-birds seemed to be losing themselves in giving praise to God.'[1]

Let us now examine some of the abundant contemporary material at our disposal and attempt to reconstruct from it an account of a typical day.

Early one morning, from some rugged city of barren Old Castile, would emerge a little procession of mule-drawn carriages, completely covered in with canvas: in one or more of these would be the Mother Foundress and the nuns whom she was taking to make the foundation: in the remainder, two or three friars who accompanied the party, and perhaps some laymen. Where friars and nuns shared a carriage, a canvas partition separated them, so that the nuns might observe their enclosure.

Their day, as nearly as conditions permitted, followed the lines of a day in the convent. Outside, the drivers would be calling to each other, singing snatches of songs, exchanging pleasantries with passers-by, and either cursing their mules or encouraging them to go faster. But in the dark, jolting interior there would be silence, broken only by the ticking of the clock which the Mother Foundress always took with her. As early as possible each day, either before they left or at one of the first towns on the route, they all heard Mass and received Communion: 'However hurried they were', says one record, 'this was never omitted.' Then there would be an awkward but orderly clambering into the high carriages; and the drivers would climb into their seats, crack their whips and recommence their songs. But before long, from inside the nuns' carriage, would come the faint tinkle of a little bell. They knew what that meant: the ladies were saying their Office. So, crossing themselves mechanically, they would drive on in silence.

Then, after what must have seemed an immense time, the muffled tinkle of the bell would be heard again, and once more

---

[1] *Libro de recreaciones* (Burgos, 1913), IX, 99; P. Silverio, *op. cit.*, VI, 237.

they would break into song. The morning wore on: and, when the sun was high, the little tinkle would sound for the midday period of self-examination. But this period the men minded less, for, when next they heard the bell, they would look for a convenient wood, or some other shady spot, where they could halt for the siesta. Here they would collect in a group, enjoy an improvised meal, take out their wineskins, and then in loud voices begin to cap each other's interminable tales. But suddenly they would stop; for out of the nuns' carriage came the Mother—sometimes just to exchange a few words with them about the roads, the weather or the possible difficulties ahead; occasionally to reprove them gently for using unseemly language; but more often to thank them in her charming way for keeping such perfect silence during a long period of prayer; and not infrequently to reward them for doing so by giving them some additional food from her meagre store. 'It was extraordinary', remarks one of her companions on those journeys, 'to see how particular the Mother was about the provision of necessaries for those who accompanied her: she . . . might have been going about on mules all her life.'

Once on their way again, the nuns said Vespers and enjoyed an hour's spiritual reading—though how they could read anything in a springless canvas-covered vehicle, travelling over roads often little better than tracks, it is hard to imagine. Before the time for Compline arrived they had covered the second long stretch of the day's journey. By this time, however, it was six o'clock, and the travellers' day was nearing its end. So, as soon as they espied the next village or town, one of the men went on to find accommodation. It was during such an interval as this that the nuns would take their period of recreation which has already been described.

Recreation over, the little caravan would find itself clattering through the cobbled streets of the town—eyed curiously, and perhaps followed expectantly, by a proportion of the youthful population. Whoever had gone on to secure the rooms would come back to meet them and guide them to the inn where they were to pass the night. We have already seen what the worst of the inns were like. At their best, they would be reasonably spacious and perhaps tolerably comfortable, with large rooms each shared by two or three of the party. Once they were all in their rooms, the nun whose turn it was to be portress would shut the door and remain near it—or if, as sometimes happened in the more primitive hostelries, there were no door, they would improvise one with frieze

32

blankets from the carriages and post a friar or a layman to keep guard outside.

On the stroke of eight, the little bell would be heard again, and then, apart from any necessary question or answer, both friars and nuns would refrain from conversation until after Prime on the next day. But, despite the earliness of their start and the fatigue of the journey, their day was not yet ended. A further hour devoted to prayer or spiritual reading would be followed by the ringing of the bell for Matins, after which came a quarter of an hour's self-examination, and the reading, by a nun appointed for the purpose, of the passage of Scripture which would form the subject of the next day's meditation. At eleven o'clock the bell rang for the last time and the nuns were free to go to bed. At five o'clock in summer, however, and at six o'clock in winter, they were up again, speculating on the hardships, or the enjoyment, which awaited them on the next stretch of the road.

[IV]

As one reads the records of these journeys, two impressions in particular dominate one's mind—the efficiency and care with which every part of every day was organized and the dominating personality of the Mother Foundress. And since it was she who was solely responsible for the organization, the two fuse into one. But no lasting results would have been achieved by mere efficiency or by the mere dominance of a personality. The greatness of Saint Teresa as a foundress derives from the fact that she was in the truest sense, and before all else, a Mother. Perhaps, to attain the fullest realization of that, one must read, and try to imagine the background of, the *Way of Perfection*, the book expressly written for her own daughters, and the *Letters*, so many of which were addressed to them. The woman freely alluded to as a saint in her lifetime and canonized only forty years after her death; the woman who pleaded with the King, who braved the wrath of the Archbishop of Seville, who talked respectfully but firmly to the General of her Order; the woman who said that, if need were, she would go and pay the dreaded Inquisition a visit of her own accord: that woman had a Mother's love of her children, a Mother's yearning to increase their numbers; a Mother's outspoken frankness with the most wayward; a Mother's tender solicitude for the youngest and weakest; a Mother's triumphant pride in the strongest and best. And it is for that reason that, in the words of the present-day General of her Order, 'her name is not only graven upon the enduring marble of history but taken on the lips of generation after generation with reverence and love'.[1]

[1] P. Silverio, cit. *CWSTJ*, I, xxxvii.

Saint Teresa in her Letters

[1]

Saint Teresa must undoubtedly have been one of the most prolific letter-writers of the sixteenth century. Nobody can estimate,
or even guess, how many letters she wrote. Those extant number,
as nearly as can be computed, four hundred and fifty-eight. But
allusions to be found in them, together with evidence of other kinds,
make it clear that they form only a small fraction of the whole. She
continually refers to the toll which letter-writing takes of her time
and energy; and it is amazing that a busy foundress could have
written so much, in view of the absorbing claims of her spiritual
life, the cares of a dozen convents, the more fundamental preoccu-
pations concerning the progress of the Reform and routine duties
of the most varied kinds which she was never without.

In assessing the magnitude of what must be called one of her
minor achievements, we must not forget that, in her day, the writing and sending of letters was a procedure more cumbrous and
more complicated than it is now easy to imagine. The large sheet
of paper, covered with the energetic, forceful script so familiar
to Teresans, was folded and refolded, sometimes after the inser-
tion of numerous enclosures, secured with a strip of paper (for
there were no envelopes) and sealed with wax. The packet was
then addressed, and the amount of porterage—or, as we should
say, postage—agreed upon with the letter-carrier written on the
cover: only a part of this was normally paid by the sender, the
rest being receivable on the letter's delivery.[1] Sometimes, when
the letter-carrier was known to be trustworthy, and the sender

---

[1] Out of this custom, when the national postal service was instituted in Spain,
grew that of paying the postman a small sum for every inland letter he delivered,
a custom even now not entirely dead.

wished to pay the whole of the charges, the balance would be enclosed in the packet, but this was exceptional.[1]

Haggling over porterage, however, was only one of the assiduous letter-writer's troubles. It was not everywhere that official couriers, who travelled on muleback, by relays, were available. Occasionally, no doubt, Saint Teresa, and others like her, had strokes of fortune. At one time, for instance, when she was living at Toledo, she became friendly with the chief courier there, who was a relative of one of her nuns, and promised her to 'perform miracles': provided packets were securely wrapped and addressed to him personally, he said, he would answer for it that none of their contents would be lost. That was wonderful: the only problem, wrote Teresa to a correspondent, was the degree of deference that had to be infused into the address:

'You must find out at your end if you have to put "Magnificent" on your letters, or how else to address the chief courier. He is in an extremely high position.'[2]

But such plain sailing was rare. Often special messengers had to be found, and their reliability assessed before they were engaged; or possibly some entirely trustworthy messenger would arrive unexpectedly with mail, and, if he could wait for a few hours before returning whence he came, there would be a hurried writing of letters intended for that destination. Reliability was all the more important when, as during the persecution of Saint Teresa's Reform, letters might easily be intercepted by the ill-intentioned; and all kinds of devices had to be adopted, such as the use of pseudonyms and the enclosing of letters to 'dangerous' persons in those to others who might be regarded as 'safe'. Further complications occurred when, as often happened, an addressee's whereabouts was unknown and any letter to him had to be enclosed in someone else's and inscribed with appropriate instructions. Many of the closing paragraphs of Saint Teresa's letters reflect anxieties unknown in an age when correspondence is dropped into postboxes and dismissed from the mind until replies arrive two or three days later.

To have written so many letters under such unfavourable condi-

[1] *LL* 118 (301). Throughout this essay the bracketed figures immediately following references beginning with *LL* are to the pages of the edition mentioned on p. 15, above.
[2] *LL* 107 (271).

tions would itself be an achievement, even were they not intrinsically of note. That many of them should be long is less remarkable, for, when an opportunity to send a letter occurred, the writer would often have no idea when a messenger would next become available and would want to say as much as possible. Perhaps the greatest surprise to the reader of the collection is that so few of the letters should be concerned with the life of the spirit. Though, as we shall see, they touch from time to time on spiritual topics, they mainly reflect the active side of the writer's life, as also, with comparable exceptions, do the *Foundations*. Their unique value and merit is to give us a picture of Saint Teresa's world unsurpassed in vividness, to bring to life a large number of the individuals with whom she habitually had to do, and, above all, to give us a brilliant, full-length portrait of herself.

[II]

All but six of Saint Teresa's extant letters were written during the last twenty years of her life (1562–82)—that is to say, after the foundation, at Ávila, of the first convent of her Discalced Reform; all but nine are later than 1567, the year in which she was encouraged by the General of her Order to begin founding elsewhere; and more than half the collection bear dates between December 1575 and June 1580—the most critical period in the Reform's history. The collection thus forms a background to many dramatic events which took place during that history and at the same time supplies a commentary upon them.

The story of the growth of the Reform during the sixteenth century is almost continuously one of conflict and stress, divided sharply into two periods. From 1562 to 1580, over and above the difficulties which would beset any movement backed by so little money or influence, Saint Teresa and her collaborators had to contend with the unceasing opposition of the Calced friars, who had no wish to be reformed, and said so with ever-increasing vigour, and of various people in positions of authority who supported them. This phase of history ended in 1580 with the creation of a separate province for the Reform, but hardly had that been effected when new complications, which had been threatening for some little time, asserted themselves within the Reform itself. The years from 1580 to 1594 are years of dramatic development. From being a province, the Reform became first a Congregation of its

Order separate from the Observance and finally an Order with complete independence. And the rapidity of this evolution was fully justified by its accelerated growth. Between 1562 and the end of 1580 were founded fourteen convents and twelve priories or colleges; between 1581 and the end of 1594, nineteen convents and forty-seven priories or colleges. Yet that same period was one of bitter internal strife centring in a feud between two leaders of the Reform, Jerónimo de la Madre de Dios and Nicolás de Jesús María, generally known by their respective surnames of Gracián and Doria. Gracián was a well-connected and able young idealist, of great personal charm, who, joining the Reform at twenty-seven, had a meteoric career which in nine years brought him, over the heads of many of his seniors, to the provincialate. Doria, an older man, had the disadvantages of being an Italian, of not having set foot in Spain till he was thirty, and of having joined the Order five years later than his rival. But he was a born administrator who, before entering the religious life, had had a prosperous career in business; and of the ruthlessness essential then, as now, to success in big business he had an ample share. Once, therefore, he had decided that Gracián must go, it was only a matter of time until he went. The conflict culminated in Gracián's expulsion from the Discalced Congregation (as it then was), in 1592, and the phase of Carmelite history of which it was a part closed with the unexpected death of Doria two years later.

As Saint Teresa's letters end, a few days before her death, in 1582, it is the first of the two phases that they chiefly illustrate. With her keen insight into character, and her affection and admiration for Gracián, who captivated her from their first meeting, she may quite possibly, even so early, have sensed the incipient enmity that was so soon to declare itself between two men of diverse and brilliant gifts, who, she hoped, would with great advantage to the the Reform collaborate.

'I thought him [Doria] really sensible, and a good person to go to for advice, and a servant of God, though he has not that graciousness and serenity that God has given to Paul [*i.e.*, Gracián] . . . He will fully recognize how valuable Paul is and he is quite resolved to follow him in everything, and I was very glad to see that. In many respects, if Paul gets on well with him . . . it will be very advantageous for them both to be of one mind, and it will be the greatest relief to me.'[1]

[1] *LL* 282 (670).

But it was not until nearly seven months after her death, at the Chapter of Almodóvar, that Doria's hostility towards Gracián manifested itself openly, and not until he was elected Provincial, in 1585, that the campaign *à outrance* against him began. She was therefore never to appreciate the unconscious irony latent in a remark which she penned to Gracián shortly before the Alcalá 'Separation' Chapter of 1581:

'You would find Father Nicolao [Doria] very useful, I assure you. Whatever happens, his advice is always good, and anyone who has suffered so much from others, as your Reverence has, will be very glad to have a companion *who will not cause you any suffering at all.*'[1]

The conflict between the Calced and the Discalced, on the other hand, may be followed, right through the *Letters*, in great detail. After the first Reformed foundation had been made, in face of much local opposition, at Ávila, five years elapsed before a second convent was founded, at Medina del Campo, but six more sprang up between 1568 and 1571, as well as three priories, and a college, for men. Then, on the women's side, came a three-year halt while Saint Teresa was occupied with restoring material security, discipline and spirituality to the convent of the Incarnation, Ávila, where all her early life had been spent, and where she had been sent, in October 1571, as Prioress. Four more priories, however, were founded during 1572–3, and from 1574 to 1576 there was progress on both fronts, with the foundation of four more convents and three priories.

It was now that what Saint Teresa calls the 'great storm of trials' broke upon the Reform, continuing for nearly four years, during which time, apart from a college for friars at Baeza, no new houses were founded. Even before 1576 there had been much contention, not merely on account of local conditions in some of the places where foundations had been made, but throughout the Spanish provinces of the Carmelite Order. The narrative which can so easily be read between the lines of the *Letters* follows all the twists and turns of the conflict, the complicated nature of which is attributable largely to a curious system then prevalent of dual ecclesiastical jurisdiction. The original Avilan community, for example, was subject, from 1562 to 1577, not to the General of the Order, but to the Ordinary, whereas all the later communities were placed under the General. In 1567, the Calced friars of

[1] *LL* 349 (806–7). Italics mine.

39

Andalusia, at their own request, were placed under the Ordinary by the Pope, who appointed two Dominicans as Visitors to the entire Order, to act quite independently of the General. Thus began the dual-control system, now embarrassing, now accommodating, according to circumstances, for the one side or the other. In 1575, for example, Saint Teresa, after having unwittingly disobeyed the General's orders to make no foundations in Andalusia, by making one at Beas de Segura, just inside the Andalusian border, was sent by Gracián, at that time the Pope's Commissary, to found a convent in the very heart of Andalusia, at Seville, and, taking the Pope's authority to be superior to the General's, she obeyed him. At the end of that year, when the General ordered her to leave Seville for a convent of her own choice in Castile, and, once there, to stay, Gracián, in his capacity as Apostolic Commissary, gave her a counter-order not to leave Seville till the following spring, and again she obeyed him. Into all this confusion, of which these are only isolated instances, were precipitated the envy, hatred and malice of the friars of the Mitigated Rule, who, seeing the Reform growing so rapidly, were apprehensive of its spreading throughout the Order. From ineffective protest they passed to indefensible violence and open rebellion. Dramatic scenes, in rapid succession, now enliven the story. The Calced friars of Seville refuse to obey Gracián, who comes to them as Visitor appointed by the Papal Nuncio. The Calced Provincial of Castile, forbidding the re-election of Saint Teresa as Prioress of the Incarnation, presides at the election and excommunicates the fifty-five nuns who vote for her. Saint John of the Cross, a mainstay of the Reform, is kidnapped, and imprisoned at Toledo, where threats, bribes and physical violence are used in turn, all vainly, to make him return to the Observance.

On a higher level, too, the conflicting forces can now be clearly discerned. On the side of the friars of the Mitigated Rule is the General, once friendly to the Reform, but since the Beas episode becoming increasingly alienated from it, who in March 1576 sends to Spain an able friar named Tostado to enforce obedience to him, and to suppress certain foundations of the Reform of which the dissolution had been decreed by a recently held Chapter-General. On the side of the Reform are King Philip II, attracted both by the austerity of its Rule and the personality of its foundress, the Papal Nuncio, Ormaneto, and the President of the Royal Council, Covarrubias. Each side scores in turn. The Chapter-General just referred to, that of Piacenza, dissolves all Discalced communities outside Castile and prohibits the foundation of further houses anywhere. The leading friars of the Reform meet and refuse to obey. The Royal Council forbids Tostado to exercise his functions. Ormaneto dies, and his successor, Sega, joins the opposing party. Covarrubias dies, and his successor, Pazos, though friendly enough, proves completely ineffective. The Royal Council forbids the Discalced to obey Sega, who retaliates by excommunicating and imprisoning their leaders. At this point, the General dies, and, Tostado having returned to Rome, Sega alone continues the persecution. Then, gradually, comes a general recognition that the only solution to the conflict is the creation of a separate Discalced province. In March 1579, Philip appoints four assessors to examine the whole question; the Discalced are removed from the jurisdiction of the Observance and given a temporary Vicar-General; the assessors recommend the separation; Discalced emissaries plead the same cause at Rome; Sega is won over; the excommunications are cancelled and the imprisonments ended, and finally, on 22nd June 1580, a papal Brief creates the new province, which holds its first Chapter in the following March. During the interval of peace between the ending of the external conflict and the beginning of the internal one, Saint Teresa's life draws to its close and her letters end. The last letters are concerned mainly with the four convents —Palencia, Soria, Granada and Burgos—founded between the promulgation of the Brief of Separation and her death. To her, the creation of the new province has brought an era of unclouded peace and she thanks God that she has lived to see it.

[III]

Where such stirring events were taking place, it cannot be thought surprising that a letter-writer who combined a striking personality with an outstanding gift for expression should throw light on many obscure events and immortalize many individuals who otherwise would certainly have been forgotten. It is remarkable, when one comes to think of it, how the life of a saint like Teresa perpetuates the most trivial happenings, and illumines not only the characters of comparatively important people who cross her path, but also the humblest personalities with whom, perhaps only occasionally—sometimes even only once—she is brought into contact. It is for all the world like a fairy story: they have but to touch her and the touch makes the memory of them immortal. What a procession of nobodies crosses the Teresan stage—and not hurriedly, but at a pace slow enough to allow us to recognize and remember its individual members! The first priors and prioresses of the Reform; the Dominican Visitors; the two Nuncios; Philip's four assessors; Rubeo, the Carmelite General; Quiroga, Archbishop of Toledo—these have at least a place, even if some of them have only a modest one, in religious history. Teresa's brothers and sisters, Salcedo, Pantoja, Julián de Ávila, García de Toledo, Ramírez, Padilla, Reinoso—these, though forgotten in history, are remembered by Teresans for the closeness of their connection with the Saint. But what of Salcedo's housekeeper, Lorenzo's servant Serna, Ruiz the livestock-dealer, the faithful Serrano, Chief-Courier Figueredo, Roque de Huerta, Diego Ortiz, Báñez's novice Parda and Parda's lachrymose friend whom Saint Teresa so aptly nicknamed Weepy-Wailer? Not one of these could ever have imagined, or even have thought it credible, that his or her name would be remembered after four hundred years. And yet, to the reader of the *Letters*, each one is not merely a name, but an individual, perfectly recognizable and unlikely to be wholly forgotten.

One can read Saint Teresa's letters, then, to extract from them occasional but precious passages containing spiritual teaching. Or to learn more about the development of her Reform during the most critical years in its history. But one can also read them to get to know more about the personalities, some of them outstanding ones, who made up that history. And perhaps most people are more interested in the personalities than in anything else.

Since many of the extant letters bear no superscription, and in some of these the content gives no clue to the recipient's identity, it is impossible to ascertain the exact number of the correspondents to whom they are addressed. The total, however, is certainly not less than one hundred and twenty. Of the 458 letters, 107 are either known or believed to have been written to Gracián and 64 to María de San José, the Prioress at Seville. The remainder, with half a dozen exceptions, are fairly evenly distributed. But the number of recipients of the letters is as nothing compared with the number of persons mentioned in them. Here there is even less hope of ascertaining the precise total, since many individuals are referred to so vaguely as to be quite unidentifiable. In round numbers they cannot be fewer than eight hundred, a considerable proportion of whom are referred to scores of times; and some four hundred seemed to have sufficient personality to justify their inclusion in the biographical section of my *Handbook to the life and times of Saint Teresa and Saint John of the Cross*.[1]

Viewed thus, Saint Teresa's *Letters* resemble a huge portrait-gallery—or, to speak more appropriately, her writing being always so dynamic, a vast stage crowded with animated figures of every type. Their diversity, and the extreme clarity with which many of them are drawn, are extraordinary, the more so because these letters are all purely private—not one of them could have been written with any thought of publication and very few were intended to be read by more than one person. Their author describes clearly because she saw clearly: a professional psychologist, a man who had spent his life studying human nature, could hardly have done better.

Look first at a group of prioresses—always the Mother Foundress' special care, since it was they, more than any others, who were to turn her ideals into realities. In the foreground, the most lovable of the group, stands María de San José: impetuous, impulsive and brimming over with affectionate generosity. When Saint Teresa was with her at Seville, she found her rather difficult to collaborate with—secretive, apt to brood and somewhat lacking in frankness. But hardly has the Mother left than her young disciple —after all, she was only twenty-eight—is overwhelmed with loneliness and pours out her affection so unreservedly that, says Saint Teresa, 'I felt quite touched and forgave you on the spot. Provided you love me as much as I love you,' she goes on, 'I forgive you everything, whether in the past or in the future.'[2] And to such a mutual affection all the answers to the letters the Prioress wrote bear witness. Perhaps of no one else represented in the collection, with the exception of Jerónimo Gracián, do we learn so many intimate, trivial and lifelike details. Decidedly well-educated for a woman of her day, she liked to 'parade her Latinity' and her Biblical learning.[3] She could be obstinate and childishly wayward —about the house to which she wanted the Seville community to move, for example, or about her reinstatement after the period during which intrigue had driven her from office ('I have written her some terrible letters, but you might as well talk to a stone wall')[4].

---

[1] Of practically all the persons referred to in these Teresan essays short biographies will be found in the *Handbook*, shortly to appear.

[2] *LL* 99 (252).   [3] *LL* 137 (347), 223 (545).   [4] *LL* 290 (685).

She could be disingenuous, over-shrewd, even 'foxy'. But Saint Teresa had no reservations to make in her affection for her:

'My daughter . . . how truly I can call you by that name! For, though I have always loved you dearly, I love you so much more now that it amazes me, and so I long to see you and embrace you again and again.'[1]

If she criticized her, that was because (as she said) 'I love you and want everything you do to be a success.'[2] All things considered, there was no prioress of whom she had a higher opinion. 'Bad though you are,' she exclaims, 'I wish I had a few more like you.'[3] 'I should feel the loss of no prioress as much as of your Reverence.'[4] And in the last year of her life she pays her the supreme tribute of trust when she writes to her: 'If my opinion were acted upon, they would elect you Foundress after my death; indeed, I should be very pleased if they did so during my lifetime.'[5]

Hardly less well does the reader of Saint Teresa's letters come to know María Bautista, the Prioress of Valladolid. Here was a very different woman from the volatile María de San José. This prudent, business-like prioress was none other than that young cousin of Saint Teresa who, as a girl, had lived with her at the Incarnation and seems to have been, characteristically, the first person to have made a practical suggestion about the inauguration of the Reform, backing this suggestion with the offer of a substantial sum of money. After spending five years at Ávila and Medina, she went to Valladolid at twenty-five and lived there, serving for long periods as prioress, until her death at sixty. 'The way she keeps this house,' wrote Saint Teresa, 'and her capability in general, is something to thank God for.'[6] She seems to have developed into a somewhat assured woman: a natural organizer, a discreet and intelligent counsellor, a thrifty manager with a remarkable grasp of money matters, she was too inflexible in her standards[7] and apt to think too much of her own advice and to expect others to do the same. At Valladolid, apparently, they did, which was by no means good for her.[8] She was self-conscious, at any rate in the early years of her rule, worrying, for example, about her re-election as prioress;[9] self-centred, not looking beyond her

[1] *LL* 284 (674).   [2] *LL* 309 (727).   [3] *LL* 302 (707).   [4] *LL* 369 (844).
[5] *LL* 410 (923).   [6] *LL* 289 (681).   [7] *LL* 78a (193).   [8] *LL* 78a (193).
[9] *LL* 65 (161).

own house;[1] inclined to be 'pernickety';[2] and acquisitive to an exaggerated degree.[3] But, in reproving her for her faults, Saint Teresa so often writes lightly and laughingly that they should not perhaps be taken too seriously.[4] 'That little person of yours',[5] she is termed in a letter to the theologian Báñez—then living at Valladolid—and the picture of a diminutive, vivacious, active woman comes at once to the mind's eye. She had a facile pen and her intelligent remarks made her letters agreeable reading. 'Almost everyone's letters tire me but yours,' wrote Saint Teresa, 'but yours I find it refreshing both to receive and to answer.'[6]

A very different prioress was Brianda de San José, who ruled first at Malagón, and later at Toledo, where, four years after Saint Teresa, she died. We should probably have heard much less about her than we do but for the serious illness which she suffered for some years and which called out Saint Teresa's maternal affection and probably softened her judgments on her character. Allowing for some benevolence on the Foundress' part, we may deduce that she was devout and amiable but weak and greatly given to acting without reflection[7]—not, in short, one of the Reform's successes.

Ana de Jesús (the Venerable Anne of Jesus), on the other hand, known to us through Saint John of the Cross as well as through Saint Teresa, was an outstanding success: during the period covered by the *Letters* she was Prioress of Beas and Granada, and it was she, rather than María de San José, who, after Saint Teresa's death, stepped, by general agreement, into a position of unofficial pre-eminence. Yet, probably through the loss of certain letters, she appears as a rather more shadowy figure than one might have expected. Only three of Saint Teresa's letters to her are extant,[8] one of which, a long letter written some four months before her death, is highly critical of the procedure which she had adopted during the foundation of the Granada convent, and reveals her as the strong character that she later showed herself to be in combating Doria. A second letter reproves her for complaining 'without the least reason', but in a third, addressing her as 'my daughter and my crown', the Saint declares she can 'never thank God enough for the favour He did me in drawing your Reverence to the religious life'. In letters written to others, Saint Teresa makes comparatively infrequent references to M. Ana de Jesús, as she also

[1] *LL* 78a (193).   [2] *LL* 126 (326).   [3] *LL* 278 (662), 289 (681).
[4] *LL* 87 (210).   [5] *LL* 65 (161)..   [6] Cf. *LL* 78a (191).   [7] *LL* 95 (241).
[8] In the order given, Nos. 421, 261, and 272.

does to Saint John of the Cross: of both these characters, themselves so intimate with each other, we learn much more outside Saint Teresa's letters than through them.

Around these prioresses are grouped a number of others, mostly recognizable, but much more slightly drawn. We hear surprisingly little about Ana de los Ángeles (Gómez), the first Prioress to hold office at Malagón, and later at Toledo; and about María del Sacramento, who succeeded her at Malagón, there is nothing in the *Letters* comparable with the delicious story told of her journey with Saint Teresa to Salamanca in the nineteenth chapter of the *Foundations*.[1] Isabel de Santo Domingo, who dealt so firmly, and yet so tactfully, with the temperamental Princess of Éboli, fades out of the *Letters* after being transferred, with her community, to Segovia; all we hear of her is the Saint's trenchant comment that poverty of spirit has been killed in her by the 'excessive comforts' of Pastrana. Ana de San Alberto, the first Prioress of Caravaca, comes to life only in the letters written to her by Saint John of the Cross. Two more of Saint Teresa's cousins, Ana de la Encarnación and Inés de Jesús, sisters who, by a curious coincidence, died on the same day, were prioresses respectively of Salamanca and Medina, the latter, some eighteen months before Saint Teresa's death, being made the first Prioress at Palencia. It is strange that these women who are so frequently mentioned should be so faintly drawn; there can be no doubt in which of her prioresses Saint Teresa was most interested.

For that matter, with the exception of her sister Juana, and her niece Beatriz, Saint Teresa paints hardly any other women with vividness or realism than the four first described. Perhaps the most remarkable omission from the *Letters* is that of a full-length portrait of Ana de San Bartolomé, the first lay sister of the Reform, who in Saint Teresa's last years accompanied her on all her journeys, nursed her in her illnesses and was with her when she died. Fortunately, we have her autobiography and other documentary evidence to her strong and earnest personality, but it is a pity that Saint Teresa, who refers to her (as she could not help but do) again and again, should have left us next to no record of what she was like. Other women, only faintly drawn, of whom we might have expected to know more, are the patronesses and benefactresses of the Reform. The Duchess of Alba is almost a lay figure. Teresa de Layz, the Alba foundress, comes out more clearly in the *Founda-*

[1] *CWSTJ*, III, 93–4.

tions than in the *Letters*. The seven letters extant addressed to Doña Luisa de la Cerda reveal only the conventional great lady whom Saint Teresa treated with affectionate respect. Of Doña Guiomar de Ulloa we learn little more than in the *Life*. Of nuns, we hear a good deal about the 'wretched Vicaress', Beatriz de la Madre de Dios, who led the revolt against the Sevilian prioress, but to understand her character we must read the story of her abnormal childhood in the twenty-sixth chapter of the *Foundations*. Isabel de San Francisco we remember only by her facile pen and her over-fertile imagination ('She makes up all those rigmaroles and it never occurs to her she is saying what is not true'[1]); Isabel de San Jerónimo, her companion at Paterna, by her indiscreet talkativeness. Casilda de la Concepción, so speakingly drawn as a child in the *Foundations*, develops into something of a moral weakling before she leaves Carmel for the Franciscans at the age of nineteen. And these are the best of the remaining portraits. What reader of the *Letters* carries away more than a purely conventional idea of Blanca, the 'Portuguese nun'; of Bernarda, the 'little saint' who died young; of the 'Flemish lady', Ana de San Pedro, and her daughter; of Elena, the niece of Cardinal Quiroga; of Saint Teresa's cousin Beatriz who acted as Brianda's vicaress? These are no more real to us than the oft-mentioned 'postulant with the gold ingots', who was to have set the Seville convent 'free from worry' of a financial kind[2]—but apparently never did.

[IV]

Perhaps because of the virile strain in her own temperament, Saint Teresa continually shows herself more interested in men than in women, and her friars are depicted with much greater animation, and in much greater detail, than her nuns. The charming and versatile Gracián; the shrewd and calculating Doria; the saintly John of the Cross; the fiery and outspoken Mariano; old Antonio de Jesús with his perpetual grievances; the conscientious and fair-minded Ángel de Salazar, who found it so difficult to do his duty both by the Observance and by the Reform; the energetic Gregorio Nacianceno; the 'rock-like' Juan de Jesús; the crafty Alonso de Valdemoro, scheming against the Reform but not scrupling to ask favours from its foundress: these are only the most prominent of her friars, and it would throw this study out of all

[1] *LL* 307 (720).   [2] *LL* 162 (405).

proportion to reproduce the descriptions she gives even of these. And, as we shall see, friars are by no means the only men whose characters she dissects with such skill.

On the relations between Saint Teresa and Jerónimo Gracián a book could be written, and some day no doubt will. From the time of their first meeting (May 1575) they developed a mutual affection probably unparalleled in the records of Carmelite history. 'The good accounts I had been given of him', writes Saint Teresa, 'had made me extremely anxious to see him. But when I began to talk to him I was happier still, for . . . it seemed to me as if those who praised him to me hardly knew him at all.'[1]

It would be tedious to quote all the passages from the *Letters* in which Saint Teresa showers praises upon this young friar who was to become both her spiritual father and her spiritual son. 'To me, he is perfect, and better for our needs than anyone else we could have asked God to send us.'[2] 'He is so saintly.'[3] He 'behaves like an angel'.[4] 'Oh, my Father, praise God for granting you the gift of getting on so well with people you meet that no one seems able to take your place.'[5] 'Oh, my Father, what majesty there is in (your) words.'[6] Yet, outspoken as she is in these and in many other eulogies which could be quoted, they are not undeserved. The qualities of Gracián's which she enumerates were precisely those which, as we know from contemporary sources, struck others. Nor need we be unduly surprised that, only some two months after her first meeting with this young man of thirty, she should be recommending Philip II to put him in charge of the Reform, for most of those who were manning the new movement were young, and, even after Doria came on the scene, Gracián was looked up to by all as a born leader. In retrospect, we may think they were mistaken, but he was in fact chosen by vote as head of the newly autonomous Reform when only thirty-six.

Further, enthusiastic though Saint Teresa is in praise of her hero, she is by no means blind to his faults. On the contrary, she singles them out from the beginning with extreme accuracy. The naturalness and frankness of manner (*llaneza*), she tells him, which he has in such great measure are gifts from God, but circumspection is necessary in the use of them, and they can easily be misinterpreted —so he had better not read others the letters she writes him![7] He should have more trust than he has had in her judgment concern-

---

[1] *Foundations*, XXIV (*CWSTJ*, III, 122). [2] *LL* 72 (175). [3] *LL* 346 (800).
[4] *LL* 74 (179).   [5] *LL* 366 (840).   [6] *LL* 147 (369).   [7] *LL* 134 (346).

ing an approach to the General, instead of being persuaded, as he so easily was, by others.[1] He is over-volatile, too: 'now . . . up in the air, now in the depths of the sea'.[2] And, she asks here with deferential tentativeness, is he always careful about 'telling the whole truth'?[3] These faults, like those virtues, were as accurately assessed by Saint Teresa, at an early stage in her acquaintance with him, as they have since been by history.

Where she sometimes seems to exaggerate is in her concern for Gracián's physical welfare. A man of thirty might presumably be trusted to wear sufficient clothing and to choose his own mount— and, if occasionally he did fall off his donkey, would he, being young and active, be any the worse for it?[4] Today her constant fears lest the Calced should poison his food seem to us uncalled for: to judge from their treatment of Saint John of the Cross when they had him in their power, they preferred attrition to liquidation. But it is hard for us to recapture the atmosphere of nervous apprehensiveness which prevailed during these years of persecution; and Saint Teresa was always inclined to be over-anxious about the health of those she esteemed—as witness her concern over the Advent austerities of Báñez,[5] and over the mortifications practised by her brother Lorenzo, to whom, one would judge, they would be unlikely to do the slightest harm.

On the whole, Saint Teresa's picture of Gracián may be described as one of remarkable fidelity. In a lesser person admiration and affection might well have blinded judgment; in her they quickened it.

Doria, whom she knew far less well, she naturally draws in less detail. So active was he, however, and so deeply did he impress his personality upon the Reform, that she refers to him in her letters more frequently than to any other person except Gracián, the Seville Prioress and her brother Lorenzo. But beyond expressions of admiration at his many virtues—in particular, his efficiency—she says very little of his character. 'A sound man, full of humility and penitence, with a great regard for truth and able to win others' good will':[6] that judgment fairly represents her attitude to him. Hopefully though she writes of the possibility that he might become Gracián's valued collaborator, her recommendation that Gracián should not be distant with him[7] (which he seldom was with anybody) suggests that she may not have been as

[1] *LL* 253 (614). [2] *LL* 256 (619). [3] *LL* 283 (673). [4] *LL* 81 (202).
[5] Cf. p. 54, below. [6] *LL* 282 (670). [7] *LL* 282 (670).

D

49

happy about them as at first sight she might seem. One would never suspect from her letters, however, what was actually to happen.

To Saint John of the Cross Saint Teresa refers much less than to many persons farther from her intimacy and not a single one of all the letters which she must have written him has survived. Some, no doubt, went when he destroyed his papers at the beginning of the period of persecution. Some may have been impounded by the Calced friars when they kidnapped him.[1] And the rest? The rest he himself tore up one day because he felt himself becoming over-attached to them[2]—a sad loss to lovers and admirers of the two Saints ever since.

Yet, notwithstanding this great gap, the place which Saint John of the Cross occupies in Saint Teresa's letters is unique: except during his captivity, when all her thoughts of him are of pity, she hardly once speaks of him without paying him a glowing tribute of affection, admiration and devotion. She never mentions any of his works, as he does hers;[3] but the vividness of her allusions to his personality and character shows how near he was to her heart. The earliest of these tributes dates from pre-Duruelo days, when he was only twenty-six. And how clearly it portrays him!

'Small of stature . . . great in the sight of God. . . . A sensible person and well fitted for our way of life. . . . There is not a friar but speaks well of him, and he lives a life of great penitence. . . . The Lord seems to be leading him by the hand. . . . We have never seen the least imperfection in him. He has courage. . . . He is much given to prayer and most intelligent. . . .'[4]

That, though warm praise, is couched in measured and judicial terms and coupled with the suggestion that the young friar might get a little good advice from Francisco de Salcedo, who at that time was still a layman. But before long the Mother Foundress begins to speak of him very differently. First, she extols his sanctity. He is 'a very holy Discalced Father';[5] 'the holy Fray John of the Cross';[6] 'a divine, heavenly man';[7] *aquel santico* (the diminutive denotes his smallness of stature), 'that little saint',[8] for 'people look on him as a saint, which, in my opinion, he is and has been all

---

[1] *LL* 204 (497).   [2] *LL*, p. 18.
[3] *Spiritual Canticle*, XII, 6. *Complete Works of Saint John of the Cross* (London, Burns, Oates, 1934–5) (abbreviated *CWSJX*), II, 72.
[4] *LL* 10 (52–3).   [5] *LL* 42 (113).   [6] *LL* 43 (115).   [7] *LL* 261 (625).
[8] *LL* 224 (549).

his life'.[1] Then, his learning: as he grows older, she begins to use her favourite nickname for him—'Seneca'.[2] He 'has great experience and learning' and is 'sorely missed here by those who were brought up on his teaching'.[3] Less than ten years after she had asked Salcedo (now a priest) to advise him, we find her placing John, as 'a man of experience', above his former mentor.[4] And there is more than experience in his wisdom: 'he has the spirit of Our Lord';[5] 'he is a soul to whom God communicates His spirit.'[6] None the less, he is very human—he cannot, for example, 'endure the people' in Andalusia;[7] neither, for that matter, can Saint Teresa herself. Thus his kinship with her embraces both the trivial and the sublime:

'You would never believe how lonely I feel without him. . . . He is indeed the Father of my soul and one of those with whom it does me most good to have converse. . . . You can behave with him just as you would with me. . . .'[8]

Not even with Gracián had Saint Teresa a closer spiritual affinity than with Saint John of the Cross.

By contrast, take Antonio de Jesús—Antonio de Heredia, as he was before he joined the Reform, though it is perhaps significant that one never alludes to him by his patronymic as one does to Gracián, Doria and even Roca: he was far less of a personality than they. Perhaps he aged rapidly, for he was already fifty-seven when he joined the Reform and the story of the five clocks[9] suggests that he was both unpractical and childishly meticulous even then. Soon he began to show signs of pusillanimity and weakness in government.[10] Gentle by disposition, he was apt to vary the habitual laxity of his rule with outbreaks of severity which destroyed all respect for him.[11] In his prime, his height and fine bearing predisposed people in his favour, and it is much to his credit that, enjoying the esteem which he did in the Observance, he should have so resolutely flung aside his dignity and embraced the hardships of Duruelo.[12] But later he became rather a disappointed man. He was always the person who—rightly, according to Saint Teresa[13]— held the second office rather than the first, who was sent with some

---

[1] *LL* 204 (496).   [2] *LL* 81 ('202).   [3] *LL* 261 (625).
[4] *LL* 163 (409).   [5] *LL* 301 (703).   [6] *LL* 300 (702).   [7] *LL* 358 (830).
[8] *LL* 261 (625).   [9] *Foundations*, XIV (*CWSTJ*, III, 65).
[10] *LL* 144, 145 (363, 365).   [11] *LL* 147 (372).
[12] *Foundations*, XIV (*CWSTJ*, III, 66).   [13] *LL* 303 (710).

other friar to accompany and advise him rather than to do the work himself. The climax came, at the Separation Chapter, when, by a small margin, he lost the provincialship to Gracián. True, he was seventy-one, which was a much greater age in sixteenth-century Spain than it is in twentieth-century England; but only in his late eighties did he appear to become conscious of failing strength. Saint Teresa speaks of him a good deal more flatteringly in the *Foundations* than in the *Letters*. 'A good old man', she terms him in a letter to Philip II.[1] 'Though I am very much attached to him . . . and he is a saintly man,' she confides to Gracián, 'I cannot help realizing that God has not given him the ability for the work he is doing.'[2] It was very much in that way that she normally thought of him. While respecting him as one of her first two friars, she never gave him her fullest confidence, and, in particular, she was impatient with his puerile jealousy of Gracián's intimacy with her. 'I am told', she remarks, 'he is very much upset to find how many letters I write and how seldom I write to him';[3] and again and again she adjures her correspondents not to let Antonio know that she has written to Gracián:

'As far as possible, he should not be told how many letters I write; tell my Father to say nothing to him about it.'[4]

That is not the kind of admonition that one expects to find necessary within the Discalced Carmelite Reform.

The remaining friars are drawn in much greater detail than the lesser nuns. Partly, no doubt, this is because Saint Teresa's contacts with them were more complicated and her attitude to them was more critical, bringing out traits of their natures which in more conventional relations would not be observed. Partly, as has already been hinted, it may be because she was in any case less interested in women than in men. Some of those whom she portrays to the life have already been enumerated. There are many more: the reader of the *Letters* soon comes to know the Calced stalwart Juan Evangelista,[5] the brilliant but untrustworthy Baltasar Nieto; Ambrosio de San Pedro and his cousin Gabriel de la Asunción, Gracián's secretary Bartolomé de Jesús; Diego de la Trinidad, Roca's companion in Rome; Juan de la Miseria, the lay

---

[1] *LL* 204 (497).   [2] *LL* 230 (562).   [3] *LL* 146 (368).   [4] *LL* 159 (398).
[5] *LL* 79, 94, 111, 140, 164, 182, 207. Not to be confused with the much younger Discalced friar of that name, who was for some years the inseparable companion of Saint John of the Cross.

brother who painted Saint Teresa's portrait; Elías de San Martín, a General-to-be; Germán de San Matías, who was kidnapped with Saint John of the Cross; and any number more. Sometimes these friars are drawn in mere thumbnail sketches, but the outlines are invariably sharp and clear. Instead of examining them, however, let us turn to some more detailed portraits of the numerous members of other Orders than Carmel, of secular priests, and of laymen.

One of the most prominent of the clerics, and perhaps the one of whom Saint Teresa wrote more outspokenly than of any other, was a Portuguese, Dom Teotónio de Bragança, a younger brother of the fifth Duke of that name, who, as a boy of seventeen, joined the Society of Jesus, but left it at the time of the trouble between Saint Ignatius of Loyola and Simon Rodrigues and eventually succeeded the Cardinal-King of Portugal, Dom Henrique, as Archbishop of Évora. He first met Saint Teresa in his forties, at Salamanca, and they had a good deal to do with each other, though they never became close friends. On the one hand, Dom Teotónio often sought her advice on spiritual matters; on the other, he took such an interest in her foundations that in one place she terms him the 'protector' of the Carmelite Order. Her extant letters to him, six in all, are mainly long ones, and, except where she girds at him for addressing her, in Portuguese fashion, by titles of exaggerated respect, highly deferential. What is interesting is the way in which she talks about him to others. While recognizing his many good qualities, she depicts him as unmethodical and un-businesslike. This she had apparently failed to discover on their first acquaintance. 'Our good friend Don Teutonio is doing extremely well', she remarks, in 1575, of some negotiations in Madrid, 'and it looks as if the business will be successful.'[1] But fifteen months later she is writing very differently:

'I don't know if good Don Teutonio will do anything: it seems improbable and he is not much use at negotiations.'[2]

'I have not much confidence in Señor Don Teutonio's ability as a negotiator. He has plenty of good will, I agree, but there is little hope of his getting anything done.'[3]

Poor unready Dom Teotónio! Yet we must not forget that it was he who published the Saint's *Way of Perfection* at Évora, in the year after her death.

[1] *LL* 76 (186-7).　　　　[2] *LL* 120 (307).
[3] *LL* 121 (312). Letters 120 and 121 were written on the same day.

Another figure of commanding stature is the famous Dominican theologian, Fray Domingo Báñez. Both Saint Teresa and her Reform owed much to the Dominicans, and speaking portraits of a number of them are found in her pages. Báñez, the chief of these, was her friend from the time of the foundation of Saint Joseph's, Ávila, until her death. 'I have few (such friends as he) left now', she writes in 1581.[1] She singles him out in her correspondence by referring to him, almost exclusively, as 'my Father'— Gracián, when he comes on the scene, being '*our* Father'. A single word of criticism from him would affect her more than all that another critic could say.[2] He had every claim upon her respect and esteem. He was behind her in all her foundations: he 'loves them and looks upon them as his own'.[3] And he was invariably ready to help her in her spiritual life: 'whenever I have had any new experience', she wrote in 1576, 'I always write to him still'.[4] Concerning the health of only one person—Gracián—was she more solicitous. Her request that the Valladolid Prioress will 'find out if he is wearing enough clothes' and 'make him wrap up his feet', especially if some indisposition of his is due to immoderate penances, 'of the kind he generally does in Advent, like sleeping on the floor',[5] shows the same maternal instinct as her fears for the safety of Gracián on his donkey. Yet there have survived only four of her letters to him. Was this because the good professor, like so many of his nation, was a bad correspondent? There is a withering paragraph in a letter dated 2nd November 1576,[6] in which a friend of the Dominican Visitor, Pedro Fernández (and therefore probably a Dominican too) is stigmatized as ungrateful to her because of his laxity about letter-writing—and also as inconstant in his attachments. P. Silverio, in a note to his Spanish edition of the *Letters*,[7] assumes that this friend is Báñez: personally, I am inclined to doubt it.

But we must pass the clerics more rapidly in review if we are to gain any idea of them as a whole. To take a type quite different from both the aristocratic Bragança and the erudite Báñez, there is Garciálvarez, the Sevilian nuns' conscientious chaplain, who later caused so much trouble in the community that he had to be

---

[1] *LL* 354 (824).   [2] *LL* 53 (135).   [3] *LL* 53 (136).
[4] *Relations*, IV (*CWSTJ*, I, 322). Occasionally (*e.g.*, *LL*, p. 139) she gave him some good advice too.
[5] *LL* 90 (218–19).   [6] *LL* 126 (325–6).
[7] P. Silverio, *Obras*, etc., *op. cit.*, VII, 339.

removed. In her eulogies of him—'so perfect', 'so full of charity', 'no one connected with him could be bad'[1]—Saint Teresa may be thought to have displayed less than her usual perspicacity of judgment; but she never wrote harshly of him, and even when she could no longer approve his conduct she would dwell on his past kindnesses. Somewhat similar in type, and even more clearly drawn, is Julián de Ávila, for over forty years chaplain of Saint Teresa's first convent—'a great servant of God',[2] she writes, 'one of the best priests in Ávila'[3]—who accompanied her on most of her early journeys, but, as he grew older, disturbed her by an excessive complacency which led to a deterioration, at Saint Joseph's, of standards of discipline. Into this category, too, falls one of Saint Teresa's early confessors, Gaspar Daza, who gave the habit to the first nuns of the Reform and was a favourite of her best of all Bishops, Álvaro de Mendoza. Of a group of Jesuits, to whom Saint Teresa owed so much—including Diego de Acosta, Gaspar de Salazar, Rodrigo Álvarez, Juan de Prádanos and Pablo Hernández—the most clearly drawn is perhaps Baltasar Álvarez. Her spiritual director even before her first foundation was made, he became her lifelong friend: 'the confessor who has done me the most good', she calls him:[4] 'one of the best friends I have . . . a saint'.[5]

And what a galaxy of prelates the *Letters* display! To Rubeo, the Italian General of the Order, Saint Teresa writes with such passionate devotion and puts forth her plans with such persuasive eloquence that it is to be feared we envisage him as an unreasonable and hard-hearted old man: the Spanish *History of the Reform*, however, gives a more favourable idea of his character. The Spanish prelates with whom Saint Teresa came into contact stand out with amazing clarity. Quiroga, the Cardinal-Archbishop of Toledo, whose appointment delighted her, but who proved unexpectedly and consistently obstinate about the foundation of a convent in Madrid; Rojas, Archbishop of Seville, who at first was better disposed to the Discalced friars than to the nuns, but was eventually won over by Saint Teresa's policy of combined deference and frankness; Álvaro de Mendoza, just referred to, Bishop successively of Ávila and Palencia, who, like his sister María and his brother Bernardino, was Saint Teresa's constant friend; Vela, Archbishop of Burgos, who, though at first highly sympathetic

---

[1] *LL* 99, 108, 118 (253, 279, 302)·   [2] *Foundations*, III (*CWSTJ*, III, 8).
[3] *LL* 168 (427).   [4] *Life*, XXVI (*CWSTJ*, I, 167).   [5] *LL* 315 (739).

with the Reform, eventually proved 'wanting in courage'[1] and had to be determinedly tackled by Don Álvaro de Mendoza before the Burgos foundation could be made. More slightly, but most individually, portrayed are Alonso Velázquez, Bishop of Osma ('a great servant of God, as you can find out from anyone'[2]); Covarrubias, Bishop of Segovia and President of the Royal Council, a staunch defender of the Reform against the Nuncio Sega; his less benevolently drawn successor, Pazos—*el Pausado*, a term which I hope it does not malign Saint Teresa to render 'Slowcoach';[3] Diego de León, a Calced Carmelite appointed Bishop of Colibraso, who, like Salazar, seems to have done his best to be fair to each of the contending parties. Ormaneto and Sega, the two Nuncios, must be judged principally by their actions, as must Jerónimo Reinoso, the kindly Canon of Palencia, and a host of others.

[v]

Besides being a Mother to her Order, and to many people outside her Order whose numbers have greatly multiplied since her death, and are still growing, Saint Teresa stood in a quasi-maternal relationship to a large family of brothers and sisters, nephews and nieces, cousins, second cousins, cousins once removed—the roll is a long one even for Spain. Her father (who apparently destroyed her letters to him, as none have survived) had a son (or perhaps two sons) and a daughter by his first wife and seven sons and two daughters by his second—Teresa's mother, who died when Teresa was about thirteen. So much did some of these brothers and sisters need a mother—not to say a business manager —that Teresa never succeeded in shaking off family obligations, much as at times these oppressed her. 'All the cares of my foundations put together', she said once, 'have not made me as tired and depressed as these business matters.'[4] And again, 'I have been getting so worn out by my relatives'.[5] However, in the numerous letters which she wrote to, and about, these same relatives, she has traced portraits as sharp and clear as any in her gallery.

Her favourite brother (this by her own confession) was Lorenzo, four years her junior, who spent thirty-five of his sixty-one years of life in the Indies, where he amassed a considerable fortune. Returning to Spain five years before his death, he bought an estate

---

[1] *CWSTJ*, III, 186.　　[2] *LL* 148 (374).　　[3] *LL* 253 (616).
[4] *LL* 334 (777).　　　　[5] *LL* 346 (801).

in the country near Ávila, and thence corresponded freely with his
sister, of whose Reform, which he would dearly have liked to join,
he became a generous helper. The letters reveal him as an amiable,
kindly, well-meaning man, slightly pompous, perhaps, to the
world at large,[1] but to his elder sister humble and deferential.
Not being over-blessed with tact, his visits were apt to be 'something of an embarrassment' to a busy foundress (though, she adds,
'when . . . I tell him to go away, he goes like an angel'[2]), but she
never grudged time to help him in his sometimes rather pathetic
efforts to live a life of recollection in the midst of the world. And he
needed a good deal of help. Now he had to be restrained from giving up 'using the carpets and silver',[3] now from an undue attach-
ment to hair-shirts,[4] now from denying himself necessary sleep.
One cannot be sure how many of Saint Teresa's necrological
eulogies of him were dictated by sisterly affection, but the letters,
while not sparing his faults, certainly give the impression of a man
who 'lived a life of prayer and walked continually in the presence
of God'.[5]

With this open-hearted and open-handed Indiano are contrasted a number of Saint Teresa's other relatives. Of his two sons,
Lorenzo, the younger, who emigrated to the Indies at eighteen,
leaving behind him an illegitimate daughter, was the more like
him; Francisco, the heir, who abandoned his intention of becoming
a Carmelite almost as soon as he had conceived it, married a well-
born but penurious bride and spent the rest of his life trying to pay
his debts, presumably took after his mother. The elder Lorenzo's
gloomy brother Pedro, a congenital hypochondriac, who returned with him from the Indies, and, while living with him,
developed acute melancholia, must have irritated him beyond
endurance. A character, more carefully drawn than these, who
contrasts no less effectively with Lorenzo, is his brother-in-law,
Juan de Ovalle.

To counterbalance her wealth of brothers Saint Teresa had only
an elder half-sister, María, who hardly enters the *Letters*, and a
younger sister, Juana, who is very prominent in them. Ovalle was
Juana's husband, and between his lack of means, which to some
extent Lorenzo remedied, and his difficult temperament, which
not even Teresa could remedy, she had an unhappy time. Gentle
by disposition, with 'the soul of an angel',[6] and unfortunately

---

[1] *LL* 101 (261).   [2] *LL* 93 (232).   [3] *LL* 168 (430).   [4] *LL* 171 (436-7).
[5] *LL* 326 (758).   [6] *LL* 2 (32). Cf. *LL* 362 (833-4).

rather ineffective in crises, she could seldom do much to solve her problems beyond consulting Teresa, who, to judge from the way she lets herself go in writing of Ovalle, had little patience with him. Touchy, quarrelsome and self-important, instead of being grateful for Lorenzo's many kindnesses, he was continually grumbling because of the interest which he showed in others. 'In some respects he is a perfect baby', sighs Teresa to Lorenzo. 'I am dreadfully sorry for my sister—we have a great deal to put up with in him.'[1] However, she concludes, 'God gives other people nice dispositions precisely so that they may put up with such as he'— an idea which no doubt Lorenzo accepted as unquestioningly as any other from the same source.

Of the Ovalles' two children, Gonzalo, who died before he was thirty, seems to have been rather a colourless youth of whom very little is said. But Beatriz, the daughter, who, after Saint Teresa's death, joined the Discalced Reform and lived to be nearly eighty, had a great deal of character. She enters the *Letters* chiefly through a rumour which had spread in Alba de Tormes, where she lived, that a married man there was taking too much interest in her: his wife, at any rate, seems to have thought so. Apparently Beatriz considered the rumours ridiculous and not worth heeding, while her easygoing mother was equally disinclined for action; the father, whom one would have expected to be running round on his dignity, was also strangely inert. 'Her parents are more at fault than she is, for they let her do as she likes with them',[2] complained her aunt, and forthwith sat down and wrote letters to both mother and daughter in which she said 'dreadful things'—it is to be feared with little effect. 'The girl's parents will take no notice of anything I say to them: I say a great deal, but they tell me I am under a delusion.'[3]

Very different from the lively Beatriz was Lorenzo's demure little daughter, Teresita, her aunt's special delight and care. Arriving in Spain from America—an 'extremely bonny and lovely' child[4] —before she was nine, she went to live in a convent of the Reform, and never re-entered the world, making her profession a month after Saint Teresa's death. The first detailed picture we have of her, written shortly before her ninth birthday, is quite idyllic:

'So here she is, wearing her habit and going about the house like a little fairy. Her father is beside himself with delight and all the

---

[1] *LL* 101 (258–9).   [2] *LL* 375 (858).   [3] *LL* 381 (870).   [4] *LL* 78a (191).

nuns are charmed with her. She has the temperament of an angel, and she entertains us so well at recreation, with stories about the Indians and about her voyage—in fact, she is a better story-teller than I am. I am delighted to think she will be no trouble to any of you.'[1]

'Like a little fairy' she flits through the letters—sometimes being allowed to send a message in one or even to contribute a post-script. Her quaint sayings are repeated,[2] her affection for the nuns (who somehow seem not to have spoiled her) is described,[3] and the perfection of her behaviour is continually remarked upon.[4] One phrase—'I sometimes wish I had Teresa here, especially when we take walks in the garden'[5]—calls up a vivid picture of what the child had become to the rapidly ageing foundress. Then a cloud falls across it. Convent-bred, to a degree very rare today, Teresita, always amenable, had showed herself over-suggestible to attempts made to persuade her to leave the convent for the world. No doubt she was told that she had never known the world, and so should live in it for a time, so as to be able to compare it with the life of religion. 'She is getting quite a sad little thing', reports Saint Teresa in November 1581.[6] A few weeks later, however, she remarks that 'Teresa is well, and I think we can feel safe about her'[7] while at the end of the letter the child adds in her own hand, 'I am all right again now'.[8] To the very last Saint Teresa has her in mind; refers again and again to her coming profession, at which she had hoped to be present; and shows the utmost concern for her —'after all, though she is a good little creature, she is only a child'.[9]

Allusions have often been made to Saint Teresa's fondness for little people, whether young or old. They seemed somehow to appeal to her protective instinct, even when there was no parti-cular circumstance to call it forth. The classical instance is the 'half-friar',[10] Saint John of the Cross, to whose shortness of stature Saint Teresa is continually referring, sometimes explicitly, some-

---

[1] *LL* 79 (198).   [2] *LL* 96, 107 (248, 272).   [3] *LL* 233 (576).
[4] *LL* 107, 108 (272, 279).   [5] *LL* 289 (683).   [6] *LL* 393 (896).
[7] *LL* 397 (902).   [8] *LL* 397 (903).   [9] *LL* 426 (950).
[10] I feel quite sure that, for the reasons set out in *Spirit of Flame* (London, 1943), p. 19, the 'half-friar' in the famous saying was not Antonio de Jesús, but Saint John of the Cross.

times indirectly by the use of diminutives.[1] Even when describing his sufferings in prison she drags it in to increase the pathos; 'he has been in a little cell, which would hardly hold him, small though he is'.[2] Hardly less familiar, to the reader of the *Letters*, than the tiny Saint, is the tiny Sevilian infirmarian, Leonor de San Gabriel—'my Gabriela'—who had sent Saint Teresa a little picture, or possibly a statuette, representing Saint Paul: 'I loved it', she remarks, 'because it was tiny—like herself.'[3] M. María Bautista, as we have seen, becomes half-humorously, half affectionately, 'that little person of yours'[4]; Ribera, who was so good a friend to the Reform at Palencia, is 'that little saint of a prebendary'.[5] And this trait in Saint Teresa is particularly noticeable in her relations with children. There must have been scores of children to whom she habitually sent affectionate messages at the end of her letters—generally referring to them as 'my little ones', or, with somewhat excessive benevolence, as 'little angels'! Even in the relatively few of her letters which we have we get to know quite a number. There were the children of Diego Ortiz, notably Martín—'my Martinico', Saint Teresa calls him, or sometimes 'our patron', since he had been named after Martín Ramírez, a benefactor of the Reform; the younger brothers and sisters of Gracián; 'Lesmitos' (little Lesmes), 'Maruca' (little Mary) and the other children of Catalina de Tolosa; the 'little angel' of the widowed Gaytán (she later joined the Reform), described in one place, with refreshing unconventionality, as a 'little puss'.[6] This love of children is a trait in Saint Teresa's character which one might have guessed, but could never have fully appreciated, had one not this collection of her letters.

Particularly is she attracted to three children whom she allowed to enter the Reform very young, wearing the habit and living the life of the community, though not making their profession till they were much older. She evidently felt that they kept the nuns young. 'These angels are a great edification to us and we find them very refreshing. If there were just one of them, and no more, in every convent, I can see no inconvenience—only profit.'[7] These three favourite 'angels' were Teresita, Gracián's little sister Isabel ('my Bella') and Casilda Padilla. Of the last we read less in the *Letters*

[1] Cf. p. 50, above.   [2] *LL* 246 (601).   [3] *LL* 304 (712).

[4] *LL* 65 (161).   [5] *LL* 374 (854).   [6] *LL* 76 (187). Cf.

[7] *LL* 193 (480).   p. 134, below.

than in the *Foundations*, but of Isabel Gracián Saint Teresa paints a companion picture to that of Teresita.

Bella, 'looking very sweet',[1] donned the Discalced habit at eight, and, growing 'plump and pretty', 'a beautiful little creature',[2] evoked from Saint Teresa more and more expressions of admiration and delight. Soon, not unnaturally, she began to compare her with Teresita, and the comparison was by no means all in Teresita's favour. 'She has a gentler disposition than Teresa and she is unusually clever.'[3] It is interesting to see how this busy foundress, with the cares of all her convents upon her, at the very height of the 'great storm of trials', has time to study these two children, to muse upon their respective qualities and to write to the Seville Prioress—for her 'entertainment'[4]—a comparative estimate of the two:

'If this Bella of mine had Teresa's natural graces, and the supernatural gifts through which we have seen God working in her, she would be the better of the two, for she is her superior in intelligence and ability and has such a gentle disposition that one can mould her as one likes. . . . I have only one trouble with her, and that is that I don't know what to do about her mouth—it is a very hard mouth, and she has a very harsh laugh, and is for ever laughing. . . . Anyone who has seen how graceful Teresa is in her movements and in every other way will notice it all the more. . . . Don't say anything about this to anyone, but it would amuse you if you saw what a life I lead her over controlling her mouth. . . .

'Well, there is a picture of the two girls for you, in case you should think I am not telling the truth when I give Bella the preference. I have told it you for your entertainment.'[5]

To the present-day reader the passage affords more than entertainment. It is one of the most striking and vivid in the whole collection. It transports us to Toledo and photographs for us this elderly nun sitting silently in a corner and watching the child of eight playing at hermitages,[6] exactly as she herself had done half a century earlier,[7] her thoughts flying to Ávila, where another child whom she knew and loved equally well would be doing the same. There is much more in the *Letters* about Bella: her childish

---

[1] *LL* 109 (281).   [2] *LL* 111 (289).   [3] *LL* 118 (303).
[4] *LL* 162 (406).   [5] *LL* 162 (406).   [6] *LL* 135, 162 (346, 406).
[7] *Life*, I (*CWSTJ*, I, 11).

sayings are reported,[1] and her various occupations described,[2] much as Teresita's are. But it is the evidence of the care with which the Saint *studied* them that is remarkable.

[VI]

Yet all these numerous portraits put together are not so striking, or so memorable, as the portrait which Saint Teresa has unwittingly left us of herself. The difficulty is to attempt to reproduce it, for, between what she intentionally reveals and what we deduce, there is enough to fill a large book. One learns much about her from her objective writings—particularly from the *Foundations*. Let us see to what extent, and in what respects, the *Letters* supplement these.

Both *Life* and *Foundations* portray a very able, busy and methodical woman, who, even if she had accomplished nothing in the interior life, would be entitled, by the number, nature and variety of her practical achievements as a foundress, to the epithet 'great'. The *Letters* give us an insight into the details of that busy life, not less crowded when she was staying for long periods at one of her own houses than during the slow and trying journeys which the *Foundations* so graphically describe. Perhaps the travelling was sometimes a relief from those long days, each crammed with duties—'letters and business matters', as she puts it, 'raining down upon me';[3] receipts to be written; gifts to be acknowledged; advice to be given to prioresses; homely remedies for illnesses to be suggested, family matters to be attended to; the price of a foundation building to be negotiated. Here and there we can see how she organizes her days: first, writing letters till two o'clock in the morning and getting a 'dreadful headache'; then finding it more economical of time to follow the doctor's orders and stop writing at midnight, besides often using an amanuensis when not writing intimately.[4]

The *Letters* also afford us a much better idea of the difficulties with which she had to contend in making her foundations than we find anywhere else, except in the account given in the *Life* of the foundation of Saint Joseph's, Ávila. In her *Foundations*, it is true, she describes in detail the impediments which had to be overcome before the establishment of each house was completed, but they

[1] *LL* 136, 138, 147 (347, 352, 373).   [2] *LL* 135 (346).
[3] *LL* 400 (907).   [4] *LL* 168 (426).

could not be expected to reveal, as the *Letters* do, how, even while she was making one foundation, or was to all appearances resting from her work as a foundress, the problems of a dozen houses were pressing upon her. The *Life* and the *Foundations* give a flat picture; the picture in the *Letters* is three-dimensional.

The most constant troubles were financial. How is this house to exist without more inmates? Will the straits of that one be relieved by the entry of a wealthy postulant who may or may not prove suitable? Will another wealthy postulant already judged suitable decide to enter or not? Can So-and-so, an admirable person for the Reform, be admitted without a dowry? Generally she can:

'I take a great many (dowryless) nuns, provided they are spiritual persons, and then the Lord sends me others with dowries, which puts things right.'[1]

There is no suggestion in the letters of undue concern over these matters: in fact, 'if we are always worrying about dowries, it will be the worse for us'.[2] But there is plenty of realism—and on occasion a bluntly phrased realism, as where a parent is suspected of unwillingness to fulfil his agreed obligations. *Si más pudieren sacar, sáquenlo*: 'if you can get more out of him, get it'.[3] One could hardly have anything more definite than that.

There were also financial problems more fundamental even than these. Saint Teresa, especially in her early years as a foundress, liked to found a house 'in poverty'—*i.e.*, without any endowment —trusting for its support to God alone. But her idealism is always tempered by sound practical sense. If she founds in poverty in a city which is already full of monasteries and convents dependent upon charity, the chances of the community's survival are small. If in a village where the local landowner is well disposed, there is the risk of undue dependence upon that benefactor. If an endowment is to be accepted, careful regard must be had to any conditions attached to it. Endowed or non-endowed, enquiries must be made in all possible quarters about local conditions. These considerations will help to explain why the letters are freely sprinkled with references to potential foundations which were never made— at any rate, during Saint Teresa's lifetime.

Other troubles are disciplinary. In one house Prioress and Sub-Prioress are at loggerheads. In another, one of the major benefactors is trying to interfere with its government. In a third, the

---

[1] *LL* 19 (76).   [2] *LL* 103 (263).   [3] *LL* 131 (339).

Prioress is ill and the Vicaress set in her place is proving unsuccessful. Confessors were a fruitful source of trouble. There were seldom situations such as arose at Seville, where the confessor conspired with two discontented nuns to depose the Prioress, but it was not uncommon for the confessor to be at odds with the Prioress, or to be over-lax with the nuns, or to be lacking in tact or understanding in his direction of them. Both Saint Teresa and Saint John of the Cross have much to say about unsatisfactory confessors and Saint Teresa's letters show that they could err in their treatment, not only of proficients, but also of the spiritually immature.

And there were other troubles so varied that one never knew what would be coming next. A whole group of them had to do with the activities of the Calced, of Sega and Tostado, and with the persecutions, the crises and the complicated negotiations that preceded the division of the Order. Into these were precipitated family worries—the death of Lorenzo, the Ovalle scandal, the problem presented by the melancholy Pedro. There were present needs: 'If you know anyone . . . who will lend me a few pence, I don't want them as a gift . . . The fact is I haven't a farthing.'[1] And there were possibilities about the future, which must not be worried about, it is true, but had to be faced, and fairly weighed, for a false step taken at such a time might have unimagined consequences. No wonder, in face of all this, that Saint Teresa was apt to describe her life as a *baraúnda*—a 'hurly-burly'!

The great gift of the *Letters* to posterity, however, consists in what they tell us, not about Saint Teresa's activities, but about *herself*.

Genuine letters—*i.e.*, letters written to be read by their recipients alone, with no thought in the writer's mind of a public—have always the advantage over objective works, even if these are autobiographical, provided that they are representative, and not all written to a small number of people or covering only a very brief period of time. Few collections in existence can be more representative than one of over 450 letters, covering some twenty years, and addressed to about 120 people in widely differing stations of life, from the King and the General of the Order to a child of thirteen. We may therefore rely upon it to give us a true and balanced picture of the writer.

What first strikes one in that picture is how much it reveals of Saint Teresa's personal life and character. About her spiritual

[1] *LL* 62 (154).

progress she has more to say, as one would expect, in the *Life* and the *Interior Castle*, and even about more superficial matters, which often help one to get to know a person better than the deeper things, she is remarkably communicative in these two treatises. But in the *Letters* she casts aside all reserve and describes her health of body and soul so intimately that we get the sensation of being in her company. Only against the background which they provide can we estimate the true magnitude of her achievements.

About some of these, but for the *Letters*, we should know next to nothing. There is, for example, the triennium (1571–4) which she spent as Prioress at her old convent of the Incarnation. Accounts written by others tell of the straits, both spiritual and material, in which she found that house, and of the good which, with the aid of Saint John of the Cross, who went to it as chaplain, she did there. In the *Foundations*, since it is not relevant to her subject, she passes it over entirely; only in the *Letters* can we read her own account of her accomplishment. But more significant is the insight we get into the handicaps against which she had to struggle. Hardly was she settled at the Incarnation than she was beset by ill-health, which dogged her right through the winter—'several feverish attacks' between October and Christmas; a quartan ague for two months in the new year; quinsy and neuralgia in February and March: 'I get quite disgusted when I realize what a hopeless creature I am.'[1] But she refuses to give up and admit defeat: 'on my good days I have been able to go with the others to choir. . . . I make great efforts not to stay in bed except when I have fever.'[2] Naturally these efforts bring reaction, in the shape of physical depression. 'I miss you terribly here,' she writes to her sister, 'and feel very much alone.'[3] Yet in every letter there is a hopeful note. She is always 'all right again now',[4] or 'well—that is, well for me';[5] or at the very worst she will say, 'I don't think it will last long'.[6] And, most important of all, she can report that her 'soul is not without tranquillity',[7] an understatement which recalls the 'some fervour' to which Saint John of the Cross confesses as he sits down to write that sublimest of treatises, the *Living Flame of Love*.[8]

This example, chosen merely because on the particular period which it covers there is nothing at all in the *Foundations*, is representative of the *Letters* from beginning to end. As we read on in them, we realize that their writer was no abnormal personality, im-

---

[1] *LL* 34 (100).   [2] *LL* 33 (97).   [3] *LL* 33 (98).   [4] *LL* 30 (91).
[5] *LL* 31 (94).   [6] *LL* 33 (97).   [7] *LL* 31 (94).   [8] *CWSJX*, III, 15.

pervious to every rebuff and set-back, to whom effort came easily, but an elderly woman with poor health, tiring soon and recuperating slowly, and very conscious of her increasing age. 'Old and tired'[1] she terms herself, more than four years before her death. A year later, and the phrase 'I am tired'[2] is recurring so frequently that we begin to think of her as wearing out, and forget, till we re-read the *Foundations*, how phenomenal, during these last years, was her activity. But activity is now taking its full toll of her: 'you would be shocked to see how old I am and how little use for anything'.[3] For that matter, even when much younger, she seems by no means sure of herself. She has great misgivings about her judgment. 'Women', she says, are 'timorous creatures, most of them', and she is no exception to the rule.[4]

'I am always timorous when I have to make a decision about anything—I immediately think I am going to do everything wrong.'[5]

In fact, she is not 'very brave' about anything, she sighs, as she quotes one of her critics: 'He tells me I am like a mouse afraid of the cats.'[6] But the context of that remark, it must be confessed, does not suggest that she took it very seriously.

Such few indications of genuine weakness as we find in her occur only on the emotional side and concern her relations with Gracián. Barely eighteen months after their first meeting, she is asking him (in a passage which, rather surprisingly, he reproduces in his semi-autobiography)[7] if he loves her ('who has no one else in the world but you, her Father') more than his mother (who 'has a husband and her other children to love her').[8] As she grows older, she finds herself increasingly dependent on him and her tone becomes increasingly urgent when she begs him to write to her more often, or to come to see her. How human she is in that letter, where, referring both to herself and to him in the third person, she writes:

'She has nothing else to console her (but your friendship), and she wants no other consolation than that. And, as she herself says, she has a great many trials and is weak by nature, so that she becomes distressed when she thinks (her affection) is not repaid. ... Careless though he [*i.e.*, Gracián] may be by nature, he must

[1] *LL* 231 (567).   [2] *E.g.*, *LL* 283, 287, 336 (673, 679, 781).
[3] *LL* 410 (923).   [4] *LL* 147 (371–2).   [5] *LL* 46 (119).
[6] *LL* 216 (532).   [7] *Peregrinación de Anastasio*, Diálogo XVI.
[8] *LL* 111 (285).

66

not be so with her; for, where there is love, it cannot slumber so long.'[1]

And quite startlingly human is a later letter, written from Palencia, where she has just arrived, expecting to find Gracián there, ready to accompany her to Soria, only to discover that he has left for Valladolid and deputed the charge of her to someone else. This is how she writes to him:

'I must remind you, my Father, that, after all, the flesh is weak, and what has happened has made me sadder than I could have wished to be: it has been a great blow to me. Your Paternity might at least have postponed your departure till you could have left us in our house: a week more or less could have mattered to you very little. I have been very lonely here. . . . Everything will be distasteful to me now, for, after all, the soul feels the absence of one who both governs it and brings it relief. May all this conduce to God's service . . .!'[2]

Another aspect of Saint Teresa's personality which can be studied only in the *Letters* is that of human relations.

Readers of the *Foundations* who remember her remark that she was always inclined to deal 'quite truthfully and simply'[3] with prelates will turn with particular interest to the two letters which she wrote to Rubeo, General of the Order. These are not merely formal letters. In the first[4] she has to defend her action in having made two foundations against his orders in Andalusia and at the same time to endeavour to divert his wrath from Mariano and Gracián. In the second,[5] besides returning to those themes, she has also to explain why she has not yet obeyed his command, received two months previously, to leave Seville for Castile. P. Silverio rightly calls the earlier letter 'a model of tact and discretion';[6] it also reveals a truly courtier-like skill in dealing with a difficult situation. Beginning with a reference to the 'great joy' she felt on hearing that his Reverence was in good health, Saint Teresa dilates on the 'great love' which her nuns, 'knowing no other father', bear him—'you are all we have in the world'.[7] Then she goes straight to the Andalusian question, and, having given a brief explanation of her conduct, plunges into an impassioned

[1] *LL* 290 (683).   [2] *LL* 366 (838–9).
[3] *Foundations*, II (*CWSTJ*, III, 5).   [4] *LL* 74 (178–84).
[5] *LL* 91 (220–6).   [6] *LL* 74 (178, n. 2).   [7] *LL* 74 (178).

defence of the two friars, after which she returns, with typically Spanish hyperbole, to the theme of her love for his Reverence: 'I beg your Reverence to realize that the whole body of the Discalced Fathers mean nothing to me by comparison with anything that so much as touches your Reverence's garment.'[1]

The second letter is an even greater achievement than the first. During the intervening eight months Saint Teresa has written 'three or four' letters to the General which have not survived and her touch is now surer than before. She begins tersely, determinedly, without compliments. Gracián and Mariano, 'without a doubt', are his Reverence's 'loyal sons'—'none . . . more so'. As to herself—his Reverence's eyes must have opened wide as he read:

'When we both stand before His judgment seat, your Reverence will see what you owe to your loyal daughter, Teresa of Jesus.[2]'

Gracián: yes, he certainly accepted a commission to act as Visitor in Andalusia—she herself wishes he had declined it, as at first he had meant to do—but it came from the Nuncio (that is, from the representative of the Pope), so, she infers,[3] he could hardly have persisted in refusing it.

Then she becomes more persuasive. 'Poor Mariano', it seems, has written the General a letter which was a little less tactful than he had meant it to be. Will not Rubeo overlook it? ('He cannot express himself properly, but he assures me he never had the slightest intention of offending your Reverence.'[4]) Possibly the devil was responsible: he 'has so much to gain by the interpretation of things in his own way'. In any case, 'let your Reverence remember that children are apt to err, and that fathers must not look at their faults, but forgive them. For the love of Our Lord, I beseech your Reverence to do me this favour.'[5] That, surely, Rubeo would find irresistible; but, if not, what about this?

'Although we women are not of much use as counsellors, we are occasionally right. . . .'[6]

That said, and a good deal more on the same subject, Teresa becomes sterner again. For the General has hurt her, and, if possible without risk of angering him, he must be told so. Two months

---

[1] *LL* 74 (180).   [2] *LL* 91 (221).
[3] Later, she says so very definitely: *LL* 91 (225).   [4] *LL* 91 (222-3).
[5] *LL* 91 (223).   [6] *LL* 91 (223).

before, he had sent her the order already referred to, to leave
Seville, and he had sent it, not direct, but through the Prior of the
Calced at Seville—and this when relations between Discalced
and Calced were at their worst. Further, it had been made public
before it was conveyed to her and she had first learned of it from
elsewhere. And she has not yet obeyed it, for Gracián—deriving
his authority, via the Nuncio, from the Pope—has told her to stay
in Seville till after the winter. How does she tell Rubeo this?

With the greatest deference, but with firmness and dignity, she
states her position in words that could not conceivably give offence:

'I will certainly not hide from your Reverence that, so far as
I understand my own mind, it would have been a great kindness,
and a satisfaction to me, if you yourself had conveyed this order
to me in a letter. . . .

'In view . . . of the great love which I have for your Reverence . . ., I have been unable to help feeling hurt that I should have
been treated like someone who had been very disobedient. . . .

'Actually, even if it were not a pleasure for me to carry out your
Reverence's orders, but the severest of trials, it would not so much
as cross my mind to do anything but obey you. . . .'[1]

How, then, does she account for not having obeyed? Not by
mentioning Gracián, we may be sure: it was an unspecified 'they'
who made her postpone the journey:

'I wished to comply with your command immediately, but it
was near Christmas, and, as the journey was so long, they would
not allow me (*no me dejaron*) to go, thinking that it would not be
your Reverence's wish that I should risk an illness.'[2]

Finally, after some animadversions on the conduct of the Provincial, Salazar, to whom Rubeo's order had first been conveyed,
Saint Teresa sends the General a greeting which, though affectionate and deferential to the last degree, has an unmistakable
sting in the tail:

'If only God would grant me the favour of hearing that your
Reverence was coming (here)! At the same time, I should be very
sorry that you had to make such a trying journey.[3] So I shall have

[1] *LL* 91 (224).   [2] *LL* 91 (225).
[3] She could hardly help saying this, as she had just been excusing herself
for not making a much shorter journey than his would be during the winter,
and Rubeo was eight years her senior.

to wait for this happiness until that endless eternity, in which your Reverence will discover how much you owe to me.'[1]

These two letters to Rubeo are the outstanding examples of Saint Teresa's relations with persons in authority, but the reader will be no less delighted with her letters to King Philip II. There are one or two passages in her letters to the great in which she perhaps overdoes her deference, as where she remarks to the Duchess of Alba: 'To learn that your Excellency was suffering from a cold marred my complete enjoyment of the letter you did me the kindness of writing me.'[2] But there is none of this, and little of the diplomatic fulsomeness which adorns her letters to the General, in those which she pens to his Caesarean Majesty. With the deepest respect she combines an admirable dignity: a member of the Virgin's Order need make no apology for addressing a King—especially when she has something to say. And in three of these four letters[3] she has something very definite to say, and very definitely does she say it. In one, she is 'quite convinced' that the Discalced must be 'made into a separate province' and Gracián put in charge of it: will his Majesty 'command this to be done'?[4] In another, her 'attention has been called' to a memorial libelling Gracián which has been sent to the King: 'I beseech your Majesty, for the love of God, not to allow such infamous charges to be brought before the tribunals.'[5] Finally, there is the imprisonment of Saint John of the Cross: 'I beseech your Majesty to command that he be set free immediately.'[6]

Genuine grievances, clear-cut requests—and no apologies!

'I see that I am being very bold, but remembering that the Lord hears the poor, and that your Majesty is in the place of the Lord, I do not think you will be vexed by my importunity.'[7]

To other of her aristocratic correspondents, such as Cardinal Quiroga, Don Álvaro de Mendoza, Doña Luisa de la Cerda, and Dom Teotónio de Bragança, she writes with the same dignified deference, modified according to the degree of intimacy with them which she possessed. In a letter to the Cardinal, for example, she uses the phrase 'your most Illustrious Lordship' (the form 'Emin-

[1] LL 91 (226).   [2] LL 384 (877).
[3] LL 77, 195, 204. The fourth, Letter 45, somewhat resembles the letter to Rubeo.
[4] LL 77 (188).   [5] LL 195 (482–3).   [6] LL 204 (497).
[7] LL 77 (188).

ence' not being yet current) six times in the first ten lines,[1] and, when writing to his confessor, she addresses the letter 'to the most Illustrious Señor Licenciate Peña, Confessor to the most Illustrious Cardinal Archbishop of Toledo, my Lord'.[2] The letter in which she thanks Don Álvaro for having permitted the jurisdiction of her first convent to be made over to the Order[3] is a model combination of frankness and tact. But if we go a long way down the social scale we shall still find tact in her. Occasionally, where others would use some downright phrase, her thrusts are so ingenuous that the unwary modern reader misses the point. A delicious example occurs in a brief note to her sister Juana de Ovalle, indicating that she wants to have a private talk with her and her daughter, but not with her slightly cantankerous husband. This is how she phrases it:

'It would not be too much to ask Señor Juan de Ovalle if he would be kind enough to allow you and your daughter to come and see me, although this might involve difficulties and he might have to stay and look after the house. But he could do me the kindness of coming to see me some other day. . . . I should be very glad if he would show me this kindness.'[4]

Another masterpiece is the intimation to Don Gaspar de Villanueva, the confessor at Malagón, who has been at loggerheads with the acting-Prioress, that he will have to go:

'I shall be very sorry if you have to leave, but I realize that inward tranquillity is more important to you than pleasing me. May the Lord give us tranquillity, as He can. Amen.'[5]

An interesting study of quite a different kind will be found in three letters written at a very short interval, a few months before her death, to a Canon of Ávila, Don Pedro Castro. Dr. Castro was a college friend of Gracián's, with whose 'intelligence and charm and . . . pleasant way of speaking' Saint Teresa had been 'very much taken', though she confessed herself a little doubtful if he were entirely trustworthy.[6] Gracián having apparently reassured her as to this, she sent him her autobiography to read; and in the first of the three letters referred to she is thanking him most gracefully for his criticisms of it. Then it occurs to her that he might be asked to preach the sermon at the forthcoming profession of a

---

[1] *LL* 368 (843).   [2] *LL* 372 (849).   [3] *LL* 192 (477-9).
[4] *LL* 376 (861).   [5] *LL* 186 (473).   [6] *LL* 382 (873).

novice in whom he has shown some interest. He seems to have half-promised to do so and subsequently to have changed his mind. As a result, he receives one of the sharpest of Saint Teresa's letters. She minces no words:

'Jesus be with you. I cannot conceive why you now refuse to grant this request, and it never entered my head last night that you would do so. You knew very well what distress you would be causing that poor little creature. . . . I am not going to say any more about it to her mother: I shall merely respect your wishes. . . . There had better be no sermon at all. . .'.[1]

The direct attack was successful. Dr. Castro relented and preached the sermon; and, late that same night, after spending the whole evening in conference with Saint John of the Cross, Saint Teresa found time to write him a note of solicitous thanks:

'Jesus be with you, and may His Majesty reward you for the pleasure you have given me, and the way you have helped me, today. . . . The sisters here kiss your hands: it was a great comfort to them. Send me word if it tired you, and how you are, but do not write to me about it, for, glad as I am to see your writing, I want to tire you as little as I can, and I must have done so a great deal already.'[2]

To judge by the deposition which he subsequently made in connection with her beatification, the incident did nothing to lessen his admiration for her.

A careful study of the letters which Saint Teresa writes to each of her principal correspondents will show how she could be all things to all men. The person to whom she wrote, both most intimately and at the greatest length, was Jerónimo Gracián. It is in her letters to him, which she once asked him never to read to others, and compared to her 'conversations with God',[3] that we should know, even if she had not told us, that we come nearest to her heart. But to María de San José, the Prioress of Seville, to María Bautista of Valladolid, and to her brother Lorenzo she is no less frank and often equally intimate. To none of them—to nobody, indeed—did she ever hesitate to write bluntly and trenchantly: she was 'unbearable', she once remarked, with people she loved,[4] and, the more she loved them, the less she could endure their having any faults; and that, in a person of her temperament, was

[1] LL 389 (890–1).   [2] LL 390 (891–2).   [3] LL 134 (346).   [4] LL 302 (704).

tantamount to saying the harder she would try to uproot them.[1] The sternest letter in the whole collection is addressed to her 'daughter and crown', V. Ana de Jesús,[2] though the 'terrible letters' which she speaks of having written to Brianda, the Prioress of Malagón, may well have surpassed this. Unfortunately, only one letter written to Brianda has survived, and that a very solicitous one about her health.

No characteristic of Saint Teresa's letters endears us to her more than the unfailing courtesy with which she wrote to persons who, by ordinary social standards, were of small importance. We are unlikely ever to learn the identity of 'some girls at Ávila' to whom she wrote advising them to await their parents' consent before taking the habit, but we can well understand their prizing the lines conveying that gentle reproof, which, softened by kindly encouragement, she administers with such delicacy and consideration, signing the letter 'Your servant, Teresa of Jesus'.[3] Some time before, 'two girls who wished to join the Reform' had received a still more encouraging letter of much the same tenor, and even more exquisitely phrased.[4] The 'nun who wished to transfer to the Discalced Carmelites' might have found Saint Teresa's blank negative somewhat disconcerting had it ended with the first paragraph. But, though 'writing in a hurry', the Saint finds time to add some sound spiritual advice ending with the heartening reminder that we can love God wherever we are. 'Blessed be His Name, there is no one who can prevent us from doing that.'[5]

Even now, we have barely fringed the immense variety of the Teresan *Epistolario*. One can still enter into the spirit of the controversy on Gaspar de Salazar's alleged intention of abandoning the Society of Jesus for Carmel: we have three letters on the subject from Saint Teresa, varying as widely in tone as in content, to the Jesuit Provincial, Suárez, to the Jesuit Rector at Ávila, Gonzalo Dávila, and (most enlightening of all) to Gracián. One can savour the frank comments on men and things written, with just a suggestion of the intimacy which Saint Teresa was later to develop for Gracián, to the Salamancan professor, Domingo Báñez. A group of letters standing quite by itself is composed by the notes of condolence, each a model of its kind, addressed to correspondents as unlike as her nephew, Diego de Guzmán,[6] her aristocratic friend Doña María de Mendoza,[7] an unknown person who seems to have

---

[1] *LL* 309 (727). [2] Cf. p. 45, above. [3] *LL* 340 (787–8). [4] *LL* 249 (603).
[5] *LL* 363 (835–6).   [6] *LL* 156 (387–8).   [7] *LL* 222 (542).

been a relative of one of her nuns,[1] and the son of the Marquis of Velada, Don Sancho Dávila.[2] What strikes one most about these letters is their complete naturalness. They contain no forced phrases, no conventional compliments. With her letter to Don Diego Saint Teresa sends a present of two melons; and, after condoling with Don Sancho, she proceeds to discuss distractions in church and remedies for the toothache. But the perfect naturalness of all Saint Teresa's letters is one of their greatest charms.

It would be impossible to give an adequate account of the *Letters* without referring, at least briefly, to their humour. Any reader of Saint Teresa's other works, especially of the *Foundations*, will expect to find this. I have commented elsewhere on the frequency in those works of such phrases as 'I just laughed to myself',[3] and of a subtler allusive humour which on occasion finds its way even into passages of marked sublimity. Humour was an essential part of Saint Teresa's make-up, and it may be doubted if, except on the highest themes, she was capable of writing very much without its continually breaking through.

The variety of the forms which it takes, and of the subjects which provoke it, may be illustrated by a random selection from the contexts in which occurs the phrase 'It makes me laugh'. She laughed at the thought that in spite of indifferent health she was able to do all she had to; at the penance of reclusion imposed upon Gracián which withdrew him from the conflict with the Calced and left the others to fight on alone; at Salcedo's old housekeeper, who treated Lorenzo, the grand gentleman returned from the Indies, with such ceremony. She laughed at the Dominican Medina's bad opinion of her, at the idiosyncrasies of the Sub-Prioress at Seville, and at the idea of sending Lorenzo hair-shirts in return for dainties and gifts of money.[4] Perhaps these examples suffice to show that what really amused her most was incongruity. Whether this was directed against her or not made little or no difference; the comical aspect of it would strike her quite objectively.

'What a contrary world this is! Here he is, who could be serving your Ladyship and won't, and here am I, who should like to and can't!'[5]

To that typically Teresan comment may be added others in which

[1] *LL* 327 (763).   [2] *LL* 381 (868).   [3] *CWSTJ*, I, xv.
[4] *LL* 34, 287, 101, 53, 131, 163 (100, 679, 257, 135, 338, 412).   [5] *LL* 6 (42).

the humour is basic, but latent. She tries to be poor, but people send her so many presents that poverty becomes quite impossible.[1] She would be too happy for words, but that letters keep raining upon her—'it's always like that when I am happy'.[2] Because Gracián takes no notice of her wish not to stay at Toledo, she becomes 'as pleased as she could be' to stay—'I have a strange nature'.[3] From this sensitiveness to the incongruous springs most of her fun. How amusing that a brother of hers and Juana's could have become an important person—'his Excellency our señor brother Don Lorenzo'![4] How ridiculous that her confessor should make her eat more as a penance![5]

Other jokes take the form of bantering comments (sometimes concealing reproofs) on the faults or weaknesses of her spiritual daughters. Of María de San José—'You are a fox and I expect there is a subterfuge about it somewhere'. 'Oh, how vain you must be now that you are a semi-Provincial!'[6] Of María del Espíritu Santo, who was so scrupulous about her accounts that 'she would be quite capable of reckoning the very water'.[7] Of Ana de Jesús, who complained because the Seville prioress sent her nuns to Granada 'in a fit and proper way instead of mounting them on mules for God and the world to see'.[8] Of two unnamed nuns who had been reporting supernatural manifestations of doubtful genuineness: 'they would not', she remarks grimly, 'have had such a whirl of experiences if they had been with me'.[9] Nor does she omit to laugh at herself—at some of her verses, for instance, which 'have neither feet nor head'. 'What a brain for a foundress! But I can tell you I thought I had a great brain when I made up this.'[10] Or at the foolishness of people who call her a saint: 'I tell them they had better canonize some other nun, as the only thing they have to do is to pronounce the word.'[11] And once, on the subject of her own character, she becomes unexpectedly epigrammatic:

'It must be my nature—I could be suborned with a sardine.'[12]

She can even, on occasion, laugh at her persecutors. The Prior of the Calced at Ávila, her 'wonderful friend', 'our good Valdemoro', is the most comic of them. Considering that it was he who abducted Saint John of the Cross, it argues great benevolence in her that she can see the humorous side of him, but his pretences of

[1] *LL* 18 (69).   [2] *LL* 101 (257).   [3] *LL* 111 (289).   [4] *LL* 1d (28).
[5] *LL* 147 (373).   [6] *LL* 162 (404–5).   [7] *LL* 123 (321).   [8] *LL* 424 (947).
[9] *LL* 233 (575).   [10] *LL* 158.   [11] *LL* 297 (697).   [12] *LL* 248 (602).

friendship are so transparent that she really cannot take him seri-ously.[1] Her references to him, all tinged with amused irony, furnish an admirable illustration of the most moving type of Teresan humour, that which concerns the troubles of the Reform.

This, as will be readily understood, is almost peculiar to the *Letters*, for in the *Foundations* she was primarily the historian, and humour in history—at any rate, conscious humour—would pro-bably have seemed to her misplaced. But in her day-by-day obser-vations to intimate friends it was different. 'I thought that was a beautiful idea about sending me to the Indies', is her only com-ment when she hears that the Andalusian Calced have been spread-ing the rumour that she is to go to America. 'God forgive them: the best thing they can do is to say so many things at once that nothing they say will be believed by anyone.'[2]

Then there are continual humorous sallies in the *Letters*. One never knows when she will come out with them, or to what they will refer. They seem to spring from sheer lightheartedness. It is when full of 'amusement and happiness', for example, that she cries to Gracián:

'Oh, my Father, it was quite unnecessary for you to swear, even like a saint, much less like a carter!'[3]

Into this category come several sinister references to fish—none too reliable, in inland Castile, even today: what must it have been like, we may ask, in the sixteenth century? 'The dog-fish was nice', but 'the tunny-fish was left at Malagón—and long may it stay there!'[4] And there were those meals which Gracián had taken in hospital: 'those dreadful cod patties!'[5] Then ('Oh, my Father, I forgot to tell you!') the *curandera* came, at the request of the Medina Prioress, to treat Saint Teresa's broken arm: 'it cost her a great deal—and the treatment cost me a great deal too!'[6] There are scores of these lively and amusing remarks, which often have the verve of youth, even when the writer is well over sixty. But one notes rather sadly that, from about 1580, when her physical powers begin to decline and personal troubles crowd thick upon her, they almost wholly disappear. Instead, we read such melancholy para-doxes as, 'The farther I journey in this life, the less comfort I find',[7] or occasionally a smilingly ironic touch: 'I am well myself and

---

[1] *LL* 121, 127, 128 (312, 328, 330).   [2] *LL* 138 (354).
[3] *LL* 228 (558–9).   [4] *LL* 108 (280).   [5] *LL* 216 (532).   [6] *LL* 229 (561).
[7] *LL* 378 (863).

have become a great Prioress—as if I had nothing else to do but that!'[1] The humorous outlook on life is the same, but the vitality is disappearing.

[VII]

The more brightly, against a bubbling humour which testifies not only to a lively personality but to a life perfectly balanced and integrated, shines the spiritual quality of Saint Teresa's letters. Though they are by no means 'spiritual letters' in the conventional sense, they will always be noteworthy in religious literature because they give a full-length picture of one whose character and experience were completely permeated with spirituality.

To lay folk she habitually writes very simply. Gaytán, who owed to her his conversion from a careless life, was apt to be forgetful of her teaching ('I have told you again and again what you should do'.[2] 'I have told you this any number of times, but you have evidently forgotten'[3]), so in addressing him she sought for picturesque metaphors which he would remember:

'You must realize that in the spiritual world, as in this world, there are different kinds of weather.'

Even to as aristocratic and highly educated a lady as Doña María de Mendoza she writes simply and directly:

'Oh, if only your control over yourself were as complete as your control over others, how lightly you would esteem what this world calls trials!'[4]

Most of her exhortations of this type are given incidentally: sometimes, as the context shows, they have only just suggested themselves to her. Apart from fragments, there is no letter of this type which is concerned exclusively with spirituality or which appears to have been written with the sole aim of edification.

There was one lay person, however, to whom she acted as unofficial spiritual director, and who had promised her obedience in things spiritual—namely, her brother Lorenzo. To him the advice she gives is largely ascetic—concerning the wearing of hair-shirts, the making of vows, aridity in prayer, the taking of the discipline, the exorcism of evil spirits with holy water, the regulation of sleep,

---

[1] *LL* 382 (872).   [2] *LL* 57 (143).   [3] *LL* 66 (162).
[4] *LL* 15 (62). Cf. *LL* 35 (105).

etc.[1] Only once, when he appears to have had a supernatural experience in prayer, approximating to the Prayer of Quiet, does she instruct him at any length,[2] and then, it is interesting to note, she falls, with apparent naturalness, into the language of mystical theology. But as a rule she uses the most homely and colloquial language, salted at times with an asperity permissible in an elder sister:

'Remember what God said to Saul, and don't do anything I tell you not to.'[3]

To her prioresses, and other nuns, she writes encouragingly, or occasionally reprovingly, of their experiences in prayer, but always in quite a general way—they had their director at hand. Her role is maternal. She will remind them of things which they seem to have forgotten and suggest that they occasionally send her news about their progress towards perfection ('Do not omit to tell me how your spiritual life is progressing. I shall be glad to know about that'[4]). Once, a remark made to M. María de San José indicates that this prioress had sent her a report on her method of prayer, and also on that of one of her nuns, and Saint Teresa sandwiches a short approving comment between a reference to the debt on the Seville convent and a matter of discipline which had arisen at Paterna.[5] In another place, M. María Bautista has consulted her about certain interior trials, to which, in a letter packed with comments on all kinds of matters, she makes brief reference, after recommending a new purgative and discussing alternative methods of sending her some accounts. And here she is markedly maternal: 'the more you have of them (*i.e.*, the trials), the less notice you should take of them, for it is clear they are the result of an unstable imagination and a weak condition'. Having said this, and a little more, she goes on to refer, in a single short paragraph, to Salcedo's lawsuit and the problem of a blind novice and to send her regards to six different people.[6] These two letters are typical of Saint Teresa's spiritual counsels to her individual nuns. Of the way in which she wrote to them collectively we have examples in two letters addressed to the Seville community in the time of their great trouble.[7] No quotations from these will convey their moving beauty

[1] *LL* 171 (436), 163 (412), 158 (391), 158 (394), 168 (426), 171 (436), 168 (428), 168 (427), 171 (437).
[2] *LL* 163 (410–11). Cf. also p. 427.   [3] *LL* 171 (436).   [4] *LL* 385 (882).
[5] *LL* 173 (442–3).   [6] *LL* 126 (327).   [7] *LL* 264, 274 (629–32, 645–53).

and the depth of their affection. 'I assure you', begins the first, 'I have never loved you as much as I do now and you have never been bound to serve Our Lord as much as you are now, when He is granting you the great blessing of being able to taste something of the meaning of His Cross. . . .

'If you help yourselves, the good Jesus will help you; for, though He is asleep on the sea, when the storm rises He will still the winds. His pleasure is that we should ask Him for what we need, and so much does He love us that He is always seeking ways to help us. Blessed be His name for ever.'[1]

The correspondent to whom she writes most frequently about spiritual things is naturally Gracián, who, from his first meeting with her, was glad to profit by her long experience. Many characteristic points of her teaching will be found, if often only germinally, in these letters. Such are the disciplinary value of trials,[2] the deceptiveness of consolations (*gustos*),[3] the transition from mediation to contemplation and the signs and effects of potent prayer.[4] Evidently Gracián wrote her frequent descriptions of his spiritual experiences, on which she comments, but generally approvingly and in only a few words. She is glad, for example, that he is 'enjoying inward tranquillity', and 'making such very great progress that it really seems like something supernatural',[5] that 'amid all these storms' he 'should have the strength to make such good resolutions',[6] and that he should be granted 'illumination in the shape of such great favours'.[7]

Occasionally, it would seem, to judge from her comments, he described his experiences to her in considerable detail:

'I cannot think how Paul [*i.e.*, Gracián] can say he knows nothing about Union, for (what he says about) that bright darkness and impetus shows that that is not so.'[8]

But it is very seldom that she can be said to give him any very definite advice, apart from a solicitous recommendation that he should not devote to prayer time which he needs for sleep—and to this counsel she returns more than once, with some insistence.[9] However, she fears that, when she advises him, he may 'laugh at this foolishness', and she only puts such points to him by way of reminder.[10]

[1] *LL* 264 (629–30). [2] *LL* 115 (293). [3] *LL* 122 (316). [4] *LL* 122 (316).
[5] *LL* 115 (293). [6] *LL* 200 (492). [7] *LL* 209 (495). [8] *LL* 216 (531).
[9] *E.g.*, *LL* 203, 209 (495, 508–9).   [10] *LL* 221 (541).

From what has been said, it might be supposed that there is little spiritual profit to be derived from reading the *Letters*, and it is naturally true that there is more to be gained from the objective treatises. But, quite apart from the deeply spiritual tone of the whole collection, there are gems to be found in the most matter-of-fact of its pages. Let us end this survey by quoting a few of them—not extracts, it should be noted, from passages containing formal instruction, but occurring in the most widely differing contexts, many not spiritual at all:

'By suffering so many trials you are letting Our Lord light the fire of His love in your soul, and that fire will gradually enkindle others.'[1]

'I don't know how we can grieve for those who go to the land of safety.'[2]

'If you feel you want everybody to be praising God, that is the surest sign that your soul is occupied with Him.'[3]

'The truth is, we never really know ourselves. So the best thing must be to flee from the all to the All.'[4]

'Sometimes the ability to pray is taken from us by the mercy of God; and, for many reasons . . ., it is almost as great a mercy when He takes it away as when He gives it in abundant measure.'[5]

'Do realize that you cannot regulate all souls by the same yard-stick.'[6]

'I read in a book that, if we forsake God when He wants us, we shall not find Him when we want Him.'[7]

'Don't grasp at comforts: it is only hired soldiers who expect to be paid by the day. Serve Him without pay, as grandees serve the King.'[8]

Such extracts, each complete in itself, might with advantage be gathered together and published as a new collection of Teresan maxims.

[1] *LL* 15 (63). [2] *LL* 31 (94). [3] *LL* 57 (143). [4] *LL* 129 (334. Cf. n. 1).
[5] *LL* 158 (394). [6] *LL* 184 (465). [7] *LL* 209 (509). [8] *LL* 403 (912).

Saint Teresa's Style: A Tentative Appraisal[1]

'I just laughed to myself.'[2] If Saint Teresa's irrepressible sense of humour could bubble up at the antics of 'serious people' making 'a great fuss about niceties concerning their honour',[3] or at the craftiness shown by the devil in his making of laws by which monks and nuns 'go up and down in rank, as people do in the world',[4] what amusement would she not have found in the title of this essay! 'Saint Teresa's style', indeed! Had she not herself said all there was to say about that?

'For the love of God, let me work at my spinning-wheel and go to choir and perform the duties of the religious life, like the other sisters. I am not meant to write. I have neither the health nor the intelligence for it.'[5]

She is conscious enough of her style—'my rough style'[6]—but conscious chiefly of its badness, of its 'imperfection' and 'poverty'.[7] How, she might have asked, could it be anything else than bad? To begin with, she was a woman, devoid of learning, taking up her pen only under obedience, 'too stupid to explain anything',[8] untrained in the writer's art, with poor health and very little leisure—'almost stealing the time for writing',[9] which took her away from her more serious duties. She had an atrocious memory,

---

[1] In this essay the abbreviation *CWSTJ* (p. 15, above) is further abbreviated to '*CW*'. Round brackets are used, as elsewhere in the book, to enclose words which are not in the original and have to be supplied in translation. Square brackets enclose words of which the Spanish equivalents are found in the original, but which have to be omitted in the interests of sense.

[2] *CW*, I, xv, and p. 74, above.   [3] *Life*, XXI (*CW*, I, 134).
[4] *Way of Perfection*, XXXVI (*CW*, I, 156).   [5] *CW*, I, xxxix.
[6] *Way of Perfection*, XVI (*CW*, II, 68).   [7] *Op. cit.*, Prologue (*CW*, II, 1).
[8] *Interior Castle*, VI, iv (*CW*, II, 290).   [9] *Life*, X (*CW*, I, 61).

often forgetting what she had written a few days earlier and being constitutionally disinclined to turn back and see. Not that it mattered very much: her readers would hardly expect anything better.

'I expect many very important things will be omitted, and others will be put in which might well be left out: just as might be expected, in fact, of one with my witlessness and stupidity, and with so little quiet time. . . .'[1]

Yet, six years after her death, this poor, ignorant, forgetful woman's first editor, himself a master of Spanish prose, could refer to 'the purity and ease of her style', 'the gracefulness and skilful arrangement of the words' and 'an unaffected elegance which is delightful in the extreme' and 'doubt if there has been any writing of equal merit in our language'.[2] And today, after three and a half centuries, she is still universally eulogized, not only for what she wrote, but for the way in which she wrote it, is considered one of the leading prose-writers of the Golden Age and in many respects is held up as a model to the young writer. She herself would probably have attributed such fulsomeness to the influence of the devil. Professional writers might 'go up and down in rank', but what would a Discalced Carmelite nun be doing between the covers of a History of Spanish literature? It certainly is rather extraordinary, when one comes to think of it. . . .

[1]

The reasons for the esteem in which Saint Teresa's style is held are two. First, she was a born writer: her instinct taught her what she could never have learned in any other way. Secondly, she had a remarkable personality, which, since she wrote with almost complete naturalness, gave her writings the same force, vigour, persuasiveness and grace that characterized her dealings with all the people, high and low, whom she met. In studying her style, therefore, we shall be studying herself, and it is that, above all, which makes the task worth while.

The subject is not an easy one to treat within the limits of an essay. Most writers on Saint Teresa have been content to use such

---

[1] *Foundations*, Prologue (*CW*, III, xxiii). Cf. epilogue to *Life* (*CW*, I, 299), in which she attributes her omission to re-read this work to lack of time.

[2] Cit. *CW*, II, 371–2.

generalizations as 'artless', 'simple and unaffected', 'rich and racy', 'racy of the soil', illustrating them with a few of her popular and unconventional forms and phrases. The style being the woman, those who penetrate it farther are apt, as the Abbé Hoornaert must have realized, to stray beyond the bounds of literary expression into the realm of personal relations. But even on Saint Teresa's style considered in the narrowest sense a substantial book is waiting to be written. So rich and so amazingly varied are her modes of expression that for every word or phrase quoted in an essay of the length of this there are perhaps a hundred that invite analysis and comparison. Many discoveries, as even these few pages may perhaps show, are still unmade, but they will call for long and patient research by an investigator prepared to discard all prejudice and treat his extensive field as virgin soil.

Such an investigator will, of course, need to work from the original texts, not from translations, and will present his results in a form intelligible only to those familiar with Spanish. First, because of the differences between Spanish and English modes of writing: phrases that seem virile and forceful in the one language too often sound brusque, even crude, in the other. Secondly, because it is at best difficult, and at worst impossible, to render niceties of Spanish style in English translation.

The pages which follow are meant only to be suggestive and to stimulate the reader to further study. In choosing illustrations, I have been greatly handicapped by having to confine myself to those which come through in English: for this reason, Spanish-reading Teresans will miss many passages familiar to them which would find a prominent place in a fuller study based on original texts. In order to give the examples here used their maximum point, I have translated them all afresh, more literally than in my versions of the *Complete Works* and the *Letters*, and indeed more literally than would be acceptable in any continuous narrative. This does not mean that the versions in those volumes are less faithful than these. They are often more so, indeed; for so condensed in places is Saint Teresa's writing that its full meaning can only be brought out by a free rendering. The versions in this essay are made solely to illustrate points of style; for an adequate comprehension of any passage the reader should always go to the translation of the work from which it is taken.

[II]

About the vocabulary of Saint Teresa a good deal has been written, most of it easily accessible;[1] and, as the details are of interest chiefly to students of Spanish, only the main lines which research has taken need be indicated. In vocabulary, as in style, the keynote is naturalness. Never allowing any of her own daughters to indulge in *préciosités* unrebuked, she herself shuns any form of expression so interpretable. The manner of writing adopted by nuns, like their 'manner of talking', 'should be simple, frank and devout, rather like that of hermits and people who live in retirement. They must use none of the newfangled words—affectations, as I think people call them—which are current in a world always eager for new-fangled things. In all circumstances let them give preference to common expressions rather than to unusual ones.'[2]

No words can be found in Saint Teresa's writings, and very few constructions or stylistic devices, which may even be suspected of any taint of affectation. She eschews learned words, only a few score of which have been found in her total of close on a million. The few she does use are mainly technical terms which she cannot avoid, and which she spells either phonetically, or in the peculiar form used by the people: *e.g.*, *estasi* (for *éxtasi*: mod. *éxtasis*: 'ecstasy'); *parajismo* (*paroxismo*: 'paroxysm'); *proquesía* (*hipocresía*: 'hypocrisy'). Other words, too, which she must continually have used, she misspells, perhaps from a desire to err, if at all, in the opposite direction to affectation: *an* (for *aún*: 'yet'); *ilesia* (*iglesia*: 'church') ; *naide* (*nadie*: 'no one'); *relisión* (*religión*: 'religion'). Many of her misspellings exemplify the popular love of metathesis: *catredático* (for *catedrático*, 'professor'); *intrevalos* (*intervalos*: 'intervals'); *primitir* (*permitir*: 'permit'); *trasordinario* (*extraordinario*: 'extraordinary'). In addition to these, she uses many metathesized forms, such as *-ld-* for *-dl-* where a second person plural imperative

---

[1] *E.g.*, A. Sánchez Moguel, *El Lenguaje de Santa Teresa de Jesús* (Madrid, 1915); R. Hoornaert, *Sainte Térèse écrivain* (Paris, 1922), (*Saint Teresa in her Writings*, London, 1931); R. Menéndez Pidal, 'El estilo de Santa Teresa', in *Escorial* (1941), V, 13–30, and *La Lengua de Cristóbal Colón* (Madrid 1942,), pp. 145–74; Helmut Hatzfeld, 'El estilo nacional en los símiles de los místicos españoles y franceses', in *Nueva Revista de Filología Hispánica* (Mexico, 1947), I, 43–77.

[2] 'Method for the visitation of convents of Discalced Carmelite nuns', in *CW*, III, 251.

is followed by a conjunctive object pronoun, which in the sixteenth century were normal. Her simplifications (*e.g.*, *perfeción*, for *perfección*, 'perfection') exemplify a tendency which still continues, and has produced new forms even in the last generation.

She uses few of the technical terms of mysticism—chiefly because she writes, not abstractly, but in terms of her own experience. The phrase 'mystical theology' occurs in three places, all in the *Life*; 'mystical theology, as I believe it is called', she writes when she first introduces it,[1] and on another occasion she makes it clear why she shuns technicalities:

'The way in which this that we call union comes, and the nature of it, I do not know how to explain. It is described in mystical theology, but I am unable to use the proper terms, and I cannot understand what is meant by 'mind' (*mente*) or how this differs from "soul" or "spirit".'[2]

She does, however, use less abstract technical terms with some frequency: *éxtasis* occurs in six places, in one of which it is frequently repeated; *arrebatamiento* ('transport') and *arrobamiento* ('rapture') are common; *rapto* ('rapture') is used three times, once as a synonym of *arrobamiento* and *éxtasis*; *elevamiento* ('elevation') and its synonym *levantamiento* are found, if verbal forms are included, three and six times respectively; *vuelo de espíritu* ('flight of the spirit') occurs seven times, once as a synonym of *arrebatamiento*, *arrobamiento* and *elevamiento*; *embebecimiento* ('absorption') is used a great deal, but often figuratively; *contentos*, *gustos* and *regalos*[3] appear continually and are clearly distinguished from one another. *Mente* is never used again after the confession just quoted. The popular *hablas* is preferred to the learned *locuciones*. *Recogimiento* ('recollection') and *quietud* ('quiet') are both common: the fourth chapter of the *Life* suggests that the terms *oración* ('prayer') *de recogimiento* and *oración de quietud*, both of which are found, were derived from Osuna. Other terms used freely and easily are *oración mental* ('mental prayer'), *desposorio espiritual* ('spiritual betrothal'), *matrimonio espiritual* ('spiritual marriage'), *unión*, *oración de unión* ('prayer of union'), *visión* (*imaginaria, intelectual*) ('imaginary, intellectual vision').

Not only English readers, but even many Spanish readers, are

---

[1] *Life*, XI (*CW*, I, 64). The other two places are in *Life*, XII, XVIII (*CW*, I, 72, 106).

[2] *CW*, I, 106.   [3] *CW*, I, xxi.

unfamiliar with Teresan orthography, the texts of so many of her works being modernized. Spanish readers, however, have the advantage over English readers as regards the use of that characteristic Spanish device, the diminutive, since English has no special diminutive form and the force of the Spanish form is apt to disappear in translation. The suffixes -*ico*, -*illo*, -*ito*, -*uelo*, and a few more, normally denote smallness, but may also render a whole gamut of other meanings and emotional tones, such as affection, protectiveness, condescension, depreciation, irony, sarcasm, contempt and disgust. Though this device was not widely accepted in literary Spanish, as it is today, and by many was thought unworthy of serious writing, quite a number of the diminutives which we find in Saint Teresa were in general use. Such were *asnillo*, a little donkey; *avecita*, a little bird; *cosilla*, *cosita*, a trifle; *hormiguilla*, a little ant; *mariposita*, a little butterfly; *palomita*, a little dove; *pastorcito*, a shepherd-boy. All these Saint Teresa uses quite frequently—some of them as figures illustrating the life of prayer. The *avecita* is the unpractised soul—a fledgeling which soon grows tired, so that the Lord has to 'put it into the nest, where it may repose'.[1] The dove is the soaring soul,[2] its eyes dazzled by the Divine Sun.[3] The *cositas*, trifles 'like grains of salt', are the soul's feeble resolutions.[4] The *hormiguilla* is Saint Teresa herself;[5] and to describe her own weakness and insignificance she is prodigal of diminutives— *pecadorcilla* ('poor sinner'), *gusanillo* ('miserable worm'), *pobrecilla* ('poor little one'): these three occur within a few lines of each other.[6] The tiny convent of Saint Joseph, Ávila, on the other hand, is given a diminutive with a precisely opposite force: it is 'God's beloved little corner', *este rinconcito de Dios*.[7]

These were all current literary words in Saint Teresa's day, but she uses many which were less so, and some which were no doubt of her own invention, charging them with emotional content which another language can only approximately express. Such are *estas ayuditas*,[8] 'these puny efforts of ours'; *aquel cuidadito*,[9] 'those trifling pains we have taken'; *un disgustillo*,[10] 'a little annoyance', 'a slight feeling of frustration'; *esta encarceladita de esta pobre alma*,[11]

---

[1] *Life*, XIII, XVIII (*CW*, I, 74, 108).   [2] Psalm lv, 6 (A.V.).
[3] *Life*, XX (*CW*, I, 128, 130).   [4] *Op. cit.*, XXXIX (*CW*, I, 284).
[5] *Op. cit.*, XXXI (*CW*, I, 213).   [6] *Way of Perfection*, III (*CW*, II, 14).
[7] *Life*, XXXV (*CW*, I, 246).   [8] *Op. cit.*, XXII (*CW*, I, 142).
[9] *Op. cit.*, X (*CW*, I, 58).   [10] *Op. cit.*, XII (*CW*, I, 72).
[11] *Op. cit.*, XI (*CW*, I, 69).

'this poor little imprisoned soul', *estos temorcillos*,[1] 'these trifling fears'; *estas lagrimillas que aquí lloro*,[2] 'these few tears that I am here shedding'. These examples all occur within less than one hundred pages of a single book: many more will be given later.

Nor is Saint Teresa content to invent diminutives in describing her own spiritual life and to metaphorize the little doves and butter-flies with which she would have become familiar in her father's garden. Occasionally, in her early work, she even carries her diminutive-making into the sphere of mystical theology, writing of its technical terms as of the doves and butterflies of her childhood and of the tears and efforts and feelings of frustration in her spiritual life.

In the fifteenth chapter of the *Life*, for example, she uses an age-old figure of mystical theology in describing the Prayer of Quiet as a *centella*, or 'spark'. At once she turns it into a *centellica pequeñita*—using two diminutives: we might say 'the tiniest of tiny sparks'.[3] In the same chapter she makes a diminutive of *consideración*, a technical synonym of 'reflection' or 'meditation', and writes of 'our poor little meditations', *nuestras consideracioncillas*.[4] Here we have proof, both of the naturalness with which she wrote of mystical experiences and of the extent to which diminutive-making was a habit with her.

[III]

Closely connected with Saint Teresa's vocabulary is her use of imagery. Here, both in variety and in effectiveness, she excels. She had, like Saint Ignatius of Loyola, a pictorial imagination, and, whether or no through the influence of the Society of Jesus, she 'would try', some years before writing her *Life*, 'to make pictures of Christ inwardly' and 'to look at a field, or water, or flowers', which, she says, 'reminded me of the Creator—I mean, they awakened me, helped me to recollect myself and thus served me as a book'.[5] 'Often, when I was a beginner,' she records about this time, 'it used to give me great delight to think of my soul as a garden and of the Lord as walking in it.'[6] It is not surprising, then, that, when at a loss to explain anything, she turned naturally to simile or metaphor. 'I shall have to employ some kind of com-

---

[1] *Op. cit.*, XXXI (*CW*, I, 210). [2] *Op. cit.*, XIX (*CW*, I, 114).
[3] *Op. cit.*, XV (*CW*, I, 90). [4] *Op. cit.*, XV (*CW*, I, 95).
[5] *Life*, IX (*CW*, I, 54, 55). [6] *Op. cit.*, XIV (*CW*, I, 86).

parison', she writes, as an apology for introducing into her *Life* the similitude of the Waters.

' ... I should like to avoid doing so; but this spiritual language is so hard to use for such as, like myself, have no learning, that I shall have to seek some such means of conveying my ideas.'[1]

And, when it came to describing to her confessors ineffable experiences which characterize the higher states of prayer:

'I did nothing, in my efforts to make myself understood, but draw comparisons. . . .'[2]

'I also drew such comparisons as I could and as the Lord revealed to my understanding . . .'[3]

These comparisons she multiplies as she finds her experiences harder and harder to explain: incidentally, she unconsciously gives her readers an insight into her own interests. For she does not confine herself, as do some of her less original contemporaries, to figures like iron, wood, and coals in the fire, or the river and the sea, which generations of mystical writers had made familiar. In upwards of 420 figures of speech which she uses in her works[4] are included flowers, beasts, birds, insects, reptiles, fishes, parts of the body, landscapes, the heavens, household implements, and common objects. There are figures of war, of family life, religious life, court life, and prison life, of matrimony, of agriculture, of athleticism, of journeys by land or by sea, not to mention such unexpected figures as the game of chess, the bull-fight and the silkworm.

The most striking of these groups of figures is that which deals with soldiering. Much has been said, since Crashaw, in the preamble to his famous hymn, described Saint Teresa as 'for mascu-

---

[1] *Op. cit.*, XI (*CW*, I, 64).   [2] *Op. cit.*, XXVII (*CW*, I, 170).

[3] *Op. cit.*, XXVIII (*CW*, I, 184).

[4] This is the number collected and listed in Index II of *CW* (III, 393–7). It does not include the figures used in the *Letters*, which, however, are comparatively few. In spite of my having admitted to the index a number of pictorial illustrations which are not figures, the statistics given in the text, which must be considered as only approximately exact, would probably be put by many computators much higher. For (i) I have been somewhat conservative in judging whether or no a word is used figuratively; (ii) Scriptural figures and illustrations, if direct quotations or near-quotations, are excluded throughout; (iii) if a figure or an illustration occurs several times on one page of the translation, it is listed only once. This is admittedly an arbitrary procedure, but I can find none more satisfactory.

line courage of performance, more than a woman', of her remarkable virility. 'Be strong men', she once counselled her daughters. 'If you do all that is in you, the Lord will make you so manly that men themselves will be amazed at you.'[1] 'Strive like strong men until you die in the attempt, for you are here for nothing else than to strive.'[2] The sister of soldier brothers, she thought of life in general, and in particular of the religious life and of her own Reform, in terms of warfare. That military figures came to her naturally, and even obtruded themselves against her will, a remarkable passage in the twentieth chapter of the *Life* bears witness. Describing the effects of rapture under the figure of *passer solitarius in tecto*, she suddenly finds herself talking about battle:

'And now comes the distress of having to return to this life. Now the soul has grown new wings and has learned to fly. Now the little bird has lost its unformed feathers. Now in Christ's name the standard is raised on high . . . the captain of the fortress has mounted . . . the highest of its towers, and has reared the standard aloft there in the name of God. From his position of security he looks down on those below. No longer does he fear perils; rather he desires them, for through them, as it were, he receives the assurance of victory.'

After this, for a time, she forsakes metaphor, but, four or five lines later, unconsciously returns to it:

' . . . the soul . . . prays to the Lord, giving Him the keys of its will.'

Then, realizing that she has strayed into her favourite field again, and reverting to her earlier similitude of the garden, she exclaims:

'Behold, our gardener has become the captain of a fortress!'[3]

It will now be understood how it is that, with the exception of the figure 'road' (or 'way'), which is often quite conventional, and three other common figures, those of water, fire, and light, she uses the figure of battle more than any other—with two further exceptions, indeed, 'sun(light)' and 'flower', more than twice as often as any other. And besides those which can be grouped under the heading of battle (conflict, fight, skirmish, war, etc.), we have specific references to arms (or weapons,) arrows, banners, cannon,

[1] *Way of Perfection*, VII (*CW*, II, 35).   [2] *Op. cit.*, XX (*CW*, II, 86).
[3] *Life*, XX (*CW*, I, 127).

captains, castles, chains (or fetters), chariots, flights, fortresses, garrisons, guards, guns, heralds, horsemen, knights, marches, prisons and prisoners, ransoms, soldiers, spears, standards and standard-bearers, swords, towers, vassals, and wrestlers. This must surely be a record number of military figures to be used by a woman.

Equally familiar to readers of Saint Teresa is her affection for anything connected with water. This element is a natural enough symbol to occur to a dweller in parched Castile, where the very names of so many villages bear witness to its scarcity. As a child it had meant much to her: she had had a picture of Our Lord at the Samarian well ('which hung where I could always see it') and would pray to God, in the words of the inscription beneath it: 'Domine, da mihi aquam.'[1] Of the three most famous of her extended figures the first in chronological order is the similitude of the Waters, developed in the eleventh and following chapters of the *Life*, to which she often returns, notably in describing the Fourth and Sixth Mansions of the Interior Castle.[2] Water, as we have seen, was one of the things which most 'reminded her of the Creator',[3] and in her letters she tells us how 'refreshing' she found it to have a cell, as at Alba de Tormes, with a river view which she could enjoy from her bed,[4] or how 'companionable' was the river which fringed the road along which she travelled.[5] So, quite apart from her main references to water, she draws for her illustrations upon aqueducts, buckets, conduits, dew, floods, fountains, lakes, mists, oceans, pools, rain, rivers and river-beds, seas, sources and springs, storms and tempests, streams, vapours, water-wheels and wells. And this is natural enough; for, to quote her again:

'There are certain spiritual things which I can find no way of explaining more aptly than by this element of water; for, as I am very ignorant, and my wits give me no help, and I am so fond of this element, I have observed it more attentively than anything else.'[6]

These are the two groups of images upon which she most commonly draws. Which come next in order of frequency it would be hard to decide. Small animals, birds, and insects would be very

[1] *Op. cit.*, XXX (*CW*, I, 203).　　　　[2] *CW*, II, 236-7, 293-4.
[3] *Life*, IX (*CW*, I, 55). Cf. p. 87, above.　　　　[4] *LL* 51 (131).
[5] *LL* 378 (863).　　　　[6] *Interior Castle*, IV, ii (*CW*, II, 236).

high on the list, partly because of the extended metaphor of the silkworm in the Fifth Mansions of the *Interior Castle*; but even without this it is an observant nun who utilizes ants, bees, birds (*aves, avecitas*), butterflies, caterpillars, cobwebs, doves, eagles, flies, hedgehogs, hens, lizards, moths, reptiles, serpents, snakes, sparrows, sparrow-hawks, spiders, toads, tortoises, turtle-doves, vipers, and worms. Clearly she was as much attracted by small creatures as by small persons. The only large animals which she mentions are the donkey, the dragon, the horse, the lamb, the lion, the sheep— most of these only once or twice and with no apparent interest. Her only flowers are carnations, roses, rosemary, and thistles; her only trees and plants the apple, the ivy, the laurel, the mulberry, the olive, the palm, the *palmito*, and the vine. Flowers, trees, and plants attract her much less than living creatures. Her use of both, as well as of more general images, such as 'garden', 'fruit', 'orchard', is largely conventional. Particularly perfunctory is her use of flowers. It is only with the 'dry twigs' of the rosemary that she is concerned;[1] thistles she mentions only symbolically, in association with thorns;[2] and to the other two flowers she refers quite conventionally—'the flowers and carnations',[3] 'a bed of roses and flowers'[4]—as though she had mentioned the first two names that had occurred to her.

All these things lay close to her hand: they imply no straining after originality or effect. Next to them in importance would come images connected with or suggestive of fire (brand, brazier, candle, coal, comet, flame, fuel, furnace, spark), but these are often either stock items in the vocabulary of mysticism or words which have almost lost their figurative value. Closely related to fire-images are images connected with light—either light itself in some particular form or manifestation (daystar, illumination, lamp, lightning, spark, star, and—one of the most frequently used—sun) or objects which reflect light, such as crystal, diamond, glass, jewels or precious stones in general, mirror, and pearl. Images of darkness are frequent but are apt to stand in contraposition to those of light, in which case it is generally the latter that have the greater significance.

A comparative estimate of the frequency of metaphorical usage

---

[1] *Relations*, III (*CW*, I, 316).   [2] *Maxims*, 1 (*CW*, III, 256).
[3] *Life*, XIV (*CW*, I, 86). For another possible explanation of the choice of that flower, see *CW*, I, 86, n. 3.
[4] *Conceptions*, II (*CW*, II, 366).

in Saint Teresa's various works[1] shows that the book with the fewest illustrations is the *Foundations*. This, perhaps, we should expect of a plain narrative dealing with practical matters, and probably, if we limited ourselves to illustrations which are strictly figurative, the number would be smaller still. Not far above the *Foundations* comes the *Spiritual Relations*, a book describing the author's spiritual experiences, but also a plain narrative and containing none of those digressions which we find in the *Life* and which lend themselves so well to figured language.

These two works contain far fewer figures than any of the rest. Each page of the *Life*, even if we omit the numerous pages crammed with pictures of 'gardens' and 'waters', has nearly four times as many as each page of the *Relations*, and the average in the *Way of Perfection*, which comes next, is nearly six times as many. As we get farther and farther away from factual narrative, the proportion of figures increases. The *Conceptions of the Love of God*, which, as will be seen later, is much less expository and more hortatory in character than would be supposed from its title, has a fraction more, page for page, than the *Way of Perfection*.[2] Next comes the *Interior Castle*, which in a sense is one single extended metaphor, and, if every figure were counted, would be by far the richest. Even if we omit all the numerous references to 'castle', 'mansion', and 'marriage', the *Interior Castle* has nearly three times as many figures as the *Life*: on this basis, the average in the *Exclamations of the Soul to God* is about one-third higher still.[3] But we shall have more to say of the imagery of the *Interior Castle* later.

One of the most striking features of Saint Teresa's style is the abundance of short phrases, popular in type, which frequently, though not always, contain figures of speech, and there-

[1] The *Letters* are excluded, as before, being neither a complete work nor an objective one.

[2] In the making of this computation, the frequent references to 'cellar' and 'kiss' are omitted.

[3] The calculations in these two paragraphs are made on the number of images and illustrations on each page of the English translation in *CW*: when the same image occurs several times on one page it is counted only once. (This method is, of course, arbitrary, but as I have said above, I can think of no better one, and in any case, for the reason already given, the figures must be considered only approximate.) On this basis, the proportions are as follows: *Foundations*: 46 images to 206 pages (say 2 to 9); *Relations*: 21 to 62 (3:9); *Life*, 356 to 292 (5:4); *Way of Perfection*: 352 to 187 (2:1); *Conceptions*: 104 to 43 (5:2); *Interior Castle*: 472 to 153 (3:1); *Exclamations*: 75 to 19 (4:1).

fore are appropriately considered here. Sometimes she invents
them; sometimes they seem to be based on proverbs, or on sayings
current in her day but now no longer so. She throws them off casu-
ally as she writes, hardly ever developing them, or returning to
them even allusively. Except in the *Letters*, they nearly always have
direct reference to spiritual experience, and, for some reason that I
cannot account for, they occur much more frequently in the *Life*
than elsewhere.[1] Sometimes they are not only vivid, but (in relation to the context in which they are used) daring, and occasionally some qualifying phrase is introduced to soften them. We expect God's love *a manos llenas, a manera de decir*—'great handfuls of
it, as one might say'.[2] The soul's progress in virtue is comparable
to a *paso de gallina*, 'a hen's pace'.[3] It is God, not the soul, who
distributes the fruit of the spiritual garden, so that nothing 'sticks
to (*i.e.*, remains in) its hands'.[4] When the faculties are suspended,
the soul 'is left, as the phrase has it, in the air'.[5] The soul with
excessive spiritual ambition is apt to become 'as dry as a stick'[6]—a
picturesque way of referring to aridity. The soul that ought to be
soaring like an eagle, but aims too low, 'moves like a hen with its
feet tied'.[7] When temptations are numerous and fierce, 'it has
sometimes seemed to me that the devils behave as though they were
playing ball with the soul, so incapable is it of freeing itself from
their power'.[8] But, when God's favour shines upon it, the devil can
only 'clap his hands to his head'[9]—*i.e.*, in despair.

[IV]

To make a comprehensive study of Saint Teresa's syntax, even
in outline, is too long and complicated a task for the writer of a
brief essay. One can do no more than isolate and illustrate some of
its salient features. This section will pick out three of the more
striking of these—apostrophe, repetition, and alliteration; the
next will attempt a more general survey.

Right from the beginning of her career as a writer, Saint Teresa
has continual recourse to exclamation, and in particular to apos-

---

[1] It will be observed that all the illustrations in this paragraph are taken from
the *Life*.

[2] *Life*, XI (*CW*, I, 64). [3] *Op. cit.*, XIII (*CW*, I, 75–6).
[4] *Op. cit.*, XX (*CW*, I, 130). [5] *Op. cit.*, XXII (*CW*, I, 140).
[6] *Op. cit.*, XXII (*CW*, I, 144). [7] *Op. cit.*, XXXIX (*CW*, I, 284).
[8] *Op. cit.*, XXX (*CW*, I, 199). [9] *Op. cit.*, XXVI (*CW*, I, 166).

trophe, a practice undoubtedly attributable to her habit of writing as she thought and spoke. Her apostrophes vary from the purely ejaculatory *¡Válgame Dios!* ('God help me!'), often equivalent in Spanish conversation to no more than 'Good heavens!', to long prayers, or reflective passages in the form of apostrophes directed to God, which may either interrupt the narrative or be, as it were, caught up in it. So characteristic is this feature of her style that it alone would probably distinguish her from any other writer. The variety of forms which it assumes is no doubt due to its being absolutely natural, for the Spaniard, in speaking, instinctively avoids monotony, becoming monotonous only when he strives after effect. As we study it in one of these forms, or in another, we are following the workings of her own mind.

Here, for example, is the first chapter of the *Life*, which, after describing the death of the writer's mother, ends with an apostrophe ('O my Lord . . .')[1] of nine lines (in the English version) which shades off again into narrative. With this may be contrasted the ante-penultimate paragraph of the second chapter, which ends with the simple ejaculation: 'Blessed be Thou, Lord, Who for so long hast suffered me! Amen',[2] and a similar ending to a narrative paragraph in the third: 'May He be blessed for ever. Amen.'[3]

In the fourth chapter the narrative is broken by two long paragraphs ('O Supreme Good! O my Rest! . . .')[4] which, beneath the surface, are reflective in character, and are followed by a resumption of the narrative in its most matter-of-fact form. A long paragraph of similar type ends the sixth chapter.[5] In the seventh comes a long apostrophe ('O Lord of my soul! . . .'[6]) which also adds something to the narrative. The eighth has a passage ('O infinite goodness of my God! . . .'[7]) completely devoid of colloquialisms, verging in places upon eloquence and more literary in type than any of the foregoing. Of similar quality is the paragraph ('O my Lord and my Good! . . .')[8] near the end of the fourteenth, which is followed by a few sentences apologizing for these digressions and then accounting for them:

'Your Reverence must forgive me for wandering from my subject: as I am speaking with a purpose in my mind you must not be surprised. I am writing what comes to my soul; and at times when, as I write, the greatness of the debt I owe Him rises up before me,

[1] *CW*, I, 12. [2] *CW*, I, 16. [3] *CW*, I, 18. [4] *CW*, I, 21. [5] *CW*, I, 36.
[6] *CW*, I, 46.   [7] *CW*, I, 50–1.   [8] *CW*, I, 87.

it is only by a supreme effort that I can refrain from going on to sing praises to God.'[1]

It is hardly necessary to say that a writer who passed so easily from narrative to apostrophe or prayer passed no less (though not necessarily more) easily from narrative to reflection. Now in a paragraph, now in a single sentence, reflection invades narrative, after which the flow of the narrative continues as freely as though the reflective interpolations had been placed in the margin. It is only after a comparatively long digression that Saint Teresa thinks it necessary to catch the narrative up with a phrase like 'But, to return to what I was saying . . .'. When she does so, it is because she has become so absorbed in her reflection as to lose the thread of her story.

Some of the most striking examples of this habit, in which, in the course of a paragraph or two, the phenomenon is repeated several times, are too long for quotation. Here is a shorter one, taken from the *Foundations*, which seems to be richer in examples than any of the other books, no doubt because it contains the largest proportion of pure narrative. It occurs at the beginning of the story of Casilda de Padilla, in favour of whom her elder sister renounced her inheritance:

'From childhood she had been so devoted to prayer . . . that she valued (the estates) as little as her brother had done. God bless me! What trials, torments and lawsuits would many people have endured in order to succeed to this inheritance! Some would even have risked their lives and reputations for it. And yet these young people had no light trials to suffer before they were allowed to give it up. The world is like that, and unless we are blind we soon discover how capricious it is. In order to be free from her inheritance, however, this girl renounced it with the greatest good will in favour of her sister, who was ten or eleven years of age, and was the only remaining heir.'[2]

Saint Teresa's second stylistic habit, which may quite fairly be termed a 'device', is repetition. This is somewhat highly developed, and, as none of its forms can be adequately reproduced in a translation, it may be studied in some detail.

First, we may note many cases of *simple* repetition, the aim of which seems to be emphasis. That Saint Teresa was from child-

---

[1] *CW*, I, 88.   [2] *Foundations*, X (*CW*, III, 51).

hood given to using repetition for this purpose we know from the story in the first chapter of the *Life* (which incidentally furnishes the earliest example of the device in her writings) describing how as a child she and her brother tried to grasp the idea of eternity by repeating again and again the words: *¡Para siempre, siempre, siempre!*[1] ('For ever—ever—ever!') She uses a similar technique in her exhortations, less frequently in reflection and prayer, and least frequently of all in narrative. In these repetitions there are numberless variations of tone: generally they are intimate, kindly, motherly; but sometimes the effect is humorous, or whimsical, or brisk, or deprecatory, or even dramatic:

Entendamos bien, bien, como ello es.[2]
(Let us understand well, well, how this matter stands.)
Jamás por jamás las pude imaginar.[3]
(Never, never could I imagine them).
Crea, crea, que . . . lleva . . . peligro.[4]
(Let him believe, let him believe that . . . it is . . . dangerous).
Mire, mire por amor del Señor no la engañe.[5]
(Let (the soul) look to it, let it look to it, for love of the Lord, lest (the devil) deceive it).
De nosotros no podemos en nada, nada.[6]
(Of ourselves we can do nothing, nothing).
¡Qué de ello, qué de ello, qué de ello . . . me falta para esto![7]
(How far, how far, how far am I from this!)
¡Oh hermanas . . . acostumbraos, acostumbraos![8]
(Oh, sisters . . . get used (to this), get used (to this!)
¿Cómo puede vuestra piedad cada día, cada día, verle hacer injurias?[9]
(How can Thy Mercy, each day, each day, see Him affronted?)
Entrad, entrad, hijas mías, en lo interior. . . .[10]
(Enter, enter, my daughters, within yourselves. . . .)
Muera, muera este gusano. . . .[11]
(Let this worm die, let it die. . . .)
Mirad, mirad, que os ruega ahora el Juez. . . .[12]
(See, see, the Judge is now entreating you. . . .)

[1] *Life*, I (*CW*, I, 11).   [2] *Op. cit.*, X (*CW*, I, 59).
[3] *Op. cit.*, IX (*CW*, I, 55).   [4] *Op. cit.*, XV (*CW*, I, 89).
[5] *Op. cit.*, XIX (*CW*, I, 118).   [6] *Op. cit.*, XX (*CW*, I, 121).
[7] *Op. cit.*, XXXIX(*CW*, I, 282).   [8] *Way of Perfection*, XXVI (*CW*, II, 106)·
[9] *Op. cit.*, XXXIII (*CW*, II, 142).   [10] *Interior Castle*, III, i (*CW*, II, 222).
[11] *Op. cit.*, V, i i(*CW*, II, 254).   [12] *Exclamations*, X (*CW*, II, 411).

These examples, nearly all in hortatory contexts, comprise verbs, adverbs, pronouns, and entire phrases. Equally frequent are repetitions of nouns and adjectives: 'With great, great confusion',[1] 'Oh, humility, humility!'[2] 'Always works, works!'[3] 'Courage, courage, my daughters!'[4] 'Prayer, prayer, my sisters!'[5] And still more emphatically, 'Prayer, sisters, prayer for her!'[6] Repetitions of this type (*a un paso paso*: 'at a snail's pace';[7] *en fin, fin*: 'after all')[8] have sometimes, in translation, to be so freely paraphrased that their force entirely vanishes.

Another use of simple repetition, found in descriptive and reflective rather than in hortatory passages, seems also to aim at emphasis, though of a different kind. Here the device has a literary turn, —possibly suggested by sermons—of which the author is perhaps, at least partly, conscious:

'(The soul) is weary of the time when it considered points of *honour*, and the mistaken belief which it had that what the world calls *honour* is *honour*: it sees that it is a sheer lie. . . . It realizes that *true honour* is no *lie*, but *true*. It holds as *something* that which is *something* and as *nothing* that which is *nothing* at all; for everything is *nothing* and that which passes away and is not pleasing to God is less than *nothing*.'[9]

'. . . I shall be affording that person *pleasure*. And as this *pleasure* of giving her *pleasure* transcends my *pleasure* . . . my regret at . . . losing the *pleasure* it gave me will disappear.'[10]

'The faculties *rejoice* without knowing how they *rejoice*; the soul is enkindled in *love* without understanding how it *loves*; it knows it is *rejoicing* in that which it *loves* and knows not how it is *rejoicing* in it.'[11]

It is impossible to pass from this type of repetition without recalling the use made of it by Saint John of the Cross, who, in a famous

---

[1] *Life*, XXXV (*CW*, I, 246). The adjective is *harta*. Cf. *LL* 233 (p. 573): *Me ha dado harta harta pena . . . : harta es haber alguna mejoría* ('It has caused me great, great grief . . . : it is a great thing (to hear) there is some improvement').

[2] *Interior Castle*, III, i (*CW*, II, 222).   [3] *Op. cit.*, VII, iv (*CW*, II, 346).

[4] *LL* 264 (630).   [5] *LL* 264 (630).   [6] *LL* 274 (648).

[7] *Interior Castle*, III, ii (*CW*, II, 226).   [8] *Op. cit.*, V, ii (*CW*, II, 256).

[9] *Life*, XX (*CW*, I, 129). The italics, in this and the next two passages quoted, are mine.

[10] *Op. cit.*, XXXV (*CW*, I, 246).

[11] *Way of Perfection*, XXV (*CW*, II, 104). The word (*gozar*) translated 'rejoice in' can also be rendered 'enjoy'.

passage of the most exquisite rhythm, brought it to a point near perfection:

' . . . Thus I shall see Thee in Thy beauty and Thou wilt see me in Thy beauty; and I shall see myself in Thee in Thy beauty; and Thou wilt see Thyself in me in Thy beauty; so that thus I may be like to Thee in Thy beauty and Thou mayest be like to me in Thy beauty, and my beauty may be Thy beauty, and Thy beauty my beauty; and thus I shall be Thou in Thy beauty and Thou wilt be I in Thy beauty, because Thy beauty itself will be my beauty, and thus we shall each see the other in Thy beauty.'[1]

So much for simple repetition. But that is only a small part of Saint Teresa's resources in this field. A second type of repetition uses either two words etymologically related or two words differing in function but identical in form, apparently without any idea of word-play. In the *Life*, Chapter VIII, two paragraphs contain seven instances of 'force' as noun and as verb, and two sentences in the earlier of them have four instances of the verb 'suffer' with only a slight change of meaning.[2] These, however, are much less effective than her hammer-stroke repetitions of simple words, and it is hard to see what effect she intended to produce by them, unless again it were emphasis. Pages could be filled with brief examples of this kind:

Es un desatino que se usa en el mundo, que me desatina.[3]
(It is a bewildering folly common in the world, which bewilders me.)
Este contentamiento . . . es verdadero, y contento que se ve que nos contenta.[4]
(This contentment is genuine and a content which is seen to content us).
En estos tiempos de quietud, dejar descansar el alma con su descanso.[5]
(In these times of quiet, let the soul rest in its rest).
Sélo de algunos letrados muy letrados.[6]
(I know it from certain learned men (who are) very learned.)
Palabras . . . sin concierto, si el mismo Señor no las concierta.[7]

[1] *CWSJX*, II, 380–1.   [2] *Life*, VIII (*CW*, I, 50–1).
[3] *Op. cit.*, V (*CW*, I, 28). *Desatino* is a word difficult to translate literally: the version in the text is only an approximation.
[4] *Op. cit.*, XIV (*CW*, I, 84).   [5] *Op. cit.*, XV (*CW*, I, 92).
[6] *Op. cit.*, XV (*CW*, I, 96).   [7] *Op. cit.*, XVI (*CW*, I, 97).

(Words ... without order, unless the Lord Himself gives them order.)

¡Oh vida de mi vida y sustento que me sustentas![1]

(Oh life of my life and sustenance that sustainest me!)

¡Oh contento mío y Dios mío! ¿Qué haré yo para contentaros?[2]

(Oh, my Pleasure and my God! What shall I do to please Thee?)

Some of these repetitions are pleonastic: *muerte tan mortal*[3] (such mortal death); *lo que es verdadera verdad*[4] (that which is true truth); *muy determinada determinación*[5] (very determined determination); *flaqueza tan flaca*[6] (weakness so weak); *tinieblas más tenebrosas*[7] (darker darkness); *las grandes grandezas de Dios*[8] (the great greatnesses of God); *¡oh, qué sola soledad!*[9] (what lone loneliness!). Here the emphatic purpose is evident.

A third type of repetition involves word-play of a not very subtle kind. As a rule, it is rather more effective than the second type, but less so than the first:

Me faltaba esto a mí, por faltaros ya a Vos.[10]

(This was failing—*i.e.*, lacking to—me because I was failing—*i.e.*, being false to—Thee.)

Un alma . . . tan desalmada.[11]

(A soul . . . so impious; *lit.*, so soulless.)

Bien veía yo, Bien mío. . . .[12]

(Well did I see, my Good. . . . The pun is untranslatable.)

Hemos de . . . dar sentidos conforme al poco sentido del amor de Dios que se tiene.[13]

(We have to give meanings (*sentidos*) which are in conformity with our slight feelings (*sentidos*) of love for God.)

El . . . descanso . . . en no tener cuenta de dar cuenta de riquezas.[14]

(The peace . . . of not having to take account (*cuenta*) of rendering an account (*cuenta*) of any riches.)

---

[1] *Interior Castle*, VII, ii (*CW*, II, 336). [2] *Exclamations*, XV (*CW*, II, 417).
[3] *Life*, IX (*CW*, I, 56). [4] *Op. cit.*, XXI (*CW*, I, 135).
[5] *Way of Perfection*, XXI (*CW*, II, 89). [6] *Op. cit.*, XXI (*CW*, II, 89).
[7] *Interior Castle*, I, ii (*CW*, II, 205).
[8] *Op. cit.*, VI, viii (*CW*, II, 312). Cf. *Exclamations*, I (*CW*, II, 402).
[9] *Exclamations*, VI (*CW*, II, 406). [10] *Life*, VII (*CW*, I, 37).
[11] *Op. cit.*, XXV (*CW*, I, 159). Cf. 'queda el ánima animosa' (*op. cit.*, XIX: *CW*, I, 112).
[12] *Op. cit.*, XIX (*CW*, I, 114). [13] *Conceptions*, I (*CW*, II, 360).
[14] *Op. cit.*, II (*CW*, II, 368–9).

Otras hablan corto y no muy cortado.[1]
(Others speak in a sharp and none too refined a tone.)

Between the second and the third type of repetition comes one which at first glance suggests word-play, but does not in fact involve it:

Muchas cosas más pudiera decir en esto, Señor, para darme a entender que no me entiendo; mas, como sé que las entendéis, para qué hablo?[2]
(I could say many more things about this, Lord, to make myself understand that I do not understand myself; but, as I know that Thou understandest (*i.e.,* knowest) them, why do I speak?)

Que no, mi Dios, no, no más confianza en cosa que yo pueda querer para mí, Quered Vos de mí lo quisiereis querer, que eso quiero. . . .[3]
(But no, my God, no, no more trust in anything which I can will for myself. Do Thou will for me that which Thou willest to will, for that will I. . . .)

Repetitive in type is Saint Teresa's frequent use of series of nouns, verbs, or other parts of speech—sometimes with actual repetition of the same word, as in the first and last of the four examples which follow, sometimes without. This might be considered a semi-literary device, and it is hard to decide how far it is natural, but it is a device of the orator, rather than of the writer:

'But it is a gentle flight, a delectable flight, a noiseless flight.'[4]
'The words . . . dispose the soul, and prepare it, and move (it), and give (it) light, and comfort (it) and quiet (it).'[5]
' . . . A refreshment sweet, invigorating, delectable, tranquil.'[6]
'He can do all things, and commands all things, and rules all things, and His love fills all things.'[7]

Finally, there is a repetitive device, involving a logical ellipsis, to which Saint Teresa is greatly addicted, especially in her letters, and which is quite untranslatable. It assumes that the reader will

[1] *Way of Perfection,* XIV (*CW,* II, 58: n. 3 explains the play. The translator of Hoornaert (p. 408, n. 77) aptly renders 'curt but not courteous', though this rendering substitutes one kind of play for another.
[2] *Exclamations,* XVII (*CW,* II, 419).   [3] *Op. cit.,* XVII (*CW,* II, 419).
[4] *Life,* XX (*CW,* I, 128).   [5] *Op. cit.,* XXV (*CW,* I, 157–8).
[6] *Op. cit.,* XXV (*CW,* I, 160).
[7] *Op. cit.,* XXVIII (*CW,* I, 183). The Spanish is more emphatic, putting 'all things' first: *Todo lo puede,* etc. There may be a reminiscence of 1 Corinthians xiii, 7 in this construction.

supply a word represented in the Spanish by a pronoun—in English often by 'that' or 'so'. Even to a Spaniard it is not always clear today what word has to be supplied, and he has to look at the sentence twice before grasping its meaning. In the simplest form of the idiom the word not expressed is identical with a previous word and the substitution is easy:

Buena intención tendrán, y la obra lo será.[1]

(They will have a good intention and the work (they do) will be so—*i.e.*, good.)

. . . *Mi padre Fray Juan de la Cruz, que de veras lo es de mi alma.*[2]

(. . . my Father Fray John of the Cross, for he is indeed that (*i.e.*, the Father) of my soul.)

But when, at the beginning of a new paragraph, Saint Teresa exclaims: 'Oh my Father, and how many of them (*qué de ellos*) this house is costing me!'[3] and to discover to what 'them' refers the reader has to retrace sixteen words of the preceding paragraph before finding another 'them' and twenty-seven words in all before discovering that the substantive is *trabajos* ('trials', 'labours'), the task of interpretation becomes harder.

Saint Teresa's use of alliteration, though more curious than significant, is rather puzzling. Occasional allusive phrases, like *esas banderas y baraúndas*[4] ('all that flag-waving and excitement') are no doubt used intentionally, and certainly with effect; others, such as *trabajos y tribulaciones*[5] ('trials and tribulations'), were no doubt phrases in common currency used without thought of effect. In another group (*e.g.*, *aquella ganancia y aquel gusto*;[6] *no . . . con ganancia, sino con engaños*;[7] *fortalecida en la fe*)[8] the alliteration might be described as semi-intentional: the word *ganancia* would suggest to the writer the word *gusto* or *engaños*, while the third combination would be suggested by Scripture.

But, apart from phrases of these types, there are a very large number more which are less easily explained. They occur continually in the *Life*, rather less in the *Way of Perfection* and *Interior Castle*, a great deal in the *Exclamations*, and only rarely anywhere else. And, curiously, they are apt to occur in great density over a

---

[1] *Op. cit.*, XVI (*CW*, I, 99–100).   [2] *LL* 261 (625).   [3] *LL* 290 (684).
[4] *LL* 326 (761).   [5] *Life*, XXII (*CW*, I, 139).
[6] *Lit.:* 'that gain and that pleasure' (*Life*, XXII: *CW*, I, 137).
[7] *Lit.*, 'not . . . with gain, but with deceptions' (*Life*, XXIII: *CW*, I, 150).
[8] *Lit.*, 'fortified in the faith' (*Life*, XXV: *CW*, I, 161).

passage several paragraphs long, and then, for some time, hardly at all. We find, for example, in one sentence: *Si . . . la condición . . . por ser penoso pensar en la Pasión, no se sufre, ¿quién nos quita estar con Él . . .?* ,in the following sentence . . . *corriendo sangre, cansado por los caminos,* and just below, *cuando os ofendía; ¡mas que, conociéndoos, pensase ganar más por este camino!*[1] Or, in one paragraph of little more than one hundred words, *desde aquel día; dejarlo todo para Dios; quien había querido; no fué menester mandármelo más; determinadamente decir; como cosa . . . no . . . inconveniente; para ponerlo por obra; conforme a como me lo mandó.*[2] Or we have a run of one letter (*t: tan sin temor de todos ellos, que se me quitaron todos los medios que solía tener hasta hoy . . .*), followed by pairs of others (*v. d, m: porque, aunque algunas veces los veía, como diré después, no los he habido más casi miedo*).[3] Sometimes there are long runs of alliteration: *pues no son para todos, y parecía las publicaba yo. Creo sin culpa suya lo ha permitido el Señor, para que yo padeciese.*[4] Or: *¿Por ventura puede el pecador, para hacer sus maldades, apartarse de este palacio?*[5] Or in a passage of considerable length a single letter predominates, as in the following where the letter *s* occurs twenty-four times in forty-nine words:

'Pues si este Señor es poderoso, como veo que lo es, y sé que lo es, y que son sus esclavos los demonios, y de esto no hay que dudar, pues es fe, siendo yo sierva de este Señor y Rey; ¿qué mal me pueden ellos hacer a mí?'[6]

It is hard to consider all the alliterations (in the *Life*, at least) purely fortuitous, for the simple reason that there are so many of them. Between Chapters XXII and XXX, in particular, they strike even the casual reader. Hardly a page will be found without a crop of them. The explanation would seem to be that in her early years as a writer Saint Teresa liked such jingles as *los peligros que os pintaren—que no miran los muchos millares—poco se pierde en probarlo,*[7] and used them (with exceptions as given above) quite unconsciously. As she grew older, they appealed to her less, or possibly she came to write more carefully, and so she dropped them. Only detailed research will give a clearer picture than this.

---

[1] *Life*, XXII (*CW*, I, 138–9).
[2] *Op. cit.*, XXIV (*CW*, I, 156).
[3] *Op. cit.*, XXV (*CW*, I, 165).
[4] *Life*, XXIII (*CW*, I, 150).
[5] *Interior Castle*, VI, x (*CW*, II, 322).
[6] *Life*, XXV (*CW*, I, 164).
[7] *Way of Perfection*, XXI, XXIII.

[v]

Saint Teresa's syntax, considered as a whole, is less that of the professional writer than of the good talker. Her works—in particular, her letters—provide our principal contact with sixteenth-century Castilian as it was spoken. The word *digo* ('I say', 'I mean') is prominent in all her narratives. Sr. Menéndez Pidal, recalling the dictum of the sixteenth-century humanist, Juan de Valdés, 'I write as I talk', aptly remarks that Saint Teresa can hardly be said to write at all—she 'talks in writing'.[1] And, in doing so, she brings a whole speaking world to life. Her syntax, one might say, is emotional. On the one hand, she has few artifices; on the other, many habits not usually found in literature. The artifices we have already considered; the habits we have now to discuss.

This characteristic of Teresan syntax explains one feature of it which might seem paradoxical: the numerous long, awkward, involved, parenthetical sentences, on the one hand, and the even more numerous short, staccato, emphatic sentences, often marked by ellipses, on the other. That is a characteristic of all effective conversation. With much to say, especially if the material contains an abundance of detail, one tends to lose one's sense of form. With a few emphatic points to make, on the other hand, one's sentences become short and emphatic, and points have often to be brought out by unusual gestures. A staccato sentence like 'Either you believe this or you do not: if you do, why do you wear yourselves to death with worry?'[2] is pure conversation. So is this verbatim report of an actual dialogue, in which one seems almost to detect the cadences of the voice:

'I said to him: "Does he know about these Briefs?" He said: "Better than I do." I said: "Well, I am certain of this about him, he will not do anything which he knows is an offence against God. . . .'[3]

But equally so is this monster period:

'I found (in *The Ascent of the Mount*) all the symptoms I had when I was unable to think of anything; for that was what I was always saying, that I could not think of anything when I was experiencing

[1] 'El estilo de Santa Teresa', *ed. cit.*, p. 153. The quotation from Valdés (*Diálogo de la lengua* (Madrid, 1928), p. 150) runs: 'my style is natural, and, without any kind of affectation, I write as I talk'.

[2] *Way of Perfection*, XXIX (*CW*, II, 120).   [3] *LL* 214 (526).

that type of prayer; and I drew lines alongside the places, and gave him the book, so that he and the other cleric I have mentioned, *a holy man and a servant of God*, should look at it and tell me what I ought to do, and, if they thought I should give up prayer altogether, I would, for why should I run into these dangers, for if, after almost twenty years of prayer, I had gained nothing, but had been deluded by the devil, it would be better not to go on, although that would have been very hard for me too, for I had already found what my soul was like without prayer.'[1]

Except for the substitution of the colloquial 'that' for *esto* ('this') I have made as literal a translation as is possible of this passage, and it will be agreed that the appositional nouns which I have italicized are the only words in it that would have been in the least out of place in an ordinary conversation.

The last three quotations are all typical of Teresan syntax, and it is in her use of short sentences and long sentences, and the way in which, with experience, she learned to vary the two, that its principal interest lies. As, however, this can be more adequately studied in the next section, which considers Saint Teresa's works individually, in chronological order, no more will be said about it here.

Ellipsis, one of the best-known characteristics of Teresan syntax, can occur equally in short sentences and in long ones, and is much commoner in speech than in writing. In conversation, when ideas rush to the surface of the mind more rapidly than they can be expressed, a motion of the hand will do duty for a clause and an inflection of the voice will save many words. In conversation, the most daring aposiopesis can be made intelligible by a shrug of the shoulders. Now Saint Teresa tends to write as though her readers could seize these inflections, or see these motions, whereas even in her own day they must often have found her more vivid than readily comprehensible and the twentieth century can sometimes only conjecture her meaning. It is this which makes her so difficult to translate: first, one has to choose the most probable meaning from among several; and then to find a rendering comparable in tone.

Here is an example, taken from my preface to the *Complete Works*, in which the first translation is literal and the second supplies the words omitted which are necessary to the sense. The passage refers to nuns afflicted by melancholy and in need of discipline:

[1] *Life*, XXIII (*CW*, I, 149–50).

'I mean in some; for I have seen that, when there is whom to fear, they become docile and can.'

('I mean that it is so in some; for I have seen them become docile in the presence of someone whom they fear, and so I know that they can become so if they like.'[1])

This is an extreme case of brevity, which is not easy to interpret, even in its context, When we have no context, the meaning can only be guessed, as in this fragment of a letter of which no more is extant:

'Know that I am not what I used to be in governing. All goes with love. I do not know if that is caused by their not doing me why or by (my) having understood that it goes better thus.'[2]

Given the fact that the letter of which this is part was directed to M. María Bautista, who was apt to be inflexible in her government, I take the sense to be:

'You know, I no longer govern in the way I used to. Love does everything. I am not sure if that is because no one gives me cause to reprove her, or because I have discovered that things go better in that way.'

In most places, however, the addition of a few words will make the general meaning of the sentence clear.

'Difficulties like that only arouse devotion in me, and, *the more, the more*' (*i.e.*, the more difficulties there are, the more is the devotion they arouse in me).[3]

'All (this) went to (*i.e.*, came to the knowledge of) my confessor, for they certainly desired my improvement, *and he to find fault with me*' (*i.e.*, whereupon he began to find fault with me').[4]

Further examples will be found in the next section.

As a rule Saint Teresa's elliptical sentences, in the Spanish, are quite comprehensible; in many of them the meaning flashes to the mind long before the mind has disentangled the construction of the sentence. She frequently inverts the order of her words, generally for the purpose of emphasis, using all the licence which the flexibility of Spanish usage gives. Fortunately for their intelligibility, most of these inversions occur, as we shall see later, in short sen-

---

[1] *Foundations*, VII (*CW*, III, 39: cf. I, xviii). [2] *LL* 276 (657).
[3] *Life*, XXVIII (*CW*, I, 181). [4] *Op. cit.*, XXVIII (*CW*, I, 186).

tences of which the sense is clear, rather than in long or in elliptical ones. Translated literally into English, they sound unfamiliar, even crude, but in the original they often give a sentence added point or emphasis. This is also true of antithesis, a figure as common in Saint Teresa's prose as in the verse of her day, and much more so than in secular prose. Antitheses are apt to occur in tense, finely balanced passages and are partly inspired by her instinctive sense of artistry:

'On the one hand, I was being called by God; on the other, I was following the world. I found great pleasure in all the things of God; (and yet) I was bound to those of the world. It seems that I wanted to reconcile these two contraries, each such an enemy to the other—the life of the spirit and the pleasures and joys and pastimes of the senses.'[1]

But even here, and still more so in many other places, the antithesis is inherent in the theme. Saint Teresa has continually to throw into strong contrast pairs of opposites—'sweetness' and aridity in devotion, the spiritual life and the sensual, right and wrong, Heaven and hell, God and the devil. *No era todo nada*[2]—'everything was nothing', a 'truth which I had learned as a child'—is a phrase, first used near the beginning of the *Life*, which recurs throughout the Works again and again. In the early chapters of the *Life*, which describe the choice between two irreconcilable contraries made by the author herself, antitheses are particularly frequent. The seventh chapter, for example, already once quoted, is full of them—how full, perhaps, no one can appreciate who has not read it through from beginning to end. Examples can be cited at random:

'The devil went away with loss, and I remained with gain.'[3]
'I was so wicked and they were good.'[4]
'God grant they may not take for virtue what is sin.'[5]
'I would reveal (*descubrir*) by my actions the sort of person I was, and the Lord would cover up (*encubrir*) my evil deeds and reveal (*descubrir*) some small virtue.'[6]

---

[1] *Op. cit.*, VII (*CW*, I, 45).   [2] *Op cit.*, III (*CW*, I, 18).
[3] *Op. cit.*, VII (*CW*, I, 37–8). 'The devil would depart confounded and I would be all the better for it.'
[4] *Op. cit.*, VII (*CW*, I, 38).   [5] *Op. cit.*, VII (*CW*, I, 39).
[6] *Op. cit.*, VII (*CW*, I, 45).

'To fall, I had many friends who would help me; to rise, I found myself . . . alone.'[1]

Examples, similar in type to this, from other prose works abound:

'Oh, how much we gain if we have no desire to gain what seems to us best and so have no fear of losing!'[2]
'Looking at His greatness, let us come back to our baseness; looking at His purity, we shall see our foulness; meditating on His humility, we shall see how far we are from being humble.'[3]
'The best life that a soul can live is a life which this sorrow (for sin) turns into death.'[4]

The antithesis, as we say, is latent in the theme, but in a writer less direct in style it would be less forceful and striking in expression. Occasionally the mode of expression recalls the artificial taste of the time, which can be illustrated abundantly from either pastoral romances or *cancioneros*. The most famous example of this in all Saint Teresa's works is of course the poem with the theme-stanza:

> *I live, yet no true life I know,*
> *And, living thus expectantly,*
> *I die because I do not die.*[5]

In other of her poems, such as 'I am thine, and born for Thee . . .',[6] the antithesis conforms rather to the type found in her prose.

Inherent in the theme of the Works, too, are the oxymora and paradoxes which, as in Osuna, Saint John of the Cross and other of the Spanish mystics, often startle the reader. The soul in the third degree of prayer, as this is conceived in the *Life*, is 'rejoicing in that agony with ineffable joy. . . . This state is a glorious folly, a heavenly madness . . . delectable disquiet.' The soul utters 'a thousand holy follies', in the bliss of its 'delectable pain':

'O my true Lord and Glory, what a cross—light and yet most heavy—hast Thou prepared for those who attain to this state!'[7]
'So delectable is this distress that life holds no delight which can give greater satisfaction.'[8]

·　　　·　　　·　　　·　　　·

[1] *Op. cit.*, VII (*CW*, I, 48).　　[2] *Way of Perfection*, XVII (*CW*, II, 72).
[3] *Interior Castle*, I, ii (*CW*, II, 209).　　[4] *Exclamations*, III (*CW*, II, 404).
[5] *Poems*, I (*CW*, III, 277: cf. n. 4).　　[6] *Poems*, II (*CW*, III, 279–81).
[7] *Life*, XVI (*CW*, I, 96–8, *passim*).　　[8] *Op. cit.*, XXIX (*CW*, I, 191).

It is not only in her short, elliptical sentences and in her long, involved sentences that Saint Teresa is difficult to understand. Occasionally, especially in the *Life*, where she is still learning her trade, the words flow from her pen in the wrong order and she does not trouble (as the translator has to) to put them right:

'This your Reverences will understand, for I can say no more, with your learning.'[1]

When displacement is accompanied by ellipsis, the result is certainly a tangle:

'Everything is like a dream that I see, and it is mockery with the eyes of the body.'[2]
('Everything I see is like a dream and what I see with my bodily eyes is a mockery.')

This was too much for her first editor, Fray Luis de León, and he altered the word-order so that it read logically.

Obscurity in such sentences as these, however, is rare by comparison with that inseparable from the long parenthetical ones. Even when the parenthesis is comparatively brief, the looseness of the construction of the sentence as a whole makes its thread hard to seize:

'This procedure is so very painful that, if the master teaching him insists on his (going) without reading, which is a great help to recollection—it is necessary to anyone who proceeds in this way, however little he reads, [but] in place of mental prayer which he cannot practice—I mean that if without this aid he is made to spend much time in prayer [that] it will be impossible for him to continue for long, and will endanger his health if he persists in it, because it is a very painful thing.'[3]

Where the parenthesis itself consists of several loosely strung sentences, it sometimes carries the writer herself so far from her theme that she finds it impossible to continue the construction. Unfortunately, while her shorter parentheses, which are not particularly noteworthy, except for their number, can be reproduced in translation, any attempt to give an adequate idea of the longer ones involves not only transcription, but paraphrase and explanation. In the following relatively simple example, Saint Teresa

[1] *Op. cit.*, XVIII (*CW*, I, 106).   [2] *Op. cit.*, XXXVIII (*CW*, I, 269).
[3] *Op. cit.*, IV (*CW*, I, 24).

begins the parenthesis with an inconsequent construction, piles clause upon clause, and mixes up her pronouns, but does in the end succeed in correctly catching up the grammatical sequence:

'For I have now experience of many kinds, that, if I begin by strengthening my determination to do a thing (which, being for God's sake alone, it is His will, even when it is begun, that the soul shall experience that fear, so that our merit may be the greater, and the greater it is, if the soul achieves it, the greater will be the reward and the more delectable it becomes afterwards), His Majesty rewards it, even in this life, in ways that can be understood only by one who enjoys them.'[1]

To make the passage intelligible, one has to split it thus:

'For I know now, by experience of many kinds, that, if I strengthen my determination to do a thing for God's sake alone, it is His will that, from the very beginning, my soul shall be afraid so that my merit may be the greater; and, if I achieve my resolve, the greater my fear has been, the greater will be my reward, and the greater, too, my retrospective pleasure. Even in this life His Majesty rewards such an act in ways that can be understood only by one who enjoys them.'[2]

Apart from parentheses, the principal obstacles to an understanding of Saint Teresa's long sentences are her strings of dependent clauses. Usually these are connected by *que*, which, in modern Spanish, is normally equivalent to 'that', but in the sixteenth century has a much wider range of meanings. That these *que*-clauses need not cause any ambiguity may be illustrated by a sentence which contains eight of them. It cannot be called elegant, but it is at least so clear that it can be translated with complete literalness:

'I told him *that* I did not know, but *that* I could not help realizing *that* He was beside me, and *that* I saw and felt this clearly, and *that* the recollection of the soul was much greater in the Prayer of Quiet, and quite continuous, and *that* the effects were quite different from those *that* I had been accustomed to experience and *that* the thing was quite clear (to me).'[3]

Contrast this, in which the first *que* is redundant, the second means 'for' and the third 'that':

[1] *Life*, IV (*CW*, I, 21).   [2] *Ibid.*   [3] *Op. cit.*, XXVII (*CW*, I, 170).

'Porque muy muchas veces . . . *que* viene de indisposición corporal, *que* somos tan miserables *que* participa esta . . . alma de las miserias del cuerpo . . .'[1]

('For very frequently . . . it arises from physical indisposition, for we are such miserable creatures that this . . . soul shares in the miseries of the body . . .')

And the sentence does not end there: ten more clauses, most of them co-ordinate, follow.

Finally may be reproduced a really incredible sentence, in which *que* occurs no less than eleven times:

'He says *that*, if all the prelates there are (should) come, even the Archbishop of Granada, whom they are very much attached to, they will not make them obey, unless (by virtue of their) having jurisdiction over them; and *that*, if they say anything to him, it is to see if they agree with his opinion, and *that* they take no notice of what he says to them, and *that* he for his part has no obligation to see *that* they obey; *that*, if he should not want to discuss the matter [that] he is wronging no one, and [that] why should they take any notice of him; *that* this (question of his authority) is not the main part of the business, *that* other means are those *that* will settle it.'[2]

These are the principal characteristics of Saint Teresa's syntax, taken as a whole. We shall now examine each of her principal works in turn, in chronological order.

[VI]

Saint Teresa's first book, her *Life*, is the most interesting of her works to study from the standpoint of style, since it reveals her as a learner in the art becoming proficient with amazing rapidity. When she began it, at the age of about forty-seven, she had probably never written anything longer than a letter, and the style of the first chapter—especially the abundance of short, clipped sentences, occasionally incomplete, like jottings in a note-book—suggests that she found writing difficult. Later, she was to give vividness to her narrative by an effective use of the short sentence, but she seems to have had no such intention here:

[1] *Op. cit.*, XI (*CW*, I, 69).
[2] *LL* 85 (207). In the original there are fourteen *que*'s; two of them, however, are not conjunctions, and one I have found untranslatable.

'It helped me never to see my parents inclined to anything but virtue. They had many [*i.e.*, virtues].'

'(My father) was strictly truthful; nobody ever heard him swear or speak evil. Of the most rigid chastity.'

'(My mother) endured a life of great infirmity; most rigidly chaste.'[1]

Her longer sentences positively creak as ideas crowd in her mind and she slowly transfers them, one after another, to paper:

'I gave alms as I could; and I could (give) very little. I tried to be alone when I said my prayers, which were numerous, especially the rosary, to which my mother was very devoted, and thus made us be so.'[2]

'(My cousins) were almost of my age, a little older than I. We always went about together. They were very fond of me.'[3]

'In my vain desires for this I went to extremes. The means which were necessary to preserve it, I cared about not at all; all I was very careful about was not to be wholly lost. My father and sister were very sorry about this friendship; they often reproved me for it.'[4]

The first two chapters are full of these short, jerky sentences. By the third, Teresa is getting into her stride and uses them only occasionally, alternating them with long ones. In the fourth chapter they have practically disappeared. At the beginning of the fifth, and again at the end, they return, but with one striking exception—'My father's distress was great at not having allowed me to confess: cries and prayers to God, many'[5]—they are less brusque and more in keeping with the context. By the sixth chapter, Teresa's natural sense of artistry is asserting itself and she begins to use the short sentence for vividness. See how the effect of the description of her illness is enhanced by the rapping out of her symptoms:

'The tongue bitten to pieces . . . I felt I was all out of joint, with the greatest confusion in the head. All doubled up, like a ball, the result of the torment of those days, as unable to move arm, foot, hand, or head, as though I were dead, unless others moved me. I could move, I think, only one finger of the right hand. (For any-

---

Life, I (*CW*, I, 10).   [2] *Op. cit.*, I (*CW*, I, 11).   [3] *Op. cit.*, I (*CW*, I, 13).
Op. cit., II (*CW*, I, 14).   [5] *Op. cit.*, V (*CW*, I, 31).

one) to come to (see) me, there was no way, for I was in such distress that I could not endure it.'[1]

From this time onward she gains an ever-increasing mastery of the art of the short sentence. She uses it, not only for vividness, but, in attempting to describe her own experiences, for clarity:

'This was no kind of vision; I think they call it mystical theology. The soul is suspended so that it seems quite outside itself. The will loves; the memory, I think, is almost lost; the understanding, I think, does not reason, though not lost, but, as I say, it does not work. . . .'[2]

'We ourselves try to pass to this quiet of the will: there is no result; it is soon over, it leaves aridity.'[3]

Or to hammer in her counsels:

'Let us believe it is all for our greater good; let His Majesty guide whither He wills; we are not now ours, but His.'[4]

'Let them believe it is a mistake; I have proved and seen it.'[5]

'Let them realize they are ill; let the hour of prayer be changed; and often it will be for some days.'[6]

Or, again, for emphasis:

'I see him subject to the trials of the religious life, which are great, with penances and bad food, subject to obedience—indeed, I am sometimes downright ashamed (to think) of it; with this, bad sleep, all trial, all cross.'[7]

'(The soul must) abandon itself wholly into the arms of God. If He will take it to Heaven, let it go; if to hell, it is not distressed, as it is going with its God; if its life is wholly to end, that is its desire; if it is to live a thousand years, that too. Let His Majesty treat it as His own; it no longer belongs to itself; it is given wholly to the Lord; let it entirely cease to care.'[8]

Soon we find her using a short sentence to introduce a series of long ones:

'*I am being very bold.* Your Reverence must destroy this if you think it wrong, but, believe me, I should say it better in the (very)

[1] *Op. cit.*, VI (*CW*, I, 32).　　　　[2] *Op. cit.*, X (*CW*, I, 38).
[3] *Op. cit.*, XV (*CW*, I, 93).　　　　[4] *Op. cit.*, XI (*CW*, I, 68).
[5] *Op. cit.*, XI (*CW*, I, 69).　　　　[6] *Op. cit.*, XI (*CW*, I, 69).
[7] *Op. cit.*, XIII (*CW*, I, 82). Cf. *CW*, I, xix.　[8] *Op. cit.*, XVII (*CW*, I, 101).

presence (of kings) if I could or if I thought they would believe me, etc.'[1]

inserting several short sentences to lighten a long or heavy paragraph:

'These devils keep us in terror because we wish to be terrorized by other attachments, such as honours, and possessions, and pleasures; for then they join forces with us; since, by loving and desiring what we ought to hate, we become our own enemies, and they will do us much harm; for we make them fight against us with our own weapons, which we put into their hands when we ought to be defending ourselves with them. *That is the great pity of it.* But if we hate everything for God's sake, and embrace the Cross, and try to serve Him in truth, he will fly from these truths as from the plague. *He is a lover of lies and a lie himself. He will have no truck with one who walks in truth.*'[2]

interspersing long sentences with short:

'What with pleasures and pastimes shall we enjoy what He won for us at the cost of so much blood? *It is impossible.* And do we think that by accepting vain honours we shall be imitating Him who was despised so that we might reign for ever? *That is not the way.* We are going astray, astray, we shall never arrive there.'[3]

or ending a long exposition with a single short, clinching sentence, such as 'I sometimes find it a help to talk nonsense', 'I cannot understand this', 'May God, for His name's sake, deliver us', 'I have seen this myself', 'Blessed be Thou for ever and ever!'[4]

Occasionally she flings at the reader a series of sharp rhetorical questions, punctuated with exclamations:

'God bless me! Why is this soul still on earth? How is it not on the summit of perfection? What is this? What is impeding one who does so much for God? Oh, he is punctilious about his reputation!'[5]

That such a passage is, as it sounds, a lifelike reproduction of the inflections of her voice we may infer from similar passages in which she records, in *oratio recta*, some of her colloquies with God:

[1] *Op. cit.*, XXI (*CW*, I, 132). The italics in this and the next two quotations are mine.
[2] *Op. cit.*, XXV (*CW*, I, 165).   [3] *Op. cit.*, XXVII (*CW*, I, 175).
[4] *Op. cit.*, XVIII, XIX, XX, XXII (*CW*, I, 106, 110, 117, 126, 144).
[5] *Op. cit.*, XXXI (*CW*, I, 213).

'Sometimes in my distress I would say: My Lord, how dost Thou command me things that seem impossible? If only I were free, woman though I am—! But bound in so many ways, without money or means of getting it, for Brief or for anything, what can I do, Lord?'[1]

This gradual mastery of the short sentence is the most striking characteristic of the *Life*, which presents a straightforward narrative, diversified by reflective passages, apostrophes and lyrical outbursts such as have already been quoted. Very rarely is the author either consciously or unconsciously literary. Even her frequent lapses into the historic present, dramatic though they sound to us—

'This amazed me, but I saw that He was right; so I go to the little house and . . . found that it would just make a convent, though a very small one.'[2]

'As she was an important person, and knew that I lived in a convent where the nuns were allowed to leave the house, the Lord gives her a very great desire to see me'[3]

—were only the transference to paper of a habit still much commoner in Spanish conversation than in English.

Nor, on the other hand, had she developed all the features which were to make her style unique. There are few of her characteristic repetitions and ellipses, few even of such long and awkward parenthetical clauses as we find later. The task she had set herself was a clearly defined one—to give 'a true and clear description of everything I remember'[4]—and, save for a few digressions, for which she would duly apologize ('But what a lot I have been saying . . .!'[5] 'I have strayed far from my intention. . . .'[6] 'But what nonsense I have begun to write!'),[7] she told it plainly.

'I have ventured to put together this story of my unruly life, though I have wasted no more time or trouble than has been necessary for the writing of it, but have merely set down what has happened to me with all the simplicity and truth at my command.'[8]

---

[1] *Op. cit.*, XXXIII (*CW*, I, 229). [2] *Op. cit.*, XXXIII (*CW*, I, 229).
[3] *Op. cit.*, XXXIV (*CW*, I, 232). [4] *Op. cit.*, XXX (*CW*, I, 204).
[5] *Op. cit.*, XXVII (*CW*, I, 178). [6] *Op. cit.*, XXIX (*CW*, I, 187).
[7] *Op. cit.*, XXXVII (*CW*, I, 266). [8] *Op. cit.*, XL (*CW*, I, 299).

She was to write very differently when she had a different theme.[1]

Three years after completing the first draft of her *Life*, Saint Teresa began the *Way of Perfection*[2]—'to help the souls of my sisters to make great progress in the service of the Lord'. 'I do not know', she confessed, 'what I am going to say': all she had in mind was 'to suggest a few remedies for a number of small temptations which come from the devil';[3] she could have had no idea that nearly half her book would consist of a commentary on the Lord's Prayer. So she starts, as though she were talking to some little group of her daughters, by using short, pointed phrases, often dividing her exhortations with the 'Firstly . . . secondly . . . thirdly . . .' of the preacher, and emphasizing her points by repeating the same word—one can almost see the finger stabbing the air as one reads. Examples, especially in the first half-dozen chapters, abound:

'Oh, my sisters in Christ! . . . This is your vocation; this must be your business; these must be your desires; these your tears; these your petitions.'[4]

'Do you think, my daughters, that it is easy to have to do with the world, to live in the world, to engage in the affairs of the world, to adapt yourselves . . . to the habits of the world, and yet inwardly to be strangers to the world, and enemies of the world, like persons who are in exile? . . .'[5]

'Here all must be friends with each other, love each other, be fond of each other and help each other.'[6]

Then, as in the *Life*, the style changes. Not, this time, because the author is learning how to write more effectively, but because she is passing from such homely themes as remedies for temptations to the wider theme of mental prayer. The motions of the finger give place to ampler gestures. The sentences and paragraphs grow

[1] The *Spiritual Relations*, of which the first and the last of the six most important are separated in date by twenty-one years, are omitted from this survey as being neither continuous, like the *Letters*, nor, like the other works, a complete whole.

[2] In so short an essay as this there is not space to enter into stylistic differences between the Escorial and the Valladolid autographs (cf. *CW*, II, xix–xxi, *Mother of Carmel*, pp. 53–4). Quotations are from the text of *CW*; on the method adopted in preparing this, cf. *CW*, II, xxiv–xxvi.

[3] *Way of Perfection*, I (*CW*, II, 1–2). [4] *Op. cit.*, I (*CW*, II, 4).
[5] *Op. cit.*, III (*CW*, II, 11). [6] *Op. cit.*, IV (*CW*, II, 17).

longer; the style becomes more flowing. But other features of the style of the *Way of Perfection* do not change. There are still but few elliptical phrases and unmanageable parentheses. There are fewer apostrophes than in the *Life*, though many short ones. 'Oh, my Lord . . .!' 'Oh, my Redeemer . . .!' 'Oh, Lord of the world . . .!' and the like are found all through the book. So, too, are exclamations and appeals to her daughters. Sometimes she combines the two, as in these extracts from a passage of no more than four paragraphs:

'And supposing, my Lord, that there are others who are like myself, but have not realized this? . . . Oh, God help me, sisters! If we only knew what honour really is and what is meant by losing it! . . .'

' . . . O Lord, Lord, art Thou our Example and our Master? Yes, indeed. And wherein did Thy honour consist, O Lord, Who hast honoured us? . . .'

'For the love of God, sisters! We have lost our way. . . . Grant us, my God, to understand how little we understand ourselves.'[1]

Rhetorical questions, like these exclamations, lend the exhortations liveliness and variety:

'Do you suppose they (the hermits) were made of iron? No, they were as frail as we are.'[2]

'What does it matter if we die? How often have our bodies mocked us! Should we not occasionally mock them?'[3]

'Why do we want to serve the Lord in so doubtful a way . . .? Who is plunging you into those perils?'[4]

Sometimes she puts questions into her daughters' mouths ('But why, you will say, does the Prioress excuse us?')[5] and answers them. Sometimes, to make a point the more surely, she utters ironic exclamations:

'If they ask for another confessor it appears that that would be the end of discipline in the convent. Oh, but he is not of their Order!'[6]

Sometimes, with an unerring instinct for holding her readers' attention, she alternates short sentences and longer ones:

[1] *Op. cit.*, XXXVI (*CW*, II, 155–7).   [2] *Op. cit.*, XI (*CW*, II, 48).
[3] *Op. cit.*, XI (*CW*, II, 48).   [4] *Op. cit.*, XVIII (*CW*, II, 76).
[5] *Op. cit.*, X (*CW*, II, 45).   [6] *Op. cit.*, V (*CW*, II, 23).

'Do not think, my sisters, that by not going about to please those in the world you will lack food. *I (re-)assure you.* Never try to sustain yourselves by human artifices, or you will die of hunger, and rightly. *Eyes on your Spouse! It is for Him to sustain you.* (If) He (is) pleased, those least devoted to you will give you food, if unwillingly, as you have found by experience. If, doing this, you die of hunger, happy the nuns of Saint Joseph's! *Do not forget this, for love of the Lord.* As you forgo revenue, forgo worry about food. *If not, all is lost.*'[1]

Rather more than halfway through her book, Saint Teresa begins her exposition of the Lord's Prayer—'perhaps the most beautiful', comments Hoornaert, 'that has ever been written'—[2] and so sensitive is she to the atmosphere of her theme that almost immediately her style becomes completely transformed. So marked is this change that it can be appreciated even in translation: it will suffice to compare the twenty-fifth chapter with the twenty-sixth. The former contrasts vocal prayer with mental and in the most matter-of-fact way refers the reader to the *Life*[3] for further details. The latter opens with a fervid appeal to the nuns to take Our Lord as their Companion, which, through a passage four paragraphs long, increases in intensity:

'If you are happy, look upon your risen Lord, and the very thought of how He rose from the sepulchre will gladden you. How bright and how beautiful was He then! How majestic! How victorious! How joyful! . . .

'If you are suffering trials, or are sad, look upon Him on His way to the Garden. What sore distress He must have borne in His soul . . .! Or look upon Him bound to the Column, full of pain, His flesh all torn to pieces by His great love for you. . . . Or look upon Him bending under the weight of the Cross and not even allowed to take breath: He will look upon you with His lovely and compassionate eyes, full of tears, and in comforting your grief will forget His own . . .'[4]

Not all the remaining chapters are in this vein: even this chapter ends on a lower note: 'It is also a great help to have a good book, written in the vernacular, simply as an aid to recollection. . . .'[5]

[1] *Op. cit.*, II (*CW*, II, 5).
[2] *Saint Teresa in her Writings* (London, 1931), p. 259.
[3] Cf. *CW*, II, 105, n. 4. [4] *Way of Perfection*, XXVI (*CW*, II, 107-8).
[5] *Op. cit.*, XXVI (*CW*, II, 109-10).

But on a comparison of the two parts as a whole, the second stands out as much more literary than the first. Not only in language, but in rhythm, Saint Teresa reaches a height which in the *Life* she seldom approaches.[1] For the first time she is carried away by her theme. 'How I have enlarged on this!' begins the penultimate chapter. 'Yet not as much as I should like, for it is a delightful thing to talk of such love. What will it be to possess it?'[2] This same theme was to carry her away, for a much longer period, in the *Interior Castle*.

[VII]

Saint Teresa's next two works were probably two opuscules which cannot be certainly dated: *Exclamations of the Soul to God* (*c.* 1569) and *Conceptions of the Love of God* (*c.* 1571–3).

The *Exclamations*, a collection of seventeen post-Communion meditations, stands out from everything else that Saint Teresa wrote. It seems almost irreverent to analyse such spontaneous outpourings—'white-hot embers', as P. Silverio calls them, 'from the fire of the Saint's love, which . . . can still enkindle the hearts of those who read them'.[3] In none of her verses[4] is she so much a poet as in the rhythmical lyricism of this fervid prose:

¡Oh vida, vida! ¿Cómo puedes sustentarte estando ausente de tu Vida? En tanta soledad, ¿en qué te empleas? . . .'[5]

('O life, life! How canst thou sustain thyself when thou art absent from thy Life? In such great loneliness, how dost thou employ thyself? . . .')

As the title of the opuscule suggests, it is thickly studded with ejaculations, often interrogatory in form, which convey to the reader something of the author's intense and hardly articulate emotion:

'O long life! O grievous life! O life not lived! Oh, what complete, what helpless solitude! Then when, Lord, when? How long? What shall I do, my Good, what shall I do? Shall I perchance desire not to desire Thee?'[6]

---

[1] I have quoted one of the exceptional passages (*CW*, I, 180) in *Mother of Carmel*, p. 27.

[2] *Way of Perfection*, XLI (*CW*, II, 177).   [3] *CW*, II, 400.

[4] Except, perhaps, in 'Oh Hermosura . . . !' But that (*CW*, II, 283, n. 2) is certainly modelled closely upon profane poetry.

[5] *Exclamations*, I (*CW*, II, 402).   [6] *Op. Cit.*, VI (*CW*, II, 406–7).

Here and there it contains parallelisms and other literary devices, which, as readers of the *Life* and the *Way of Perfection* will already have suspected, seem to come naturally to this born writer:

'Thy works are holy, are just, are of inestimable worth and of great wisdom. . . .'[1]

'Here, my God, must be manifested Thy power, here Thy mercy.'

' . . . I ask Thee . . . to love one who loves Thee not, to open to one who calls Thee not. . . .'[2]

'O true Lover! With how much pity, with how much sweetness, with how much joy, with how much indulgence . . . dost Thou heal these wounds . . .!'[3]

In the early sections we find much paradox and word-play, such as was common in the literature of piety—

'I grieve . . . for the time when I lived without grief. . . .'[4]

'What shall I do, not to undo the wonders which Thou doest in me?'[5]

But these soon grow fewer and in time disappear. In their place— chiefly in the later sections—we find a great wealth of character- istically Teresan repetition. Nowhere else in the whole of the works is there proportionately so much of it:

'See, see, the Judge . . . now entreats you . . .'

'God help me, God help me . . .!'

' . . . Not to wait a year, not to wait a day, not to wait an hour, and perhaps not more than a moment . . .'

'O Christians, Christians! . . . There is still a remedy, Lord, a remedy . . .'

'O brethren, O brethren, children of this God. Let us brace ourselves, let us brace ourselves . . .'

'What is this? What is this? . . . Alas, alas, Lord . . .'[6]

These are but typical examples. The use of the device would be excessive were it not set in a context of spontaneous exaltation, giving the impression of such complete naturalness.

Though the theme of the *Conceptions of the Love of God* has a close

---

[1] *Op. cit.*, I (*CW*, II, 402).   [2] *Op. cit.*, VIII (*CW*, II, 409).
[3] *Op. cit.*, XVI (*CW*, II, 417).   [4] *Op. cit.*, I (*CW*, II, 402).
[5] *Op. cit.*, I (*CW*, II, 402).
[6] *Op. cit.*, X, XI, XIII, XIV, XV (*CW*, II, 411, 414, 415, 416).

affinity with that treated later in the *Interior Castle*, the tone and style suggest rather the *Way of Perfection*. It is an exposition of 'some of the texts from the *Songs* of Solomon'[1] written for her daughters. The short, pointed phrases, the apostrophes to God—short oftener than long—the exclamations, the appeals: all these are so frequent and conform so closely to type that illustrations are hardly necessary. Let a single one suffice:

'God help me! What are we nuns doing in our convent? For what did we leave the world? For what did we come (here)? In what can we better employ ourselves than in making dwelling-places in our souls for our Spouse, and coming to Him in time to be able to ask Him for the kiss of His mouth?'[2]

The early chapters tend to be intimate and colloquial: at one point we pass directly from an apostrophe to God (though it must be remembered that these apostrophes were quite natural to the author) to an anecdote which provides the best example of anti-climax in the whole of the works:

'I remember hearing a religious preach a most admirable sermon . . . and there was so much laughter and what he said was so completely misinterpreted . . . that I was astounded.'[3]

An indication of the colloquial level of the early part of the work, which would incline a reader to rate it low stylistically,[4] is the large number of diminutives used: in Chapter II there is a higher proportion than almost anywhere else—notable exceptions are to be found in one or two chapters of the *Foundations*. The pang felt by a spiritual person at every little thing (*cosita*) he encounters which is contrary to his profession is like the sharp prick of a tiny thorn (*espinita*), however minute (*pequeñita*).[5] Souls have their *guerrillas* ('minor conflicts') and, on emerging from 'favoured states', find 'a thousand little causes of stumbling (*tropiecillos*) and a thousand little occasions of sin (*ocasioncillas*)'.[6] In the same chapter occur *cosillas* ('trifling faults'), *pelillo* ('little hair', used figura-

---

[1] *Conceptions*, Prologue (*CW*, II, 357).   [2] *Conceptions*, II (*CW*, II, 366–7).
[3] *Op. cit.*, I (*CW*, II, 360).
[4] As Hoornaert does, for example; though I think he goes too far in calling it 'especially in the first chapters, . . . apart from a few soaring passages heavy, restrained and plodding'. (*Op. cit.*, p. 259.)
[5] *Conceptions*, II (*CW*, II, 366).   [6] *Op. cit.*, II (*CW*, II, 365, 366).

tively), *arbolillo* ('shrub'), *puntica* ('tittle') and *ocasioncita* ('just a little occasion'—*i.e.*, of sin).[1]

About halfway through the book—from the fourth chapter, which treats of the Prayer of Quiet—the author becomes absorbed in her sublime theme and the tone of her prose rises. Anecdotes, colloquialisms and diminutives almost disappear; apostrophes increase in number and become longer, images are employed and pressed home with effect, and, especially in the chapters on the Prayer of Union, there are passages of real eloquence and great beauty. It would be self-indulgence to quote the fifth and sixth chapters, where, in the original Spanish, an exquisite rhythm enhances other qualities which will be evident even in a translation.

The *Book of the Foundations*, begun in August 1573 and completed late in 1576, is the most matter-of-fact of Saint Teresa's works, occupied mainly with the practical business of the Reform, containing a far higher proportion of straightforward narrative than the *Life*, and, unlike the *Life*, saying little either of the author's own spiritual experiences or of spiritual experience in general. It abounds in digressions, ranging from a paragraph or two of reflections to anecdotal biographies extending over chapters. As in effect it is a volume of reminiscences, no reader objects to them, especially as the anecdotes, the records of the writer's own experiences and the comments on human nature are packed with wisdom and humour. The book rambles happily, and we ramble happily with it, not least because we find it so easy to read.

The language and the style of the *Foundations* are as matter-of-fact as its content, as almost any passage will show:

'One (thing) occurs to me here, and it is this: that one day, in the refectory, they gave us portions of cucumber; the piece I got was very small, and rotten inside. I called a sister quietly—one of the most intelligent and gifted we had—in order to prove her obedience, and told her to go and plant that cucumber in the little garden that each of us had. She asked me if she was to plant it upright or sideways; I told her sideways. So she went and planted it without ever realizing that it could not possibly do anything but shrivel up.'[2]

'Having reached the house, we entered a courtyard. The walls seemed to me in a very tumbledown condition, though not as bad as when I saw them by day. . . . We did not know what to do for

---

[1] *Op. cit.*, II (*CW*, II, 371, 372, 373).   [2] *Foundations*, I (*CW*, III, 2).

nails, and it was not a time at which we could buy any. So we started to look round the walls; at last, after some trouble, we found a good number. Some (began) the hanging, and we (nuns set to work) cleaning the floor, and we all worked so quickly that, by daybreak, the altar was set up and the bell hung in a gallery; and Mass was said at once.'[1]

Not only matter-of-fact is the style, but as a rule perfectly natural —suggestive, one would say today, of the letter home. Often the details of the narrative are miscellaneous in character, and sometimes inconsequent—at which we can hardly wonder after reading the opening lines of Chapter XIX:

'I have been making a long digression. When I recall anything which the Lord has been pleased for me to learn by experience, it worries me if I cannot put it down.'[2]

In keeping with its general character, the book has very few long apostrophes—just occasionally, when very much moved, the Saint cannot refrain from one; but such as there are are so short as to be hardly more than ejaculations:

'He told me privately there would be no house for us . . . (and) we should be forced into a lawsuit. But oh, God! what little power has the strongest opposition, when Thou, Lord, art pleased to bestow courage! This new difficulty seemed rather to stimulate me, etc.'[3]

' . . . She became very sad, realizing that the day was over and that all other days would come to an end in the same way. O greatness of God, which turned into hatred the happiness caused her by delight in things which must perish! She began to feel so sad that she could not hide the fact from her betrothed, etc.'[4]

The function fulfilled in the other books by long apostrophes seems to be performed by transitions from narrative to quiet reflection and thence back to narrative again. There are few emphatic repetitions—for the author is not exhorting or teaching, but narrating. On the other hand, there are probably more diminutives in the *Foundations* than (with the exception of the *Letters*) in all the other works put together. They include the well-known phrase, applied to the first Reformed convents, 'these little dovecotes (*palomarcitos*)

[1] *Op. cit.*, III (*CW*, III, 11).   [2] *Op. cit.*, XIX (*CW*, III, 92).
[3] *Op. cit.*, III (*CW*, III, 9).   [4] *Op. cit.*, X (*CW*, III, 52).

of the Virgin Our Lady';[5] the equally familiar 'little Bethlehem of a porch' (*portalito de Belén*), applied to the chapel of the priory at Duruelo;[2] and the 'little lambs (*ovejitas*: lit., little sheep) of the Virgin',[3] used of the Discalced nuns. Again and again the diminutive is applied to women (*mujercitas, mujercillas, pobrecillas*), once to a friar (*frailecico*), and on various occasions to most of the features or attributes of convent life, the house (*casilla*), the little church (*iglesita*), the diminutive courtyard (*patiecillo*), the tiny bell (*campanilla*), the modest kitchen (*cocinilla*), and the meagre bundle of wood available for a fire (*hacecito de leña*). The use of the diminutive form in the *Foundations* would repay more detailed study.

The *Interior Castle*, a treatise on the Mystic Way at once comprehensive and sublime, was written in something like twelve weeks,[4] with an intensity which many of the author's contemporaries described as supernatural. It would be understandable if such a book had no stylistic merits at all—if the words had flowed in torrents from the pen in long, formless periods, so that it was hard to read, not only because of the sublimity of its content but because of its style. It is true that its first chapter begins with a far from well-balanced sentence of sixty-three words, and that the first page of a current Spanish edition contains only thirteen sentences while the first page of the *Life*, in the same edition, contains twenty. It is also true that there are more, and longer, parenthetical sentences in this book than in either the *Life* or the *Way of Perfection*, but the total number is still not large, and, though the translator is often perplexed by them, it is doubtful if they puzzle the average reader.

The unexpected and remarkable truth is that, of all Saint Teresa's works, despite the rapidity and intensity with which she wrote it, and despite her absorption in her high argument, the *Interior Castle* is, both constructionally and stylistically, by far the best. It is the only one of her books in which she seems to start with a preconceived plan, simple, clearly developed and never obscured by the comparatively few and unimportant digressions. In style, as in content, it is a work of great maturity. It combines three types of writing: the autobiographical (for much of it, like the *Life*, describes Saint Teresa's own spiritual experiences); the hortatory (for she finds time in it, as in the *Way of Perfection*, to give counsels

[1] *Op. cit.*, IV (*CW*, III, 17).   [2] *Op. cit.*, XIV (*CW*, III, 66).
[3] *Op. cit.*, XVIII (*CW*, III, 89).   [4] *CW*, II, 195.

to her daughters); and the expository, where she outlines the Mystic Way, as she had outlined parts of it in the *Life* and the *Way of Perfection*. And it combines all the best of those books and of those three manners. _____

It has an amazing variety. Saint Teresa's art has by now become so instinctive with her that she passes without the slightest effort from one manner to another. The long apostrophes are very few, but there are many short ones, often no more than ejaculations, not interrupting the trend of the thought. Short and long sentences are balanced with consummate skill:

'Oh, Jesus! Will anyone say that he has no desire for so great a good, especially when he has got over the most troublesome (part of the way to it)? No, no one. We all say we desire it; but, if the Lord is to take complete possession of the soul, more than that is necessary.'[1]

'To see, then, the restlessness of this little butterfly—though it has never been quieter or more at rest in its life! Here is something to praise God for—namely, that it knows not where to settle and make its abode—for it has had such an abode that everything it sees on earth leaves it dissatisfied, especially when God has again and again given it this wine which almost every time has brought it new blessings. It sets no store now by the things it did when it was a worm—that is, by the gradual weaving of the cocoon. It has taken wings: how can it be satisfied with crawling along when it can fly?'[2]

'Oh, poor little butterfly, bound by so many chains, which prevent you from flying as you will! Have pity on her, my God, and see to it that she may in some measure be able to fulfil her desires, to Thy honour and glory. Remember not the slightness of her merits and the baseness of her nature. Mighty art Thou, Lord, to make the great sea draw back, and the great Jordan, and to allow the Children of Israel to pass over them. (And yet Thou needest) have no pity on them, for, with the aid of Thy strength, she can endure many trials. And this she is determined to do: she desires to suffer them.'[3]

The short, lively sentences so strikingly characteristic of the *Way of Perfection* are found in equal number here:

'Let us strive, my sisters, for the love of the Lord; let us leave

[1] *Interior Castle*, III, i (*CW*, II, 221).   [2] *Op. cit.*, V, ii (*CW*, II, 255).
[3] *Op. cit.*, VI, vi (*CW*, II, 298).

our reason and our fears in His hands; let us forget this natural weakness, which can cause us so much concern. The care of these bodies, let our superiors see to it. That is their business: ours is only to journey speedily to see the Lord.'[1]

'The Lord is just. If the fault is not ours, His Majesty will give you in other ways what He denies you in this—His Majesty knows why. His secrets are deep-hidden. But at least what He does will be best for us, without any doubt.'[2]

'We are His, sisters; may He do with us as He will and lead us by whatever way He pleases.'[3]

So, too, are the short rhetorical questions and exclamations:

'What, then, is this? Whence does it come? I will tell you.'[4]

'What do you think His will is, daughters? That we should be altogether perfect, so as to be one with Him and with the Father, as in His Majesty's prayer. See how far we are from attaining this!'[5]

'Oh, what blessed madness, sisters! If only God would give it to us all!'[6]

Of the imagery of the *Interior Castle* there is far more to be said than can find a place in a brief survey. The statistics already given, which show that, with the possible exception of the *Exclamations*, it is the richest of Saint Teresa's works in images, say very little. They convey no idea, for example, of the contrasts in imagery, of the quick succession in which figure after figure is fired, as it were, at the reader in the hope of explaining the inexplicable; of the effect produced by the Saint's more homely and unconventional comparisons. Of the skill in the presentation of sustained images befitting a work which, after all, is itself one long image; of the masterly development—exciting, yet restrained—of the justly famous similitude of the silkworm; and of the impress which it leaves on the latter part of the book through the image of the 'butterfly', or 'little dove'. The *Interior Castle* is, in short, a treatise of quite exceptional pictorial quality.

And there are other characteristics of the book, either wholly or in part stylistic, which enhance its beauty. Not only the images, but the numerous anecdotes and the modes of address have made

---

[1] *Op. cit.*, III, ii (*CW*, II, 226).   [2] *Op. cit.*, III, ii (*CW*, II, 228).
[3] *Op. cit.*, IV, ii (*CW*, II, 239).   [4] *Op. cit.*, V, ii (*CW*, II, 257).
[5] *Op. cit.*, V, iii (*CW*, II, 261).   [6] *Op. cit.*, VI, vi (*CW*, II, 301).

it perhaps the most popular book, wholly mystical in nature, ever written. Saint Teresa never loses sight of the daughters for whom it is primarily meant. She addresses them directly, asks them the most pointed questions, puts objections ('But, you will say next . . .') into their mouths and admits them to her personal intimacy. She forgets what she has just been saying; she is not clever enough to explain her meaning; she has a poor memory; and the noises in her head are so loud that she is beginning to wonder what is going on in it.[1] Can ever a treatise so sublime have had so homely a background?

Of Saint Teresa's *Letters* the two most striking features are their number and their scope. The collection of 458, including only a small proportion of fragments, covers a period of just over forty-one years,[2] and the recipients vary from members of the writer's own family and friars and nuns of the Reform to bishops, aristocrats, the General of the Order and the King of Spain. We should therefore expect them to differ greatly in style, as in fact they do. The modes of subscriptions range from 'Your Lordship's unworthy servant and subject' to a blunt 'Yours' (*Suya*): the superscriptions abound in superlatives like *Ilustrísimo* and *Reverendísimo*; and in one letter, of barely more than a page, addressed to the Cardinal Archbishop of Toledo, the phrase 'your most Illustrious Lordship' occurs no less than fifteen times. There are signs that, in addressing the great of this world, Saint Teresa has taken some pains, not only over deference, but over clarity. It is not here, however, that she is at her most characteristic, but rather in the very large majority of the letters written to close acquaintances, relatives and individual friends.

So little difference is there between Teresa the author and Teresa the letter-writer that it is as easy to trace the evolution of her style in the *Letters* as in the *Life*, the *Way of Perfection* and the *Interior Castle*. If we begin reading the collection at the beginning, we get the impression of a long, rambling narrative, made up of enormous sentences full of loosely strung phrases and clauses—the writer, one would think, has no sense of style at all. Here is a liter-

---

[1] *Op. cit.*, VI, iv; III, i; IV, i; IV, ii; IV, i (*CW*, II, 288, 221, 232, 236, 234).

[2] The first twenty years of this period, however, are represented by only one letter and five short notes; the remainder of the letters extend from 29th November 1561 to 15th September 1582, three weeks before the Saint's death.

ally translated extract from the first of her long letters extant, written to her brother Lorenzo in the Indies:

'But, as I have written to you already at great length, for many reasons and causes which I have been unable to avoid, because they are inspirations from God, so that they are not suitable for a letter, I only say that holy and learned persons think that I have an obligation not to be cowardly, but to put all I can into this task, which is to found a convent, where there will be only fifteen nuns, without possibility of adding to the number, in the strictest enclosure, so that they will never go out and will see no one without having veils in front of their faces, founded upon prayer and mortification, as I have written to you more fully, and I will send you another letter by Antonio Morán, when he goes.'[1]

But this was written to the correspondent with whom she was more completely natural than with anyone else. 'You must not give yourself the trouble of re-reading the letters you write me', she tells him, sixteen years later. 'I never re-read mine. If a word here or there should have a letter missing, just put it in, and I will do the same for you.'[2] Further, the long letter just quoted was written before Saint Teresa's first book was begun, and we have already seen how quickly her natural gifts as a writer developed once she gave them play. From time to time, when ideas were crowding into her brain, and perhaps a courier was waiting for her bundle of letters, she tended to revert to these long, formless and even ungrammatical periods, which, did the translator not put them into some kind of order, would be the English reader's despair. After she had become accustomed to writing, her epistolary style evolves more slowly and its most characteristic feature becomes, and remains, the same use of short sentences and the same balancing of short sentences with long ones that we have found in the objective works. The short sentences are in the main vivacious, sometimes elliptical and always marked by great word-economy.

'So your Ladyship must be brave; think what the Lord suffered at this season. Life is short; our trials last but a moment.'[3]
'There is little to do: the house is near this one. Don't let it trouble you. May God repay you for your advice. I think I understood what you crossed out.'[4]
'I am well, and my Isabel is a real delight to us. Her gentle and

[1] *LL* 2 (29).   [2] *LL* 163 (412).   [3] *LL* 15 (63).   [4] *LL* 64 (158).

merry nature is a rare thing. Yesterday Señora Doña Juana wrote to me. They are all well.'[1]

'Once done, done for good. For a few days, all is outcry; but punish some and the rest will be quiet. Women are like that, timorous creatures, most of them.'[2]

'The writing, by my daughter Gabriela. I should like to write to all; I have no head.'[3]

There is a very characteristic sentence of this type which, in one form or another, occurs again and again:

'I don't deserve it, but only cross and more cross.'[4]

'If it is not God's will, well and good, but only cross and more cross.'[5]

'I realize that I deserve only cross and more cross.'[6]

But, as Saint Teresa's epistolary style is sometimes spoken of as though it were uniformly staccato, it should be added that in her most usual type of paragraph, one, or sometimes two, short sentences are found in the middle of longer ones:

'I was delighted that our most Reverend Father General arranged that matter so nicely. *He is wise and holy. God guard him.* His Majesty knows how much I should have liked to stay in your house longer.'[7]

'Your Lordship will already know that they are sending Father Domingo as Prior to Trujillo, where they elected him, and that those of Salamanca have sent to beg the Father Provincial to let him remain. *They do not know what he will do.*

'*It is a trying region for his health.* If your Ladyship should see the Father Provincial of the Dominicans, scold him from me, for he was a very long time in Salamanca and never came to see me.'[8]

'She has great talent (for her age it seems impossible) and much prayer, for the Lord has shown her favour since she took the habit. *Great her contentment and humility: it is a rare thing.* Both say that they will commend your Lordship to Our Lord very particularly.'[9]

---

[1] *LL* 122 (315).   [2] *LL* 147 (371–2).

[3] *LL* 274 (651). ('The actual writing should be done by my daughter Gabriela. I should like to write to all the sisters, but my head is not fit for it.')

[4] *LL* 253 (617). *I.e.*, 'but only one cross after another'.

[5] *LL* 305 (716).   [6] *LL* 308 (724).

[7] *LL* 24 (82). The italics here and in the next two quotations are mine.

[8] *LL* 30 (92–3).   [9] *LL* 70 (170).

This brevity involves frequent ellipses. Much has been written about Saint Teresa's elliptical manner, which, marked though it is in some of her objective work, is naturally most marked of all in her letters. The exact meaning of her most complicated passages has puzzled even Spanish Carmelites from her own Castile. Many others, at first sight, are Greek to anyone else.

Her late brother-in-law, Martín de Guzmán, for example, has been fairly successful in a lawsuit, but some difficulty is being experienced about the property of her dead father. This, literally, is how she tells her brother Lorenzo about it:

'But Martín de Guzmán . . . got his way, and judgment was given for him, though not well; and to ask again for what my father (may he have glory!) sold, no patience remains to me.'[1]

('. . . Now they are asking again for the property which was sold by my father—may he be in glory! I have lost all patience.')

In another place she discusses the character of her friend Dom Teotónio de Bragança.

'Without that, I have no more confidence in his being a great negotiator. That he has great will, yes; possibility, little.'[2]

('Apart from that, I have not much confidence in his ability as a negotiator. He has plenty of good will, I agree; but there is little hope of his getting anything done.')

And, two days later, she is writing to Gracián about his interior life, under the fiction that the reference is to a third person[3]—the 'Paul' who is really Gracián himself:

'Forgive me so long a message, for the love you have for Paul allows it, and, if you think this that I say good, tell it him, and if not, no; but I say that which I should wish myself. I tell you it is a great thing works and good conscience.'[4]

('Forgive me for sending such a long message. Your love for Paul must be my excuse. If you think what I have said is good, you must pass it on to him; if not, don't. I am just telling you my own

---

[1] *LL* 2 (31).   [2] *LL* 121 (312). Cf. p. 53, above.

[3] On this fiction, see *LL*, pp. 197, n. 5, 264. I am inclined to think that she practises the habit, not only out of caution, but also partly to hide a natural embarrassment in showing her affection for Gracián in so deliberate a medium as a letter, and perhaps, too, because, with her childlike love of invention, she liked it for its own sake.

[4] *LL* 122 (317)

feelings about it. I assure you there are two great things—good works and a clear conscience.')

But the most characteristic of Saint Teresa's ellipses occur like those at the beginning of the *Life*, in short sentences, and are quite intelligible.

'He will certainly write to your Ladyship when there is someone by whom',[1] (*i.e.*, by whom to send the letter).
'She is very happy and here with her'[2] (*i.e.*, we here are pleased with her).
'You are only wasting your time, but as little humble (*i.e.*, as you have so little humility) you will not believe me.'[3]
'Julián de Ávila is lost for him and all'[4] (*i.e.*, '. . . is lost in admiration for him, and so are all the rest').
'It was never his intention, so far as I know, that I should come for good: mine, yes'[5] (*i.e.*, that was *my* idea).
'If we were faithful to God . . . only for the authority He gives (and the more, the more), it would be the greatest gain.'[6]
('If we were faithful to God . . . only for the sake of the authority He gives to His servants—and the greater the authority, the more faithful we should be—our faithfulness would still bring us great gain.')
'If it is not put right, it would be dangerous. And if there were something!'[7] (*i.e.*, And what a great deal there is to put right!).

The love for such elliptical sentences, as well as for inversion, often used in conjunction with ellipsis, increases as the years go by. It would be difficult to establish the precise extent of this tendency, since there would be no general agreement as to precisely when a sentence becomes elliptical and border-line cases abound. But the general trend is unmistakable.

The practice of inversion is a specific instance of a trait which can be illustrated only inadequately in translation—the extreme flexibility of Saint Teresa's style. A language in which almost any word can occupy almost any position in a sentence affords ample opportunities for this habit and she certainly takes full advantage of them. 'Ambition I believe he has none',[8] she writes. 'Well am I, and restful have I found it without this disturbance.'[9] 'Sheet of

---

[1] *LL* 6 (47).   [2] *LL* 49 (126).   [3] *LL* 54 (139).   [4] *LL* 72 (175).
[5] *LL* 90 (217).   [6] *LL* 147 (369).   [7] *LL* 163 (408).   [8] *LL* 74 (179).
[9] *LL* 100 (255).

paper with signature came none.'[1] 'All your documents I received.'[2] 'The enclosed letter from the Seville prioress (you must) read.'[3] 'Great thing is truth.'[4] 'Much like a Christian he bears it.'[5] Sometimes the inversions are spread over a whole sentence:

'Never have I health, nor wish to have it had I; a great desire to have already left this exile, yes I have. . . .'[6]

By this time the reader who knows the *Letters* only in translation will begin to understand why in the original they are occasionally difficult. The reader who attacks them in Spanish may at first find the inversions irritating; but, once accustomed to them, he will find that they greatly enhance the *Letters*' variety and vivacity.

Closely connected with the elliptical habit is the device, already described, of substituting a pronoun for some noun already once used and occasionally using it in a different sense. Thus, writing to thank her brother Lorenzo for his kindness to their sister, she remarks on the latter's *trabajos de necesidad* (*i.e.*, trials arising from need) and continues: *Yo no la tengo de nada* ('I have it not of anything', where 'it' (*la*) refers back to *necesidad*, 'need').[7] Sometimes, when a verb and a noun are identical in form, she uses the pronoun for the noun corresponding to the verb:

'May He grant you as many and as happy new years as I wish (*deseo*) you. I had it greatly (*i.e.*, I had a great *wish* (*deseo*)) to see your writing.'[8]

One of the commonest uses of this contraction is with the noun *merced* ('favour', 'honour'). *Vuestra merced* (today contracted to *usted*) was (and still is) the normal pronoun of address in polite conversation. The *Letters* abound in phrases like these:

'*Suplico a vuestra merced me la haga* (*i.e.*, *me haga la merced*) *de venirse presto.*'[9]

('I beg your Honour to do me it (*i.e.*, to do me the honour) of coming quickly.')

The substitutive device also tends to increase in frequency as Saint Teresa grows older.

Another happy product of Saint Teresa's skill in the art of word-

---

[1] *LL* 122 (319). [2] *LL* 257 (620). [3] *LL* 168 (429). [4] *LL* 298 (701).
[5] *LL* 283 (672). [6] *LL* 74 (182: cf. n. 6). [7] *LL* 19 (74). [8] *LL* 70 (168).
[9] *LL* 47 (123). It should be added, however, that Saint Teresa often repeats the noun *merced*, as in the fourth paragraph of this same letter.

economy is the brief, incisive phrase, pregnant with meaning, and fully appreciable only in the original Spanish, if now and then so brief as with the passage of centuries to have become obscure. *Andar remendada* ('to go about patched'), used by the Saint of herself, loses force when we render it 'to go about in a patched habit'.[1] *Hombre de suerte y de verdad* ('a man of luck and truth') can be paraphrased only as 'just the right sort of man, thoroughly reliable'.[2] 'To go off with hands to head' (*con las manos en la cabeza*)[3] is a vivid image for despair—especially when used, as here, of the devil. 'He had arrived well'[4] (*bien logrado fué*: 'he had fought the good fight', 'he had lived to a ripe old age') is a satisfying epitaph. All these are readily understandable. Even Spaniards, however, find it difficult to interpret 'in all of which I see a "yes-no"' (*en todos veo un 'sí-no'*),[5] a phrase intelligible only in its context. In another place Saint Teresa declares herself apprehensive of *tanta señoría y baraúnda*,[6] 'all the fashionable people (I should have to meet) and (all the) fuss (there would be)'—one of the tersest phrases I have ever encountered in Spanish. Running it close is *para principios y negocios*,[7] which, in its context, means 'when one is making a beginning and negotiations are in progress'.

Repetitions conforming to all the types enumerated above are frequent. Simple repetition, used for emphasis (*harto harto*, somewhat stronger than 'very, very';[8] *más, más virtud*, 'far more virtue'),[9] is the least so, except for the oft-repeated *amén, amén*, or even *amén, amén, amén*,[10] occurring sometimes in the middle of a paragraph, though more often at the end. The rather pointless, and sometimes pleonastic, repetitive variations, such as 'very dangerous perils',[11] 'burdened with a very great burden',[12] 'any surer way to the assurance',[13] 'charmed with his charming ways',[14] are much more common; but they are mere habits of writing, with probably no intention of word-play.

Occasionally Saint Teresa indulges in quite complicated wordplay, which, in a correspondent with such a natural manner, might seem surprising. Some of the most noteworthy examples deserve examination. The play in the phrase *unos gustos para*

---

[1] *LL* 2 (29).

[2] *LL* 2 (30). An alternative idiomatic rendering of *hombre de suerte* would be 'a Heaven-sent man'.

[3] *LL* 14 (60). This image is also used in the *Life*.

[4] *LL* 19 (74).   [5] *LL* 17 (67).   [6] *LL* 60 (150).   [7] *LL* 78a (192).

[8] *LL* 62 (153).   [9] *LL* 132 (342).   [10] *LL* 166 (419).   [11] *LL* 32 (96).

[12] *LL* 134 (346).   [13] *LL* 40 (111).   [14] *LL* 67 (165).

nuestro gusto no más,[1] written to Gracián, may have been unintentional: it derives its point from the fact that, while *gusto* means 'pleasure', *gustos*, as well as meaning 'pleasures', is a technical term for 'consolations' in prayer. So, I fancy, was the comment made to the Valladolid prioress on a nun who had gone out of her mind (*juicio*): 'See how wonderful are the judgments (*juicios*) of God.'[2] But there must have been purpose in the untranslatable *Nunca me cansan, sino que me descansan de otros cansancios*,[3] addressed, strange to say, to the Sevilian prioress, María de San José, who, it will be remembered, was somewhat *précieuse* in her own letters. Another, *que se gane con este ganado*,[4] seems to be a little sisterly quip directed at Lorenzo. It may have been a favourite one of hers, as three years or more earlier we find her perpetrating it in a letter to María de San José. One Antonio Ruiz, owed three hundred ducats by the Seville community, needed to gain (*ganar*) some money to buy food for his *ganado* (livestock), and Teresa thought she would approach her brother Lorenzo, who would gain (*ganar*) by helping him. This seems rather laboured, but no doubt some of María de San José's puns were worse still. An example, the more puzzling because of its context, occurs in a letter to her early patroness, Doña Luisa de la Cerda. The object of the letter is to comfort Doña Luisa at a time of heavy trial, when one would have thought a play upon words out of place. Yet she writes: 'You long since put paid (*tiene . . . dado carta de pago*) to the pleasures of this life, though you may not think yourself well paid (*muy pagada*) in having to suffer.'[5] Such a phrase illustrates once more Saint Teresa's unpredictableness.

The diminutives of the *Letters*, though fewer perhaps than one would expect in writing largely colloquial and often intimate, are none the less a delight. They include many applied to little people, who for Saint Teresa, as we have said, had always a special attraction. The Leonor de San Ángelo (*Leonorica*)[6] of whom we know next to nothing was presumably one of these. Others were her niece Teresa ('*Teresica*'), a 'sensible little woman' (*cordecita*)[7] of nine, 'dreadfully sad' (*tristecilla*)[8] at leaving the Seville sisters;

---

[1] *LL* 122 (316). *Lit.*: 'a few pleasures for our pleasure only'.   [2] *LL* 93 (231).

[3] *LL* 137 (347). 'Your letters never tire me: in fact, they cure me of the tiredness caused by other things.' The literal translation, preserving the word-play, would be: 'They never tire me, but they untire me from other tirings.'

[4] *LL* 310 (730). 'That this sheep-deal will be profitable.' *Ganar* means 'gain' and *ganado* can denote any kind of livestock.

[5] *LL* 31 (95).   [6] *LL* 309 (726: cf. n. 1).   [7] *LL* 233 (576).   [8] *LL* 96 (247).

Saint John of the Cross, at once Saint Teresa's 'little Seneca' (*Senequita*)[1] and 'little saint' (*santico*),[2] immured in his 'miserable little cell' (*carcelilla*)[3] at Toledo; Gracián's little sister, Isabelita,[4] described as *muy gordita*,[5] 'plump', 'chubby';[6] Gaytán's daughter, *nuestra sabandijita*[7] ('little reptile': in English, reptiles not being considered lovable, one has to say 'little puss'); a 'little saint' (*santica*)[8] of a nun who died young; the 'little slave girl' (*esclavilla*)[9] who wanted to join the Reform; and many more.

More or less depreciatory are *lugarcillos*,[10] 'tiny villages . . . dreadful places to make foundations in'; *bandillo*[11] (diminutive of *bando*, 'party strife'), 'petty bickering'; *ingratilla*[12] ('ungrateful little thing'), applied to the sometimes querulous Sevilian prioress; *prioritas*[13] ('inexperienced prioresses'); *monjillas* ('poor nuns') and *mujercillas* ('weak women'), two terms frequently used by Saint Teresa, the second, on occasion, of herself:[14] once or twice she describes herself in even stronger terms as a *pobre vejezuela*[15] ('poor little old woman'). Affectionate references are made, by means of diminutives, to the most dissimilar persons: to some young friars (*frailecitos*),[16] for example, who were 'real saints'; to *Blasico*[17] ('little Blas'), the sacristan of the convent at Seville; and to Lorenzo's son *Francisquito*[18]— the diminutive can only be translated as 'Frankie', though at the time the term was used of him he was seventeen.

These are the outstanding characteristics of the *Letters*: in a bird's eye survey it would be inappropriate to point to such traits as are found only here and there. Long sentences, involved sentences, and parentheses (though not as a rule long ones) are fairly frequent, but such obscurities as we find are generally due less to length than to brevity. There are curious cases of lapses of memory not surprising in a correspondent who never re-read what she wrote. In one place, for example, she breaks off a sentence in the middle and then passes directly to some other subject: obviously, she has been interrupted, and, when she sits down to her desk again, a new idea is already in her mind. In another place she

---

[1] *LL* 202, 1. n. The source of this phrase is MS. 13,482 (B. Nac., Madrid).
[2] *LL* 224 (549).   [3] *LL* 246 (601).   [4] *LL* 216 (535).   [5] *LL* 311 (731).
[6] This diminutive of *gordo* (fat) is generally used as a compliment in Spain, though often with irony.
[7] *LL* 76 (187).   [8] *LL* 180 (459).   [9] *LL* 183 (463).   [10] *LL* 231 (568).
[11] *LL* 303 (710).   [12] *LL* 143 (361).   [13] *LL* 131 (340), 231 (567).
[14] *LL* 234 (578).   [15] *LL* 277 (658), 278 (660).   [16] *LL* 127 (329).
[17] *LL* 149 (377).   [18] *LL* 158 (393).

repeats in one paragraph what she has already said in the last—probably for the same reason. All such traits bring her nearer to us than any conventional letter-writer could possibly come.

[IX]

In these writings of hers, then, Saint Teresa gives us abundance, both of material and of variety. She can appeal to every type of reader, whatever his moods. In the *Life* she aptly intersperses descriptions of her spiritual experiences with more objective autobiography, so that from the first we know her both from without and from within. In the *Way of Perfection* she passes from exhortation and teaching to exposition, adopting throughout an emphatic and decisive manner of presentation very different from the more discursive tone of the *Life*. The *Exclamations*, fervid, rhythmical and lyrical, brings us nearer than any other of her works to her inmost soul. The *Conceptions* and the *Way of Perfection* are more alike in style than any other two of her writings, though parts of the *Relations* closely resemble parts of the *Life*. The *Foundations*, with its leisurely pace and its inconsequent manner, will attract the reader who is interested chiefly in the history of the Discalced Carmelite Reform and the character of its foundress. The most mature of Saint Teresa's works, both in content and in style, and at the same time the most varied, is the *Interior Castle*. It recalls in places the finest and most spiritual pages of the *Life*, the fervour and the eloquence of which it carries to a much higher power; its hortatory passages sometimes equal, and sometimes surpass, those of the *Way of Perfection*. Its sublimest passages far outshine those of the *Exclamations*. I do not hesitate to repeat that I think it 'one of the greatest mystical works in Christian literature'.[1]

[1] *Mother of Carmel*, p. 39.

PART II

The Historical Problem of Spanish Mysticism
Mysticism in the Poetry of Fray Luis de León
Mysticism in the Poetry of the Golden Age

The Historical Problem of Spanish Mysticism[1]

[I]

The two outstanding features in the history of Spanish mysticism are the amazing extent of its output and the relatively short period of time within which this output was confined. The amount of the output is not perhaps surprising: Spanish writers have always been extremely—often excessively—productive, and the fertility of the mystics is paralleled by that of the dramatists of the Golden Age and of the novelists who wrote between 1870 and 1920. But other periods in Spanish literary history have been distinguished in drama and in prose fiction, whereas mysticism has had no second period of greatness. If we except books written in Catalan, modern works of devotion and text-books of mystical theology,[2] the publication of mystical works in Spain began with García de Cisneros' *Book of Exercises for the Spiritual Life* (1500)[3] and ended, in frank decline, with Molinos' *Spiritual Guide*, in 1675. Such was the flood of works on mystical theology which appeared in Spanish during these 175 years that its like has never since been seen in any country in the world.

[1] The origin of this essay will be found in an article by Professor Otis H. Green in the *Hispanic Review* (Philadelphia, 1938), VI, 93–103, and in a commentary upon it which I wrote for the same periodical (1942, X, 18–33). Part of the essay was read as a paper to the Oxford Society for Historical Theology and another part was incorporated in a lecture given to the Consejo Superior de Investigaciones Científicas in April 1947. References to Professor Green's article are given in footnotes after the word 'Green'.

[2] Under this head will be included compendiums which summarize, restate, and reapply the teachings of the great mystics, as well as critical works, often imbued with the mystical spirit, such as those of Seisdedos Sanz and Arintero.

[3] See *Studies of the Spanish Mystics* (London, 1927–30), II, 1–37.

To these facts may be added two others which help to define the period further. First, while the average level of all these authors below the first thirty or forty is not high (and no one can appreciate the depths to which they descend who has not read some of the worst), the two greatest of all, Saint Teresa and Saint John of the Cross, have scarcely been surpassed in their particular field in the whole of post-Biblical Christian history. Secondly, the mystical leaven permeated contemporary doctrinal manuals, Biblical commentaries and various types of ascetic prose, to say nothing of sacred and even secular verse.[1] Both qualitatively and quantitatively, then, the influence of the mystical spirit over this long period, stretching from the beginning of the Spanish Renaissance to the end of the Golden Age, is greater than might at first sight appear.

The historical problem relating to Spanish mysticism is not the brevity of the period during which it flourished, for its Golden Age is longer than that of Spanish drama, despite the attraction which drama has for the Spanish genius. Prose fiction, too, to say nothing of lyric poetry, flourished for a shorter time than mystical literature. There seems little that calls for explanation in the fact that, after burning for nearly two centuries, and for about one-third of that time with an intensity unparalleled anywhere in post-Renaissance Europe, mystical literature in Spain should have died slowly down, and, for the next two and a half centuries, burned no more.

Nor is the primary problem which confronts us the late emergence of Castilian mysticism, for, though it may seem curious that in the age of Dante, Eckhart, Tauler, Suso, Ruysbroeck, Hilton, Julian of Norwich, Saint Catherine of Siena and Ramon Lull there should have been no mystical output in Castilian, the explanation, which is historical, lies close at hand. During the centuries of crusade and reconquest Spanish idealism found its natural outlet in another direction: the best way of showing devotion to God was to play one's part in routing His enemies. And here, again, there is a parallel in pure literature: Spanish drama, which was to become so notable a feature of Spain's literary history, had developed little farther, before the sixteenth century, than Spanish mysticism.

No: the problem we have to solve is why, after touching such great heights, and exercising so wide and so profound an influence,

[1] See pp. 153–93, below.

Castilian mysticism should have almost completely disappeared, leaving hardly a trace. Eighteenth-century literature, it may be said, was somewhat secular in character; but the Salamancan School, which flourished during the second part of that century, was largely inspired by Fray Luis de León, and yet it shows no appreciation of such of its Master's poems as the semi-mystical 'Alma región luciente'.[1] With the Romantics of the early nineteenth century, religion begins to take a larger place in literature, but it is invariably the somewhat florid institutionalism of Rivas and Zorrilla, never the experiential religion of the Carmelite Saints. 'Even today', wrote Pidal, in his essay on Malón de Chaide (1840), 'many smile derisively at the mention of the title of a mystical work or the name of a religious writer.'[2] Later in the century, many leading Spanish writers are interested in varying aspects of religion—*e.g.*, Balmes, La Avellaneda, Rosalía Castro and the Campoamor of the *Drama Universal*—but none of them is in the least influenced by mysticism. Never, during the nineteenth century, did the mystics enjoy a rehabilitation comparable with that of the principal secular writers who were their contemporaries.[3] The greatness of their achievement—even its nature, in fact—was simply not understood. Fray Luis de León was translated by Maury and reprinted by López de Sedano, Quintana and Böhl von Faber, but to all of these he was merely a Hebraist or a Horatian. In Eugenio de Ochoa's *Thesaurus of Spanish Mystical Writers* (Paris, 1847) little distinction is drawn between the mystical and the ascetic. Even as literature, the writings of the greatest mystics were not appreciated. The anonymous author of a prologue to the works of Saint John of the Cross in the *Biblioteca de Autores Españoles* (XXVII, xix) describes him as inferior to Saint Teresa—even to Luis de Granada—'not only in his ideas, but also in his language and style. He is languid, incorrect, careless in phraseology; his apostrophes are frequent and monotonous; his periods unequal; his combinations of words inharmonious.' Indeed, declares the prologist, though superior to the writers named in the 'energy and vivacity of his sentiment', he is inferior to them in 'intellectual capacity'.

[1] Cf. pp.169–72, below.
[2] P. J. Pidal, *Estudios literarios* (Madrid, 1890), II, 169. Cf. also pp. 168–9, 172–5, *passim*.
[3] See my *History of the Romantic Movement in Spain* (Cambridge, 1940), II, 277–8.

Finally, we have to observe that, in post-Romantic Spain, only Catalan, of the Peninsular literatures, produced—in Jacinto Verdaguer[1]—a poet who has some claim to the title 'mystical'; and I do not think that claim is a very strong one. And, in the Spain of today, although religious fervour stands at a high level, and, so far as one can gather, the number of genuine contemplatives is increasing, the effect of this upon Spanish literature has been negligible.

Such are the facts which seem to me to constitute the historical problem of Spanish mysticism.

Before we attempt its solution, however, we must make one highly relevant observation of a general kind. The mystical spirit, the mystical progress, the mystical life—all these are the most intensely personal matters conceivable. If with many people religion itself is not now, as it was once, a theme for everyday conversation; if many writers, though profoundly religious, deliberately refrain from introducing their spiritual experiences into their writings: still less may we expect to read freely of the deepest intimacies that pass between God and the soul, even where it is possible to describe them. We should never have known of Saint Teresa's spiritual life had not her directors ordered her—sometimes peremptorily—to write of it. Nor can we suppose that she found it possible to set down the whole story. 'Of that breathing of God,' wrote Saint John of the Cross in the closing paragraph of his sublimest book, *Living Flame of Love*, 'I should not wish to speak, neither do I desire now to speak; for I see clearly that I cannot say aught concerning it, and that, were I to speak of it, it would seem less than it is'.[2] The mystical life is a life of the sternest endeavour directed towards the least easily attainable, though the most clearly pictured, of goals, and as a general rule those who have the fullest and profoundest experience of it speak about it least.

Only at a time, then, when religious feelings were deeply stirred, as they were in the decades following the Reconquest, should we expect to find any substantial amount of subjective writing on the mystical life, and only such mystics as unite profundity of experience and facility of expression are ever likely to leave a record of their contacts with Reality.

[1] See *Saint John of the Cross, etc.* (London, 1946), pp. 133–43.
[2] *Living Flame of Love*, IV, 17 (*CWSJX*, III, 113).

[11]

A solution to the problem will certainly not be found by postulating, as some have done, a disharmony between mysticism and the Spanish temperament. On the contrary, no observant student of the mystics can live for long in Spain without discovering that the two have the closest of affinities. This is a judgment which has been passed by numerous writers. 'Lo místico es lo español',[1] was the equation enunciated by Ángel Ganivet.[2] Mysticism, he adds, 'is so deeply rooted in Spain that we cannot take a step in life without having it as our companion':[3] it is the 'true centre' of Christianity as conceived by the Spaniard.[4] And few, if any, of Ganivet's contemporaries can be said to rival him for insight into the temperament of his fellow-countrymen. Andrés González-Blanco affirms that 'Castile is a race of mystics. . . . We have been mystics to the marrow. . . . Our race has certainly been inoculated with mysticism.' And, glancing at something like the very problem now occupying us, he attributes 'the rarity of mystical poetry in the garden of our Parnassus' to an incapacity, not for the mystical quest, but for mystical expression.[5] When the Argentine critic, Manuel Gálvez, speaks of the 'mysticism latent' in the Castilian, and goes so far as to say: 'It might be affirmed that all mystics love Castile and that everyone who loves Castile has something of the mystic about him,'[6] he is recording observations made in Spain itself by a foreigner of Spanish stock and the impressions which, over a long period, he has gathered from Spanish art and literature.[7] Other foreigners who visit Spain, whether men of letters or no, continually remark upon traits and incidents which illustrate the mystical element in Spanish character, though they often fail to realize the connection between mysticism and the phenomena they are describing. They observe in the Spaniard's attitude to life an intense idealism which, while fully recognizing life's realities (for on these Spaniards always retain a firm hold), is for ever impelling him to fix his gaze upon the object of his desire, and to allow no considerations, whether material or spiritual, to

[1] *Granada la bella* (Madrid, 1905), p. 53.
[2] *Saint John of the Cross, etc.* (London, 1946), pp. 158–68.
[3] *Granada la bella*, p. 56. [4] *Op. cit.*, p. 55.
[5] *Las Mejores Poesías Místicas en lengua castellana* (Madrid, 1916), pp. v, xix, xx.
[6] *El Solar de la raza* (5th ed., Madrid, 1920), pp. 40–1.
[7] Cf. *op. cit.*, pp. 40, 142–3, *et passim*.

deflect him from his purpose.[1] The Spaniard loathes compromise, and, if his strong sense of reality tells him that he will be ruined unless he abandons his ideals, he will quietly resign himself to accepting ruin. This is no rhetoric, but a simple statement of fact of which, during the Civil War of 1936–9 and the years immediately following its close, illustrations could be found by the thousand. It is no accident that Spain should have had three civil wars in just over a century, the first two considerably less inspired by dynastic motives than a superficial glance at the history-book would suggest, the third almost purely ideological.

This idealism, of course, is not mysticism, but it is the atmosphere in which mysticism best thrives. And the foreigner who grows intimate with Spaniards of many classes and types soon realizes how characteristic it is, too, of their attitude to religion. First, Spain has hardly any of the multitudinous religious denominations which jostle each other in Great Britain and the United States: with the huge majority of Spaniards it is Catholicism, the traditional channel through which their forefathers have sought God, or nothing. And of the majority who remain faithful to their forefathers' creed, a large number, beneath what may look like an inflexible, and, some might suspect, a conventional, institutionalism, live what is in reality a rudimentary form of the mystical life as known to the most profound contemplatives. Even so heterodox an observer as Havelock Ellis could not but be struck, on entering any Spanish church, with 'the ecstatic attitude of devotion which the worshippers sometimes fall into without thought of any observer'.[2] One has only to spend a short time in such a church, in the early hours of any morning, to grasp one of the first principles of the mystical life. Closer acquaintance with individual Spaniards will show that, in numerous cases, much more than the first principle is there, and that not merely the formal practices of religion, but the life and character, are permeated with the recollectedness, the tranquillity, the singleness of purpose and the passionate devotion of the mystic. The iron demands made upon the lovers of God by Saint John of the Cross, which, viewed against a background of Regent Street, Fifth Avenue or the Rue de la Paix, seem so terrifyingly inhuman, become matters of stern but perfectly practicable self-discipline when applied to the descendants of the men who waited for eight centuries to storm Granada or who poured out their blood

[1] Cf. Gálvez, *op. cit.*, pp. 41–2.   [2] *The Soul of Spain* (London, 1908), p. 13.

to bring pagan races into what they believed to be the one fold.

No, it is from no lack of affinity between the Spaniards and the mystical ideal that our problem arises. Let us look at some of the other solutions that have been suggested.

[III]

At one time a solution would have been sought in the contention that Spanish mysticism was derived from writers in the north of Europe—an idea first popularized by Menéndez Pelayo, though, as far as I know, he never made that assertion in so many words and in places he seems implicitly to contradict it. He goes no farther than to proffer the guarded suggestion that workers on the history of Spanish mysticism should 'fix their eyes primarily (*ante todo*) on this far-away period of German influence and of the incubation of the school in Spain'.[1] What he is definite about is his opposition to the 'absurd opinion of Rousselot, who denies all influence of German mysticism in Spain' and his attribution of the growth of heretical mystical tendencies to northern influences.[2] Others have been less cautious. Rafael Altamira, a noted historian but in no way a specialist in religious history, is rash enough to describe Spanish mysticism as a 'German importation',[3] and Américo Castro, who is not even a trained historian, considers this as 'true beyond a doubt':

'Mysticism is an importation which comes to us from the north —from the Rhineland and the Low Countries. When mystical fervour was extinguished there, the magnificent anachronism began to develop here in Spain.'[4]

But, even before Castro wrote, that theory had been completely disposed of by a serious student of the subject, Dr. Pierre Groult, who, after examining the relevant texts, gave his judgment that there was influence, but no formative influence, and certainly no 'importation'. Even for Spanish illuminism the Low Countries

---

[1] *Historia de las ideas estéticas en España*, 3rd ed., (Madrid, 1920), III, 117. Cit. Green, pp. 94–5.

[2] *Historia de los heterodoxos españoles*, ed. Artigas (Madrid, 1928), V, 208–9. Cit. Green, p. 95.

[3] *Psicología del pueblo español* (Barcelona, 1918), p. 105.

[4] *Santa Teresa y otros ensayos* (Madrid, 1929), pp. 10, 18.

had 'no special responsibility'. And, as for mysticism proper, 'Northern literature played no preponderant *rôle* in the Peninsula during the primitive period. . . . Works written in the Netherlands were known and esteemed in Spain, but, except as regards Cisneros, no evidence exists that they were ever seriously utilized.'[1]

Other scholars have attributed the sudden rise and vogue of mystical literature in Spain 'to the rebirth of Platonic philosophy in the Renaissance'.[2] Professor Otis Green, who has examined this suggestion with some care, believes it to be due to a misinterpretation of Menéndez Pelayo. It commends itself, one may add, to critics who are anxious to deny the existence of a supernatural element in mystical experience or to minimize its force. But Professor Green's answer to it, based upon Menéndez Pelayo, is that 'all that portion of Platonic teaching which could be assimilated by Christian mysticism had long since found its way into the works of the Church Fathers'.[3] I have no doubt that he is right; for both the closeness and the unanimity with which the Spanish mystics, and most of their contemporaries among the ascetics, adhere to the Fathers, are very noticeable.

Another type of explanation put forward by Professor Green regards the 'appearance and development' of Spanish mysticism 'as having been conditioned by causes which were essentially social'.[4] 'It was all a part of the campaign against Protestantism', he reports W. R. Inge as saying—but, even if we accept Inge as an authority on Spanish religious history, we should note that that remark, in its context,[5] refers to the Discalced Carmelites' external activities and 'voluntary austerities', not to their mystical teaching. Professor Green also quotes a rather hazardous generalization by Aubrey Bell, to the effect that Spaniards have an innate ascetic stoicism which 'in moments of intense crisis . . . flames up into mystic ecstasy.'[6] Observing rightly that religious life, not only in Spain but in all Europe, was in a state of crisis in the mid-sixteenth century, he makes a short quotation from Luis de Granada and a longer one from Saint Teresa, and concludes that 'mysticism is thus seen to be a reform movement'.[7]

Now there is no doubt that social conditions, and particularly

---

[1] *Les Mystiques des Pays-Bas et la littérature espagnole du seizième siècle* (Louvain, 1927), pp. 269–70.

[2] Green, p. 97.   [3] Green, p. 98.   [4] Green, p. 99.

[5] *Christian Mysticism* (London, 1899), p. 224.

[6] Green, p. 100.   [7] Green, p. 101.

the need for reform within the Church, intensified and gave added effect to the Discalced reforms within the Franciscan and Carmelite Orders, which in their turn provided the greatest of the mystics with an audience of maximum receptivity. The Counter-Reformation, too, cannot have failed to stimulate the fervour of the mystics, and probably helped to give frequent touches of mystical colour and warmth to ascetic writers who, in another age, might have been tedious and uninspired, and who are far more numerous in Spain than the pure mystics. But, considering the early date of the first of these mystical writers—nearly half a century earlier than that of the Council of Trent—and the peculiarly personal nature of the mystical task, it seems difficult to regard the 'mystical movement', except in quite a minor degree, as a 'reform movement' or 'a means of attacking the atrophy of Spanish and European religious life and of defending that religious life, and the institutions in which it was incorporated, from the onslaught of an enemy from the outside'.[1]

A similar answer may be given to a further suggestion of this type, made by Pedro Sainz Rodríguez at the end of his historical sketch of Spanish mysticism:

'At the conclusion of the Reconquest, Castilian mysticism developed in Spain, in an atmosphere of great exaltation in which religious faith and culture were converted into political ideals, and with this conversion coincided the shock of a series of influences of mystical and philosophical doctrines.'[2]

It is tempting to find the reason for the sudden eruption of mystical ardour in the exaltation consequent upon the recovery of Moorish Spain for Christendom and to set down Neo-Platonism and northern mysticism (together with the impetus given by the Counter-Reformation) as the influences which combined with this exaltation to popularize mystical theology. This explanation, especially in its fullest form, is more adequate than the last, since it accounts for the progress made before 1550. But it, too, seems to take insufficient note of the personal element, the part played by this being of the very essence of the matter.

Professor Green ends by proposing for the problem a solution which is partly his own—previously hinted at, he remarks, only

[1] Green, p. 101.
[2] *Introducción a la historia de la literatura mística en España* (Madrid, n.d. [1927]), p. 283.

by Etchegoyen.[1] One element, he claims, is decisive—'the element of genius';[2] and by that he seems to mean principally the genius of Saint Teresa. 'What fruit, we may very well ask, would have been yielded by the writing of Osuna, Estella, Laredo, Granada, Alcántara, if Teresa de Jesús had not reached out to them in search of some message that would help her to analyse and express her mystical experience?'[3] This may have been intended as a rhetorical question, but it is in reality one that can be answered, from our knowledge of those writers and their public, with some degree of confidence. The writings of these men would have yielded considerable fruit, though chiefly within the respective Orders of each; the fame of Luis de Granada and Saint Peter of Alcántara would have passed, precisely as in fact it did, beyond the boundaries of Spain.[4] But none of the five would have been read so widely, or have had so much influence on writers outside their own Orders, had not Saint Teresa used them, commended them, quoted them, and swept them up, as it were, into the great mystical current in which her own influence surpasses that of any of her contemporaries in force, as does that of Saint John of the Cross in depth. She draws together individuals who might other-wise never have been read or thought of in conjunction with one another. She fuses diverse temperaments; absorbs, reconciles, and re-expresses apparently divergent ideas. Were it not for the clearly marked differences in mystical thought which persist in certain of the religious Orders, it might be said that she found Spanish mysticism a movement and left it a school.

This consideration, which lays due stress upon the personal and individual nature of the mystical experience, takes us nearer the heart of the question than any other. It does not, however, throw much light on the fact that never, since the Golden Age, has the mystical spirit permeated any body of literary work in Spain, or on the little understanding and appreciation of the greatest Spanish mystics which has been shown there between the end of the seventeenth century and the beginning of the twentieth. To satisfy

---

[1] *L'Amour divin. Essai sur les sources de Sainte Thérèse* (Bordeaux-Paris, 1923), p. 108.

[2] Green, p. 101.   [3] Green, p. 102.

[4] See particulars of some forty translations of the works of Luis de Granada into English and French, in my *Studies of the Spanish Mystics* (London, 1927–30), I, 425–9, and of seventeen translations of Saint Peter of Alcántara's *Tratado de la oración y meditación* into English, French, Italian, and Portuguese, in *op. cit.*, II, 412–13.

at least some part of those requirements we shall have to go deeper still.

[IV]

Any solution of the problem must of necessity, I think, be a complex one, since so many factors are involved—historical, social, religious, literary. One method of approach would be to solve its various parts separately.

First of all comes the suddenness of the mystical eruption, and this may certainly be explained by the exaltation due to the Reconquest, together, perhaps, indirectly, with the intellectual stimulus of the Renaissance, which was beginning to revivify Spanish literature.

Secondly, there is the length of the period during which mysticism flourished, and this is explicable by the strong impetus given to it, at a point which otherwise might have been the beginning of a rapid decline, by the Carmelite Saints. It is a striking fact, that, before Saint Teresa wrote even the earliest of her works, six of her chief contemporaries had completed either some or all of their main contributions to mystical literature.

Thirdly, the fervour of this remarkable manifestation of mysticism may be accounted for by the emotions engendered in the Carmelites, and in others, by the Reformation and the Counter-Reformation, and also, I think, by the intensity normal in Spanish religious experience, so often observed and commented upon by foreigners.

Fourthly, the richness of the content of Spanish mysticism is due partly to the strong injection of personal experience which it received, chiefly from Carmel, and partly to the numerous external sources from which it drew—the Scriptures, the Fathers, the Northern mystics and the Neo-Platonists.

Fifthly, the nature and the slow pace of the decline are attributable to the strong influence of the Carmelite School persisting after the deaths of Saint Teresa (1582) and Saint John of the Cross (1591) and also reproducing itself indirectly through other Orders.

Finally, the failure of the movement to reappear in a similar form is clearly due to the fact that nothing approaching a similar conjunction of conditions ever occurred again.

Another approach would be to regard the Golden Age of Spanish mysticism from two distinct standpoints. It gives birth to writings primarily experiential, and to others which are, at least in part, systematic works on mystical theology. It is not only in the period of decline—the years between the death of Saint John of the Cross and the publication of Molinos' *Spiritual Guide*—that the codifiers are at work: there are codifications, based on the Fathers and the Northern mystics, from the time of García de Cisneros onwards. The rise of mystical theology of an objective type can be ascribed to the external causes already rehearsed; that of the profoundly experiential type is attributable to a particular kind of genius. The existence of a Golden Age is due to the fact that in this particular period, as never before or since, these external conditions happened to coincide with the appearance of great religious and literary genius. The failure of mysticism to penetrate later literature means that, on the one hand, the demands of individual experience on objective theology had already been met, and that, on the other, religious genius and literary genius did not again in any marked degree coincide. In men of letters who were strongly mystical by temperament, that trait was unhappily inarticulate, as, after all, it is in most people—even in many who possess it in generous measure. The fact that mysticism in Spain has always been specifically Catholic in type may have shackled a few somewhat unorthodox writers who give the impression of having been mystics *in posse*.

It will perhaps only be putting the same thing into different words to say that the Golden Age of mysticism should be looked upon, not as a literary or a social movement, but as the vogue of a certain type of thought into which was suddenly precipitated a religious revival. Its greatness, certainly, and to some extent its length also, were proportionate to its experiential quality.

Religious revivals make their appearances with notorious and unaccountable irregularity. Again and again social conditions or national emotions suggest that some kind of corporate manifestation of the religious consciousness is imminent—and yet that manifestation never comes. The coal, the wood, the paper are laid on the hearth; there are times when even the match is struck; but the fuel fails to catch fire. Something is lacking; a something commonly described as genius, though the mystics themselves would call it Divine grace.

In the sixteenth century the fuel was laid, the match applied and there came the fire. Why did it not come earlier? Why has it not come since?

It is indeed strange that, in the thirteenth century, Ramon Lull failed to kindle a greater fire in Catalonia or in Castile.[1] He supplied the spark, but there was insufficient fuel, and indeed, he himself to some extent smothered what fire he produced. Temperamentally he was a true mystic, but he was too much else as well. Those two opuscules, the *Book of the Lover and the Beloved* and the *Art of Contemplation*, embedded in *Blanquerna*; the *Tree of the Philosophy of Love*; the finest passages in the *Book of Contemplation*; the best of the poems—all these, until quite recent years, have been buried beneath the huge mass of his other works, probably not fewer than five hundred. What should have been the wide and intense influence of a natural mystic was metamorphosed into a series of ephemeral reputations, each more fantastic than the last. The 'fool of love' became famous rather as the inventor of 'arts', or methods, of infallible and irrefutable demonstration of the truth of the Christian faith which would convert the whole world. And then, after his death, he proceeded to become notorious as a naturalist, a troubadour, an alchemist, a navigator—a discoverer of all kinds of things, from nitric acid to America. Had he lived, not in the Catalonia of James the Conqueror and his sons, but in the Castile of Cardinal Cisneros and Philip II, his place in the history of religion would have been a very different one.

Since the decline of the mystical Golden Age, there have been more sparks, but again too little fuel. Hardly ever, until quite recent years, has Spain been in a condition for any kind of religious revival, and men who in other times might have led some form of mystical movement have failed to attract followers or even to make themselves articulate. In pure literature, mystical affinities can be detected in the essayist and novelist Juan Valera, which, had he lived in another epoch, he might have developed, in the poet José María Gabriel y Galán and in the novelist Ricardo León. More pronouncedly mystical, though still literary in type, are Restituto del Valle-Ruiz, and, in Catalan, Mn. Miquel Costa i Llobera and Mn. Llorenç Riber. These names, to which others might be added, take account only of those known to the world of letters—not of holy and humble men of heart, living obscurely and contentedly in religious houses, looking inward and upward rather than outward, their only legacy to the world the seeds they have planted in the hearts of others. Yet such might the preacher

[1] I refer here to *influence*, not to vogue. The latter is touched upon by Pedro Sainz Rodríguez (*Introducción*, etc., pp. 187-9), and treated more fully in my *Ramon Lull, a Biography* (London, 1929), pp. 376-400.

Luis de Granada have been, for he was sixty-three when he published the first of his long works and about eighty-five when he finished the last; Teresa, the Avilan nun, unknown outside the smallest of circles until she was nearly fifty; Bernardino de Laredo, a simple lay brother; and scores of others. But it just chanced that they lived in an era of revival, and they became famous.

It will be inferred, and rightly, that I do not in the least despair of a fresh revival of the latent mysticism of Spain during the present century. Even at the beginning of the century the Argentinian Gálvez could write:

'Is the day coming when this country will experience a renaissance of mysticism? It would not be at all surprising. All over Europe just now one feels the breath of spiritual unrest, of religion, of mysticism.'[1]

What he wrote of Europe as a whole is singularly applicable to Spain. During the past few decades persecution and destruction have rekindled love; the spiritual ground lost to the rapid encroachment of materialism has been reclaimed by suffering; and in the religious life of Spain there has come into being a regenerative and reformative force, though it is as yet too early to pronounce upon its permanence.

But it seems not at all impossible that a new Saint Teresa or Saint John of the Cross should arise in Spain. Historical phenomena do undoubtedly, from time to time, reproduce themselves.

[1] Gálvez, *op. cit.*, p. 142.

Mysticism in the Poetry of Fray Luis de León

Within the broad framework of common usage, as opposed to the narrower limits of precise and formal Catholic tradition, the word 'mystical' is susceptible of a number of interpretations. Loosely, it is often applied to any writing which embodies intimations of an extra-normal consciousness, is marked by a deep spirituality or is religious in anything more than a superficial or an institutional sense. Such popular interpretations, however, cannot be admitted in any serious discussion.

But even if we exclude these, and rely upon a definition which is valid in the domain of mystical theology, we are still faced with a considerable ambiguity. Are we to allow the title of 'mystic' only to such writers as Saint Teresa and Saint John of the Cross, who received from God such favours as He confers upon His few most ardent lovers, which frequently manifest themselves in super-normal physical phenomena? If so, must there be direct evidence of such experiences in their writings or will it suffice that the evidence should have come down to us at second hand and should relate to their lives alone? In the latter case, we should be able to extend our definition to include, for example, the founder of the Society of Jesus, whose *Spiritual Exercises* are in spirit profoundly mystical, yet for the evidence of mystical favours in whose life we have to go beyond his writings, to the *Acta Sanctorum* and to such biographers as Bartoli and Ribadeneira. Or, again, can the title of 'mystical writer' be fairly given to one who, like Fray Luis de Granada, deals in the main with ascetic topics and only occasionally touches upon the mystical? Or to one, like Pedro Malón de Chaide, who presents a theme in which the mystical ideal is latent and which appeals to the many as well as to the few? Or to the very numerous writers who appear in Spain at the beginning of the seventeenth century and who in an entirely objective way summarize and codify the writings of the great mystics of the six-teenth—writing, in fact, something like text-books of mystical theology?

When Menéndez Pelayo made his often quoted computation that Spain had given the world some three hundred mystical writers and some three thousand mystical works, it may be taken for granted that he was including all these classes and probably also many writers, such as Hernando de Talavera, the first Archbishop of Granada, Hernando de Zárate and Alejo de Vene-gas, in whose writings it is hard to find anything suggestive of direct mystical experience at all. For some fifteen years, I myself spent several months annually searching in the libraries of Spain, and sometimes in those of Italy, France, and Belgium, for works of these writers. And my manuscript bibliography, which excludes those found on examination to be purely ascetic, contains no more than one hundred and forty authors.

For the purpose of this study of the Augustinian, Fray Luis de León, a somewhat narrower definition is desirable. Critics who have denied him the title of 'mystic' seem generally to have meant that they are unable to find in his writings any suggestion of first-hand mystical experience, and that, where he refers to such experi-ence, he is merely repeating what he has read in the works of others. In maintaining that he has every right to that title I claim that there are indications in his prose writings, if nothing more, that he was familiar with mystical experience, either in his own life or at the very least in the lives of other people with whom he was well acquainted. In this examination of his original poetry my aim will be, not to suggest that he translated supernormal experiences of his own into verse, but to discover how far, if at all, he treated in his verse the same purely mystical or semi-mystical themes with which he deals in his prose. Before coming, then, to the poems, it will be necessary to treat in summary form the more general ques-tion already referred to.

[II]

In the first volume of my *Studies of the Spanish Mystics*[1] I discussed the claim made on behalf of Fray Luis de León that he should be

[1] London, 1927, pp. 318–39. Revised edition, London, 1951, pp. 258–76.

reckoned among the mystics of Spain, a claim which has been opposed by Coster, Salcedo Ruiz and a few other critics and was demurred to by a small number of reviewers of my own book. My conclusion, which the intervening years have in no way altered, was that, whichever of the foregoing definitions of the word 'mystic' we may adopt, the writings of Fray Luis have won him the unquestionable right to inclusion within that category. It will not be difficult to summarize the arguments which can be used on both sides.

1. Against Fray Luis, Coster quotes a passage from his Latin works, the final words of which might seem at first sight conclusive:

'Atque hactenus verborum, quem diximus sonum persecuti sumus, et quasi in scena res ageretur, suas cuique personae voces dedimus, sive potius a Salomone datas sumus interpretati: jam sub iis personis, et corporeorum amorum imaginibus, quid arcani, ac divini lateat aggrediamur dicere pro eo quantum nobis Deus intelligentiae, ac sermonis concesserit. Est enim magna res, et plane super hominis vires, et denique ejusmodi, ut vix possit intelligi, nisi ab iis, qui eam non tam doctoris alicujus voce quam ipsa re, et suavi amoris experimento a Deo didicerunt, de quorum numero non esse me, et fateor et doleo.'[1]

But closer examination will make us less inclined to draw a definite conclusion from this evidence. In the first place, the date of the passage can hardly be later than 1580, whereas the earliest editions of the *Names of Christ*, the work on which the claim for the admission of Fray Luis to the company of the mystics must principally be based,[2] did not appear till 1583 and 1585 respectively. Secondly, it is altogether too bold a proceeding to base a deduction of this kind upon an interpretation of the 'magna res' of the passage which equates it with 'any direct mystical experience whatsoever'. Precisely what it is the context does not make clear. The phrase may refer to the Spiritual Betrothal, or it may refer to the highest of all the grades of union—to the Seventh Mansions of Saint Teresa. There is no justification whatever for taking it to mean that all mystical experience was foreign to Fray Luis. On the contrary, there is ample reason for believing that, although in writing of

[1] *Opera*, etc. (Salamanca, 1891–5), II, 39.

[2] Though Azorín says of that book (in one sense correctly): 'No vemos en él un tratado de filosofía, ni siquiera de misticismo' (*Los Dos Luises* (Madrid, 1921), p. 123).

mystical theology he normally preserved the most strictly academic objectivity, he had in fact experienced in his own life much of which he wrote so impersonally. The late Aubrey Bell, who devoted many years to the study of Luis de León and examined his works, both in Latin and Spanish, with this very question in mind, gave it as his opinion that he had clearly 'progressed far along the Mystic Way, and that, if his writings are not to be called mystical, the number of Spanish works deserving that title will have to be much restricted. He had listened to the "turturea Spiritus Sancti vox gemitibus inenarrabilibus"; he was not unversed "en los resplandores de la contemplación y en los arrobamientos del espíritu"; he had tasted the "blandura y dulzor" of communing with God.'[1] I fully share this opinion.

2. A second argument directed against the inclusion of Fray Luis de León within the mystical category is that many of the mystical passages in his works are certainly derivative and that there is no proof that any one of them is original. It may be doubted, however, if there is a single Christian mystic, in any country, who does not frequently quote from the works of others to illustrate his theme, for the mystical experience is so many-sided in its manifestations and yet those to whom it becomes familiar are so unanimous as to its genuineness that it invites quotation; after all, Saint Teresa is probably the most personal of all mystical writers, and yet volumes have been written on her comparatively scanty sources. If Fray Luis is less subjective than she, his reticence does not necessarily connote lack of experience. He uses authorities far less than the really derivative writers on mystical theology in the generation following his death, who, incidentally, make considerable use of him, as does also a writer as near to him in time as Fray Juan de los Ángeles.[2] Finally, the demand that every writer on mystical theology shall give proof in his writings of having enjoyed direct mystical experiences is entirely unreasonable. Many of the most sublime passages in that most sublime of Christian mystics, Saint John of the Cross, bear no certificate of subjectivity, as one might say, in the shape of the first personal pronoun. In the last resort, the test here must be one of personal impression; and to me, at least, it is as inconceivable that Fray Luis had not some personal experience in mind when he wrote the most eloquent passages in the chapters 'Bridegroom' and 'Prince of Peace' in the

[1] Aubrey F. G. Bell, *Luis de Leon* (Oxford, 1925), p. 225.
[2] *Studies of the Spanish Mystics*, 1927, I, 398–401; 1951, I, 323–5.

Names of Christ as that he never himself fled from the 'vain world's roar'[1] or knew the delights of 'humble fare'.[2]

3. In some critics a certain prejudice has been created against Fray Luis de León by the existence in his work of elements far removed from experiential religion and even considered by some to be in conflict with it. Miguel de Unamuno, for example, who could appreciate one aspect of the temperament of Fray Luis better than others, describes his humanism as 'tempering his native Castilian mysticism', and looks upon him essentially, it would seem, as 'Platonic, Horatian and Virgilian, a soul in whom epicureanism and stoicism merged in Christianity, a lover of harmony, tranquillity and peace'.[3] There is a good deal to be said on this question, of which only the main points can here be considered.

It is perfectly true, not only that Fray Luis shows the very marked influences referred to by Unamuno, but that he appears to attach very little importance to asceticism. In his prose he seems less anxious to recommend bodily mortification than to warn his readers against its abuse.[4] In his verse he sets aside the ideals of asceticism in favour of those of comfort and moderation: ample sleep, simple but pleasant food, a sympathetic environment. More than one of his poems might have been written by any pagan author. But, while it is admittedly unusual to find a Horatian who is a mystic, there is nothing inconsistent in the idea of a dual personality such as we may postulate in Fray Luis. Many writers have held a doctrine poetically, and in no other way, and still more have been two entirely distinct persons in their lives and in their writings. Even Saint Teresa, an apostle of detachment and austerity, has a lighter side to her character and moods in which she freely indulges her whims and prejudices and of which we continually catch glimpses in her letters and occasionally elsewhere:

[1] 'El mundanal ruido' ('A la vida retirada'). Except where otherwise indicated, translations of Luis de León's poems are based upon Aubrey F. G. Bell, *Lyrics of Luis de León* (London, 1928). The translator generously allowed me to adapt his versions at my discretion.

[2] . . . *una pobrecilla*
mesa, de amable paz bien abastada
('A la vida retirada').

[3] 'En torno al casticismo' (*Ensayos* (Madrid, 1916), I, 167).

[4] Cf. *Nombres de Cristo*, ed. Onís (Madrid, 1914–21), III, 185–6. See reference to the ode 'A la vida religiosa' below.

'Now you will reprove me for talking about games, as we do not play them in this house and are forbidden to do so. That will show you what kind of a mother God has given you—she even knows about vanities like this!'[1]

A more marked dualism is to be found in Fray Luis de León, but, instead of inveighing against the Andalusians, or making good-humoured fun of companions in religion, as Saint Teresa so often did, he retreats into the world of poetry (and he was a poet to the core) and of Horatianism, and there he develops an ideal which he follows much less passionately than he follows the mystical ideal,[2] but none the less with evident satisfaction. If he was not perhaps as much given to bodily mortification as were some of his contemporaries of whose self-flagellations pious biographers relate impressive stories, he must have practised constant mortification of the spirit: only this, in a man of his temperament, can explain the superhuman self-restraint of which the well-known 'Decíamos ayer . . .' anecdote[3] gives evidence. And, as Saint John of the Cross so often reminds us, it is spiritual rather than physical mortification which leads the lover of God through the Dark Night of Sense to the delights of Illumination and Union.

4. Some readers of Fray Luis de León, however, are also disconcerted by the lack of system which they find in his description of the Mystic Way. There is no succession of 'grades of love', no regular alternation of periods of illumination and periods of darkness, no series of 'mansions', each conveying an ever-deeper experience of Divine intimacy. Both in the *Names of Christ* and in the more spiritual and sublime of the lyrics, the reader feels lost in a region which, though a 'fair land of radiant light', is also a region of somewhat vague aspirations and yearnings: his very path is often hidden from him and his goal is by no means always clear.

It would be more correct to say that, though Fray Luis does in fact map out the mystical path, using the traditional divisions, it is not here that he is at his best or his most characteristic. Two well-known passages in the *Names of Christ*, from the chapters 'Way'[4]

[1] *Way of Perfection*, XVI (*CWSTJ*, II, 63).
[2] So I think, but there are those who would differ. The late W. J. Entwistle, for example (*Modern Language Review* (1927), XXII, 54), describes the 'Vida retirada' as Fray Luis' 'greatest poem' and 'the product of his deepest emotion'. I should be bound to dissent from both these judgments, which are, of course, entirely of a personal kind.
[3] *Studies of the Spanish Mystics*, 1927, I, 293–4; 1951, I, 239–40.
[4] *Nombres de Cristo, ed. cit.*, I, 118.

and 'Prince of Peace',[1] which need not be reproduced here, will illustrate this. Further, I have discussed Fray Luis' conception of the Mystic Way at some length elsewhere and shown that he has in his own mind a clear conception of mystical progress.[2] This conception is not, however, as essential to his idea of the contemplative life as it is to the ideas held by certain other writers. Fray Luis' writings, in fact, represent a perfectly legitimate and well-defined type of mysticism, fundamental to which are the following elements: (i) continual striving after union with God; (ii) purgation through spiritual mortification; (iii) the use of Nature and of other created things (notably music) as means towards the attainment of the traditional stage of illumination; (iv) an ultimate goal (which some, not without reason, may take as approximating to the Fifth rather than to the Seventh Mansions of Saint Teresa) in which considerable stress is laid upon the personality, and there is little suggestion of absorption in the Deity.

[III]

If we now take up Fray Luis de León's poems with a view to discovering how far they reflect the mystical ideas of his prose, we shall have to aim at extreme precision and avoid generalizations. I find it impossible, after a careful study of the poems, to agree with Menéndez Pelayo that 'the poetry of Fray Luis de León is entirely mystical in character'[3], and it is hard to find any definition of mysticism, other than the vaguest of all those given above, which will justify us in agreeing with Pfandl's dictum that seven of the lyrics 'merit being described as of mystical inspiration'.[4]

While, in spite of recent researches, the canon of Luis de León's poetical works cannot be said to be as yet definitely established, we may, I think, safely leave out of account the lyric 'To the religious life' ('A thousand thoughts were mine . . .'), the authenticity of which has for some time been looked upon with suspicion, principally on the grounds of language. Though as recent a critic as Coster[5] considers it genuine, it is more commonly taken as being

[1] *Op. cit., ed. cit.*, II, 186 *sq.*

[2] *Studies of the Spanish Mystics*, 1927, I, 329–39; 1951, I, 268–76.

[3] *Horacio en España*, cit., *Poesías de Fray Luis de León, con anotaciones inéditas de D. Marcelino Menéndez y Pelayo* (Madrid, 1928), I, 41.

[4] *Geschichte der spanischen Nationalliteratur*, etc. (cf. p. 267, n. 1, below), p. 145; Spanish ed., p. 160.

[5] *Revue hispanique*, XLVI, 203.

the work of a disciple or imitator of Fray Luis: 'it has many touches of Luis de León's style and thought, and, if not by his own hand, must be the work of an excellent poet intimately acquainted with his lyrics' is the judgment of Aubrey Bell.[1] To my mind, P. Llobera gave it the *coup de gráce* in 1932.[2] If we may reject it, it is a most striking fact that, of all the poems commonly included in editions of this poet, it is the one which has most to say of asceticism and bodily mortification. One might suppose that one of the Augustinian professor's disciples had felt that the Master had said too little about this and had endeavoured to supply the deficiency. There is something very un-Leonine about such stanzas as:

> *The cilice, closely knit*
> *With sharp and cruel bristles, that he wears*
> *Close to his skin is fit*
> *To wean him from the cares*
> *Wherewith blind love the hearts of men ensnares.*

> *To him the cruel scourge*
> *Is welcome, with its knots of twisted wire,*
> *For it the heart can purge*
> *Of the corrupt desire*
> *That still outruns the right in senseless fire.*[3]

This seems to be the only poem of disputed authenticity which would otherwise have fallen to be considered here in some detail. The remainder of those which seem to me relevant are nine in number.

Only the briefest mention need be made of the short poem 'On

---

[1] *Modern Language Review* (hereafter abbreviated *MLR*) (1926), XXI, 176.

[2] *Obras poéticas de Fr. Luis de León* (Cuenca, 1932), I, 386–7. This edition is used throughout for references in the following pages.

[3] Bell, *Lyrics*, etc., *ed. cit.*, pp. 25, 27.

> *El cilicio tejido*
> *de punzadoras cerdas de animales,*
> *que al cuerpo está ceñido,*
> *aparta de los males*
> *que causa el ciego amor a los mortales.*

> *La disciplina dura*
> *de retorcido alambre le da gusto,*
> *pues cura la locura*
> *del estragado gusto*
> *que huye a rienda suelta de lo justo.*

leaving prison', which has the interest of combining the two ideals chiefly found in Fray Luis—the Horatian (ll. 3–7) and the contemplative (ll. 8–9). Solitude, which figures prominently in this poem,[1] becomes the main theme of the ode 'To retirement' ('At length, O harbour sure...'), which was probably written, whether at the same time or no,[2] under the influence of similar sentiments. In the fourth stanza there seems to be more feeling than we often find in Luis de León's poems:

> *Receive me in thy height;*
> *Receive thou me as from the erring host*
> *Of men I take my flight....*[3]

And the same may be said of the personal references throughout the poem. One might have expected, with such a theme, to find at least some influence of the mystical spirit. But there is none: the poet is completely occupied with himself; not so much as the name of God appears in the whole poem.

'Night serene' ('When I behold the sky...')[4] takes us a little nearer the mystical life, though not as near as one might suppose from the epithets which have been lavished upon it. It has at least qualities which relate it to the greatest mystical literature. One is the presentation of a high ideal, the grandeur of which is enhanced by contrast (ll. 1–5, 36–40): the

> *dwelling of great might,*
> *Temple of lovely light incomparable...*[5]

—to attain to some intimacy with which the poet adjures his readers to make that effort ('Oh, mortal men, awake.... Oh, skyward lift your eyes!')[6] is a continual preoccupation of the Spanish mystics.[7] Another is the attitude of contempt for the world—'this dark, low prison-house', 'this life that flatters', etc.[8]—which is part

---

[1] 'Con solo Dios ... y a solas su vida pasa.' *Ed. cit.*, I, 365. *Lyrics*, p. 83.

[2] *Lyrics*, pp. 93, 95. Aubrey Bell (*MLR*, XXI, 173) places the two at the end of 1576 and some time in 1577 (perhaps the summer) respectively. William J. Entwistle (*MLR*, XXII, 182) makes the dates respectively 'December 1576, or very early in 1577' and 'spring or early summer' of 1577.

[3] *Recíbeme en tu cumbre,*
recíbeme, que huyo perseguido
la errada muchedumbre....

[4] *Lyrics*, pp. 99 *sq.*   [5] *Ed. cit.*, I, 161.   [6] *Ed. cit.*, I, 163.

[7] Cf. my *Spanish Mysticism* (London, 1924), pp. 43–5.

[8] 'Esta cárcel baja, escura', 'aquesa lisonjera vida'. *Ed. cit.*, I, 162–3.

of the necessary preparation for the mystical life and the antithesis of the Horatian position. A third is the occasional use of the language of mystical theology. At the beginning of the poem, for example, there is the juxtaposition of 'sorrow and love' ('amor y pena')[1] and the 'ansia ardiente' ('burning fever', 'fire of yearning') which recalls the 'con ansias en amores inflamada' ('kindling with love in flame of yearning keen') of Saint John of the Cross; at the end, the exaltation of Divine Love,

with glories and delight encompassèd.[2]

But, in spite of all this, it is only in the widest of the senses applicable to the word—a sense which we have agreed to discard—that the poem 'Night serene' can be described as mystical. The ideal set forth in it is not union with God—a God not far from each one of us, closer than breathing, immanent in His works and ready to receive and absorb within Himself the purified soul. No: Fray Luis' thought is fixed, not on immanence, but on transcendence. His Heaven is far away—a 'heavenly eternal sphere', whose characteristics are 'greatness', 'brightness', 'beauty'. There is nothing intimate about it; and, as the poem grows lovelier, it also grows more remote. A genuinely mystical poem, like the 'Dark Night' or the 'Spiritual Canticle' of Saint John of the Cross, leads us, often without our knowing it, to a very climax of intimacy. Here, on the contrary, we feel much farther from the ideal at the end than at the beginning. The description and the enumeration of 'those eternal splendours' (l. 42) is rendered more remote than ever by a return (l. 61) to the contrast between the baseness of earth and the sublimity of Heaven:

Here dwelleth sweet content,
Here reigneth peace. . . .[3]

The following stanza still further intensifies the sense of the unapproachable ideal:

---

[1] Which we find also in the 'Elisa' ode:

> *De amor guiada y pena*
> *penetra el techo extraño. . . .*
> *(Ed. cit.,* I, 128.)

[2] *de glorias y deleites rodeado. Ed. cit.,* I, 170.

[3] *Aquí vive el contento,*
aquí reina la paz. . . . Ed. cit., I, 170.

> *Here beauty infinite*
> *Unveils itself, and light, quintessence pure,*
> *Transparent gleams: no night*
> *Its radiance may obscure;*
> *Spring's flower'd splendour here is ever sure.*[1]

As for the final stanza, with its five ecstatic apostrophes, of which Bell, in his fine appreciation of them, says, 'the impression is not of thinness but of intensity',[2] it cannot, I think, be denied that the impression left by such a conclusion is also of the extremely remote, if not even of the completely unattainable.

Similar in some respects to 'Night serene' is the famous poem 'To Francisco de Salinas' ('Calm grows the air around . . .'),[3] in which the poet is inspired, not by hosts of stars, but by waves of music, and where his Platonic inspiration has also been popularly miscalled mystical. P. Llobera thinks it necessary to state his belief, as Professor de Onís had done before him, 'that this ode has reference, not to celestial harmony, but to the harmony of music'.[4] This, no doubt, is true enough, but music (that 'sound divine') and Nature run together frequently in Fray Luis' mind,[5] and he often uses music to illustrate his characteristic love of harmony and order in the spiritual life. It is difficult to be precise in a matter in which the poet himself did not aim at preciseness (as the mystics invariably do), but to represent the soul as cleaving the air 'till it attains unto the highest sphere' and listening to a 'new mode' ('*otro* modo': my italics) of

> *music that wells*
> *Undying, and all other kinds excels*

certainly seems to be invading the realms of 'celestial harmony'.

In this poem, too, as in 'Night serene,' a number of expressions are used which belong properly to mystical literature. Such is the passage:

> *Through sea of melody*
> *In rapture sweet the soul doth onward glide*
> *And sinks there finally,*

---

[1] *Ibid.* There are four absolutes in the Spanish: 'inmensa hermosura . . . toda'; 'clarísima luz pura'; 'que jamás anochece'; 'eterna primavera'.
[2] *Luis de León, ed. cit.*, p. 238.   [3] *Lyrics*, pp. 131, 133.   [4] *Ed. cit.*, I, 69.
[5] Cf., for example, his exposition of Job xxxviii, 37.

Until whate'er betide
Beyond it to its senses is denied[1]

where an image is employed common to all Christian mystics current in Spanish literature as early as Ramon Lull,[2] and particularly well known during the Golden Age through a phrase first used by Bernardino de Laredo and expounded by Juan de los Ángeles in his *Conquista del Reino de Dios*:

Oh, the ocean's joys to know:
To be engulf'd and not to row![3]

Directly afterwards come the figures of the *arrobamiento* ('Oh, heavenly ravishment! . . . Oh, sweet oblivion!') and of 'life-giving death'[4] which are familiar to every reader of (for example) Saint Teresa. The final phrase has also a ring familiar in treatises on the Purgative Way.

We now come to the poems on more directly religious themes, in which, however, the mystical note is not necessarily more frequently heard. More than half of the ode 'To Elisa'[5] is devoted to the story of the Magdalen, on which, nearly twenty years after Fray Luis' poem was written, Malón de Chaide published a treatise (*The Conversion of the Magdalen*) strongly tinctured with mystical sentiment.[6] Yet, fruitful though this theme might be, there is hardly a hint in the poem of the mystical approach to God. In the lines (51 sq.) beginning with the words 'Sorrow and love her guides' ('De amor guiada y pena . . .') there is a vague reminiscence of Saint John of the Cross's 'Dark Night'; and perhaps,

---

[1] *Aquí la alma navega*
por un mar de dulzura, y finalmente
en él ansí se anega, . . .
  que ningún accidente
  extraño y peregrino oye y siente. Ed. cit., I, 74–5.

[2] E.g., *Libre d'amic e amat*, § 234: 'Amor és mar tribulada de ondes e de vents, qui no ha port ni ribatge. Pereix l'amic en la mar. . . .'

[3]   *¡Quién supiese navegar*
    y engolfado no remar!

Subida del Monte Sión, Bk. III, Chap. 40. Cit. Juan de los Ángeles, *Conquista del Reino de Dios*, Diálogo VIII, § 7. Cf. *Studies of the Spanish Mystics* (London, 1930), Vol. II, p. 70.

[4]   *¡Oh desmayo dichoso!*
    ¡Oh muerte que das vida! ¡Oh dulce olvido!
        Ed. cit., I, 75.

[5] Also entitled 'A una señora pasada la mocedad'. *Lyrics*, pp. 41 sq.

[6] *Studies of the Spanish Mystics*, (1930), II, 266–78.

though in spirit rather than in language, there are reminiscences of the 'Spiritual Canticle'. But I would not insist so much on parallels like Fray Luis'

> May she, so quick to offend,
> Now in Thy service labour . . .[1]

and Saint John of the Cross's

> My soul is well content
> To serve her spouse with all her wealth and might[2]

as on the spirit of complete detachment and self-surrender which pervades the entire poem.

'The Ascension' ('O Shepherd, dost Thou leave . . .?' '¿Y dejas, Pastor santo . . .?')[3] though one of Fray Luis' most inspired poems, full of a fervour admirably restrained, and artistically almost perfect, is rather disappointing from the standpoint from which we are now judging it. Its author's normal objectivity (to which his frequent use of the first personal pronoun must not blind us) here becomes positively plastic. The poem is supposed to have been composed in the cells of the Inquisition, and it always gives me the impression of an attempt made by the author to picture the scene which he is describing with the utmost possible vividness. Bell expresses a similar idea when he suggests that Fray Luis may have been working on his recollection of some painting: 'one seems to see and hear the upward sweep of wings as in El Greco's Assumption and Giotto's Ascension'.[4] Sr. Valbuena Prat, who so often sheds some new light on a familiar poem, aptly observes that it is Horatian in technique: 'The way it begins in medias res, the questions, the restrained movement, all remind one of Horace.'[5] Intrinsically, this critic's judgment, though I cannot entirely endorse it, is a refreshing change from the type of eulogy which is content to remark that the poet 'nowhere displays more unction, more ecstatic piety'[6] than here. Sr. Valbuena Prat thinks

[1] La que sudó en tu ofensa
trabaje en tu servicio.
Ed. cit., I, 131.
[2] Mi alma se ha empleado,
y todo mi caudal en su servicio.
Cántico espiritual, xx.
[3] Lyrics, pp. 71, 73.   [4] MLR, XXI, 172.
[5] Historia de la literatura española (Barcelona, 1937), I, 502.
[6] J. Fitzmaurice-Kelly, Fray Luis de León (Oxford, 1921), p. 219.

that, despite his profundity of sentiment, Fray Luis does not here reach his greatest heights and that the technical perfection of the poem is 'inferior to the sincere serenity of Fray Luis at his best.'[1] To me the poem seems to enshrine the highest degree of both sincerity and serenity, but I cannot discover in it the smallest suggestion of the mystical spirit. Even of the phraseology this is true.[2] In the four additional stanzas to be found in one manuscript, and thought to be the work of one of Fray Luis' disciples, there are distinct indications that the second artist was not merely trying to paint the lily of the first, but was aiming at providing the poem with a semi-mystical conclusion.[3] The theme of the soul which breaks the chains that bind it to the earth so that it may follow its Beloved is essentially mystical, as far as it goes: so, too, are the addressing of Christ as 'sweet Bridegroom', the contrasting of dark night with illumination and the notion that true life consists in the presence of Christ.[4] These additional stanzas may be thought to spoil the unity of the original poem, but there can be little doubt that they had their source in the feeling that, as it stood, the poem left its readers, like the disciples, 'in this deep vale obscure . . . how poor, how blind!'[5]

The longer ode 'All Saints' ('What saint or most renowned

---

[1] *Loc. cit.*

[2] The sea-image in ll. 16–17 is not used in the mystical sense quoted above. The reference to 'los ojos que vieron de tu rostro la hermosura' (ll. 11–12) suggests at first sight the

> Gocémonos, Amado,
> *y vámonos a ver en tu hermosura*

of the 'Cántico espiritual'. But here, too, the words are taken in a different sense.

[3] *Ed. cit.*, I. 286–7.

[4] *¡Qué! ¿temes la salida?*
¿Podrá el terreno amor más que la ausencia
de tu querer y vida?
Sin cuerpo no es violencia
vivir, mas es sin Cristo y su presencia.

> *Dulce Señor y amigo,*
> *dulce Padre y Hermano, dulce Esposo,*
> *en pos de ti yo sigo,*
> *O puesto en tenebroso*
> *O puesto en lugar claro y glorioso.*

[5] *en este valle hondo, oscuro . . .*
¡ cuán pobres y cuán ciegos . . . !

166

Virtue . . .?'[1], also connected with the Inquisition prison, is an evident imitation of Horace's ode 'Quem virum aut heroa' (*Carm.*, I, 12), and would find no place in this survey were it not for the last three stanzas, in which, after having addressed himself to the Son of God, to Our Lady, to the angels and to certain of the saints, Fray Luis prays with deep emotion for Divine comfort in his imprisonment. 'Unto this heart give peace', he cries,

> *Which throbs with pain and grief in darkest night;*
> *But, once it gains release,*
> *Will sweeter song indite,*
> *Praising Thy name, Thy beauty, and Thy might.*[2]

This penultimate stanza (and the final stanza is similar to it in spirit) is in no sense mystical: on the contrary, the author is too much preoccupied with his own troubles to rise to those heights. But his description of himself in the 'darkest night' is too striking for us to avoid remarking that it was in another such dark night, at Toledo, only a few months after Fray Luis had been acquitted, that Saint John of the Cross wrote two or more of his own immortal poems. The irrelevance of this observation to our main theme will perhaps be pardoned in view of the interest of the suggestion that the Carmelite saint, who may have made the personal acquaintance of the Salamancan professor some ten years earlier, and certainly knew a great deal about him, could have read or heard of the verses which Fray Luis had written in prison, and, being himself arrested and imprisoned very shortly afterwards, should have occupied his own time in the same way.

The last two poems now to be considered are the most interesting for our subject. The ode to Felipe Ruiz beginning 'When from this prison drear . . .?' ('¿Cuándo será que pueda . . .?')[3] is one of the poems on which thoughtless writers shower the adjective 'mystical', probably on account of the reference in the fifth line to

[1] *Ed. cit.*, I, 288–308: '¿Qué santo o qué gloriosa Virtud . . . ?' *Lyrics*, pp. 35 *sq.*
[2] *Ed. cit.*, I, 307:

> *Da paz a aqueste pecho,*
> *que hierve con dolor en noche escura;*
> *que fuera deste estrecho*
> *diré con más dulzura*
> *tu nombre, tu grandeza y hermosura.*

[3] *Lyrics*, pp. 105 ff.

'the contemplation of pure truth, untouched by sorrow'.[1] A typical example of this comes from a usually sound critic, the late Ludwig Pfandl, who describes the theme of the ode as 'the mystical yearning for the beyond'.[2] But that is precisely what it is not—'yearning', by all means, but certainly not 'mystical'. For, to begin with, the aim of the true mystic is not only the attainment of the Beatific Vision after death, but union with Divine Reality on earth: and, in the second place, his desire for both union and vision is essentially and solely the lover's desire for the Beloved—for companionship and union with Him and even for incorporation and absorption in Him. The aspirations of Fray Luis, by comparison with these, are, however attractively expressed, of a puerile kind. When he arrives in Heaven he will be like an inquisitive child— or shall we say a child of the Renaissance?—wanting to *see* and *know* the reason of everything. 'Allí . . . *veré*', 'There . . . I shall *see*', is his theme. He wants to *see* how the Divine power laid the foundations of the earth, to *see* the columns by which the earth is sustained, to *know* why there are storms and earthquakes, to *see* the sources of springs and rivers, to *know* the causes and the effects of heat and cold—and so on, to the very end of the poem. It is all highly individual—almost an exaltation of individuality. The true mystic, on the other hand, so completely sinks his individuality that he is often accused of preaching excessive passivity and tending to pantheism.

Most instructive of all is the final stanza. Working up to a climax, the poet arrives in imagination at the 'highest sphere' and its 'mansions' (*moradas*: the word used, throughout her *Interior Castle*, by Saint Teresa). One remembers how, in 'the centre and midst' of Saint Teresa's mansions, 'is the chiefest mansion, where the most secret things pass between God and the soul'.[3] 'Between God and the soul'! We have to descend a long way from Saint Teresa's earthly paradise to the 'highest sphere' of Fray Luis' Heaven. For his 'mansions' are merely 'of joy and of delight', surrounded by a vague atmosphere of 'light and gold', inhabited, not, like Saint Teresa's innermost mansion, by God alone, (Who is

---

[1] 'Contemplar la verdad pura sin duelo.' *Ed. cit.*, I, 192. For 'sin duelo' (*lit.*, 'without grief'—the reference may be to the effort of striving) some manuscripts have 'sin velo', 'without a veil', but for several reasons the reading I have given seems to me preferable.

[2] Pfandl, *op. cit.*, German ed., p. 143; Spanish ed., p. 158.

[3] *Moradas*, I, 1 (*CWSTJ*, II, 202).

the God of Job, mentioned by name only twice in the whole of the poem, and then in connection with snow and clouds), but merely by 'blest spirits'.[1]

By contrast, in 'The Heavenly Life' ('Alma región luciente . . ')[2] we have the only one of Fray Luis' poems which has any claim to be called mystical in conception. Pfandl, in the phrase just quoted, couples it, astonishingly, with the ode to Felipe Ruiz, but to it, at least, his definition is applicable enough. Bell calls it 'one of León's most mystical poems':[3] it is even more than that. If Sr. Valbuena Prat goes a little far in describing it as penetrating 'to the heights of mysticism'[4]—for there are heights far beyond these —his hyperbole is not without justification. I quote the poem, in a version of my own, in its entirety.

> *Fair land of radiant light,*
> *Fields of the blest, to winter's frost unknown*
> *And the sun's scorching might;*
> *Soil ever newly sown,*
> *Bearing eternal joy unto its own:*
>
> *See the Good Shepherd come!*
> *Snow-white and purple blooms enwreathe His head*
> *As to their heavenly home,*
> *To fields well-waterèd,*
> *Staffless and slingless His lov'd flocks are led.*
>
> *He leads His sheep on high*
> *Till, glad at heart, their pasture-land they view,*
> *Where roses cannot die*
> *And flow'rs are fresh with dew,*
> *For ever cropp'd and yet for ever new.*
>
> *Within the mountain's fold,*
> *Faithful, He bathes them in the torrent's flood,*
> *Laves them in joy untold,*
> *Gives them abundant food:*
> *Shepherd and Pasture He, and all their Good.*

[1] *Ed. cit.*, I, 203. The stanza, in the Spanish, reads:

> *Veré sin movimiento*
> *en la más alta esfera las moradas*
> *del gozo y del contento,*
> *de oro y luz labradas,*
> *de espíritus dichosos habitadas.*

[2] *Lyrics*, pp. 97, 99.   [3] *MLR*, XXI, 175.   [4] Valbuena Prat, *op. cit.*, p. 502.

And when at length the sun
Has reached the zenith of his mighty sphere,
The hour of rest begun,
He to His flock draws near,
And with sweet sound delights His sacred ear.

He strikes the sonorous lyre,
And lo! the soul thrills to its deathless strain!
Dissolving in its fire,
It counts pure gold but vain,
Plunging within it ever and again.

O sound! O voice divine!
Might some faint note of this descend to me,
Transport my will in Thine,
Unite it utterly
Until it blend, O heavenly Love, in Thee.

Dear Love, did I but know
The pasture where Thy noontide rest would be,
I'd break my toils below,
And never stray from Thee,
But with Thy flock remain, for ever free.[1]

Many pages would be needed for an appreciation which would bring out all the various beauties, both of thought and of artistry, in this magnificent poem, to my mind the most nearly perfect, though not the longest or the most impressive, that Fray Luis de León ever wrote. We must, however, confine ourselves to stressing its mystical quality. It looks at first like a companion picture to that of the Ascension, for with even greater vividness it describes Christ ascended into Heaven, that 'fair land of radiant light', where, amid eternal springtime, His head crowned (a picturesque though not an original touch) with purple and white flowers, He leads His flock 'staffless and slingless' ('My sheep hear My voice and follow Me') to green pastures. It is, I think, rather an exaggeration to say, as W. J. Entwistle once said, that 'the second, third and fourth verses . . . are León's paraphrase' of Psalm xxiii;[2] for not only is there much detail in each poem not to be found in the other, but in the Psalm there is a 'rod' and a 'staff'. However, it is true that, down to the end of the fourth stanza, the thought is largely

---

[1] *Ed. cit.*, I, 230–44.   [2] *MLR*, XXII, 59.

Biblical. Then, as we come to the 'abundant food'—'mesa llena': perhaps the 'table prepared before me' of Psalm xxiii, where the sustained image suffers a similar rather disconcerting modification —the mystical nature of the poem suddenly becomes apparent.[1] At the beginning of the stanza ('Within the mountain's fold . . .') there has been a distinct suggestion of the mystical inner chamber and the refreshing stream, such as we find, for example, in the 'Spiritual Canticle':

> *Within the mountain's fold,*
> *Faithful He bathes them in the torrent's flood,*
> *Leaves them in joy untold . . .*[2]

> *. . . And in thy beauty see ourselves portray'd,*
> *Where purest waters spring,*
> *Rippling o'er hill and glade,*
> *Then enter farther in the forest's shade.*[3]

But now we come upon the entirely mystical line:
> *Shepherd and Pasture He, and all their Good.*[4]

It is, of course, open to any commentator to interpret this phrase as a reference to the Eucharist (though I observe that P. Llobera does not do so); but, if perhaps this thought can hardly have been absent from the poet's mind, the applicability is much more extensive. In brief, the reference is to the whole process of inter-communion between Soul and Spouse which characterizes the state of union and which the mystics commonly describe under such symbols as those of the two candle-flames, of coal and fire, of river and ocean. The fact that the primary application is to the next life seems unimportant, for the whole of the remainder of the poem is susceptible of a secondary interpretation also.

Next come the references, so familiar to all readers of the

---

[1] *Ed. cit.*, I, 239.

[2] *Ya dentro a la montaña*
del alto bien las guía; ya en la vena
del gozo fiel las baña. . . .
        Ed. cit., I, 239.

[3] *Y vámonos a ver en tu hermosura*
al monte o al collado,
do mana el agua pura;
entremos más adentro en la espesura.
        'Cántico espiritual', xxxvi.

[4] *Ed. cit.*, I, 239: 'Pastor y pasto él solo y suerte buena.'

mystics, to a rest from labour ('a rest most busy,' as an English
mystic once called it), to the voice of the Beloved (in this case it is
the 'deathless sweetness' of the 'sonorous lyre' as played by Him)
which causes the Lover's heart to burn, and to the swoon of love—
i.e., rapture or ecstasy.

Finally, at the beginning of the penultimate stanza, in what I
think is one of the most moving moments in the whole of Fray
Luis' poetry, the author, in a striking apostrophe, makes explicit
the secondary interpretation of which no sensitive reader would
fail already to have become conscious, and begs that he himself
may be given nothing less than the grace of union—perpetual
union (*i.e.*, the Seventh Mansions), the final words of the poem
suggest—while still on earth:

> *O sound! O voice divine!*
> *Might some faint note of this descend to me,*
> *Transport my will in Thine,*
> *Unite it utterly*
> *Until it blend, O Heavenly Love, in Thee!*
>
> *Dear love, did I but know*
> *The pasture where Thy noontide rest would be,*
> *I'd break my toils below,*
> *And never stray from Thee*
> *But with Thy flock remain, for ever free.*[1]

In these few pages we have examined the principal poems on
which Fray Luis de León's claims to be called a mystical poet must
mainly rest. Our conclusions can be expressed very briefly. Only
once does he give us anything like a clear and full description of
any single stage or experience of the mystical life. Quite frequently
he uses mystical language and much of his work is impregnated

---

[1] *¡Oh son! ¡Oh voz! ¡Siquiera*
pequeña parte alguna decendiese
en mi sentido, y fuera
de sí el alma pusiese
y toda en ti, oh Amor, la convirtiese!

Conocería dónde
sesteas, dulce Esposo, y desatada
desta prisión adonde
padece, a tu manada
viviera junta, sin vagar errada.
Ed. cit., I, 242.

with the mystical spirit. But there are other elements in his rich and many-sided work than those of mysticism, and there are aspects of his poetic temperament which sometimes seem to be definitely at variance with it. We cannot, with the learned and enthusiastic Augustinian historian P. Ignacio Monasterio, speak indiscriminately of the 'mysticism to be found in his loveliest poems, "The Life removed", "To Francisco de Salinas", "Night serene", etc.,' in which 'if he does not surpass the mystical flights of Saint Teresa and Saint John of the Cross, he at least equals them'.[1] But we can certainly hold, with Menéndez Pelayo, that mystical authors formed a large part of his spiritual food and believe that his greatest achievement in this sphere is, not so much that he reproduced or poetized their ideas, as that (to continue in the words of the critic just quoted) 'he learned from the sublimity of their thought, with which he combines that serenity, lucidity and mellow warmth (*suave calor*) which everywhere dominate his poetry'.[2]

[1] *Místicos agustinos españoles* (Madrid, 1929), I, 189.
[2] *Poesías de Fray Luis de León* (Madrid, 1928), I, 35–6.

Mysticism in the Poetry of the Golden Age

In a previous essay I remarked that the mystical leaven, during the Golden Age, permeated sacred and even secular verse. The poet who would be most generally cited as exemplifying this permeation is Fray Luis de León, whose verse, however, as we have seen, except in the poem of the Heavenly Life,[1] betrays very little direct mystical influence. It may be of interest to examine the works of some other writers of the time less commonly thought of as mystical and to discover how far this influence shows itself in their poetry.

[1]

The Spanish author who wrote the largest quantity of sacred verse during the Golden Age is undoubtedly Lope de Vega (1562–1635).[2] This statement may surprise even those who are moderately familiar with Spanish literature, for Lope de Vega is generally thought of as the world's most prolific dramatist: some four hundred and fifty of his plays are still extant, and, three years before his death, he claimed to have written no less than fifteen hundred. But his non-dramatic work is also voluminous, and of the twenty-one volumes of it in the standard edition[3] a considerable proportion—notably the *Sacred Poems* (*Rimas sacras*) and the *Loving Soliloquies of a Soul to God*—are inspired by religion.[4]

---

[1] Cf. p. 169–72, above.

[2] See my *Saint John of the Cross, etc.* (London, 1946), pp. 85–96.

[3] *Colección de las obras sueltas, assí en prosa como en verso, de D. Frey Lope Félix de Vega Carpio, etc.* (Madrid, Sancha, 1776–9). References are given to this edition, the letters (a), (b) denoting the first and the second poem on the page respectively.

[4] For the *Rimas sacras*, see Vol. XIII of Sancha's edition; the other poems examined are contained in Vols. X, XVI, XVII, XIX of that edition and in

Not much of it, however, is concerned with the mystical life, of which it is improbable that Lope de Vega had any personal experience. Though he became a Franciscan tertiary in his fiftieth year, and was ordained priest soon afterwards, his life, essentially that of a man of the world, was studded with amorous incidents which, from our modern standpoint, do him no credit. Avid, it would seem, of experience, and continually moved by passion, devout or mundane, he would pass easily from extreme licence to extreme penitence, and vice versa. It is scarcely possible to question his sincerity: no man who was only conventionally religious could have written the sonnet 'Shepherd divine'[1] with its appealing and impressive climax:

> Shepherd, whom love can slay, I pray Thee hear;
> Flee not before the blackness of my sin,
> But, since the weary soul to Thee is dear,
> Stay, quell the fears that compass me within.
> Yet why say 'Stay' when Thou art at the door,
> Waiting with piercèd feet for evermore?

Or what is surely one of the most passionate of all poems of penitence:

> Oh, what am I that Thou should'st seek me more?
> Jesus, my Lord, what love Thy heart must fill
> To make Thee spend the nights so dank and chill,
> The nights of darkest winter, at my door!
>   Hard was my heart—I kept Thee in the street!
> With crazy notions was my mind imbued;
> Cold as the ice was my ingratitude,
> Freezing the blood-drops on Thy piercèd feet.
>   How often did my guardian angel say:
> 'See, where He's waiting. Shall He wait in vain?
> What wondrous love is this that thus can stay!'
>   How often, Beauteous Lord, did I complain:
> 'Tomorrow let me open, not today,'
> And, on the morrow, said the same again.

the *Romancero espiritual para recrearse el alma con Dios* (Pamplona, 1624), reprinted in facsimile (1903) by the Hispanic Society of America. Fuller references than are given in this essay will be found in *Bulletin of Spanish Studies* (Liverpool, 1944–5), XXI, 217–23, XXII, 34–43.

[1] Quoted in *Saint John of the Cross, etc.*, pp. 88–9.

The dominant theme in his devotional verse, then, is repentance
—a theme presented under four aspects. First, he describes the gulf
that stretches between sinful man and the All-Holy God—*l'infiniment grand et l'infiniment petit*. Secondly, he dwells on the tragedy of
his own sinful and wasted years, which often leads him to reflections on the vanity of the world. Thirdly, his realization of this
sinfulness takes the form of deep remorse. Fourthly, he expresses
his consciousness of the generosity of Divine forgiveness. These four
aspects are so closely connected that it is seldom possible to isolate
one of them from the rest: sometimes, indeed, all four can be
illustrated in a single poem, such as the well-known sonnet on the
Mass:

> *I see Thee in my hands, Eternal King,*
> *I raise the stainless Victim up on high;*
> *And then from my unworthiness I fly*
> *And of Thy wondrous lovingkindness sing.*
> *Now shrinks my soul from grace so vast and free,*
> *Now it dissolves in floods of loving tears.*
> *I sigh with grief; I tremble with my fears:*
> *So oft, my Lord, have I offended Thee!*
> *Oh, look upon me with that human gaze,*
> *For, basely, though I've left the paths divine,*
> *'Tis vain imaginings have turn'd my ways.*
> *Let not my wretchedness so far decline*
> *That one whose hands, unworthy, Thee upraise*
> *Should ever be abandon'd, Lord, by Thine.*

Within this framework there would be ample place for the mystical ideal, for it is precisely the realization of the greatness of God
and the nothingness of man that inspires the mystic's attempts at
self-adjustment. But there is practically no allusion in the *Sacred
Poems*, either personal or objective, to the Mystic Way. One sonnet
(199a) refers in detail to a journey, but the context shows that it is
the journey of life. Another (176b), with its stress on introspection
and interior conflict, is suggestive of the experiences of the Purgative Way, but gives no hint of anything beyond it. When Lope
de Vega uses mystical language, he is generally either writing in a
non-mystical sense or repeating commonplaces from other authors.
His constant playing upon the themes of death-in-life and life-in-
death has not the deep significance of Saint Teresa's and Saint
John of the Cross's poems on the refrain:

> *I live, yet no true life I know,*
> *And, living thus expectantly,*
> *I die because I do not die.*[1]

Except in one place (183a), where it preludes a meditation on the Crucifixion, his use of this theme is suggestive rather of the conventionality of the Cancioneros.

The closing lines of a poem entitled 'Ex Divo Bernardo' (106–7):

> *Thou, O my Christ, my Own,*
> *Thou art the only Good for which I yearn.*
> *From all but Thee I turn*
> *And fix my hopes on following Thee alone.*
> *I have no need but Thee*
> *To serve Thee's life and health eternally*

are in consonance with the mystical spirit, though no more. The same inspiration is found in several sonnets on the theme 'God, Centre of the soul.' Into one of them (82a) is interwoven, with the threads of repentance and remorse, that of aspiration:

> *Were but my love in truth a blazing flame*
> *How soon 'twould journey to its sphere on high!*
> *But 'tis a comet shooting through the sky,*
> *Ere sinking to the earth from which it came.*
> *How do I yearn for Thy Divine embrace*
> *When for my guilt with heavy fear I sigh!*
> *And, if my love has not the strength to fly,*
> *Where can it find an earthly resting-place?*

The Augustinian figure of the soul seeking its centre, on which this sonnet closes—

> *But tell me, Lord, if I am far from Thee,*
> *And in its centre alone the soul can rest,*
> *In what place is there any rest for me?*

—was evidently an attractive one to Lope: it occurs again at least twice (177a, 195b), and the second time we hear the genuine note of mystical desire:

> *And if the soul its will should wholly bend*
> *To find that centre where its search can end,*
> *How must it love that Good, all good excelling!*
> *Since none has rest who makes not Christ his dwelling.*

[1] *CWSTJ*, III, 277–9; *CWSJX*, II, 450–1.

Yet one can never escape the feeling that this language is at best the expression of a mood—one of the most pronounced of the reflections of the sun upon the prism of a many-sided temperament. For a moment the Goal is clearly in sight; but in another moment it is dimmed and even half-obscured; and before long it has disappeared again, to reappear only uncertainly.

The way to the Goal, too, is hidden. Apart from the few references just quoted, there is no suggestion of a progress along the Mystic Way. A sequence of eight sonnets (88–92) to Saint Teresa, who was both beatified and canonized in Lope's lifetime, refers to various incidents in her life, historical or legendary, such as the Transverberation, but all the emphasis is on visions and locutions, and there is no sign of acquaintance with, or, for that matter, interest in, her teaching. The last sonnet of the sequence uses mystical language, but this strikes one as quite devoid of feeling and the context in which it occurs is conventional in the extreme.

It is not so much here that one finds whatever of the mystical spirit there may be in the *Sacred Poems* as in the depth of the love which they reveal and the fervour of their aspirations. In his most spiritual moments Lope de Vega may be termed a mystic *in posse*. His aspirations, it is true, are not to union, like Saint John of the Cross's, nor to vision, like Luis de León's, but mainly to service and to worthier living. Yet their intensity and the yearnings after intimacy with God which accompany them give them a semi-mystical quality. One can recognize the true lover in their hyperboles (190b); in their fond pleadings (219b); in their frequent whispers of endearment—'Jesús dulcísimo', 'Jesús mío'; in their rhetorical questions (191b):

> *Oh, sweet my Life, had but my soul for Thee*
> *Such loving fervour as is Thine by right!*
> *But where to find a love that's infinite*
> *To match Thine own Divine Infinity?*

And there are times when this Divine love not only lends him wings, but makes verbal music (192a):

> *Luz que ilumina el sol, las once esferas,*
> *luz ¿quién es luz, sino tu luz hermosa?*

> (*Light that dost light the sun and all the spheres,*
> *Light—where is light save in thy light so fair?*)

Yet, though he mounts on these wings, he cannot sustain his gaze, and, again like Saint Augustine, he is left with only a loving memory and a yearning for what he has savoured, but is as yet unable to feed upon.

[11]

The work by virtue of which the term 'mystical' is most commonly applied to Lope de Vega's sacred verse is the *Loving Soliloquies of a Soul to God* [1]—'the most energetic attempt that he made', says Vossler, 'to seek the most personal expression possible for his devotion'. [2] Published in 1626, the *Soliloquies* consist of verses followed by passages of prose many times their length and supposed to have been translated from the Latin by one Gabriel Padecopeo, whose name is an anagrammatic pseudonym for Lope de Vega Carpio. A biographical sketch of this imaginary author describes him as a soldier returned from active service who, after various experiences in the world, decided to retire from it also, and, during a short period spent in retreat, wrote these *Soliloquies*, together with one hundred short prayers, in prose, appended to them. Lope himself was now in Holy Orders, and the faintly theological colouring of the verse prologue might suggest that he no longer wrote religious verse like that of the *Sacred Poems*. But, in fact, the reader will find little change.

The dominant theme is again repentance, and each of its four aspects enumerated above can be so easily glimpsed that further analysis is unnecessary. A note heard in the *Soliloquies*, however, which seldom occurs in the *Sacred Poems*, is that of aspiration. There is a constant reaching out towards the unattained, and perhaps unattainable. There is a yearning for death which will bring true life —one of the mystic's most frequent themes. There are vague longings inspired by love, and centred in God, but otherwise hardly definable (1, 26)—so powerful that at times they defeat their own ends:

'I shall indeed be able to love Thee, but who can love Thee as Thou Thyself lovest? At the least, my God, I can content myself with loving Thee to the limit of human capacity. Yet alas! I know not how to love Thee, my Life, for I find so much to love in Thy Divine perfections that when I attempt to imagine them they overwhelm me (*me anego*)'(31).

[1] *Ed. cit.*, XVII, 1–93. The bracketed references are to pages of this volume.
[2] *Lope de Vega und sein Zeitalter* (München, 1932), p. 173; *Lope de Vega y su tiempo* (Madrid, 1933), p. 197.

Now this verb *anegarse* is a common one with the mystics, who use it, with *deshacerse, embeberse* and others, in a quite literal sense, to denote absorption of the personality within the life of Union.[1] Lope adopts it, though with a different meaning, as he also adopts the mystical word *desmayo*, swoon. Here it is, for example, in the Fifth Soliloquy (47), decked out in metaphor. Christ is a garden: 'all lilies and roses art Thou, all gardens and fountains'. The entry to the garden is through a quickset hedge, but none the less the soul will enter, to pluck the roses:

> Then let me enter, Lord, I pray,
> To pluck these roses, wondrous fair,
> And let my soul find comfort there,
> For with its love it faints away.

In the Seventh Soliloquy (65–7), a similar line of thought is followed, again in allegorical form, but at greater length. The soul—that is, the writer—has left Egypt and reached the Promised Land. His guiding star, the Virgin Mother, has led him to the pierced Side—which once more, with brusque change of figure, becomes a garden. In this there bloom a thousand divine flowers, the fragrance of which revives him from a swoon. Such terminology, however, though allied to the language of mysticism, is not that of the true mystic. It suggests the repetition of words one has heard and read rather than the incorporation of the experiences they represent into one's own experience. And the air of unreality about such language is intensified by the Baroque or semi-Baroque forms of expression which it would be irrelevant to discuss here but which occur more frequently at this stage of Lope's career than earlier.

Nevertheless, it is in the verses intercalated in the prose part of the Seventh Soliloquy that Lope uses this language with the greatest effect. In sincerity they reach the level of the few greatest sonnets of the *Sacred Poems* and in literary merit they are not far below them. They go beyond Augustinian mysticism—

'Lord of my life, if the soul finds rest in Thee alone, as in its true centre, wherein can it find rest if it seeks not Thee?'[2]

—almost to the point reached by Saint John of the Cross at which words fail him and he can take refuge only in metaphor. They

---

[1] Luis de León also uses it, in the seventh stanza of his poem 'Calm grows the air around . . .'. Cf. p. 164, above.

[2] From the ninety-fifth of the hundred ejaculatory prayers referred to above.

speak, that is to say—though not with Saint John of the Cross's literalness—of transformation:

> *Oh, were my love so strong that I might die*
> *In love's sublime access,*
> *Transformèd in the Bridegroom's deep distress,*
> *For no true love, 'tis plain,*
> *Could see Thee dead, and yet alive remain.*

And even of deification, using the word *endiosar* (deify) in a way hardly translatable into English,[1] but yet somewhat vaguely, so that one cannot be sure how far the poet is merely being metaphorical.

These are the semi-mystical passages of the greatest significance to be found in Lope de Vega's poetry. They show that he was carried along from time to time by the mystical current of the day, but give no indication that it had any genuine meaning for him. His other poems of this type confirm that impression. A 'Discourse in praise of Saint Teresa of Jesus' (XVII, 231–44) is full of allusions to Saint Teresa's mystical experiences but is wholly impersonal. In Volume X the religious verse is purely conventional; in Volume XIX there are only occasional devout sonnets and some ballads written round the figure of Bras, Gil and Llorente—a type of poem, familiar to readers of Saint Teresa, in which Lope de Vega outclasses many of his contemporaries, but simply because he is more of a poet than they. The 'Spiritual Ballads' (*Romancero espiritual*) are not only almost devoid of the mystical spirit but are so heavily overlaid with hyperbole, verbiage and Baroque imagery that one doubts even their sincerity.

Finally, there is the *Shepherds of Bethlehem*, a prose narrative of events connected with the Nativity, interrupted by numerous Biblical digressions and permeated with an atmosphere of vaguely pastoral idealism, which falls within our orbit because of the lyrics which diversify the prose. Written about 1611, during a lull in his love-life and before he had taken Orders, it was dedicated to his infant son Carlos Félix, to whose childish footsteps, so the dedication implies, it was to serve as a guide. In such a book we should hardly expect to find any mystical language: nowhere in Lope's work would this be less in place. The unwary reader might suspect

---

[1] The relevant line is *porque te humanas tú para endiosarme* (*lit.*, 'because Thou makest Thyself human in order to deify me'), but the context, embodying a trivial conceit on the word zero, makes the author's intention suspect.

mystical intention, at least in the wider sense of that adjective, in a few poems like the carols:

> *Kings from the land of the sunrise,*
> *This is the land of the Sun.*
> *Brightest of dawns is breaking;*
> *Fairest of days has begun.*
> *Cease looking up at the heavens,*
> *Following the star divine,*
> *For where you are now the Sun is*
> *And the stars no longer shine.*

and

> *'Whither goest thou, Mary,*
> *Maiden and mother fair?*
> *Lonely is yonder hillside;*
> *Night may surprise thee there.*
> *See how the day is dying:*
> *Grievous may be thy plight.'*
> 'She within whom the Sun shines
> Has no fear of night.'

> *'See all the stars appearing*
> *Now that the daylight dies.*
> *Greater becomes thy beauty;*
> *Lovelier seem thine eyes.*
> *Yet do I fear when darkness*
> *Makes thine the only light.'*
> 'She within whom the Sun shines
> Has no fear of night.'

But there is no ground, either in the poems themselves or in their context, for supposing that this was in the author's mind. In the *Shepherds of Bethlehem*, if nowhere else, Lope de Vega was as unmystical a religious poet as his age produced.

[III]

Baltasar del Alcázar (1530–1606) is about the last author in whom most people would look for any trace of the influence of mysticism. A soldier by calling, he was rewarded, first with a governorship and later with a post in the household of the Count of Gelves. As a poet, he wrote solely for pleasure, and never published his verses, or even kept them; he made his solid reputation, which has never declined, by his wit, humour and satire; his best-known poem is entitled 'Cena jocosa' ('The Jolly Supper') and the nickname given to him in his lifetime was 'the Sevilian Martial'.[1] It is a striking illustration of the essentially religious temperament of the Spanish people that this master of a highly secular art should have penned a small number of devotional poems worthy of preservation. How they survived his indifference to the fate of his verses one cannot imagine. Possibly we have to thank the 'solicitude and diligence' of his friend Pacheco, who has left it on record that, 'whenever he visited him, he wrote down something of what he had stored in the treasure-house of his felicitous memory'.[2] Or did Alcázar attach greater importance to his religious verse than to the poems which he wrote in a lighter vein? It would not be surprising if he did.

Speaking generally, we can divide this religious verse into three groups. First, *villancicos*, or carols, which were very popular at that time, on the Incarnation or the Blessed Sacrament. Secondly, a group of sonnets, inclining to the doctrinal or to the moral, such as those in which, in almost medieval fashion, the body talks with the soul. Thirdly, a number of poems of a more personal type, breathing a spirit of pure and selfless devotion. Only the last class here concerns us.

The first of these poems is addressed to a crucifix: some, perhaps, would describe it as evangelical rather than mystical, but at least it is instinct with the mystical spirit that stretches out toward God:

> *Give me grace that, with the blest,*
> *When this weary life is o'er,*
> *I may live for evermore*
> *Where Thy blessed feet do rest.*[3]

The same characteristic can be found in a poem of the *enfado* type,[4] which applies a convention that was common among popular poets to the theme of the misery of life without the Beloved. 'My possessions and my wealth offend me', runs the argument; 'my

---

[1] References in this section are to *Poesías de Baltasar del Alcázar* (Madrid, Real Academia Española, 1910).

[2] *Op. cit.*, pp. lvi–lvii.   [3] *Op. cit.*, pp. 157–9.

[4] *Enfadarse*: to be offended, angry. In this somewhat artificial type of poem (normally satirical) each stanza begins with this verb, *i.e.*, voices a grievance or a complaint.

reputation and my position offend me. It offends me to see how tenuous is my happiness—if, indeed, there can be any happiness save in possessing Thee.' But, he adds, he has one consolation:

> *Yet, though complaining ever and again,*
> *One thing, my Lord—one only—comforts me,*
> *That I should please Thee most when I complain,*
> *That all my plaints should have their source in Thee.*[1]

Other poems of this personal and experiential type are to be found among the sonnets, which, in the Spanish edition of Alcázar's work, are arranged in such a way that the moral and doctrinal poems gradually shade into the personal. The first seven are almost objective. Into the next three, somewhat in the Lopean vein, enters the note of contrition. The next, 'At the moment of Communion', speaks of greater intimacy:

> *Enter this house of mine so dark and cold,*
> *Bring light and warmth, desertless though I be.*
> *Come, O my Lord, come as a Guest to me,*
> *Welcom'd with tears of love and joy untold.*[2]

But the most striking sonnet of the group is the twelfth and last, bearing the simple title ' To Jesus':

> *Jesus, Thy ever-holy Name I bless;*
> *Jesus, may all my will stretch out to Thee;*
> *Jesus, my soul's desire for ever be;*
> *Jesus, as God and Man I Thee confess;*
>
> *Jesus, my speech of Thee shall e'er be praise;*
> *Jesus, for Thee with living faith I'll fight;*
> *Jesus, Thy law shall be my sole delight;*
> *Jesus, I'll glory in Thee all my days.*
>
> *Jesus, Thy Being may I contemplate;*
> *Jesus, my heart shall kindle with Thee near;*
> *Jesus, on Thee my thought shall meditate;*
> *Jesus, I'll love Thee, Thou to me so dear;*
> *Jesus, within Thee be my soul's estate;*
> *Jesus, whene'er I call Thee, do Thou hear.*[3]

[1] *Op. cit.*, pp. 159–60.   [2] *Op. cit.*, p. 166.
[3] *Op. cit.*, p. 167. In the original, the verb in every line except the first, fourth, and fourteenth is in the subjunctive, but this would be clumsy and monotonous if rendered literally into English. In some lines I have therefore substituted the future indicative.

For its simplicity and sincerity, for its economy of words and for the evocative power of its spirituality, this sonnet must be put at the very head of Alcázar's religious verse. Clearly, too, it is written under the influence of the mystics. True, it can be described as mystical only in its spirit. It prays that the soul may ever desire God and expresses the wish to fight for God; it then goes farther and begs that the thought may meditate upon Him and the understanding contemplate Him. There would not seem, however, to be any idea of progression as between meditation and contemplation, since they are referred to in the reverse order to that in which they naturally occur: probably the word 'contemplation' is used in a Lullian rather than in a Teresan sense. With the sestet of the sonnet comes an intensification of the poet's emotion, weakening only in the last line. 'Were the authorship of the sonnet unknown,' remarks Rodríguez Marín, 'we might well conjecture it to be the work of Saint John of the Cross or Saint Teresa.'[1] He is right so far as its context is concerned, though its technical merits, one might suppose, would prevent its ever being seriously attributed to Saint Teresa.

[IV]

A minor poet who made his mark in religious verse, and also in religious drama, is Josef de Valdivielso (c. 1560–1638).[2] The one-act plays of Valdivielso, of the type, very popular in the Spain of his day, known as the *auto sacramental*, are some of the best of their kind ever written by poets not in other respects of the first rank. Some of his hymns to the Blessed Sacrament have a moving simplicity and candour. Even his twenty-four-canto poem to Saint Joseph, though tedious as a whole, can show some fine flashes. But it is his poems of popular inspiration, which have been compared to the paintings of Murillo, that reveal him at his best. Here the traditional Gil, Antón and Bras make a welcome reappearance to express the authentic spirit of popular devotion.

Without giving any indication of being himself a contemplative —without indeed being in the fullest sense a mystical poet— Valdivielso strikingly illustrates the prevalence in Spain at this time of mystical ideas and language. His inspiration, too, is that of

---

[1] *Op. cit.*, p. lxxvii.
[2] References are to his *Romancero espiritual*, ed. Mir (Madrid, 1880), pp. 67–9.

the famous sonnet, 'I am not mov'd, my God, to love of Thee'[1]—a love which is of the essence of mysticism. There are numerous references in his verse to this treasure-house of mystical theology, the Song of Solomon, and the figure of Bride and Spouse enters it so freely that ideas which are of the essence of mysticism creep in, almost unobserved.'[2] On the other hand, it might be urged that the emphasis is less on the lover's striving after the Beloved than on the Beloved's wooing of the Lover:

> *When I'm awake, Thou woo'st me;*
> *Thou watchest when I sleep;*
> *Thou follow'st when I flee Thee,*
> *Thy straying child to keep.*[3]

> *At my door, to woo me,*
> *My Spouse takes up His place.*
> *Lovely are His features;*
> *I adore His grace.*[4]

This last trait is particularly characteristic of the doctrinal stanzas to Saint John the Evangelist, 'On the *In principio erat Verbum*',[5] which recall the similarly entitled stanzas of Saint John of the Cross.[6] In referring elsewhere to these and other of the poems of the Carmelite Saint, I have noted the divorce which he effects between doctrine and poetry.[7] There is no such divorce here. In places the language of the two poets is almost identical, but, whereas Saint John of the Cross maintains a sober, almost prosaic level of style throughout his stanzas, Valdivielso, from the very beginning, soars into the realms of imagination. The Evangelist is a 'seraph of love', breasting the waves of love's ocean, rising upon the wings of the Sun until he reaches the Sun itself.

Where Valdivielso comes nearest to being a mystical poet is in

---

[1] Translated in my *Studies of the Spanish Mystics* (London, 1927 and 1951), I, vi. Characteristic poems of that type in Valdivielso are 'Romance de los trabajos' and 'Romance de un alma a los pies de un crucifijo' (*op. cit.*, pp. 71–3).

[2] *Op. cit.*, pp. 117, 175–6, 197–9, 231–3.

[3] 'Romance de los trabajos' (*op. cit.*, p. 6). The word translated 'woo' is *rondar*, which denotes peregrinations by youths round streets inhabited by their ladies, to whom they offer gallantries.

[4] 'Seguidillas al Santísimo Sacramento' (*op. cit.*, pp. 201–2).

[5] *Op. cit.*, pp. 51–3.

[6] *The Poems of Saint John of the Cross* (London, 1947), pp. 40–67.

[7] *Spirit of Flame* (London, 1943), pp. 41–2.

his treatment of the theme of transformation or deification—*i.e.*, the most intimate experience of the Spiritual Marriage. Sometimes this treatment is merely allusive, as in his speculation on the state of blessedness enjoyed by Our Lady:

> *If the best of gifts were given*
> *To the best this world that trod,*
> *If they lived transform'd in union,*
> *God in her, and she in God . . .*[1]

or in the panegyric of Saint John the Evangelist:

> *With the love that dwells in union,*
> *Transformation's work begun,*
> *Christ, transform'd in John, His lover,*
> *Made the two to be as one.*
> *Death himself grew pale and fearful*
> *As he came to keep his tryst,*
> *For he saw, that John, his victim,*
> *Was both life and God in Christ.*[2]

More often it refers, in most definite—even exaggerated—language, to the relations between God and the devout soul after Communion. Not only does the soul, after partaking of God, 'remain in God, and God in her', not only has God 'become the life of the soul', but 'the soul has become a new God' (*el alma un nuevo Dios hecha*).[3] In one poem Valdivielso heaps figure upon figure, either taken direct, or adapted, from the Song of Solomon, before coming to this climax:

> *Open to me, my dove;*
> *Come, let us sup together.*
> *Nowhere are bread and wine*
> *Better—no, not in Heaven.*
> *I shall remain in thee.*
> *And thou in Me shalt abide.*
> *Eat of Me, Who am God*
> *And thou shalt be ev'n as I.*[4]

In another he ends upon a Scriptural text (Galatians ii, 20) used

---

[1] Valdivielso, *ed. cit.*, p. 1. The second 'best' is feminine.
[2] *Op. cit.*, p. 204.   [3] *Op. cit.*, pp. 56–7.
[4] 'Serrana de mis deseos' (*op. cit.*, p. 225). Assonance, and not rhyme, in the even lines is found in the Spanish.

by the mystics again and again to describe mystical union, and applies it to this particular kind of 'transformation'.

> *I enter'd straight into that breast*
> *In which the altar has been made,*
> *And where that Bread Divine is laid*
> *Which here within my soul doth rest.*
> *Of God partaking, God was I,*[1]
> *For what I eat, that shall I be,*
> *And, since my God converteth me,*
> *Of that conversion shall I cry:*
> *'So now I live, and yet not I,*
> *For this my God doth live in me.'*[2]

Inspired by the Most Holy Sacrament, but not, however, referring solely or even specifically to it, are some sentiments on transformation expressed in *octavas*, as admirable in their content as in their form. This is perhaps the most mystical of all Valdivielso's poems. It begins by describing Christ as uniting the soul to Himself with a 'fast knot', as wounding it with arrows of love and as enkindling it with love's fire. The last stanza, with its most daring conclusion, rarely equalled even by the mystics, may be quoted in full:

> *Since Thou art God of love, Oh, make me love Thee;*
> *Receive me in Thyself, now Thou hast found me,*
> *Fain would I have Thee bound—do Thou then bind me;*
> *And, with love's arrows that Thou holdest, wound me.*
> *O Fire of love, in love's strong furnace prove me;*
> *Unite me with Thyself, Whose love's around me.*
> *Pierc'd is Thy breast; within it do Thou take me,*
> *Unmake in me the man; God do Thou make me.*[3]

[v]

Pedro Espinosa (1578–1650), for long thought of merely as an anthologist, but studied increasingly for his original work since it was edited by Rodríguez Marín,[4] is the latest in date of the poets here discussed, beginning to write just as the Golden Age was turn-

---

[1] 'Quedé Dios hecho'

[2] 'A una conversión' (*op. cit.*, p. 108).

[3] 'Hombre me deshaced, y Dios hacedme.' 'Octavas al Santísimo Sacramento' (*op. cit.*, pp. 131–2).

[4] *Obras*, ed. F. Rodríguez Marín (Madrid, 1909)—the edition here used. Cf. Rodríguez Marín's *Pedro Espinosa* (Madrid, 1907).

ing from the spontaneous to the Baroque. A native of Antequera, he mixed with Granadine poets before travelling north and making the acquaintance of the leading writers in Castile. As a youth he fell in love with an Antequeran lady, who disappointed him by marrying a business man, and, when her husband died, threw him into despair by marrying again. Hopelessly disillusioned before he was thirty, he turned for comfort to religion, went into a lengthy retreat in a hermitage near his native city and in due course was ordained.

Though in a well-known sonnet[1] he attacks the prevalent mode of cultism, he himself is not free from either cultism or conceptism, and in his propensity to the Baroque he marks a definite point of advance in the progression from Herrera to Góngora.[2] Most of his poems on religious subjects conform to that type: in decorativeness, brilliance of imagery and sumptuousness of colour they equal, and sometimes even outdo, his secular verse. Nothing that he ever wrote, for example, is more advanced in this respect than the sonnet 'To the Assumption of the Virgin Mary'.[3] He begins this in an atmosphere of exuberant light and colour, goes on to evoke a quite Oriental exoticism and finally draws a churrigueresque picture of the Virgin, clothed in the sun, with the moon at her feet, surrounded by seraphim and choirs of angels who sing as Christ seats her at His side.

Even when he is less ornate, the intimate themes which inspire Christian poets seem, at first glance, to make little impression upon him. A sonnet on the Blessed Sacrament, for example,[4] combines literary conceptism with unexceptionable religious orthodoxy, but is completely devoid of emotion and almost so of poetry. Another, 'To Jesus Christ on the Cross', is, except for a single phrase, completely objective. And so, for page after page, and poem after poem, one could go on.

But closer scrutiny will reveal another Espinosa—more personal and intimate in his religious attitude, more simple and sincere in expression—whom the purely literary critic is apt to ignore. Perhaps, from his own standpoint, the critic is right: there is less power

[1] 'Rompe la niebla de una gruta escura. . . .'
[2] For a detailed treatment of Espinosa's work, see Audrey Lumsden, in *Spanish Golden Age Poetry and Drama* (Liverpool, 1946), pp. 40–62.
[3] Studied in detail by Audrey Lumsden in *Bulletin of Spanish Studies* (1942), XIX, 101–3.
[4] Espinosa, *op. cit.*, p. 40.

in Espinosa when he renounces ornateness and discards his technical devices. But at least he can create an atmosphere in which the mystical spirit flourishes in an atmosphere of sincere feeling intensified at times to fervour. Sometimes one finds the two manners present in the same poem. In the sonnet 'To the Ascension of the Lord'[1] the 'cloud' which, in the Biblical narrative, 'received Him out of their sight', has to be a 'golden cloud', and its origin cannot be natural: by some strange process it is

> *engendered by the weeping for Thy absence.*

So much is in harmony with the literary evolution of the day, but the poet also strikes the personal note by his opening words:

> *Jesus, my love . . .*

and, when he has rendered due homage to incipient Gongorism, he pours out his soul in a profession of penitence and faith. A similar juxtaposition of Espinosa's two manners is found in some verses on solitude[2] in which, before plunging into a wealth of colour and flower imagery, he delivers himself of the striking line:

> *No quiero más que soledad y Cristo*[3]

and proceeds to develop a contrast found in the works of most devout writers:

> *Ah, what is this, my Christ? I fancy-free,*
> *Thou overwhelmèd in a storm of woes?*
> *Thou, wounded and fast-nail'd upon a tree;*
> *I, feeding eagerly on worldly shows?*
> *I, prais'd by men; Thou, used despitefully?*
> *Thou, crown'd with thorns; I with the fragrant rose?*

Similar in spirit to this poem is a striking 'prayer', of only five lines, which, with an economy of language rare in Espinosa, establishes a personal relation between the soul and Christ such as any of the mystics could have claimed as his own:

> *I hail Thee present and yet absent yearn,*
> *Oh, see what tears I shed for Thy return!*
> *Thy hermit languishes in country drear:*
> *Sweet Jesus, to my fervent cries give ear.*
> *Blind, for my Sun, poor, for my Wealth I burn.*[4]

---

[1] *Op. cit.*, p. 39.   [2] 'Soledad de Pedro de Jesús, presbítero' (*op. cit.*, p. 73).

[3] *Lit.*, 'I want no more than solitude and Christ', but the literal rendering gives no idea of the force of the Spanish.

[4] *Op. cit.*, p. 42.

In the poems addressed to Saint Ignatius of Loyola at the time of his beatification and canonization there are suggestions of fervent love, but they are everywhere overlaid by a characteristically florid art, and, as they are partly dependent on the formula '*Ignatius* is *ignis*', the references to fire and heat may be interpreted as excursions in conceptism. One is the more inclined to suspect this kind of fervour because of the numerous artificialities in these poems—the profession of allegiance to the Saint, for example, which is followed by an almost puerile play upon the title of the Society of Jesus.[1]

There are a number of other passages, however, which bring us very close to the mystical life—notably, two of the poems curiously named 'Psalms', perhaps because the point of departure for each may have been suggested by one of the Psalms of David. In the first of these, the poet avows his sincere, personal, ardent desire for God:

> *And everything I see*
> *Spurs me to love of Thee,*
> *To kindle my affections in love's fire;*
> *Yet keener than my love is my desire.*[2]

The starting-point of this poem is Psalm xix, 1 ('The heavens declare the glory of God . . .') and it is the wonders of Nature (ornately presented, to be sure) that incite this desire. But they do their work well. Whether the poet be thinking of this life or the next, his cry is always: 'Where shall I find Him?'

> *Where hast thou hid thyself,*
> *Beloved . . .?*
> *I'll seek my love straightway. . . .*

Thus Saint John of the Cross.[3] This is Espinosa:

[1] *Op. cit.*, pp. 53–4. The Society was called in Spanish *Compañía*. The lines run:

> Santo Ignacio, Santo Ignacio,
> que a la fe y la caridad,
> dais un mundo por ciudad,
> yo os ofrezco el alma mía;
> que cuanto no es Compañía
> es desierto y soledad.

[2] *Op. cit.*, pp. 60–1.

[3] 'Spiritual Canticle', i, iii (*The Poems of Saint John of the Cross* (London, 1947), pp. 5, 7).

> *Glory, O Lord, Thy presence is to me.*
> *Whither art gone, whither art gone, my life?*
> *Where shall I find Thee? Whither dost Thou hide?'* [1]

True, it is of vision that he is speaking, not of union. The fragrance of the Beloved refreshes him; the remembrance of Him heals him; but only the sight of Him can satisfy. [2] His soul faints with love and cries out:

> *Where shall I find Thee, for I cannot see*
> *Him, Him the fair One, Him, for whom I yearn?* [3]

But there are notable similarities with Saint John of the Cross's 'Spiritual Canticle', so obvious that they need not be insisted upon:

> *Come, Lord, my soul is lost in love.*
>
> *I hear Thy voice and so I take new strength,*
> *But, since I find Thee not,*
> *I scatter my complaints upon the wind.*
>
> *. . . my soul,*
> *wounded with love . . .* [4]

The second 'Psalm', inspired by a genuinely mystical conception of love, goes farther. Beginning with an exhortation to the love of God, it breaks at once into an apostrophe to the Spouse:

> *¡Oh mi Esposo gentil, oh, dulce Esposo!* [5]

to Whom it refers in language probably suggested by the Song of Solomon. Amid a profusion of images—the fire, the arrow, the wine, etc.—commonly used by the Mystics, come references to the suspension of the faculties and the absorption of Union:

> *And may Thy lightning-flash forthwith consume me.*
>
> *The generous wine bereft me of my senses.*
>
> *Nor stay'd I in myself, nor was my soul in me.*
>
> *Hide me and overwhelm me in Thy flames;*
> *Make me, O Lord, one spirit with Thyself,*
> *Beloved, my Beloved. . . .*

[1] Espinosa, *op. cit.*, p. 62.   [2] Espinosa, *op. cit.*, p. 62.
[3] Espinosa, *op. cit.*, p. 62.
[4] Espinosa, *op. cit.*, p. 62. Cf. Saint John of the Cross: 'Spiritual Canticle', i–vi.
[5] 'My gentle Bridegroom, oh, my Bridegroom sweet!' (*op. cit.*, p. 63).

After this, the 'Psalm' goes off into the beauties of Nature, though the theme of desire never entirely leaves it, if once more it is desire for vision rather than for union.

[VI]

It would be difficult to find four poets within a single epoch who differ more widely among themselves—in the quantity and quality of their output, in the nature of their genius, and in the attitude that each takes to religion—than Lope de Vega, Alcázar, Valdivielso and Espinosa. Yet even this brief survey is sufficient to show that they were all influenced by the language of the mystics, and, in differing degrees, touched by the mystical spirit. None of them, however, in the strict sense referred to in the last essay, is a mystic. We do not deduce—such an idea hardly even occurs to us—that, because the language of Valdivielso is more advanced than that of the other three, he enjoyed a deeper spiritual experience. But all four exemplify the devotional note which is continually heard in Golden Age verse and all four manifest deep penitence, ardent love and desires (if only vague desires) for something closer to Christ than the foot of the Cross and the hope of Heaven.

PART III

New Light on Saint John of the Cross

New Light on Saint John of the Cross

(i) LIFE AND TIMES

The quatercentenary of the birth of Saint John of the Cross, which fell in 1942, seemed at first to have produced little noteworthy literature.[1] But, in Spain, centenary literature, like many another form of activity, blooms late, and outside Spain the world was at war; so it was not for some time that the extent of the contributions of scholarship to the quatercentenary became apparent. The best of these can now be grouped in three classes, according as they deal with the Saint's life and times, his commentaries and his poems. On the last group I have already written in a previous volume:[2] some addenda will be found in the second section of this essay. The first is dealt with in this section. The second is too technical to treat here in any detail. Briefly, it comprises (*a*) doctrinal studies, such as P. Gabriel de Sainte Marie-Madeleine's *Saint John of the Cross, Doctor of Divine Love*,[3] P. Efrén's *San Juan de la Cruz y el Misterio de la Santísima Trinidad*,[4] and a number of the contributions to the omnibus volume *Sanjuanistica* (Rome, 1943); (*b*) works dealing with the authorship and chronology of the second redaction of the commentary on the *Spiritual Canticle*. The controversy on this last subject, started thirty years ago by Dom Philippe Chevallier, has continued, now fiercely, now intermittently, without leading to any agreement; in 1948 it was forcefully reopened by M. Krynen (*Le Cantique Spirituel de Saint Jean de la Croix commenté et refondu au XVIIe siècle*) and is once more in full swing.[5] It should be added that critical activity has been

---

[1] *Saint John of the Cross, etc.*, p. 50.   [2] *Op. cit.*, pp. 50–3.

[3] *Op. cit.*, pp. 41–3. The book was also published in French and in Italian.

[4] Zaragoza, 1947.

[5] A bibliography of the controversy will be found in the second edition of my *Complete Works of Saint John of the Cross*, Vol. III, pp. 419–39 (v. p. 406, l.6.)

greatly stimulated by new reviews founded by the Carmelites—
Revista de Espiritualidad (Madrid, 1941–), *Ephemerides Carmeliticae*
(Florence, 1947–)—as well as by many others—*e.g.*, *Revista
española de teología* (1941–), *Verdad y Vida* (1943–), *Vida religiosa*
(1944–)—which provide ample outlet for exposition and discussion.

[1]

On the life and times of Saint John of the Cross two works in
particular stand out. The first is the huge fourteen-volume History
of the Discalced Carmelite Reform (*Historia del Carmen Descalzo*),
written by P. Silverio de Santa Teresa, now General of his Order.
Since it appeared during the decade of Civil War and World War
which cut off Spain from most other countries, it is only recently
that this has become generally known. Its vastness, no doubt, will
deter all but the most persevering student. It has a number of
faults: it is loosely constructed and at times insufficiently co-
ordinated; its indices need to be fuller; its style inclines to diffuse-
ness and prolixity; and it often confuses various friars—and, still
more, various nuns—whose names in religion are the same. But it
gives the first clear and detailed picture ever to be drawn of the
background of Saint John of the Cross's activities, and in its fifth
volume, devoted entirely to his life and works, the author is able
to give adequate space to the discussion of intricate, perhaps
insoluble, problems.

Secondly, there is the biography of Saint John of the Cross,
written by P. Crisógono de Jesús Sacramentado, and published, in
the year after that scholar's untimely death, as the preface to a new
edition of the Works in the series 'Biblioteca de Autores Cris-
tianos'.[1] It is unfortunate that this work, of five hundred closely
printed pages, was not first published independently: it has unde-
servedly lost prestige, and failed to attract due attention, by the
inconspicuousness of its appearance. That being so, it will not be
out of place to say a word about its author.

Crisógono Lorenzo Garrachón was born at Villamorisca, a
village in the province of Palencia, on November 24th 1904. Like
Saint John of the Cross, he went to school at Medina del Campo,
where he showed an unusual mental precocity. He made his profession as a Discalced Carmelite at sixteen, and, after studying

---

[1] *Vida y obras de San Juan de la Cruz.* Abbreviated, in the footnotes to this
essay, *Vida.* A second and revised edition was published in 1950.

philosophy and theology at Ávila and Toledo, was ordained priest at twenty-two. He had then just completed his first substantial book, a two-volume study of Saint John of the Cross as thinker and writer (*San Juan de la Cruz: Su obra científica y su obra literaria*), which he kept in manuscript for two years, and published, by order of his superiors, only in 1929. It is obviously the work of a very young man, and parts of it were handled rather severely, especially by foreign critics, not without justification. But its marked individuality, its intuitive brilliance and its breadth of outlook gave promise of a large body of valuable work to come. In 1930 appeared a less extensive book, *La Escuela mística carmelitana*, which, without entering into great detail, made a comprehensive survey of the writers of Saint Teresa's school from her own day to this. When the Second Republic's persecution of the religious Orders began, he was sent to Louvain, to study, lecture and write, and both there, and later, when he returned to Spain to teach theology in Carmelite colleges, he turned out an immense number of manuals, articles, lectures and sermons—sacrificing much, it might be thought, to the enthusiasm and fluency which have ruined the scholarship of many a Spaniard. It is true that he had an amazing superficial energy—the energy proceeding from a youthfulness which he never lost. When I first met him, he was twenty-five, and looked like an overgrown sixteen: he talked rapidly, nervously, passing from one subject to another with feverish intensity. One who knew him intimately, almost to the day of his death, described him to me as 'the friar who never grew up'. But that did not mean that his mind was not maturing. While for the moment he was producing such things as were demanded of him, mainly of a popular kind, he was planning and writing parts of long-term books, drafts of which were found, after his death, among his papers: a 'Critique of Scholasticism', a 'History of Christian Mysticism', a 'History of Spanish Philosophy'.

After the end of the Civil War, he came to the front as an administrator. In 1941 he became the first editor of the *Revista de Espiritualidad*, and secretary of the National Committee formed to organize the celebrations of the quatercentenary. With the labours which these tasks entailed he combined the execution of a task outlined by the Congreso Sanjuanista of 1928 which he had long wished to fulfil—the writing of a rigorously critical biography of Saint John of the Cross, on a scale never before attempted. This entailed endless journeys, patient investigations into the intricacies of sixteenth-century religious history, long periods spent in libraries of all kinds, from the vast Biblioteca Nacional in Madrid to the few shelves of dusty tomes which constituted the literary stock of the smallest convent. To these activities had to be added editorial duties, committees, lectures, missions and retreats—and it was at the end of a retreat, in the small town of Usúrbil, near San Sebastián, that he had a sudden attack of septicaemia and died. By a strange coincidence, it was on the day of his death that a tribunal appointed to report on works written for the quatercentenary awarded his biography of Saint John of the Cross the National Prize.

[11]

To a man with a mind so agile that he could compose on the typewriter as rapidly as though he were typing to dictation, and who seldom—too seldom—blotted a line, the discipline which he imposed upon himself when he began work on his biography must have been unimaginably severe. 'Not a fact has been set down without documentary proof; not a place described without a personal visit':[1] those are the first words of his introduction. Well over two thousand documents, many of them previously unpublished, are cited in the footnotes, and these have been used for the most trivial historical details—and even, in places, for descriptions of scenery—in an attempt to carry the reader back into the authentic sixteenth century. This essay, however, will deal only with those of the main facts of Saint John of the Cross's life on which this biography gives fresh information.[2]

The Saint's childhood was even more straitened than has been supposed. The fifteen-forties, says an almost contemporary biographer, were 'sterile years, when bread was not to be had for love or money'.[3] John's father died, after a painful illness of two years, when the boy was only a few months old, and the mother had still three young sons when she set out on foot to seek help from her husband's relatives, before deciding to shape her own destiny and find

[1] *Vida*, p. 7.

[2] For the reader's convenience, I follow, and give footnote references to, the narrative as recorded in my *Spirit of Flame* (London, 1943; abbreviated *SF*), of which I shall hope, in due time, to publish a revised edition incorporating new material now available.

[3] *Vida*, p. 21, n. 23.

work in Arévalo.[1] It was in about 1551, when they left Arévalo for Medina, that their fortunes began to mend. There were certainly only two sons now. Francisco, the elder, whom some nine years earlier the mother had made an unsuccessful attempt to leave with his father's childless uncle[2], had learned a trade and married a wife, who, like him, became a comfort and help to the mother. Juan, as we know, went as a boarder into a kind of orphanage, ambitiously named the 'College of Doctrine'; and it seems to have been here, and not, as was previously thought, earlier, that he tried his hand at carpentering, tailoring, sculpture and painting, as the instruction given was of a vocational, as well as of a doctrinal kind.[3] Here, too, as we also know, he found a generous patron, who, in return for his services, adopted him and sent him to a college recently[4] founded by the Society of Jesus. P. Crisógono puts the date of his entry into this College as late as 1559 (when he was seventeen) and keeps him there for four years.[5] These dates, however, are little more than guesses.

His entry into the Carmelite Order (1563) was for some reason —possibly because his patron was pressing him to be ordained to a chaplaincy in his hospital—made 'very secretly'.[6] The prevalent belief that he took the habit on Saint Matthias' day has no more foundation than the conjecture that he was born on Saint John the Baptist's day: manuscript sources affirm that he entered the Order soon after the end of the college year, and, as the novitiate lasted exactly a year, and he is known to have been professed between May and October, a day in the summer seems more likely.[7]

One curious detail, unearthed from a manuscript in the Vatican, will be of particular interest to students of Saint John of the Cross's poetry. 'In gratitude for the favour which Our Lord had shown him of making him worthy to live in the said Order, beneath the protection of His most holy Mother, he composed some stanzas in heroic verse and in the pastoral style', later 'expounding them with such spirituality as to make manifest what experience he had

---

[1] This corrects SF, p. 12. There is some doubt as to when Luis, the weakling, died; cf. Vida, p. 26, with P. Silverio, Historia del Carmen Descalzo (Burgos, 1936: abbreviated HCD), Vol. V, p. 8, n. 1.

[2] Vida, p. 24; cf. Baruzi, pp. 75–6.   [3] Vida, p. 35. Cf. SF, p. 12.

[4] HCD, V, 21, gives the date as 1555, but all other authorities seem to agree on 1551.

[5] Vida, pp. 43–4. Cf. SF, p. 13.   [6] Vida, p. 52.

[7] P. Silverio (HCD, V, 26) suggests August or September. P. Crisógono refrains from making any guess (Vida, p. 56).

of prayer and converse with God '.[1] The period referred to is the year of his novitiate; and, as none of his extant poems tallies with the description, the verses may merely have been some class exercise. The really striking part of the evidence is the statement that the spirituality of his expositions was recognized when he was only twenty-one.

[III]

The next part of the Saint's life—his three years (1564–7) as an *artista*[2] at Salamanca University and his meeting, in the Long Vacation of 1567, with Saint Teresa[3]—has already been studied in detail. Further information about his academic environment and new testimony to the respect in which he was held for his uprightness and austerity add nothing essential to the story. He has now made his profession, received priest's orders, decided against becoming a Carthusian,[4] been accepted by Saint Teresa for her Reform, taken a year's theological course (1567–8) at Salamanca[5] and spent some weeks with the Mother Foundress at her foundation at Valladolid. On 28th November 1568 the youth of twenty-six took the habit of the Reform in the little house at Duruelo,[6] with Antonio de Jesús, the ex-prior of the Observance at Medina, and with (in Saint Teresa's words),[7] 'a young man not in orders', who seems to have been a deacon.[8]

Some doubt has been thrown upon the statement, frequently made, that, during part (probably the early part) of the time which Saint John spent at Duruelo, his mother, his brother Francisco and his brother's wife lived there, the mother doing the cooking, the brother the cleaning, and the sister-in-law the washing.[9] Two reliable manuscripts, however, give this information, though it must be admitted that, on practical grounds, the story seems unlikely.[10] Another manuscript describes Francisco as living with John and accompanying him on his preaching tours,[11] and from the fact that no friar is spoken of as going with them P. Crisógono deduces that this took place during the period when

[1] *Vida*, p. 59, nn. 33–4.   [2] *Vida*, pp. 64–5; Baruzi, (see p. 232, below) pp. 98–9.
[3] *SF*, pp. 14–19.
[4] There is also evidence (*Vida*, p. 91, n. 25) that he had considered becoming a Discalced Franciscan.
[5] *Vida*, p. 92, nn. 28–30.
[6] *SF*, pp. 22–4. On a conflict of opinion here, see *Vida*, p. 97, n. 56.
[7] *SF*, p. 23.   [8] *Vida*, p. 102.   [9] *Vida*, p. 102, n. 68; *HCD*, V, 56–7.
[10] *Vida*, pp. 9, 10–11; *HCD*, V, 57, n. 1.   [11] *Vida*, p. 101, n. 68.

John was alone in the house, preparing it for the inauguration.[1] Had there been enough work at that time for two women, one would have assumed that the other visit also took place then.

Officially, the Duruelo house was not recognized as a priory until the Castilian Provincial, Fray Alonso González, who had presided at the inauguration, paid it a return visit, probably in the spring of 1569.[2] Less than a year after this, a chance invitation given to Fray Antonio to preach in the neighbouring village of Mancera de Abajo led to the transference there of the Duruelo community.[3] The narrative of the activities of Saint John of the Cross during the next two years is rather confused, but, as only various comings and goings are involved,[4] we can pass on to the summer of 1572, when he went to Ávila as confessor to Saint Teresa's old convent of the Incarnation, remaining there for five years.[5]

As Saint Teresa, who had been sent there as Prioress in the previous year, reported the good effects of his ministry in a letter dated September 1572,[6] we cannot be far wrong in assuming that he went there during the summer. What does seem to be wrong is the statement, previously repeated by most of his biographers, that the friar who went with him was P. Germán de San Matías.[7] The reason for this supposition is the undoubted fact that, when he was kidnapped by the Calced in December 1577, P. Germán, kidnapped with him, was his companion. But P. Germán was certainly at Pastrana as late as 25th April 1573.[8] The name of Saint John's original companion is not known. At first they lived in the priory of the Observance; then, more suitably, in a small house near the Incarnation, prepared for them by Saint Teresa. There were seven Discalced friars living with him while he was at the priory, and it is likely that he had two or three colleagues in turn at the Incarnation before P. Germán.

The abduction of December 1577 was not the first act of its

---

[1] *Vida*, p. 102, n. 68.   [2] *Vida*, p. 107.   [3] *SF*, pp. 27–8.

[4] See, for example, *Vida*, p. 112, n. 10; p. 120, n. 41. I have attempted to clarify the narrative in my *Handbook to the Life and Times of Saint Teresa and Saint John of the Cross*.

[5] *SF*, pp. 29–30.   [6] *LL* 39.

[7] *SF*, p. 29. P. Bruno, it is true (*Saint John of the Cross* (London, 1932), p. 410), queries it, and P. Silverio (*HCD*, V, 61) says only that Germán was with him 'most of the time', but P. Crisógono is the first to go into the matter in detail.

[8] *Vida*, p. 133, n. 34.

kind. Some two years previously, the Calced friars, growing alarmed at the rapid spread of the Reform, had conceived the wrong-headed idea of killing it by capturing its leaders and compelling them, if they could, to return to the Observance. In the winter of 1575–6[1] the Prior of the Calced house in Ávila had John kidnapped, together with his companion (who at that time seems to have been one Francisco de los Apóstoles),[2] and carried off to Medina del Campo. Their incarceration was soon over, for the Papal Nuncio, Niccolò Ormaneto, a good friend of the Reform, ordered their liberation. But in June 1577 Ormaneto died, and, his successor, Filippo Sega, being hostile, it was fairly certain that the Calced would make another attempt to seize the leader of the Reform, who, according to one manuscript,[3] had anticipated this and suggested leaving the Incarnation, but was overruled. The second abduction took place on the night of 2nd December 1577.[4] Documents long since known describe in detail Saint John's sufferings in the Toledo priory, where he was immured for eight months;[5] a few details, however, can be added. At Ávila, where he was first imprisoned, the guards were sufficiently lax for him to be able to escape for long enough to get back to his house and destroy most of his papers[6]—including letters from Saint Teresa, one may suppose, since not one of these is extant.[7] It was very different at Toledo. He must have been taken there with great secrecy, for as late as the middle of January Saint Teresa testified that no one knew where he was;[8] he himself, indeed, had been blindfolded on the journey.[9] After being publicly accused of having contravened rules made at the Chapter-General held at Piacenza in May 1575, he was vainly adjured, first with threats and then with bribes, to change his habit: the sources tell us that he was offered, among other things, a priorship, a large cell, a good library and even a

[1] Some time before February 1576. See Saint Teresa, *LL* 91, written in that month, the language of which does not suggest that the abduction had taken place very recently.

[2] *Vida*, p. 159, n. 25. *HCD*, V, 93, simply takes it for granted that the second friar was P. Germán. Actually it may well have been after this incident that Germán took Francisco's place.

[3] *Vida*, p. 160, n. 30.

[4] *Vida*, p. 162, n. 39. *HCD*, V, 99, gives the date as December 3, but the earlier day seems to me the likelier.

[5] *SF*, pp. 37–8.

[6] *HCD*, V, 100, throws doubt upon this story. Cf. Saint Teresa, *LL* 204 (p. 497).

[7] Others he destroyed later as an act of abnegation: see *LL*, p. 18.

[8] *LL* 210.   [9] *Vida*, p. 170, n. 4.

cross of gold. To which last offer he replied: 'One that seeks Christ in nakedness needs no trinkets of gold.'[1] All failing, he was treated with the utmost severity, though the pretence of legal procedure was still maintained. He had been convicted of contumacy, the punishment for which was incarceration in the cell provided for that purpose during the good pleasure of the General—or, in this case, of his duly appointed representative, Fray Jerónimo Tostado. When the news came that Germán, imprisoned elsewhere, had escaped, John was removed to a cell considered safer, presumably because it led out of a guest-room, where there would be friars sleeping even at night.[2] The darkness, the starvation diet, the periodical floggings—all these have been described at length already.[3] The testimonies of witnesses during the beatification processes add abundant detail. 'Say what they like about him, he is a saint', the younger friars would whisper to themselves as they saw him suffer.[4]

In May 1578, about five months after his abduction, he was given a new gaoler, a young Father from Valladolid, Juan de Santa María, whose own testimony is still extant. It was this gaoler who gave him paper and ink 'because he wished to pass the time by composing a few things profitable to devotion'.[5] Several nuns, and others, who saw much of him later have detailed what he wrote.[6] One specifies the 'Spiritual Canticle'. Another (or rather four signing jointly), 'stanzas on the mystery of the Most Holy Trinity.' A third says that, after his escape, the Saint recited, 'out of his head', three *romances* on the Gospel *In principio erat Verbum*—presumably the stanzas on the Trinity just mentioned. A fourth reports him as having said that he wrote the 'Spiritual Canticle' in prison and also the stanzas on *Super flumina Babylonis*. Only one witness says that he wrote the poem 'Dark night' in prison; and, as this evidence adds that he also wrote the commentary there, which he is known to have begun much later, it may well be that he did not write the verses either.

One somewhat longer testimony adds a new poem and goes into further detail. 'When the holy Father left his prison', deposes M. Magdalena del Espíritu Santo, 'he took with him a little book

---

[1] *Vida*, p. 173, nn. 17, 18.

[2] Some authorities say that he remained in the same cell, which was made more secure, but the balance of the evidence is against this. *Vida*, p. 174, n. 20.

[3] *SF*, pp. 39–40.   [4] *Vida*, p. 178, n. 43.   [5] *SF*, p. 40; *Vida*, p. 182, n. 69.

[6] *Vida*, p. 183, n. 71. Cf. *SF*, pp. 40–5.

(*cuaderno*) in which he had written, while there, some *romances* based upon the Gospel *In principio erat Verbum*, and some verses which say 'How well I know the fount that freely flows, Although 'tis night', and the stanzas or *liras* that begin 'Whither hast vanishèd?' as far as the words 'Daughters of Jewry'.[1] P. Crisógono throws doubt on the *cuaderno* in view of the testimony that the Saint recited the verses to the nuns from memory, while they copied them down. I see no reason why he should not have preferred reciting to reading, and the copying proves nothing at all. The stanza beginning 'Daughters of Jewry' is numbered 31 in the first (Sanlúcar) redaction of the commentary and 18 in the second (Jaén) redaction, and the phrase is generally taken as meaning that the number of stanzas he wrote in prison was thirty.[2]

[IV]

We now come to the narrative of the Saint's escape from the Toledo priory, which nearly all biographers have obscured by stories of supernatural locutions and visions of Our Lady guiding him to safety. It may not be out of place to quote one of the most recent of them.

'On the following night Our Lady appeared to the poor little Brother; she was resplendent with beauty and glory—marvellously more lovely than the Byzantine Virgin of the *Sagrario* with her royal mantle embroidered with eighty thousand pearls. To the prisoner . . . she said:
'"Have patience, my son, for thy trials will soon cease, thou shalt leave this prison, say Mass, and be consoled."'

. . . . .

'One day . . . Mary let him see, in spirit, a window, high up in the gallery overlooking the Tagus, and told him that he would descend from it, and that she would help him. She also showed him how to unscrew the two locks of his prison, the lock of the dungeon and that of the hall. . . .'[3]
'It is an acknowledged historical fact: "Our Lady had set him free."'[4]

---

[1] *CWSJX*, III, 319.   [2] Cf. here *SF*, p. 41, n. 2.
[3] P. Bruno, O.D.C., *Saint John of the Cross* (London, 1932), pp. 178–80.
[4] *Op. cit.*, p. 185, and the question-begging footnote on that page.

The first of these stories, which may well be true, comes, though at second hand, from the Saint himself. But the rest is surely fantastic—and in any case, as we saw, John had learned at school how to handle a screwdriver. P. Silverio[1] and P. Crisógono,[2] to their great credit, both sweep the narrative clear of such fantasies and limit themselves to discussing whether or no the screwdriver was provided by the friar-gaoler. Baruzi leaves this question open:[3] the two Carmelite historians, weighing the evidence in favour of the gaoler's complicity against the severity of the constitutional penalties for conniving at a prisoner's escape, incline to the negative. To me, the narrative, as pieced together from contemporary evidence, is more suggestive of complicity than of mere benevolence. Here, in brief, it is.

Knowing no more of the geography of the priory than the way from his cell to the refectory, John had first to get his bearings. This he did by persuading the gaoler to let him empty his own slops, so that 'the cell door was left open while the friars were at dinner, this seeming to him[4] the most convenient hour for not being seen.'[5] Having thus examined the lie of the land, and found a suitable window for his escape, he spent some time, on another day, in unscrewing and rescrewing the bolts of his door till the holes were so much enlarged that he could do it at will. Not long before, the gaoler had given him needle, thread and a pair of scissors for mending his habit: possibly the ex-carpenter's apprentice utilized the scissors as a screwdriver. On a third occasion, he took some of the thread, weighted it with a stone (who gave him this?) and let it down from the window till he had the height of the window from the ground. Then, returning to the cell, he calculated that, by tearing his blankets into strips, he could make a serviceable rope only ten feet less than the required length—for him, short though he was, this meant a drop of only five.

If the gaoler observed nothing of all this, he must indeed have

---

[1] *HCD*, V, 123–4.

[2] *Vida*, pp. 185–6. P. 186, n. 79, reproduces two of the most authoritative testimonies, neither of which introduces the supernatural.

[3] 'Il est possible que la fuite ait été favorisée por le geôlier. Mais il est possible aussi que Jean de la Croix l'ait préparée par ses seules forces' (*Saint Jean de la Croix* (Paris, 1924), p. 192).

[4] To John or to the gaoler? The Spanish text leaves the interpretation open.

[5] *Vida*, p. 186, n. 80. The gaoler himself, however, deposed that the door was left open while the friars were at their siesta. He ought to have known, though of course the incident was many years old.

been unfit for his task; but what are we to say of the incident, related by the gaoler himself, which followed?

'On one of the last days when he was in prison, the holy father Fray John called this witness, begged his forgiveness, and, in gratitude for the tasks which he had done for him, offered him a crucifix, which had been given him by a certain person,[1] and, over and above its intrinsic worth, was of value for having belonged to that person. It was a cross of exquisite wood, and carved in relief on it were the instruments of the Passion of Christ our Lord, and the figure of Christ crucified nailed to it was in bronze. This saint was accustomed to wear it beneath his scapular, over his heart; and this witness received this gift from him, which he still has and keeps.'[2]

At least, surely, this must have told the young friar to what use John had put his scissors and thread, and his daily outings. The last act should have been equally revealing. The blankets were now strips sewn together, as the gaoler, when bringing the prisoner his supper, apparently failed to notice. According to one account, he had forgotten the water, and, while he went to get it, John loosened the bolts, which, when he locked him in for the night, he also failed to notice.[3] Another, written by a nun with charming naïveté, says that, 'when they bolted (the door), God inspired him to insert his finger, and thus it was not secured'.[4] Whichever version we adopt, the rest was easy. The prisoner (and the gaoler) had forgotten no detail: John had even begged a lamp (the cell having previously been unlit),[5] the hook of which he needed for attaching his rope to the window-sill. He was able to choose a night when, as some guests were sleeping in the room into which his cell opened, the door leading from that cell into the corridor had not been closed, because of the heat.[6] Taking off his habit, and throwing it down, he lowered himself slowly, 'clinging to the rope with his hands and both knees'[7]—no brief description could be more vivid —and, coming to the end of it, dropped the remaining five feet on

---

[1] Saint Teresa.   [2] *Vida*, p. 188, n. 86.   [3] *Vida*, p. 190, n. 94.
[4] P. Silverio, *Obras, etc.*, IV, 364; *CWSJX*, III, 342.
[5] Baruzi (p. 187, n. 8) quotes two MS. sources which imply that he had no artificial light at all, and one which says that 'sometimes (*alguna vez*) they would give him a small lamp (*candil*) by which to read his Hours'.
[6] *HCD*, V, 126–7, puts this point well; cf. *Vida*, pp. 190–1.
[7] *Vida*, p. 192.

to the city wall. Shaken by the drop and exhausted by the efforts he had made, he crawled along the wall and made his way down into an enclosed courtyard. He knew where he was now. That kindly gaoler had been describing the lie of the land to him (why, if not to help him to escape?). A contemporary account makes the position clear:

'He started to go round the courtyard and see if there were any way of getting out into the street, but found that the walls were very high and the door was closed. The religious in whose care he had been had told him that there was a convent near the priory (where he had been imprisoned). He remembered that, and said to himself: "Supposing this should be the courtyard of that convent!" He looked again more carefully and found that it was.'[1]

The documents graphically describe his feelings. It would never do for him to be discovered at dawn in a courtyard two of whose sides were formed by the walls of the priory and the convent. If the nuns found him, they would hand him over to the friars; if he got into the friars' hands again 'he was afraid they would kill him'. He thought of 'crying out to the friars and begging them to have pity on him and take him back'. He even 'tried to get back by the way he had come, but, try as he would, he could not'.[2] Then, in one corner of the wall, he saw some gaps which might serve him as footholds. Clambering slowly up, and dropping down again, he found himself at last in the street.

Thus run the accounts given by religious most of whom had heard them from his own lips. They agree almost exactly; they constantly use such phrases as 'he told me', 'we heard him say'; and, if we allow that Saint John of the Cross, after so many privations, had exceptional powers of endurance, we shall find them quite convincing. They quote him as saying that he got over that wall by means of the holes in it, 'without knowing how', and that 'it seemed to him' (as well it might) 'a miracle'.[3] The hagiographers, however, tell another story. A typical one leaves nothing to be desired in glamour:

'A very beautiful light was sent to him, surrounded by a resplendent cloud, emitting rays of the sweetest brightness (*de suavísima claridad*). It might have been a column of fire or a cloud of light. . . . As he stood before it, he heard a voice proceeding from

---

[1] *Vida*, p. 193, n. 103.   [2] *Vida*, p. 193, nn. 105–6.   [3] *Vida*, p. 194, n. 107.

it, saying "Follow me". Strengthened by this Divine inspiration and protection, he went after the light and followed it as far as the wall . . . and there the light disappeared'.[1]

Let our most modern hagiographer's version of another document complete the story:

'The wall was very high. He leant against it, his courage gone, when he was suddenly *taken up and lifted over the wall*. When he found himself in the little street the light had disappeared, leaving him in a dazzled condition, which, he says, lasted for two or three days.'[2]

[v]

Having got the little Saint over the wall, whether by means of footholes or of supernatural propulsion, we almost lose sight of him till he reaches his desired haven—Saint Teresa's own convent: doubly hers, for she had founded it nine years previously and had selected it for her retirement in 1576 when the General had told her to retire to a convent of her choice in Castile and make no more foundations. We get one fleeting glimpse of him, crossing the Plaza de Zocodover, where the market-women, half-dozing beneath the dim lights of their stalls, as they waited for early custom, hurled uncomplimentary epithets at the ragged, cowlless little figure till they lost sight of him.[3] Then we catch sight of him stopping at an open door where a torch is burning, and asking leave to come into the vestibule and rest there till morning. They let him in and he stays till eight, when the streets are busy, and he can easily find his way to the convent unnoticed. The scenes there on his arrival are described in contemporary documents with the greatest fullness, but these have already been reproduced, and, as they raise no problem, may be passed over. Staying in the convent all day, he left that evening, disguised as a secular priest, for the home of one of the Cathedral canons and a good friend of the Reform, Don Pedro González de Mendoza.[4] The inevitable physical reaction followed. Nearly eight weeks later, when he set out to

[1] Jerónimo de San José. In *Vida*, p. 194, n. 108.

[2] P. Bruno, p. 183, from José de Jesús María (Quiroga), to which P. Crisógono gives a reference only, evidently thinking it not worth quoting. The italics in the quotation are mine.

[3] *Vida*, p. 194, nn. 110, 111.

[4] Not to be confused with a Bishop of Salamanca of the same name, who had died in 1574.

attend a Chapter-General at Almodóvar, the Canon refused to let him go alone and sent two of his servants with him. And Teresa was troubled at his going at all. 'I have been dreadfully distressed to hear what a time Fray John has gone through', she wrote, 'and how they have allowed him to go down there so soon, ill as he is. Please God he may not be taken from us by death. . . . You will have few left like him, if he dies.'[1]

In the same letter she expressed the hope that he would go no farther than Almodóvar, which is only a few miles south of Ciudad Real. But although, with characteristic womanly insistence, she begged Gracián ('as a favour to me') to 'see that he is looked after . . . and not allowed to go on any farther' ('Don't neglect to tell them about it, and see it is not forgotten'),[2] no notice was taken of her requests, and, in any case, Gracián, for some unknown reason, seems not to have attended the Chapter at all.[3] We need not suppose that the friars were anything but sympathetic with his condition: one manuscript describes how they told off a certain Pedro de Jesús to attend to his physical needs, and another asserts that their object in sending him as Vicar to El Calvario, near Beas, was to eliminate any risk of his being kidnapped once again.[4] He was still accompanied by Don Pedro's servants when he started for the south. Only at Beas did they leave him, when he decided to spend 'a few days' at the convent of the Reform before completing his journey.[5]

Years afterwards, the Beas nuns could testify to the Saint's lamentable state of health when he reached them: he was 'weak

---

[1] *LL* 247.

[2] *Ibid.* P. Silverio's dating of this letter seems to me more accurate than P. Crisógono's. Saint Teresa does not say, as the latter asserts, that Saint John had arrived, and if she did not write till the Chapter was beginning, she could hardly have expected her letter to have any effect.

[3] Cf. *LL* 253 (616, n. 3); *Vida*, p. 202, n. 2.

[4] P. Crisógono (*Vida*, pp. 208–9, n. 24) discusses in detail a visit made by Saint John of the Cross to Medina del Campo, which has puzzled biographers, believing that it occurred after the first abduction of 1576 (when he was actually imprisoned at Medina), and not after the second. The only difficulty about this inference is that each of the testimonies quoted says that he was accompanied by Fray Germán de San Matías, who had been imprisoned with him, and as far as we know, Germán was seized with him only on the second occasion. On the other hand, they were not imprisoned together in 1577–8, and there is no proof that they were not both abducted on each occasion. On the whole, I think P. Crisógono's theory is the best.

[5] *SF*, pp. 50–1.

and weary'; 'terribly weak', 'like a dead man, with nothing but skin on his bones, so exhausted that he could hardly speak'.[1] But at Beas, in the congenial companionship of M. Ana de Jesús and her spiritually-minded nuns, he found both spiritual employment and spiritual relaxation. And it was 'a milestone' in his life, 'as well as a resting-place';[2] for it was here, apparently, that he first began to write down expository comments on his verses. On his converse with the Beas nuns, both during his stay and when he went over periodically from El Calvario to hear their confessions,[3] nothing new of great importance remains to be said. His duties at El Calvario lasted for about seven months, during which time he began writing his commentaries on the poems in earnest. In June 1579 he founded a college of the Reform at Baeza,[4] and remained there for about three years, though for the latter part of that period he also held the office of Prior at Los Mártires, Granada. On these years P. Crisógono gives a mass of detail, some of it descriptive, some anecdotal, but little, if anything, which adds clearness or sharpness to the outline we already have.[5]

[VI]

The next stage in the life of Saint John of the Cross begins soon after the separation of the Discalced from the Observance (22nd June 1580). At the first Discalced Chapter (3rd March 1581) properly so called (the two Almodóvar Chapters having been illegal), he was given his first administrative Office in the Reform, that of Third Definitor, and, for some ten years, he held such offices almost continuously. P. Crisógono, in describing these years, very wisely goes into detail concerning the history of the Discalced province, for, without a knowledge of this, much that happened is inexplicable. To those who read no Spanish, my *Handbook of the Life and Times of Saint Teresa and Saint John of the Cross* should serve somewhat the same purpose.

The most noteworthy event which occurred during Saint John of the Cross's first year of office was a visit which he made to Ávila, under an order from Diego de la Trinidad, whom Gracián, now Provincial, had made his Vicar in Andalusia, to attempt to bring

---

[1] *Vida*, p. 211, n. 30. [2] *SF*, p. 51. [3] *SF*, p. 52. [4] *SF*, p. 59.

[5] There are conflicting opinions on the numbers, and the names, of the friars whom St. John of the Cross took with him to make the Baeza foundation. P. Crisógono (*Vida*, pp. 235–7) carries the discussion a little farther.

Saint Teresa south to make a foundation in the important city of Granada. The visit was made very expeditiously—though less so than we might gather from P. Silverio, who inclines to put his arrival on November 28th,[1] and his departure, with the nuns whom Saint Teresa, unable to go herself, sent by him, on the next morning. P. Crisógono points out that, before the nuns could be sent, permission would have to be obtained from Gracián, then in Salamanca, which could hardly have taken less than three days, and presumably some preliminary conversations had been necessary before it was decided whom to send.[2] Still, as John's final conversation with Teresa was held on November 28th, and the order authorizing his visit had been signed, in Andalusia, only fifteen days earlier, no time had been lost in carrying the order out. The visit must indeed have been a memorable one, for John had not seen Teresa since before his abduction, close on four years before, and he was never to see her again.

Precisely when Saint John took up residence at Los Mártires is not certain. Though he was appointed at the Alcalá Chapter of 1581, two documents give the date of his election by the community, one as 1582, and one as March 1582,[3] so that, when he arrived at Granada with the nuns on 20th January 1582,[4] it is probable that this was his first appearance there. On the other hand, P. Juan Evangelista, Saint John of the Cross's very close companion, says definitely that he had been Prior for eighteen months when he (P. Juan) took the habit at Christmas 1582, which would antedate his election to June 1581.[5] Yet there is no documentary evidence that he was in Granada before January 1582, and Diego de la Trinidad's order of 13th November 1581 describes him as Rector of Baeza. It looks, therefore, as if he was elected by the community in March 1582 (or, less probably, elected in June 1581, and confirmed, after his arrival, in March 1582), his engagements having prevented his entering into residence earlier. As the new Alcalá constitutions ruled that superiors should remain in office for three years but might be elected to another house at any time after the first two years, there is no inconsistency between this hypothesis and his retaining the rectorship at Baeza till June 1582.

Detail regarding the years spent at Los Mártires is particularly abundant, and for two reasons. First, he resided there for a con-

---

[1] *HCD*, IV, 647, n. [2] *Vida*, p. 284, n. 35. [3] *HCD*, V, 219. [4] *SF*, p. 64.
[5] *Vida*, pp. 290-1, n. 4. But P. Crisógono, in putting forward this evidence, himself underlines P. Juan's vagueness in the matter of dates.

siderable time—as Prior till 1584, and again from 1587, on his reappointment by the Chapter of Valladolid, and at other times intermittently. Secondly, when the depositions for the beatification process were taken (1614–18), there were still many living who had known him at Los Mártires. So P. Crisógono has no difficulty in bringing out of his documentary treasure-house things new and old. Some of the simplest and most attractive anecdotes are concerned with the friars' contact with nature. As at El Calvario, Saint John of the Cross took the community a great deal into the country, either for pure recreation or in order to teach them. But at Granada, with its magnificent panoramas of the Sierra Nevada, of which one of the finest could be seen only a few hundred yards above Los Mártires, there was scenery less intimate, but more impressive, than he had found anywhere else. And he made use of it to the full. 'A friar once asked him why he was so much in the habit of taking them out into the country. And he replied that it was because, if they stayed indoors, they would always be wanting to go out.'[1] That, no doubt, was the truth, but hardly the whole truth. Its complement is indicated by the story of how he took the community some way up the slopes of the Sierra Nevada, and then sent them off each in a different direction with instructions to spend the time in prayer.

[VII]

It was the Chapter of Almodóvar, which opened on 1st May 1583, that first disclosed the rift which was later to develop into a complete split between Saint John of the Cross and the policy associated with the name of Nicolás Doria. Most of the Saint's biographers have made it clear that he had to suffer two periods of persecution—the first, which culminated in the abduction and the Toledo imprisonment, from the friars of the Observance; the second, from his own Discalced brethren. The motive for the first has in the past been made clear enough, but not always the motive for the second.

Briefly, John was an idealist, if, in the main, a practical one; Doria, who, until his middle thirties, had been a successful banker, was an organizer and a man of the world. Gracián, too, was an idealist, and from the fundamental antipathy which existed between him and Doria arose the deplorable conflict which ended

[1] *Vida*, p. 307, n. 81.

with his expulsion from the Discalced Reform. John by no means always agreed with Gracián: at this very Chapter, for example, he opposed the extension of the Reform, which was essentially contemplative, to countries which he considered unprepared for it,[1] whereas Gracián eagerly sponsored attempts made to implant the Reform in darkest Africa. Still, in the main, John and Gracián thought alike and John's disgrace was followed closely by Gracián's dismissal.

At the Almodóvar Chapter, John deprecated two measures, both of which were carried against him: one, the inauguration of missionary work; the other, the eligibility of priors for re-election.[2] He may have been right on the first point, but he was surely over-idealistic as to the second. A young movement cannot at first avoid overworking its few outstanding men and there were not many friars suitable for being given authority.

Though Saint John of the Cross spoke (as apparently he generally did on these occasions) 'with great energy and animation'[3]— even more so than usual[4]—his double defeat seems to have aroused less attention than the violent attack—the first of many— made by Doria on Gracián for his allegedly bad government. In this duel Saint John is not recorded as having taken any active part, and, the Chapter ended, he returned to Granada, having been confirmed in his office for a further term. For two years he lived peaceably, finishing his *Ascent of Mount Carmel* and 'Spiritual Canticle', which he had begun at El Calvario, and composing the *Living Flame of Love*.[5] At the Lisbon-Pastrana Chapter of 1585, which chose Doria to succeed Gracián as Provincial,[6] and at which, according to one authority, Saint John of the Cross again opposed the re-election of superiors,[7] he was elected Second Definitor and Vicar-Provincial for Andalusia. Received by the Andalusian houses, as the chronicler says, with 'general applause',[8] he began a period of visitations which, with the making of five new founda-

---

[1] This we know both from the Saint's biographer, P. Jerónimo de San José, and from the historian of the Reform, P. Francisco de Santa María. *HCD*, V, 257–8, reproduces the testimony of these authors and attempts to estimate its reliability. *Vida*, p. 316, n. 124, is frankly sceptical about P. Jerónimo's account of the debate, and it is clear that P. Francisco was following him.

[2] Cf. *HCD*, V, 254, n. 1.

[3] A contemporary testimony: *Vida*, p. 315, n. 120.

[4] That is, if we can trust P. Jerónimo and P. Francisco (*HCD*, V, 260–1 and 260, n. 1).

[5] *SF*, pp. 68–70.   [6] *SF*, p. 71.   [7] *HCD*, V, 449.   [8] *Vida*, p. 364, n. 25.

tions, occupied him for more than two years of his vicariate. But, amid the general applause, it would appear, could be heard some murmurings. In the Seville house were two precocious young friars—Diego Evangelista and Francisco Crisóstomo—much sought after and continually leaving their priory to fulfil invitations to preach. Diego, who had made his profession at sixteen, was only twenty-five; Francisco was probably not much older. Saint John reminded them that the Order was a contemplative one, and recommended them to spend more time in the priory in accordance with the spirit of the Reform. In their defence it must be said that Gracián, their late Provincial, also fancied himself in the pulpit, and had not set too good an example.[1] But they appear to have developed a resentment against their Vicar-Provincial which neither the substance nor the manner of his correction justified.[2] And the enmity which he had unwittingly sown in their hearts was to bear fruit all too soon.

A meeting of the Definitory, in Madrid, called by Doria in 1586 to suggest some minor changes in organization, showed the new Provincial that he could impose his will even on a dissenting majority, and, fortified by this knowledge, he now began to plan large-scale reorganization. None of it was ready for the Chapter of 1587, held at Valladolid in April of that year, and, except for one contentious proposal which aroused considerable excitement, the business transacted there went hardly beyond routine. No significance probably attaches to the fact that while again re-elected Prior of Los Mártires (against his will and against his principles) he was not re-elected Definitor or Vicar-Provincial, for at the Madrid Chapter of 1588 he was again given high office.[3] This Chapter was in reality a Chapter-General. In the preceding July, Doria had achieved the first stage of his ambitions for the Reform by obtaining from the Pope a new constitution making it a Congregation, under a Vicar-General elected by itself for a six-year term, who would be subject only to the General of the entire Order, and introducing a new system of centralized government. This was to be carried out by a tribunal called the Consulta, consisting of the Vicar-General and six elected *consiliarios*, but the Vicar-General was to be authorized, on occasion, to act alone, which was what Doria, obviously cast for that role, wanted.

Before summoning the Chapter-General, which duly elected

[1] Cf. here *Vida*, p. 365, n. 26.
[2] Cf. the testimony reported in *Vida*, p. 400, n. 30.　　　　[3] *SF*, p. 73.

him to the desired office, though by only 32 votes out of 50, Doria had begun his campaign against Gracián, and persuaded his Definitors (of whom John, it will be remembered, was not one) to impose severe penalties upon him and deprive him of active and passive voice at the next two Chapters-General. This done, Doria saw his way clear for action, and it is significant, and may also be thought surprising, that Saint John of the Cross should have been elected a *consiliario*, First Definitor, and Deputy Vicar-General. Normally this would have seemed perfectly natural, since John was one of the first two friars of the Reform and had also had long experience of government. But, in the special circumstances, what did it mean? The election would hardly have been made against Doria's will, or, indeed, without his definite approval. Did he expect that John would take his side against Gracián, or did he believe that, during the time John was out of office, Gracián had to all intents been successfully disposed of and need not be taken into account any more? The latter theory seems the more probable: in that case it would be understandable that Doria should want John, almost certainly his ablest colleague,[1] to hold the senior position under the new régime, and to act as his personal deputy.

That, at any rate, was what happened, and, from the conventional standpoint, the years 1588–90 marked John's highest point of success. It was decided to establish the Consulta's headquarters at Segovia, and John, who had been instrumental in founding a priory there in May 1586, was transferred from Los Mártires as Prior of Segovia, and, during Doria's frequent absences on visitations, took his place.

For nearly three years all went well. True, there was much unrest in the Reform: Doria's visitations were often unpopular; Gracián did his utmost both to vindicate himself and to decry the new organization; the nuns of the Congregation were dissatisfied with its policy, and later, under M. Ana de Jesús, actively opposed Doria's plans. John did what he could to carry out his superior's wishes and also to placate the nuns, who, to a woman, were his devoted adherents. But he must have found his position very difficult, especially when the nuns petitioned the Pope to appoint him

---

[1] As I read the characters of these friars, the only man of comparable ability, other than Doria and Gracián, was Roca and he, besides being over-inflexible in his methods, had neither John's seniority nor his experience.

their Commissary. No information exists concerning the relations between John and Doria during the years 1590–1, but we may be sure that, when a Chapter-General was called for June 1591 and John prophesied to the Segovian Prioress that it would 'throw him into a corner, like an old rag', he had good reasons, other than supernatural revelations, for his apprehensions.[1]

If not earlier, the situation had certainly become tense by June 1590, the date of a Chapter-General extraordinary, at which John was re-elected a *consiliario* and a Definitor.[2] Doria, greatly exasperated with the attitude of the nuns, had proposed to the Chapter that they should be thrown over altogether. John spoke up for them, and no doubt angered Doria as much as he impressed the assembly. The Vicar-General had learned that Gracián, from the distant Lisbon priory to which he had been sent, had been intervening in the nuns' favour and no doubt he thought that their proposal about the Commissary had originated in the mind of John himself, or in the minds of John and Gracián together. Even more serious than this was the conflict between John and Doria over Gracián. As we have seen, John did not approve and could not have approved all the acts of his late Provincial, but he deplored the animus being shown against him and the tendency which was developing to wash this particular piece of linen in public.[3] Not only did he strongly deprecate this, but he went so far as to absent himself from a meeting of the Definitors at which the matter was to be discussed. One of the letters which he wrote to Doria about it, reports Fray Juan Evangelista, 'was such that, when he read it to me, I urged him strongly not to send it, as it would only give offence. But he would not agree, and told me that it was for God's glory, and also that, being a Definitor, he had an obligation in the matter.'[4]

The year that passed between the two Chapters, then, cannot have been a happy one, and, whatever Doria's outward behaviour to John, there can be little doubt that he went to the 1591 Chapter determined to get rid of him. Whether unexpectedly or not, he found two ready allies there. Who the first was, we cannot tell; the chronicler of the Chapter says only that he was a fellow-Definitor.[5] P. Crisógono thinks that it may have been Antonio de

[1] *Vida*, p. 416. Cf. *SF*, pp. 74–5.
[2] So the historians have it, but cf. the MS. testimony in *Vida*, p. 417, n. 4.
[3] *Vida*, p. 420, n. 12.   [4] *Vida*, p. 421, n. 14.
[5] *Vida*, p. 421, n. 16.

Jesús,[1] now an old man of eighty-one, full of grievances, or the fiery Ambrosio Mariano: but he only suggests these because nothing whatever is known of Saint John's relations with the other three.[2] Actually the chronicler gives no evidence of animosity or rancour, merely remarking that, 'during exchanges of opinion he had several passages at arms (*dares y tomares*) with one of the Definitors'.[3] Still, his opponent would no doubt be ready to ally himself with Doria, and with the Saint's other opponent, Diego Evangelista. That rancorous young friar, who in the preceding year had been made Vicar of a newly founded priory, was appointed a Definitor and a *consiliario* at this Chapter. John was not re-elected to either post. According to the chronicler just quoted, he was dropped principally because a friar without any office could not conceivably be appointed Commissary to the nuns,[4] and it was this development, which might have split the Congregation, that Doria was particularly anxious to avoid. John, in no way abashed by being passed over, made numerous contributions to the debates which, as he spoke with his accustomed energy,[5] would, from a worldly point of view, have done him only harm. He protested against the growing tendency of the Dorian régime to multiply rules. He defended the nuns. He stated the case for Gracián. Some supported him, but the majority were for Doria, and his arguments were of no effect.

One can imagine how, within Doria's active brain, plans were forming, even during the discussions, for getting this contumacious friar quickly and permanently out of the way. John had no objection whatever to being got out of the way: he was even willing to take a hand in the process. A Discalced Carmelite province had recently been formed in Mexico and the Fathers there had petitioned the Consulta for twelve more friars. Without waiting to be asked, he offered to be one of them. Doria must have been delighted: how much easier, he may have thought, to run a religious Order than to run a business—for in the business world one's enemies are not given to such ready self-liquidation. The patent

---

[1] Ana de Peñalosa had warned the Saint that same summer against over-intimacy with Antonio (see *CWSJX*, 2nd ed., Letter 28).

[2] Luis de San Jerónimo, Juan Bautista *el Andaluz*, and Gregorio de San Ángelo.

[3] *Vida*, p. 421, n. 16.

[4] *Vida*, p. 422, n. 18.

[5] *De la manera que siempre*. This detail comes from the historian of the Reform (*Vida*, p. 423, n. 23).

recording Fray John's offer and its acceptance can still be read.[1] However, shortly after the Chapter ended, a papal Brief was received which ruled out the appointment of a Commissary to the nuns altogether. So Mexico was forgotten, and Doria even offered to reinstate John as Superior at Segovia. But John, not without fears that he would be compelled to go, refused.[2] He was thereupon sent to Andalusia. 'God has been very gracious to me', he remarked. 'I shall now be able to attend exclusively to my soul.'[3]

[VIII]

Nothing had any power to touch him now; he had peace where he lived.[4] Had it not been so, he would have been appalled at his enemies' machinations. Doria, an organizer with no time for indulging private grudges, had lost interest in one who could do him no more harm. Not so the 'imprudent and choleric youth (*mozo*)'[5] Diego Evangelista. That his former superior should have been deprived of office was not enough for him. A trivial anecdote which has come down to us[6] shows that, even in little things, he was determined that he should suffer humiliation and pain. Before long he was engaged in large-scale defamation. Becoming intimate with Doria, he was sent by him to visit houses of the Reform and gather information to be used against Gracián, and he profited by this opportunity to collect and spread scandal against Saint John of the Cross, with a view, it seems clear, to bringing about his expulsion from the Congregation.[7] The lengths to which he went have already been fully described.[8] Concentrating on the convents, he elicited statements which he twisted into accusations, offering the nuns gifts, threatening them with excommunication and for-

---

[1] *Vida*, pp. 423–4.   [2] See *CWSJX*, Letter 21 (6th July 1591).

[3] *Vida*, p. 424, n. 27.

[4] Saint Teresa, *Interior Castle*, IV, i (*CWSTJ*, II, 235).

[5] A contemporary description, cit. *Vida*, p. 439, n. 81; *HCD*, V, 633, n. 1.

[6] *Vida*, p. 427, n. 33.

[7] P. Silverio (*Obras SJX*, IV, 291 n.) seems to suggest (for he is not as definite as P. Crisógono, *Vida*, p. 437, n. 72, implies) that Diego's campaign did not begin till after Saint John of the Cross went to Úbeda, late in September 1591. As elsewhere, however, he describes it as beginning a month after his going to La Peñuela (*HCD*, V, 627), this must be a slip. There is abundant documentary evidence for its being placed in the La Peñuela period.

[8] See, e.g., P. Bruno, pp. 334–5. P. Silverio (*HCD*, V, 627–47) and P. Crisógono (*Vida*, pp. 437–41) are fuller, but add little that is more damning; and the very brevity of P. Bruno's narrative adds to its effect.

bidding them to consult their confessors. By one means and another he obtained the most fantastic admissions, which seem too childish to merit credence.[1]

Doria's part in all this has come in for much merited criticism.[2] Being a hard-headed man of the world, and a good judge of character, he cannot conceivably have believed these stories. He could be sharp enough on occasion: why did he not administer a sharp rebuke to his malevolent Definitor and bring the campaign to an end? That he was gravely culpable all commentators agree: the only question in doubt is whether or no he gave his tacit approval to this perversion of justice, or even initiated it. P. Silverio, though unwilling to make so serious a charge without conclusive evidence, admits that, on any other hypothesis, 'it seems next to impossible' that Diego should have acted as he did.[3] We know that, during Diego's visitations, the Vicar-General was constantly receiving written reports and complaints, some of which are still in existence. When he received Diego's memorandum containing the sum total of the allegations, he is said to have remarked mildly that the Visitor had somewhat exceeded his functions.[4] But he kept the memorandum, which remained in the archives of the Reform until in 1594, the year in which both Doria and Diego met with their untimely deaths, the newly elected General, P. Elías de San Martín, had it burned in his presence.[5]

The last person, however, who seemed to be troubling himself about either the Vicar-General or his Visitor was their saintly victim. There are few signs that he was not completely impervious to the slanders. To rumours of his forthcoming expulsion his answer came pat:

'They cannot take the habit from me save for incorrigibility or disobedience, and I am quite prepared to amend my ways in all wherein I have strayed, and to be obedient, whatever the penance they give me.'[6]

'God allows this', he wrote to the Prioress of Caravaca, 'for the glory of His elect. In silence and hope will be our strength.'[7] He was urged to make a formal complaint to Doria, but he would not. For he was at peace. He had been allowed by Doria, and by Antonio de Jesús, now the Andalusian Vicar-Provincial, to go to

[1] E.g., *Vida*, p. 439, n. 84.   [2] *SF*, pp. 76–7.   [3] *HCD*, V, 648.
[4] *Vida*, p. 441, n. 90.   [5] *Vida*, p. 441, n. 91.
[6] *CWSJX*, 2nd ed., Letter 27.   [7] *CWSJX*, 2nd ed., Letter 25.

whatever part of Andalusia he liked. He chose the most solitary of the priories of the Reform, built on a wooded and heath-clad spur of the Sierra Morena, formerly the site of a remote hermitage, La Peñuela. 'I get on better among the stones', he said, 'than with men.'[1]

A letter which he wrote to Ana de Peñalosa nine days after his arrival there, rediscovered and published only in 1950,[2] complements the picture which the biographies give of his life there with some vivid detail, furnishing a revealing insight into his state of mind. Immediately on his arrival, he had written putting himself at the disposal of the Vicar-Provincial, who was at Baeza;[3] and, when he wrote to Doña Ana, had evidently just received a reply saying that before long he would probably be moved. However he remarked, almost light-heartedly, he found himself very well, and no news was good news; meanwhile 'the desert is an admirable training-ground'.

'The vastness of the desert is a great help both to the soul and to the body, though my soul is in a very poor way. It must be the Lord's will that the soul also should have its spiritual desert: let whatever best pleases Him be very welcome, for His Majesty well knows what we are of ourselves.'

Then he goes on to describe how he has spent the morning, with the rest of the community, in gathering chick-peas, which some other day will have to be shelled.[4] And he adds a curious remark: 'It is pleasant to handle these inanimate creatures—pleasanter than being handled by living creatures ourselves.' Evidently the manhandling he had received at the Madrid Chapter had left some bruises.[5]

---

[1] *Vida*, p. 429, n. 39. Cf. *SF*, pp. 76–7. *HCD*, V, 657, n. 2, suggests another reason for his choice of La Peñuela which seems to me not very likely.

[2] It is included in the second edition of *CWSJX* as Letter 24.

[3] The gist of the correspondence, from a MS. source, is given in *Vida*, p. 431, n. 48. The original letters have not survived.

[4] Rocky and desolate though the country was, P. Crisógono (*Vida*, p. 432, n. 51) shows from contemporary testimony that the friars had made it yield a good deal: at this time there was a large vineyard, an olive-grove and fifty acres of corn. They must have sold most of this produce.

[5] Either from La Peñuela or from Úbeda he wrote to P. Juan Evangelista, begging for his prayers and making his own the Biblical phrase, *Filii matris meae pugnaverunt contra me*.

Since this and the previous section aim, not at giving a full description of Saint John's last days, but at tracing the causes, and the course, of what may be termed the 'second persecution', little need be added to the well-known outline of the final stages of the Saint's life.

When, after some six months at La Peñuela, he fell seriously ill, and, refusing to be taken to Baeza, where he had numerous friends, chose to go for treatment to Úbeda,[1] he must have known, or at least guessed, that he was submitting himself to still one more series of humiliations. To judge from another letter which he wrote to Ana de Peñalosa, he thought lightly of this 'slight bout of fever'.

'If it does not go I think I shall need medical aid; but I go with the intention of returning again, for in truth I am deriving great good from this holy retreat.'[2]

But he presumably knew that the Prior at Úbeda was Diego Evangelista's companion, Francisco Crisóstomo, passionate of temper and *rigidísimo*[3] in government, and he would not have been surprised when he met with a scowling welcome. The documents are eloquent of the treatment which he received there:

'The cell where he died was the smallest and poorest in the priory, with nothing in it but a poor bed and a crucifix.

'Ill as he was, the Prior made him accompany the community, and, one day, when he excused himself from going to the refectory, the said Prior sent for him and gave him a stern rebuke.'[4]

The accounts of his sufferings, aggravated now by erysipelas, are excruciating even to read. Hardly less intolerable to the sufferer would have seemed the Prior's behaviour. When the sick man could no longer leave his bed, he would come and taunt him, denying him other visitors, and depriving him of nourishing food on the pretext of expense. Hearing of his unhappy plight, the friars at La Peñuela sent him provisions; their Prior, indeed, came over himself to see him. At last, one of the Úbeda friars, forbidden by the Prior to render him services, wrote the Vicar-Provincial a full

---

[1] *SF*, p. 78.

[2] *CWSJX*, 2nd ed., Letter 28. He said, writing on September 21, that he was leaving on the next day, but he did not, in fact (*Vida*, p. 445, n. 1), set out until a week later (September 28).

[3] *Vida*, p. 449, n. 17.   [4] *Vida*, pp. 449–50, nn. 21–3.

account of what was happening. Antonio might not always, in the past, have been a faultless companion, but he was too large-hearted a man to think of grudges at a time like this, and, despite his eighty-one years, he came over post-haste to see that John was made as comfortable as could be.[1] It is pleasant to record that Francisco, unlike Diego, repented of his harshness, coming, on the last day of the Saint's life, and apologizing (with a typically Spanish face-saving excuse) for having neglected him 'because the house was so poor'.[2] The Saint's gentle and generous answer quite broke him down and during the few hours that remained he was constantly seen kneeling at the dying man's bedside.

(ii) POEMS

[IX]

In the year 1830, the poet and critic Quintana remarked that Saint John of the Cross's poems were 'far outside the range of literary criticism'.[3] A generation later, a French critic described him as 'caring nothing for literary beauty . . . never suspecting that . . . one can write poetry for poetry's sake. He speaks in verse as the bird sings, as the heart prays.'[4]

So far has criticism reacted from this imperfect and erroneous conception of Saint John of the Cross that he is now acknowledged to be one of the greatest artists in the history of Spanish poetry. And, since the publication of P. Crisógono's biography, further progress has been made in the study of his technique, notably through the discovery of two secular poems on the basis of which he composed verses *a lo divino*. Such adaptations were, of course, quite common. We know that Saint John of the Cross was acquainted with Sebastián de Córdoba's allegorizations of Boscán and Garcilaso de la Vega,[5] and in my *Complete Works of Saint*

---

[1] *SF*, p. 79. He arrived on November 27, the eve of the anniversary of the foundation of Duruelo, reminding the sick man of what had happened twenty-four years before. P. Crisógono (p. 464, n. 87) corrects this and says it was the twenty-seventh anniversary. He, too, is wrong: it was the twenty-third.

[2] Vida, p. 469, n. 107.

[3] *Poesías selectas castellanas* (Madrid, 1830), Vol. I, p. 269.

[4] P. Rousselot, *Les Mystiques espagnols* (Paris, 1867), pp. 382–3. Quoted more fully in my *Saint John of the Cross, etc.* (London, 1946), p. 37.

[5] Cf. p. 232, below.

Teresa of Jesus I cited two possible profane sources for one of her poems ('O Loveliness, that dost exceed . . .'), which is so unlike her usual manner as to make the existence of such an original almost certain. For some time Spanish critics have been searching in contemporary song-books and elsewhere for sources of the minor poems of Saint John of the Cross, and with marked success.

Already, in 1942, in a book entitled *La Poesía de San Juan de la Cruz*, on which I have already commented,[1] Don Dámaso Alonso had indicated the source of the 'ballad with a Divine meaning', the English translation of which begins:

> *For all the beauty man can gain*
> *Never my life away I'll fling,*
> *But rather for some other thing*
> *Which happy chance may well attain.*[2]

In 1580, eleven years before Saint John of the Cross's death, a minor poet named Pedro de Padilla published, in a kind of *Golden Treasury* (*Thesoro de varias poesías*), a ballad similar to this in construction, and based upon four lines which, except that for 'all the beauty' it has 'the sole beauty', are absolutely identical with those just quoted. The *Treasury*, if its gold was by no means pure, merited praise from Cervantes, five years after its publication, in his *Galatea*, and, twenty years later, turns up in Don Quixote's library, where the Curate comments unfavourably upon its bulk.[3] Padilla's poem (which may not have been composed by himself)[4] relates entirely to human love, though it has less of passion than of edification, its burden being that a woman, however beautiful to look upon, needs 'some other thing' (*un no sé qué*: the French *je ne sais quoi*) to complete her perfection. The fact that, shortly after publishing his *Treasury*, Padilla became a Carmelite, and published an entire *Spiritual Garden* of poems *a lo divino*, forms an additional link between him and Saint John of the Cross.

A poem for which, in 1942, Sr. Alonso suspected a secular original is the very striking one built on the quatrain:

[1] See *Saint John of the Cross, etc.*, pp. 50–3. I abbreviate, in footnotes, *DA*. The same author's *Poesía española* (Madrid, 1950) is referred to as *DAP*.

[2] Poems, XX, in P. Silverio's edition and in my translation.

[3] 'If there were not so many of them [the *varias poesías*]', said the curate, 'they would be more relished.' (*Don Quixote*, I, vi.)

[4] In any case, the opening quatrain is found elsewhere (*DAP*, p. 252, n. 34).

Upon love's chase I went my way,
Not void of hope, began to fly,
And soar'd aloft, so high, so high,
That in the end I reach'd my prey.[1]

The theme occurs in Gil Vicente, Juan del Encina and other Spanish poets, who treat it erotically, and, in 1944, Don Francisco López Estrada found in a collection dated 1562 a love-poem which came nearer to Saint John of the Cross than anything previously known.[2] But, as no source had been traced for the initial quatrain, Don Dámaso Alonso concluded, in 1942, that it was 'probably original.'[3] Then, one day, quite unexpectedly, in the National Library of Spain, he discovered a manuscript which showed that he had been wrong. Here, at the beginning of a secular love-poem, of unknown authorship, was, with but two slight changes, Saint John's own quatrain:

Upon love's chase I went my way,
All void of hope, began to fly,
And rose aloft, so high, so high,
That in the end I reach'd my prey.[4]

There can be no mistake about this. Saint John of the Cross took that quatrain, copied it, and glossed it *a lo divino*, almost certainly using for the purpose the poem from the 1562 collection referred to above, and possibly some other poems as well:

But the most remarkable discovery concerns the poem generally known as the 'Pastorcico':

A shepherd boy his grief is brooding o'er . . .[5]

This poem, of five stanzas, is a pastoral allegory of the Redemption. In modern times it has been greatly admired for its simplicity, its haunting air of melancholy and its bold adaptation of a conventional pastoral love-theme. It stands quite apart from all Saint John's other poems. Until 1949 it was believed to embody reminiscences of Garcilaso (through Córdoba), but in other respects to be original.[6] And then, as unexpectedly as Don Dámaso Alonso

[1] Poems, VI, in the editions cited above.

[2] Diego Ramírez Pagán, *Floresta de varia poesía* (Valencia, 1562). See Francisco López Estrada, in *Revista de Filología Española* (Madrid, 1944), XXVIII, 473-7.

[3] *DA*, p. 119.   [4] *DAP*, p. 254.   [5] Poems, VII, in the editions cited above.

[6] *DA*, pp. 55-60. M. de Montoliu (*Literatura Castellana* (Barcelona, 1930), pp. 348-9) vaguely relates the refrain of this poem with a phrase in Montemayor's *Diana*, but I do not take this very seriously. (Cf. *DA*, p. 256, n. 19.)

in Madrid, Don José Manuel Blecua, one of Spain's foremost
investigators in the field of Golden Age poetry, found a poem in a
late-sixteenth-century MS. belonging to the National Library
of France containing four stanzas, parts of which are almost
identical with those of Saint John of the Cross.[1] In translation,
the two poems read as follows:

A (Anonymous Author)

1. *A shepherd-boy his grief is brooding o'er,*
   Alone, uncomforted, disconsolate.
   His thought is firm upon his heart's true mate;
   His breast with love is stricken very sore.

2. *He weeps not that she thinks of him no more,*
   For mere neglect could ne'er affright him so,
   He weeps because, his heart brought very low,
   His breast with love is stricken very sore.

3. *Then cries the shepherd-boy, 'What woe's in store*
   For this true lover when his love's away,
   Whose heart is in her presence night and day,
   Whose breast with love is stricken very sore!'

4. *He thinks he'll see his shepherdess no more,*
   That fair one living in an alien land,
   And so he lays him down upon the sand;
   His breast with love is stricken very sore.

B (Saint John of the Cross)

1. *A shepherd-boy his grief is brooding o'er,*
   Alone, uncomforted, disconsolate.
   His thought is fix'd upon his heart's true mate;
   His breast with love is stricken very sore.

2. *He weeps not for some love-wound giv'n of yore,*
   For no such thing could pain and grieve him so,
   E'en though it overcharg'd his heart with woe:
   He weeps because she thinks of him no more.

3. *And so, because she thinks of him no more*
   —That shepherd-maid of his, so fair to see—
   He lets his alien foes treat cruelly
   That breast that love has stricken very sore.

[1] José Manuel Blecua, in *Revista de Filología Española* (Madrid, 1949),
XXXIII, 378–80.

4. '*Woe*,' *cries the shepherd-boy,* '*woe be in store*
   For him that's come betwixt my love and me,
   So that she wishes not to know or see
   This breast that love has stricken very sore.'

5. *Then climbs he slowly, when much time is o'er,*
   Into a tree, with fair arms wide outspread,
   And, clinging to that treee, forthwith is dead.
   For, lo! his breast was stricken very sore.

These translations give a good general idea of the degree of similarity between the two poems. A detailed comparison will be facilitated by more nearly exact prose versions of A and B, the readings of A being given in italics:

1 B. A little shepherd, alone, is grieved, far removed from pleasure and contentment, and his thought is fixed (A: *firm*) upon his shepherdess, and his breast sorely hurt with love.

2 B. He does not weep because love has wounded him, for it does not grieve him to see himself afflicted thus, though he is wounded in the heart; but he weeps because he thinks he is forgotten.

2 A. *He does not weep because he thinks he is forgotten, for he has no fear of forgetfulness, but because his heart is worn out* (rendido), *and his breast sorely hurt with love.*

3 B. For only from the thought that he is forgotten by his fair shepherdess, in (his) great grief he allows himself to be ill-treated in an alien land, his breast (being) sorely hurt with love.

3 A. *But, says the little shepherd*: '*Unhappy (am I). What shall I do when the evil of absence comes, since I have my heart in presence and my breast sorely hurt with love?*'

4 B. And, says the little shepherd: 'Ah, unhappy he who has made absence between (me and) my love, (so that she) does not wish to enjoy my presence and my breast is sorely hurt for love of her!'

4 A. *Now he imagines himself parted from his fair shepherdess in an alien land, and he remains stretched out on the sand,*[1] *and his breast (is) sorely hurt with love.*

5 B. And at the end of a long time he has climbed up into a tree, where he opened his fair arms, and has remained dead, clinging to them, his breast sorely hurt with love.

[1] No doubt the bank of a river is meant.

Impossible though it must always be to make an exact comparison between two poems on the basis of a translation of them, these prose renderings are, I think, sufficiently literal for our purpose. The first stanzas, except that A has the diminutive form *pastorcillo* and B *pastorcico*, are absolutely identical.[1] In the second stanza B takes the first line of A and substitutes it, with one change, for the refrain; the first and second lines of B are original, as is the third, except that it takes the word *corazón* ('heart') from the third line of A. The third stanza of B, taking from A only the refrain and two phrases (*bella pastora*, 'fair shepherdess', and *en tierra ajena*, ('in an alien land') from A's fourth stanza, atones for having discarded A's refrain in the second stanza by repeating the line it had substituted for it, and thus both pulling the poem together and emphasizing the idea which A had dismissed lightly, but which in B is an essential one. The fourth stanza of B copies the refrain of A and also takes from A the substance of the first line of its third stanza and, rather curiously, the rhyme-words of the first three lines of that stanza: *desdichado, ausencia, presencia*. The fifth stanza of B, apart from the refrain, has no connection with A. Don Dámaso Alonso thinks that it is an imitation ('it cannot be a coincidence', are his words) of a passage from Córdoba's adaptation of Garcilaso's Second Eclogue, which, translated literally, describes 'a shepherd, alone, raised up on that tree, with face and brow wounded and covered with thorns'.[2]

Sr. Blecua, having collated the two poems, makes only the briefest comment upon them,[3] and Sr. Alonso merely remarks that Saint John of the Cross 'has done no more than alter a few words and add the last stanza, which charges the entire poem with Divine meaning'.[4] I think, however, that he does much more than that, and a consideration of his treatment of his model may destroy one's initial regret that his 'Pastorcico' is not as original as one had supposed.

The chief merits of A are the attractiveness of its refrain, which comes out even in translation, and the air of gentle melancholy pervading the whole poem, which depends chiefly on an element unreproducible in English, the suave consonant-combinations of the original. Its content, however, reveals its inferiority. The love-

[1] The reading 'firm' (*firme*) for 'fixed' (*puesto*) is not an exception, as it is found in one of the MS. collections in which Saint John's poem occurs.

[2] *DA*, pp. 58–9. Cf. *DAP*, p. 256.

[3] *Revista de Filología Española* (1949), XXXIII, 380.   [4] *DAP*, p. 258.

stricken shepherd-boy weeps for his wounds, and for the state of his own heart, but not for his 'fair shepherdess's' forgetfulness. He dreads her approaching departure, and, imagining her already in a foreign land, flings himself on the ground and 'remains stretched out on the sand'—at which point the poem abruptly ends. A conventional situation, a psychological improbability and an unconvincing picture. There is no force behind the poem, no body in it—merely a typical pastoral unreality.

What does Saint John of the Cross do with this unsatisfactory model? Two things. He gives to unreality life and a sublime meaning; and he turns a pointless story into a five-act drama. Let us consider his drama an act—*i.e.*, a stanza—at a time.

1. *Christ's love for Humanity*. This stanza the Saint transcribes without alteration; we cannot doubt that it was this that first struck him by its effectiveness as an allegory. Christ's thought (runs the argument) is fixed upon the soul; His loving heart is sorely grieved.

2. *Christ's grief and its cause*. Why is He grieved? Here, so early in the poem, Saint John of the Cross has to part company with his model. The anonymous author attributes the shepherd's grief, not to the shepherdess's forgetfulness of him, but to his own condition. If the poem is to be an allegory of the Redemption, this will not do; the cause must be Humanity's neglect of God. So, sacrificing the refrain to the argument, Saint John of the Cross attributes Christ's grief, not to the wounds of love (for these, however deep they were, would not so afflict Him), but to Humanity's having forsaken Him.

3. *Christ comes to earth* . . . The next stage of the story can only be Christ's coming to a *tierra ajena* (cf. the 'strange land' of Psalm cxxxvii, 4, where He is ill-treated and still suffers and grieves. This stanza also has to be supplied by the adaptor.

4. . . . *Laments over Humanity* . . . The first line of the lament (which recalls Christ's lament over Jerusalem) follows the source very closely, but the second and third lines are original and introduce the third character in the drama.[1]

5. . . . *And dies on the Cross*. . . . This addition of a further stanza to the poem was of course imperative. The stanza, apart from the refrain, is, unless we adopt the theory of Dámaso Alonso, quite original. But I can see no reason for doing so. Saint John of the

[1] For the identity of this character cf. Poems, VII, n. 3, in *C.W.S.J.X.* 2nd ed. II, 430, and *Hispanic Review* (1952), XX 248–53

Cross had to describe the Crucifixion in terms of the shepherd-allegory. How else could he represent the Cross than as a tree? If the idea had not occurred to him independently—and it would seem obvious enough—it would surely have been suggested to him by Scripture, which has the figure in all its detail—the grief, the ill-treatment, even the shepherd and the sheep?

'Christ also suffered for us . . . Who, when He was reviled, reviled not again . . . Who His own Self bare our sins in His own body on the tree. . . . For ye were as sheep going astray, but are now returned unto the Shepherd and Bishop of your souls.'[1]

Contrast the closeness of the language of the 'Pastorcico' and that of this well-known passage with the disparity between it and the lines from Córdoba. Saint John of the Cross has neither the crown of thorns, nor the wounds in the face and brow, while neither the passing of time, nor the spreading wide of the 'fair arms', nor the clinging to the tree is found in Córdoba. I think there can be no doubt as to our conclusion.

[x]

This example of an alleged borrowing which, as I see it, is no borrowing at all, brings us to a very important theme connected with the literary aspect of Saint John of the Cross's work on which sufficient research has now been done to make possible at least tentative conclusions. This is the relation that may have existed between Saint John's poems and those of Boscán, Garcilaso de la Vega and the allegorized version of Boscán-Garcilaso made by Sebastián de Córdoba.

Discussion on this subject began after the publication by P. Gerardo de San Juan de la Cruz, C.D., in his edition—the earliest critical edition—of Saint John of the Cross's *Complete Works* (1912–14) of a note appended to the text of the poem 'Living Flame of Love' at the beginning of the commentary upon it. The poem is written in a metre resembling the *lira* (*i.e.*, the stanza of the 'Spiritual Canticle' and the 'Dark Night', introduced into Spanish by Garcilaso de la Vega), but containing six lines instead of five, and the note remarks that 'the arrangement of these *liras* resembles that of those which in Boscán are adapted in a spiritual

---

[1] 1 Saint Peter ii, 21, 23–5. For 'tree', see *Hispanic Review, art. cit.*, p. 253.

sense', quoting three lines of a Spanish poem in illustration of the fact, and continuing:

'In these (lines) there are six feet (*sic*), of which the fourth rhymes with the first, the fifth with the second and sixth with the third.'

The reference is not to the works of Boscán, but to an allegorical adaptation of the combined works of Boscán and Garcilaso de la Vega made by one Sebastián de Córdoba, of Úbeda, and first published at Granada in 1575. The three lines are also found in Córdoba. Strange to say, although this note occurs in six of the seven manuscripts of the first redaction of the *Living Flame* and in all five known manuscripts of the second redaction, it was excluded, no doubt from motives of piety, from all the editions, until it was unearthed and published by P. Gerardo.

Though, as early as 1881, Menéndez Pelayo had commented on Saint John of the Cross's use of a Garcilasan stanza, it seems to have been the discovery of this note which first aroused interest in the possibility that he might have drawn upon contemporary poetry. If he consciously made use of Garcilaso's *lira*, and later modified it through the influence of Córdoba, might he not have been indebted to Córdoba in other ways also? And, if to Córdoba, why not to Garcilaso, and to Boscán, directly? So, in 1924, Jean Baruzi, in his *Saint Jean de la Croix et le problème de l'expérience mystique*, hazarded very tentatively the opinion that we owe a few (some half-dozen, in fact) of Saint John of the Cross's well-known lines to Garcilaso–Córdoba, or even to Garcilaso's works in their original form. Five years later, the young Carmelite, P. Crisógono de Jesús Sacramentado, made an enthusiastic entry into the field[1] with several further discoveries, as well as with generalizations which are anything but tentative. Where Baruzi had written of his parallel quotations: 'On n'oserait voir . . . un modèle', 'On oserait encore moins rapprocher . . .', merely adding 'Et pourtant, nous entendons je ne sais quelles affinités musicales lointaines',[2] P. Crisógono takes one's critical breath away by observing not merely of some parallel in particular, but of the entire poem 'Living Flame of Love':

'The whole style of the stanzas of the "Living Flame", so full of

[1] *San Juan de la Cruz, su obra científica y su obra literaria* (Madrid, 1929). Cf. p. 198, above.

[2] Baruzi, *op. cit.*, pp. 120, 121.

232

exclamations, convinces us that its author took from Garcilaso not only the metre of his verses but also their air and manner of expression; sometimes even words and epithets. . . .'[1]

He even goes so far as to call one of the parallels which he notes a 'most lovely imitation' of Garcilaso.[2]

There, for some years, the matter rested, and no new parallels of any great significance were discovered until the publication of Don Dámaso Alonso's *La Poesía de San Juan de la Cruz.* To the value of this 'small book of notable quality' I have already paid tribute[3] and such criticisms of it as I shall now make will refer solely to the matter at present under discussion. Even here it was of great service; for it cited almost as many new parallels as those already known, as well as throwing fresh light on some of the latter. But any reader with experience in the elusive field of literary influences may well feel that, for so practised a critic, Sr. Alonso, in his deductions, goes unduly far. He talks, for example, of a 'dense background of Garcilasan imitation', of imitations perpetrated 'of set purpose', of 'absolute certainty' and of 'conclusions so clear-cut as to be almost mathematically exact'.[4] A few of his parallels are undoubtedly very close ones: it would be hard to believe that Saint John of the Cross's

> *El* aspirar *del aire,*
> el canto *de la* dulce Filomena

('The breathing of the air, the song of the sweet Philomel')[5]

did not derive from Garcilaso's

> . . . *el viento* espira,
> Filomena *sospira en* dulce canto

(' . . . the wind breathes, Philomel sighs in sweet song'),[6]

especially as the lines in Garcilaso are followed by a reference to the turtle-dove reminiscent of 'Spiritual Canticle', xxxiv, and then by two lines which contain all four of the chief words in 'Spiritual Canticle', iv, 3–4. Sr. Alonso, however, is, I think, unduly influenced by this and one or two other striking parallels. He claims that the strong links in his chain 'vitalize' the weak ones,[7] and,

---

[1] P. Crisógono, *op. cit.,* II, 26. [2] *Op. cit.,* II, 27.
[3] *Saint John of the Cross, etc.* (London, 1946), pp. 50–3.
[4] *DA,* pp. 44, 46, 45, 94. [5] 'Spiritual Canticle', xxxix, 1–2.
[6] Eclogue II, 1146–7.
[7] Cf. *Saint John of the Cross, etc.* (London, 1946), p. 52.

both in this book and in his later *Poesía española*, he conveys the impression that the matter is settled beyond dispute. Saint John of the Cross, he concludes, 'imitated' both Garcilaso and Córdoba: 'the majority (of the parallels adduced) *undoubtedly* proceed from direct contact'.[1]

So high, and deservedly so, is Sr. Alonso's reputation in Spain that reviewers of his two books unquestioningly accepted both his theory of vitalization and his implications of finality. 'After this book', wrote one such, 'it seems that there can be no more to say.'[2] But the writer was wrong. There was (and perhaps still is) a great deal more to say. The strong links in the chain are so few and the weak links so many that the entire evidence needs full and critical consideration. Elsewhere[3] I have examined it in detail and reached conclusions which can be summarized as follows.

Twenty-six parallels in all have been found between Saint John of the Cross on the one hand, and either Boscán or Garcilaso or Córdoba on the other. Of these I can describe only one (the Filomena passage just cited) as close enough to justify a verdict of possible conscious and direct influence. Six more may be described as possible, or occasionally probable, reminiscences. The other nineteen are weak cases of reminiscence, four of which are not supported, or are even apologized for, by the very critics who adduce them.

Of the seven more or less close parallels one is with Boscán and five are with Garcilaso: the only parallels with Córdoba which have been found come into the category 'weak'. This is at once a surprising discovery and a welcome one. Surprising, because critics have made so much of Córdoba's supposed influence on Saint John of the Cross that it had almost become taken for granted: 'he read (Córdoba's book) with care (*detenidamente*)', writes Sr. Alonso: it was his 'spiritual companion'; 'he undoubtedly used, loved and imitated it'.[4] Welcome, because it confirms one's feeling that so great a poet could not have been seriously influenced by a journeyman parodist, still less have consciously imitated him.

The facts seem to be that Saint John of the Cross knew Córdoba's book well enough to quote once from it and use one of its stanzas as a model. As Granada is a long way from Ávila, where he was living

---

[1] *DAP*, p. 272. Italics mine.

[2] R. M. de Hornedo, in *Razón y Fe* (Madrid, 1943), CXXVII, 322.

[3] "The alleged debts of San Juan de la Cruz to Boscán and Garcilaso de la Vega." In *Hispanic Review* (1953) XXI.

[4] *DA*, pp. 81, 50, 76.

from before the date of its publication until December 1577, it is doubtful if he saw it, either in its first edition (1575) or in its second (1577), before he went south, after his escape from prison, in October 1578. There is no conclusive evidence that he used anything in it except the stanzaic form.

His debts to the authentic Garcilaso, however, seem to have been more considerable. Of the sixteen parallels found, six — as well as one with the authentic Boscán—are fairly close ones, which would suggest that Saint John of the Cross was familiar with the first edition of the joint works of Boscán and Garcilaso published by Boscán's widow. At the same time, since all but one of the parallels point to reminiscence rather than to conscious imitation, it would seem likely that his reading of that volume had taken place long before the writing of any of his verse.

External evidence would also support this view. Humanly speaking, it is hardly possible that so avid a reader should not have encountered the works of Boscán and Garcilaso in boyhood, since he had lived for a dozen or more years in the very town (Medina del Campo) where they had only recently been published. After taking the Carmelite habit in 1563, on the other hand, he would have read little or no secular poetry, and, so far as we are aware, none of the poems for phrases in which parallels have been found were written before 1578. The intervening fifteen years were filled with philosophical and theological studies, with evangelization, pastoral work and the business of the Discalced Carmelite Reform, and with the all-absorbing task of pressing forward along the Mystic Way. Surely during those years he would have forgotten most of his Garcilaso, with the exception of lines which remained in the memory by virtue of their vivid imagery or their imperishable music. Was there not among these lines that passage from the Second Eclogue which contained so many of the motifs found in the 'Spiritual Canticle'—the 'gently moving air,' the sweet song of Philomel, the dove, the green flower-spangled fields, the clear pure spring? Far more probable than that he imitated Garcilaso of set purpose seems to me the theory that, long ago, as a boy, he had read those verses till he knew them by heart, and now, as slowly, and perhaps at infrequent intervals, he wrote his first long poem, they came back to him unbidden, perhaps even unrecognized. It is, I believe, along such lines as these that we may hope to explain the influence exerted by Boscán and Garcilaso on Saint John of the Cross.

PART IV

Cervantes in England
Cervantes on England
Cervantes Criticism outside Spain

Cervantes in England[1]

'Cervantes and England': 'Shakespeare and Spain'. Those are two evocative and attractive themes for study; and, if scientific investigation of them has yielded little result, they at least allow full play for the imagination. Here are the two supremely inspired creative writers of the modern world, whose careers are not only almost exactly contemporaneous, but fall squarely within their respective nations' principal period of literary splendour. During the greater part of the careers of Cervantes and Shakespeare, these two nations, the rival powers of sixteenth-century Europe, are at war with each other: neither author, therefore, can have the opportunity to learn much about the other's country. Despite valiant attempts which have been made to show that Shakespeare had a considerable knowledge of Spain, and perhaps even of the Spanish language, it must be held as doubtful if more has been proved than that he incorporated in his vocabulary a few common Spanish words, a few current Spanish allusions and a few conventional or proverbial Spanish phrases.

Cervantes, the four-hundredth anniversary of whose birth we are now celebrating, seems to have known even less of England. I say 'seems' because, even had he known more, he would probably never have told us so. He was not the man to go exploring the sea-coast of Bohemia: what interested him was humanity—not so much the respects in which geographical boundaries separate some of us from others as the traits which all of us, whether Spanish, English, French, Italian or German, have in common. But once in his life—probably towards the end of his life, after the conclusion of an Anglo-Spanish peace—he made, in his Exemplary novel,

---

[1] An address delivered at the University of Liverpool on 3rd November 1947, in commemoration of the quatercentenary of the birth of Cervantes.

La Española inglesa, a charming and generous gesture to our country, which we, to our eternal gain, had the grace to repay. It is our acknowledgment of this gesture that I propose here to describe.

The welcome given by England to Cervantes' greatest work can be paralleled by no other country in the world. There will not be time in this lecture to follow the fortunes in our country of the *Exemplary Novels*, or of its author's minor works, but at least some idea can be given of the place which has been accorded in our literature to *Don Quijote*. That immortal novel was received with immediate acclamation, which has not died even today. 'England', wrote the best-known of our British Cervantists some forty years ago, 'was the first foreign country to mention *Don Quijote*, the first to translate the book, the first country in Europe to present it decently garbed in its native tongue, the first to indicate the birthplace of the author, the first to provide a biography of him, the first to publish a commentary on *Don Quijote*, and the first to issue a critical edition of the text.'[1]

Without pretending, or attempting, to follow the vogue of *Don Quijote* in England chronologically and in detail, let us illustrate it by glancing in turn at a few of Cervantes' principal translators, who, as it happens, have the additional interest of being noteworthy as individuals.

The earliest of them is Thomas Shelton, of whose life and personality very little is known: he was long confused with a contemporary of the same name who followed the profession of stenography. Our Shelton appears to have had a considerable acquaintance with Spanish, but how he acquired it we cannot say. Almost all our knowledge of him, indeed, is gathered from the preface to his translation.

At that time, Spanish books were reaching England chiefly by way of the Low Countries and the copy of *Don Quijote* which Shelton used for his version belonged to an edition reprinted at Brussels in 1607. That it was made for someone living outside England is proved by various allusions, and also by phrases such as 'as we say in England'. This person is believed to have been a certain Richard Verstegan, who lived at Antwerp and sent many foreign books to England. But all Shelton tells us is that he translated the book 'through the importunity of a very dear friend, who was desirous to understand the subject'. The work was done about

[1] James Fitzmaurice-Kelly, in *Proceedings of the British Academy* (1905-6), p. 29.

the year 1607, and done very quickly—'in the space of forty days', so he declares, in which case he must have been an extremely rapid worker. The friend was allowed to read the translation: but then, adds the translator, 'I cast it aside, where it lay long time neglected in a corner, and so little regarded by me that I never once set my hand to revise or correct it'. After about four years, however, other friends of his came to hear about the translation and urged him to publish it. He was now engaged in 'many affairs' and told them that he had no time to read it through and correct the errors which he probably knew were to be found in it. So he eventually agreed to publication on condition that some person would undertake to do this for him.

It was in 1612 that his six-hundred-page volume appeared. 'The History of the valorous and witty knight-errant Don Quijote de la Mancha. Translated out of the Spanish.' Thus the title-page: no more. Perhaps Shelton was ashamed of the work which he had done so hastily and thrown aside so carelessly, so long before: at any rate his name appears only at the foot of the dedication 'to his very good lord, the lord of Walton'. And he had some reason. His facility as a translator seems to have been more remarkable than his accuracy. Again and again his version is the loosest possible paraphrase and even worse are its frequent lapses into over-literalness. Like a schoolboy, he is continually led astray by the similarity in appearance between pairs of words with different meanings. *Sucesos*, which means 'events', he translates by 'successes'. *Desmayarse*, to him, is always 'dismay', instead of 'faint' or 'swoon'. *Admirar* is 'admire', to which verb it corresponds in fact very seldom. A second edition of his translation, revised by another hand, was published in 1620, the year in which appeared his version of *Don Quijote*, Part II. But only about one-quarter of the changes made by the reviser show any improvement on the original and a modern critic has described the revision as 'superficial and careless'.[1]

None the less, Shelton was reprinted (in four volumes) as recently as 1896, and he can still be read with pleasure. For, in the first place, he was a genuine man of letters, and in addition he had the good fortune to live in an age when English prose was at its highest level of merit: his book is almost exactly contemporary with the Authorized Version of the Bible. He reflects, in some degree,

---

[1] Edwin B. Knowles, Jr., 'The First and Second Editions of Shelton's *Don Quixote*, Part I: a Collation and Dating', in *Hispanic Review* (1941), IX, 252-65.

the felicity and sonority of that masterpiece. He has a typically rich Elizabethan vocabulary. He abounds in phrases which, though not always correct, are virile and idiomatic. His translation has thus a value of its own. In the second place, he lived in Cervantes' own day, and, as we can tell from his notes, had great sympathy with his subject. There is a certain quality about a version of a great work made by a contemporary of its author which no version made in a later age can possibly possess. And then, for English readers, Shelton's version acquires a halo of semi-sanctity from the high degree of probability that, supposing Shakespeare to have been acquainted with the *Quijote*, as Middleton, Fletcher and Jonson certainly were, it is in this version that he must have read him.

Shelton (if we enter to his credit Stevens' translation of 1706, which was avowedly based on him) held the field for almost a century, his only rival being Philips' version ('made English according to the humour of our modern language') of 1686, which a nineteenth-century critic called 'not so much a translation as a travesty'. But in the last year of the seventeenth century appeared a new version, the work (according to the title-page) of 'many hands and published by Peter Motteux, servant to his Majesty'.

This translator, who had the English Christian names of 'Peter Antony' and the French surname of 'Motteux', was born at Rouen in 1660, emigrated to England at twenty-five, upon the revocation of the Edict of Nantes, and, after some time spent in commerce, took up publishing and writing. During 1692–3 he was editor of a review called *The Gentleman's Journal*, and in 1693— after giving light to an undistinguished version of Malebranche— he reprinted Sir Thomas Urquhart's translation of the first two books of Rabelais' masterpiece (1653), together with a third, also by Urquhart, in the following year publishing his own version of Books IV and V. After translating two unimportant works from the French, he turned to the writing of comedies, by which, to many students of English literature, he is best known, and not until the end of the century did he bring out another translation, that of the *Quijote*.

This was not one large volume, but, in Motteux's own words, 'four little portable duodecimos': 'the book', he added, 'being more for diversion than for study, is therefore more proper for the pocket than the closet'. Preceded by an impressive list of subscribers, the first two volumes appeared in 1700; the third and fourth in 1703. By 1712 the book was in its third edition. In his introduction, Motteux set a fashion which has been followed by most of his successors—that of censuring those who had attempted the same task before him. 'I have engaged', he writes, 'to rescue the hero of Cervantes out of the hands of his former translators and to set him free to seek happier adventures in a more proper dress.' Without going so far as to accuse Shelton, as a later translator, Jarvis, unjustly does, of using as model an Italian translation (which, in fact, was published ten years after Shelton's own), he declares, very uncharitably, that it 'falls short of the purity of the English tongue even of that time'. He tells only half the truth when he complains that 'the first translators generally kept so close to the author that they were obscure', though he has a good case against Stevens, whom he condemns for 'hastily furbishing up' a version which, as we have seen, was itself hastily written.

Motteux's own translation has been much attacked and much defended. For myself, I must say that if I had to read Cervantes in English for pure pleasure, I would rather read him in Shelton. The 'grand style' of the Elizabethans better reflects Cervantes' manner than the sprightliness of the 'various hands', which I suspect were in the main one hand, and though Motteux had undoubtedly a great sense of humour, it was a coarser, more superficial humour than Cervantes'—very much more suited to the translator of Rabelais. He tends to put too much of himself into his work; to indulge in open burlesque, where Cervantes hints and suggests. And such subjectivity is one of the worst vices of a translator.

Yet this version, which has been so violently attacked—Ormsby, in the last century, went so far as to call it 'worse than worthless'—had a success incomparably greater than Shelton's. In the eighteenth century, whose taste it well suited, it went into ten editions. In the nineteenth it was given a new life by Lockhart, who used it, in a slightly revised form, as a text for his annotations. In this new dress, Motteux went into a dozen fresh editions during the nineteenth century, and into several more during the twentieth —the latest I have seen was published in 1934. Add to this evidence of popularity the praise of Lockhart, Prescott and Ticknor, the last-named of whom, while censuring its undue freedom, calls it 'on the whole, the most agreeable and the best',[1] and you will

[1] *History of Spanish Literature* (Boston, 1849), III, 419–20.

see that, whatever one's personal feelings about it may be, it will always have to be seriously reckoned with.

We may pass very briefly over an extraordinary piece of work which appeared in 1711, and which I mention at all only as a curiosity. This was a 'merry' translation, made by one Edward Ward, of 'the life and notable adventures of that renowned knight Don Quijote de la Mancha,' into 'Hudibrastic verse'. To us the idea of the transformation of the *Quijote* into one thousand pages of iambic tetrameters rhyming throughout in couplets is simply ridiculous, and I can assure you that the reality is more than ridiculous—it is horrible. But Ward was a great admirer of Samuel Butler, and, seeing nothing in the *Quijote* beyond an amusing story, he thought it (to quote his preface) an 'excellent subject for a Hudibrastic poem, well worthy of a Butler's genius, whose matchless pen has made his memory immortal'.[1] Ward, poor soul, hoped that his verse paraphrase might make him 'a sharer in Cervantes' lasting reputation'. Needless to say, it did not: it seems rather to have plunged him into oblivion.

Leaving him there, we come to a third notable translator of the *Quijote*, who, like Shelton and Motteux, had personality. This was Charles Jervas, or Jarvis (*c.* 1675–1739), an Irishman who by profession was a portrait-painter, and who, though an acquaintance of Pope, Swift, and other leading men of letters, appears to have embarked on no literary venture save this. Testimony of his own day represents him as a man of overweening vanity: there is a story that he copied a Titian, and then, believing himself to have surpassed the original, stood back to compare the two and cried: 'Poor little Tit! How he would stare!' His contemporaries apparently refused to take his project of translating the *Quijote* very seriously. Sir John Hawkins, in his introduction to the works of Samuel Johnson (London, 1787), records that Jarvis 'laboured at it many years, could make little progress, for, being a painter by profession, he had not been accustomed to write and had no style'. While Pope, who declared that Jarvis knew no Spanish, made the blunt observation, in a letter to Swift dated 14th December 1725, that 'Jarvis and his *Don Quijote* are both finished'.

Hawkins believed that the two large tomes were the work of a man called Broughton, and that Jarvis merely gave them his name,

[1] On *Hudibras* and *Don Quijote*, see Edward M. Wilson, 'Cervantes and English Literature of the Seventeenth Century', in *Bulletin Hispanique* (1948), L, 45–52.

but there is no sort of evidence for this, and the probability is that Broughton revised the work for the press, since it was not published until 1742—seventeen years, that is to say, after Pope reports it as having been completed, and three years after Jarvis' death. The fact that it is the most faithful to the original of the three versions as yet surveyed makes it difficult to believe that it was the work of a man who knew no Spanish; for the early French translations were as free as the English ones, and anyone translating from them (or from the Italian, which Jarvis would hardly do since he censures Shelton for having, as he believes, done it) would find himself a very long way from Cervantes. His style, it is true, is undistinguished and pedestrian—which is a relief after parts of the last-named translation and that to be considered next. But he makes determined efforts to interpret difficult phrases and render delicate shades of meaning, and the success which attended him was not, I think, undeserved.

The translator of the *Quijote* best known to students of English literature for his original work was Tobias Smollett. It is said that the originator of this translation was not the author, but the publisher, who, noting the considerable success of Jarvis' posthumous version, considered how he could rival it, and bethought him of a popular novelist, whose temperament and predilections he quite erroneously believed to be similar to Cervantes'. Thus Smollett's translation was conceived, and in 1755, thirteen years after Jarvis', it was born.

If this account of its conception be correct, the publisher knew little of Cervantes, who, thanks to Philips, Motteux and Ward, had come to be considered by most English people a cheerful buffoon. The author of *Don Quijote* was not the first writer of genius, and is not the last, to have been so misinterpreted. Smollett's art, though by no means despicable, was completely unlike his. His style is vigorous and hearty; his humour broad to the point of farce, and often extremely coarse.

However, Smollett, having evidently no idea of his inadequacy for the task proposed to him, made his translation, basing it to a large extent on Jarvis',[1] and, after spending four years (according to his own statement) in revising it, produced it in two volumes. It is a free translation, endeavouring to 'retain the spirit and ideas'

[1] Cf. C. Rocco Linsalata, 'Tobias Smollett's Translation of *Don Quijote*', in *The Cervantes Quadricentennial at the University of Texas* (Austin, Texas, n.d.), pp. 55–68.

of the original, without 'servilely adhering to its literal expression'. Smollett's principal aim, according to his preface, is to preserve what he terms 'that ludicrous solemnity and self-importance by which the inimitable Cervantes has distinguished the character of Don Quixote'. The word 'ludicrous' is very typical. It suggests situations and incidents at which one laughs heartily, and Smollett throws back his head and laughs heartily all the time. His real affinity is with the picaresque. His novel *Roderick Random* is inspired by *Gil Blas*, which he adapted with considerable skill, and he might have been extremely successful with Quevedo. But, whatever one may think of the spirit of his translation, nothing can obscure the fact that he was a master of the English language, and, considered as English, his was the best version of *Don Quijote* that had come out yet.

All this time had been appearing numerous versions other than those which we have glanced at. And now comes a deluge of translations of various kinds, made with various motives, and none of them having any claim to distinction. Most are either reprints of previous ones, perhaps with a few trifling emendations, and all with title-pages presenting new names or other attractions to commend them to the public. Here, for example, in 1818, is the *Quijote* in four large volumes, 'embellished with carvings from pictures painted by Robert Smirke Esq., R.A.' The numerous full-page engravings give the impression of being far more important than the text, and the name of the translator, the artist's sister Mary, can only be discovered at the end of the dedicatory letter.

Then there is the Motteux-Lockhart version (1822) already referred to, the object of which is to 'preserve the merits of Motteux and get rid of his faults'. In his biographical preface to this version the translator of so many Spanish ballads makes bold to assert that Cervantes, as a novelist, has 'found but one rival' in the whole world. We ask ourselves wonderingly who that can be, for we had supposed the author of the *Quijote* to be above all challenge. And then we recall that Lockhart was the son-in-law of the novelist who in Spanish reviews of the early nineteenth century used to be called the 'Cervantes of Scotland'—Sir Walter Scott.

Lockhart, in his preface, reacts strongly against the idea, universally held in England even down to his time, that Cervantes wrote the *Quijote*, in Smollett's words, 'to ridicule and discredit those absurd romances, filled with the most nauseous improbability and unnatural extravagance, which were a disgrace to commonsense and reason'. Or, as Byron epigrammatically but even more in-exactly put it, that 'Cervantes smiled Spain's chivalry away'. With equal vigour Lockhart reacts against the Motteux-Smollett conception of Cervantes as a superior kind of buffoon, and in his judgment of Cervantes' hero—'one of the greatest triumphs of his (Cervantes') skill'—he shows signs of approaching a more modern standpoint:

'We pity the delusion, we laugh at the situation, but we revere, in spite of every ludicrous accompaniment, and of every insane exertion, the noble spirit of the Castilian gentleman; and we feel, in every page, that we are perusing the work . . . of a calm and enlightened mind.'

Cervantes, that is to say, is more, not only than a successful buffoon, but even than a great national humorist. His genius is universal. His great novel, while 'the peculiar property as well as the peculiar pride of the Spaniards', is fundamentally 'the pro-perty and pride of the whole of the cultivated world'.

The somewhat pretentious-looking three-volume translation of Duffield (1881)—described by him as 'a new translation from the originals of 1605 and 1608', with numerous notes derived from J. A. Pellicer, Diego Clemencín and others—reveals to us a new Cervantes: the hero of nineteenth-century romanticism. That literary phase, in the sense in which it is normally understood, had long since passed away, but Duffield had not moved with the age. A Romantic born out of due time, he goes farther than Lockhart, and not only castigates 'the thoughtless and the vulgar' who for two and a half centuries have regarded *Don Quijote* as 'a piece of unmatched buffoonery' but idealizes its author into a peerless crusader, the hero of a hundred battles—one who

'knew the nature of the fight he waged and had assurance of the victory that would follow; who, single-handed and bereft of sym-pathy at the time he most needed it, kept a steady light shining—the light of justice and honour'.

The 'only living faith' to be found in Spain in Cervantes' day 'was a faith in the miraculous deeds of the Cid, in Amadis of Gaul, in the Twelve Peers'. The whole country 'was given up to that form of delirium which comes from the unnatural excitement of the fancy'. No other force could do anything against this: it was left for Cervantes to work a 'wonderful miracle'.

So we are back to the Cervantes of Byron, but with a difference. Not with a serene or cryptic smile, but riding into the fray on his white horse, and in his hand a Book, this knight of justice and honour drove delirium out of the land. Wherefore, concludes the translator, 'the time has come when his great work should be read not only for the beauty of its excellence, for the charm of its style, for its sweet humour and tender compassion', but because its author 'was one of the most renowned refiners of taste and manners of whom Christendom can boast'.

In the same year Duffield published further fruits of his Cervantine studies, which, he claimed, had occupied him for twenty years, in the shape of a little work entitled *Don Quijote, his Critics and Commentators: A Handy Book for General Readers*, which described Cervantes' supposed aim, still more comprehensively, as the working of a 'moral, social, political and religious reformation'. Romanticism, you will say, at its very worst; and you will be right. But the Romantic manner had almost passed away. Duffield had his admirers, such as the *British Quarterly Review*, which thanked him very heartily for 'purifying this Christian and high-purposed author from the infamous uncleannesses which have been fathered upon his great genius and noble name'. But he seems to have had comparatively few readers, and in the same decade there appeared yet another translation which, both regarded as a version of the original work and from the standpoint of interpretation, was superior to everything that had preceded it.

To be exact, two more translations appeared in this decade: one of four volumes, by John Ormsby, in 1885, and one of five, by Henry Edward Watts, in 1888. If I speak chiefly of Ormsby, I must not be taken as despising the considerable achievement of Watts, who not only prefaced his work with the conventional biography of Cervantes, but added to it five appendices, one of which was a substantial annotated bibliography and another an index to the text of the *Quijote*—'a service', as the translator correctly remarked, 'which no English edition has ever before done for Cervantes'. Though not a writer by trade, and though forced to do most of his work over a period of eighteen years, amid 'the turmoil of a harassing and jealous profession', he was a most meticulous translator, whom no serious student of the subject can ignore. But Ormsby was the more interesting personality, and his version, too, on the whole deserves its greater popularity.

John Ormsby (1829–95) was an Irishman whose ancestors had

migrated to Ireland from eastern England during the reign of Elizabeth. As a young man, he came to England and studied law, but his literary tastes led him to take up writing: he was also a great Alpinist and traveller. And his favourite travel-ground was Spain, of which country he knew many of the less frequented and even of the wildest regions. It was in this way that he became drawn to Spanish literature, to which, had he been less of a dilettante, he might have rendered even greater services.

His first attempt at translation was a version of the *Poema del Cid* —at that time, if we except some fragmentary renderings made by the Duque de Rivas' friend, John Hookham Frere, the only one in our language. The lateness of this beginning he redeemed by following it up almost immediately with his translation of the *Quijote*. No doubt he worked at this the more assiduously because soon after publishing his *Cid* he became almost totally deaf and in the world of Cervantes he found the most congenial companionship. One can well believe this, for he is not only commendably accurate, but also remarkably well informed. His appendices (notably that on the proverbs of *Don Quijote*) are as valuable as those of Watts and his version is truer to the spirit of the original.

A great admirer of Shelton, he had first proposed merely to republish that translator's 'racy old version,' whose charm 'no modern translation, however skilful or correct, could possess'. Only a contemporary, he thought, could 'feel' the 'vitality' of Cervantes' book as Shelton had done. But reflection convinced him that, in the critical days of the late nineteenth century, a version so hastily made, so long ago, would be unable to hold its own: the chief argument in favour of its being reprinted would inevitably be sentiment. Reviewing subsequent versions as we have done, together with others—one an 'impudent imposture'; another an abridgment; a third mere 'patchwork'—he could find none that was satisfactory. He was forced, therefore, either to abandon his project or to make one for himself.

He worked rapidly, though not hastily, and his work was comparatively soon done. It has been reprinted again and again, and deservedly. Ormsby was a skilled translator, with a good knowledge of Spanish, both literary and colloquial, a high ideal of the translator's responsibilities and a scholarly regard for shades of meaning both in Cervantes' language and in his own. 'Faithful, vigorous, direct and vivacious', wrote the greatest of our British

Cervantists, 'his rendering gives the English reader the best impression of Cervantes' incomparable book.'[1]

But no less noteworthy is Ormsby's attitude to Cervantes' masterpiece. Gone is the age which regarded the book as merely comic—'a queer droll book, full of laughable incidents and absurd situations'. Gone, too, is the age which thought of it as a political allegory. Gone even—despite its so recent manifestation—is the Romantic age. When he began the book that was to give the *coup de grâce* to a 'degrading mockery' of chivalry, says Ormsby, Cervantes had in his mind 'no deep design or elaborate plan'. This was to have been a mere tale like the short ones he had already written. But it grew on him—and to what a masterpiece it grew! Ormsby's understanding of Cervantes is matched by his sanity of outlook and his ability to appreciate Cervantes' humour, powers of observation and self-effacement before his characters. This introductory essay was one of the best things that had been written in English upon its subject down to that time.

Cursory as this survey has been, I hope it may have presented a clear, though necessarily an unfinished, picture of the six or seven principal British translators of the *Quijote* over a period of two hundred and seventy-five years. Of Shelton, the grave Elizabethan who barely emerges out of the shadows. Of the Anglo-French Motteux, publisher and writer of comedies. Of the self-conscious portrait-painter Jarvis. Of the boisterous novelist Smollett. Of the Romantic Duffield, the meticulous Watts and the much-travelled Ormsby. But I would end by describing to you a later figure than these, clearer to me than any other, since him alone of them I knew, who, though a commentator and biographer of Cervantes rather than a translator, is connected in a curious way with several of the translators. I mean my predecessor in the Gilmour Chair at this University, James Fitzmaurice-Kelly (1857–1923).

Like Ormsby, Fitzmaurice-Kelly was an Irishman, and, till almost the end of his life, a bachelor. Intended for the Catholic priesthood, he found that he had no vocation, either for the Church or, later, for medicine, so, with his taste for writing, he drifted into journalism, and, having also a gift for languages, he decided to specialize in the language of some European country. Perhaps from

[1] James Fitzmaurice-Kelly, in *The Complete Works of Miguel de Cervantes Saavedra* (Glasgow, 1901), III, xxxvi.

personal predilection, perhaps from the chance of being able to reside for a time in Spain, he chose Spanish. And from the beginning his favourite author was Cervantes. When only thirty-five, he published his *Life of Miguel de Cervantes Saavedra*, which, coming from a young man with no university education, shows a remarkably high degree of scholarship. At first, however, in a country from which the Hispanic tradition had departed and with no outstanding Hispanic scholar whom it could call its own, he became better known as a writer for the general educated public. He wrote of James I of Aragon, of the *Celestina*, of the picaresque novel, of the *Diana*, of lyric poetry, of Fray Luis de León, of Lope de Vega, of Iriarte, of Noroña, of nineteenth-century Spanish history, of Espronceda, of Rubén Darío, and (not least important) of great Hispanists whose names were unknown in this country until he published their obituaries. More important, when still barely over forty, he brought out his *History of Spanish Literature*, which, in its Spanish form, went into eight editions in twenty years and was also translated into French and German. Finally, he produced two anthologies—one in verse, preceded by a brilliant introductory essay, and one in prose and verse, containing a brief but cogent critical study of each author.

He did all this superlatively well; for, although with time he came to excel in exact scholarship, he was by nature less an exact scholar than a gifted writer. His sense of balance and proportion, his precision of expression, his feeling for the graceful, the pointed or the epigrammatic phrase—all were enlisted in the service of Hispanic culture and all helped to popularize Hispanic culture in England. 'He is no dryasdust erudite,' wrote Menéndez Pelayo of him, very justly, 'but a fine and sensitive man of letters, a critic with taste and feeling for poetry, and with a keen instinct for originality and beauty, who expresses his aesthetic enthusiasm with eloquence and, indeed, ardour. Even within the limits of a handbook he contrives to avoid aridity and can be read with pleasure.'[1]

There were, as I have said, hardly any Hispanists in England at this time, and there was no chair of Spanish in any English university. So when, in 1908, a benefactor endowed the first of such chairs—that of the University of Liverpool—there was no difference of opinion as to who should fill it. This handsome and

---

[1] Introduction to Fitzmaurice-Kelly's *Historia de la literatura española*, ed. Bonilla y San Martín (Madrid, 1901), p. xx.

distinguished Irishman, with the pointed beard, the finely moulded features and the air of quiet reserve, soon became a well-known figure in university circles, and it was difficult to realize that he had not lived in a university all his life. Fitmaurice-Kelly came in England to represent Spain, and, before long, to represent, above everything else, Cervantine studies. His biography of Cervantes, after a life of twenty years, was republished in a new, enlarged and up-to-date form, and later translated into Spanish. He lectured before the British Academy on the occasion of the tercentenary of *Don Quijote* (1905) and again on that of the tercentenary of Cervantes' death (1916). In the latter year he was called to the University of London, where a Chair of Spanish, bearing Cervantes' name, was founded to commemorate the tercentenary. He wrote on Cervantes' vogue or influence in France, in Rumania and in Japan. He edited reprints of no less than three English translations of Cervantes—those of Shelton, Jarvis and Ormsby. He collaborated with Ormsby in an edition of the *Quijote* and edited the Complete Works of Cervantes in English translation. In 1920, only three years before his death, he published a comprehensive review of recent Cervantine studies, showing that, although he never forgot the claims of the unlearned, he kept abreast of modern scholarship as well.

In offering you, therefore, these brief pictures of the English translators of Cervantes, I have no hesitation in asking you to award your highest admiration to my great predecessor in this University, to one who so successfully combined the very diverse gifts of the popularizer and the investigator; who, without translating Cervantes, became his foremost British interpreter; and whose name will be spoken of with respect and admiration wherever Cervantine studies are pursued and known.

Cervantes on England[1]

Cervantes' collection of twelve short stories entitled *Exemplary Novels* has enjoyed far less popularity in this country than *Don Quijote*. Published in Spain in 1613, it soon became known in England, and, in 1640, six of the stories[2] were translated by James Mabbe, a Hispanist who had previously published versions of works as unlike as the picaresque novel *Guzmán de Alfarache* (1622) and the semi-mystical *Devout Contemplations* by Cristóbal de Fonseca (1629). Numerous other books containing one or more of these tales were published in the seventeenth and eighteenth centuries, but only in the middle of the nineteenth did there appear a very imperfect version of the whole,[3] and not until 1902 an adequate translation, from the pen of Norman MacColl.

This neglect is strange, for, had *Don Quijote* never been written, the *Exemplary Novels*, several of which are little masterpieces, would have sufficed to give their author a secure place high in modern literature. Possibly the adjective in the title was felt to be slightly repellent. It suggests a collection of highly moral tales—'I have given them the name "Exemplary",' wrote Cervantes to the gentle reader, 'and, if thou lookest carefully there is not one from which cannot be derived a profitable example. If in any way it could chance that the perusal of these novels could tempt any reader of them to an evil desire or thought, I would rather cut off the hand with which I wrote them than bring them out in public.' The moral,

---

[1] This essay is based upon a lecture delivered at the University of Valencia on 17th April 1947 in commemoration of the quatercentenary of the birth of Cervantes.

[2] Including the story which is the subject of this essay and which he alters considerably. See Frank Pierce, 'James Mabbe and *La Española inglesa*', in *Revue de littérature comparée* (1949), XXIII, 80–5.

[3] *The Exemplary Novels of Miguel de Cervantes Saavedra*, trans. Walter K. Kelly (London, Bohn, 1846), 2nd ed., enlarged, 1855; reprinted 1881, 1894.

however, is never obtrusive: often it is hardly observable; and Cervantes himself describes his stories as eminently fitted for recreation.

Part of their charm lies in their variety—for not all the 'troubled spirits' to whose needs the author claims in his preface to be ministering will find solace in stories of an identical type. Attempts have been made, with unequal degrees of success, to date them, and some critics have tried to divide into successive 'periods' the total span of about fifteen years during which they were being written. Here it will suffice to indicate their remarkable range. Some are highly realistic, inclining to the picaresque; notably the story of low life in Seville entitled *Rinconete and Cortadillo*, and the vivacious *Illustrious Kitchenmaid*. Some are satirical; and even these differ strikingly in tone: *The Licentiate Vidriera*, for example, is in various respects at opposite poles from *The Dogs' Colloquy*. Some (*e.g.*, *The Trick Marriage* and *The Jealous Extremaduran*) may be classed as domestic drama: one, at least, *The Force of Blood*, is outstandingly dramatic. Several are romantic and idealistic. *The Liberal Lover*, *The Two Maidens*, *The English Spanish Lady*. In parts of these, as throughout in *The Little Gipsy-Girl*, Cervantes attempts to blend the ideal with the real—not always very happily; of gipsy life and customs, for example, he knew very much less than of the underworld of Seville.

[1]

This essay deals with a novel in the last group, *La Española inglesa*, a title which I have translated *The English Spanish Lady*.[1] The story represents an interesting attempt to depict our own country and people. Charming though it is, it cannot be called one of the best of the *Exemplary Novels*,[2] albeit external evidence suggests that it must have been one of the latest of them. The action begins in 1596, the date of the sack of Cádiz by the Earl of Essex,

[1] MacColl has 'The Spanish-English lady', but the misleading hyphen, suggestive of mixed nationality, is not in the original, and, since *inglesa* is the adjective qualifying *Española*, 'Spanish' should stand nearer the noun than 'English'. The most literal translation would be 'The English Spanishwoman', did that noun exist. Cervantes obviously intended his title to be paradoxical.

[2] As good Cervantists as Schevill and Bonilla (*Novelas ejemplares* (Madrid, 1922–5), III, 383) called it a 'solemn piece of child's play (*niñería*) based on purely chance happenings, the unlikeliest imaginable'. It found a staunch defender in Pfandl (*Geschichte, etc.*, German ed., p. 303; Spanish ed., p. 337). See Rafael Lapesa, 'En torno a "La Española inglesa" y el "Persiles"', in *Homenaje a Cervantes* (Valencia, 1950), p. 496.

and ends, according to the chronology of the narrative itself,[1] about seventeen or eighteen years later—a year, that is to say, after the date of the publication of the collection as a whole. This means either that Cervantes went astray in his dating of the event on which the plot is built, or that, as is more probable, he failed to observe that he was allowing too much time to elapse between the various episodes. If we assume the latter alternative, the tale may have been written at any moment after the conclusion of peace between Spain and England in 1605, but the balance of probability would still favour its being late in the period 1605–13, since, heedless though the author may have been of the precise years in which he was dating the different parts of the action, he can hardly have failed to observe that he was bringing his conclusion perilously near the time at which he was writing.[2]

A good deal of the character of the story can be gathered from an outline of the plot. The heroine, a Spanish girl of seven, named Isabela, is carried off to London by Clotaldo, the well-born English 'captain of a squadron of ships',[3] who, as the author again and again pointedly reminds us, was a 'secret Catholic'. She is brought up in his own family. When she reaches the mature age of twelve, Ricaredo, the son of the house, who is six years older, falls in love with her. Though his parents have been intending to marry him to a 'wealthy Scottish maiden', they consent to the match, and, after an interval of two years, the wedding is about to take place when an unexpected contretemps postpones it.

Four days before the date for which it has been fixed, Clotaldo bethinks himself of informing Queen Elizabeth, 'since among those of illustrious lineage no marriage takes place without her good-will and consent'. As though conscious of the shortness of the notice, Cervantes explains that Isabela's parents 'had no

[1] Isabel's father describes his daughter as having been captured fifteen years since, at a point more than two years before the end of the story. But Cervantes may have been confusing the attack on Cádiz made in 1596 with an earlier one of 1587. There are several definite inconsistencies of date in the story, so one more would not be surprising.

[2] This is my own view, and I do not think the thesis of Mack Singleton ('Date of "La Española inglesa"', *Hispania* (U.S.A.) 1947, XXX, 329–35), that the novel was written about 1596, tenable. Lapesa (*op. cit.*, pp. 505–7) discusses the question of date in some detail. Internal evidence would certainly favour a date when Elizabeth was long dead, the Gunpowder Plot and its consequences had been forgotten, and James was proposing to marry his heir to a Spanish princess.

[3] The translations throughout this essay are my own.

doubt that she would give her leave, so they delayed asking for it'. The Queen, however, sending for her, is amazed at such a 'new marvel of beauty' and somewhat imperiously insists upon post-poning the wedding, and keeping the bride at Court, until Ricaredo, by some doughty deed, shall have proved himself worthy of her.

To so characteristic a display of masterfulness there is no answer; so, although 'the bride's trousseau was all ready and the relatives and friends had been invited, 'the unfortunate bridegroom obe-diently accepts a command in the navy bestowed upon him by the Queen then and there, under a 'General' who soon afterwards succumbs to an apoplectic stroke while on the high seas. Ricaredo —'delighted, though not at the General's loss'—steps into his dead commander's place, successfully engages some Turkish galleys and takes a Portuguese ship, manned by Spaniards,[1] which they have previously captured. Urged to kill the Spaniards, so as to 'take the great ship to London without fear or anxiety', he refuses to do so, providing them instead with money and landing them in Spain. One of them, however, asks to be taken to England, together with his wife, so that they may search for a daughter lost fifteen years before, who proves, of course, to be Isabela. He gets his wish, and Ricaredo, on going to the Queen to claim his reward, takes both the father and the mother into her presence. The usual mole, located conveniently behind the girl's right ear, having estab-lished her identity, general recognition is followed by general rejoicing, and one might suppose that there was nothing left for Ricaredo and Isabela to do but to get married and live happily ever after.

But this story, unlike some others in the collection, contains an abundance of incident, and the moment has now arrived for com-plications, The villain appears—a certain Count Arnesto, son of the Mistress of the Queen's Robes, twenty-two years of age, 'arrogant, haughty and self-confident'. 'His soul having been enkindled by the light of Isabela's eyes', he has already aspired to her hand and been rewarded with 'many and notable marks of her disdain'. When his rival appears, he challenges him to a duel, but is arrested and imprisoned, whereupon his mother attempts to poison the bride. At the Queen's instances her own doctors attend her and save her life, but her illness has destroyed her beauty, and,

---

[1] At this time Spain and Portugal were united as a single kingdom, under Philip III of Spain.

when she returns to Clotaldo's house, she resembles 'the richest of jewels enclosed in a case of rough wood'. Ricaredo's parents, having set eyes on her, decide, without his knowledge, to 'send for the Scottish maiden', adjudging her to be the next best thing to Isabela in beauty. Though some eight years have passed since her super-session, she proves still to be available, but Ricaredo is naturally faithful to Isabela, and, sending her, with her parents, back to Spain, he counters his parents' designs by announcing that he will 'on no account marry or give his hand to the Scottish bride till he has been to Rome to make it right with his conscience'. To Isabela he makes a promise to come to Spain in two years' time and claim her.

Eighteen months have passed when one day Isabela, now in Seville, with her beauty fully restored, hears from Ricaredo's mother that Arnesto, banished from England by Queen Elizabeth, has treacherously killed Ricaredo in France. Not doubting the truth of the news, she resolves to become a nun, and, on the second anniversary of her lover's departure, is about to take the veil when a man appears, 'dressed like those who come back ransomed from captivity', and cries in a loud voice: 'Stop, I am alive.' It is, of course, Ricaredo, who has returned at the last moment to reward her constancy. Arnesto had only wounded him; he had escaped to the coast, been captured (like Cervantes himself) by Turks and taken to Algiers, and finally ransomed and landed at Valencia. Thence he had travelled to Seville, for the dénouement and the long-postponed wedding, which is now celebrated, lest further mischances should befall, 'within a week'. It only remains for Cervantes to point the mellow moral of a charming tale—'how much may be accomplished by virtue, and how much by beauty, the which things, either separately or united in one person, can turn the heart even of an enemy, and also how from the greatest adversity Heaven can bring the greatest profit'.

[11]

'Durchaus rein romantisch'—to quote Friedrich von Schlegel's description of Spanish poetry—is this most idealistic of Cervantes' exemplary tales. Wherever one tests it, it conforms to type. Its coin-cidences: the millionth chance which unites Ricaredo with Isabela's parents on the high seas; his arrival at Seville just as she has set 'one foot within the portress' lodge of the convent'. Its antitheses:

both the constant contraposition of Catholic and Protestant, Christian and infidel, palace and convent, virtue and vice, and such crudely Hugoesque contrasts as that between Isabela in health and after her beauty had been destroyed:

' . . . Lovelier than imagination could conceive . . . Like a star or exhalation that is wont to move through the region of fire on a serene and tranquil night, or like the sun's rays which break through between two mountains at daybreak.'

' . . . Without eyebrows, eyelashes or hair, her face swollen up, her complexion ruined, her skin puffed up, her eyes watering. So hideous, indeed, did she become that although until then she had been a miracle of beauty, she now seemed a monster of ugliness.'

Above all, its characterization. None of the personages, viewed from the standpoint of real life, has any individuality. Can they indeed, we ask, have been conceived by the creator of Rinconete and Cortadillo? Typical is the description, in the final scene, of Ricaredo, by now a seasoned traveller and hard-bitten man of action in his late thirties. As presented to us he is merely the Englishman of any Spaniard's imagination. His round blue cap has fallen off, revealing 'a confused mass of curly golden hair and a pink and white complexion, like carmine and snow, signs which immediately marked him out in the sight of all as a foreigner'. His benevolence and generosity do more than that: they mark him out as being scarcely human. What sort of lover is it whose bride a jealous woman has all but murdered, and who yet says 'many things in defence' of the culprit, 'entreating that she should be pardoned, since the excuses that she made were sufficient to lead to the forgiveness of hurts still greater'? When one reads what the 'excuses' in fact were, one almost suspects irony in the remark that his grief had 'brought him near to the point of losing his reason, such were the things that he did'.

Why do we accept these impossible people, follow their fortunes, if not exactly with breathless excitement, at least with genuine pleasure, and take in every detail of their appearance and personality as we should the faces and dresses of the old-world figures on the canvas of some great painter?

To the two parts of this question there seem to be two separate answers. One concerns the story; the other, the actors in it.

Our interest in the story is undoubtedly attributable to the author's wholly un-Romantic concern with its construction, at first sight by no means obvious. This has been effectively revealed by Don Joaquín Casalduero; and, though both here and elsewhere in his suggestive work on the *Exemplary Novels*[1] there are places where I must dissent from him, it is only right to pay tribute to his penetrating insight. Cervantes may or may not have intended to write a 'composición tetramembre' with 'ritmos binario y ternario',[2] but he must certainly have aimed at achieving a perfect symmetry of construction, at creating an orderly, if artificial, world; and the reader, caught up, as it were, by the rhythm of the plot, enters unconsciously into the author's mind, expects and accepts the conventions of the story and would probably experience a feeling of genuine disillusion if some *deus ex machina* brought it to a premature close. One never becomes conscious of the symmetry until one looks for it, but, as soon as its existence becomes apparent, one realizes to what an extent it dominates the plot. Thus, the novel has four parts or 'acts', laid, respectively, in London, on the high seas, in London and in Seville. In the first act Ricaredo falls ill; in the third, Isabela. Both in the first act, and again in the third, an incident arises to delay the wedding a few days before it is due to take place, thus adding to the force of the climax. Isabela figures in two incidents describable as processions: *viz.*, when, in the first act, she goes to the Royal Palace in London; and when, in the last, she goes to the Sevilian convent. Twice, in the first act and in the third, the 'Scottish maiden' enters the story as Isabela's unconscious rival. The father takes Isabela from her parents and carries her off to London; the son restores her to her parents and soon afterwards sends her back to Spain. The quadripartite plan and the pairs of connected or contrasted actions, as deliberate as the advance and the retire of a slow and stately dance, are quite unmistakable. Sr. Casalduero's superposition upon these elements of the 'ternary' movement, on the other hand, seems to me oversubtle, and, when he carries it into the realm of ideas, interpreting it as a 'mystical neoplatonism' and 'a luminous ladder leading to pure Idea, to the soul', definitely false. He even goes so far as to liken Ricaredo's first and second declarations of love and the final reunion with Isabela to 'the three steps of the mystical ladder: *purgatio, illuminatio, unio*'.[3] This interpretation is taken up by Don Francisco Sánchez-Castañer, who carries the symbolization even

[1] *Sentido y forma de las 'Novelas ejemplares'* (Buenos Aires, 1943).
[2] *Op. cit.*, p. 93.   [3] *Op. cit.*, pp. 100–1.

farther, though admitting that it 'may seem slightly forced'.[1] I feel sure that this path is leading us in the wrong direction, away from the true nature of the story, and the intention of its creator. In any case, enough has been said to show why we can find a genuine interest in the action.

As to the characters, they have a frankly superficial, but quite irresistible, charm. Since he was idealizing his hero and heroine, and nothing in literature is more monotonous than generalized idealization, Cervantes took care to endow them with picturesqueness in the highest possible degree. Isabela, the loveliest child in Cádiz, adds to her beauty, as she passes into womanhood, accomplishments, modesty and grace. Her creator attends to every detail as he attires her for her visit to the royal palace: the Spanish gown of green satin and cloth of gold, the train, the pearls, the diamond girdle and collar, the headdress and the fan. It is a charming Herreran hyperbole which likens her, as she advances alone through the spacious hall, to a 'star of exhalation, that is wont to move through the region of fire on a serene and tranquil night'.[2] No less charming, this time for its simplicity, is the description of her approach and her address to the Queen, and affecting is the picture of the leave-taking between her and her lover—'she stood so still that it seemed as though an alabaster statue were weeping'. Later pictures, of which the appeal varies vastly in kind, but hardly at all in degree, abound.

Worthy to stand beside her is Ricaredo. 'Leaping' from his boat, and waiting for no escort other than the cheering crowd, he hurries to greet his lady and salute his Queen. A splendid figure, in his Milanese armour and broad-brimmed hat adorned with feathers, he is likened, by some of the onlookers, to Mars, by others to a male Venus. He, too, is the central figure in some charming and distinctive scenes—one, for example, in which the child tries his sword and uses his armour as a mirror; another, in which, before her envious courtiers, the Queen seats him on a velvet stool by her side.

Artificial Isabela and Ricaredo may be, but they wear their artificiality with a singular grace.

[1] *La Española inglesa*, ed. prologada por E. Allison Peers y Francisco Sánchez-Castañer (Valencia, 1948), p. 24.
[2] Cf. p. 258, above.

[III]

Two curious features of the story are the frequency with which
it alludes to the English and the Spanish languages and the attitude
which it takes to religion. I am inclined to think that these two
apparently dissimilar characteristics have a fundamental relation
to each other. Let us examine them in detail.

The language-motif is found on the very first page. Isabela, torn
from her Spanish home, was brought up to speak English, but
'did not lose her Spanish', because Clotaldo 'took care to bring
Spaniards home in secret to talk with her', so that 'without forgetting her own language she spoke English as though she had
been born in London'. Brought before the Queen, she 'addressed
her in the English tongue', eliciting the reply, 'Speak to me in
Spanish, maiden, for I understand it well and shall enjoy hearing
it'. She does not, however, venture to address Isabela's parents in
that tongue. Ricaredo has apparently learned some Spanish from
Isabela, for he addresses the Spaniards on the captured vessel in
their own language; but he is not very fluent, for, in relating his
story on his arrival at Seville, he thinks it 'wiser to rely upon the
fluency and discretion of Isabela instead of on his own, as he did
not speak the Castilian tongue very skilfully'. He does, nevertheless, give a long and detailed account of his complicated adventures, presumably in Spanish. The letter sent to Isabela giving the
false news of Ricaredo's death is 'written in English' but she
'reads it in Spanish'—a detail one would think unnecessary.

The religious atmosphere of the story, a peculiarly self-conscious
Catholicism, pervades it from beginning to end. Clotaldo's family
is 'Catholic in secret, although in public they appeared to follow
the opinion of their Queen'. Ricaredo is 'very sound in the
truths of the Catholic faith'—as soon becomes clear. It is 'as a
true Catholic Christian' that he gives his promise to marry Isabela
and 'by the Catholic faith which my Christian parents taught me'
that he later confirms it. The fear of having to 'unsheath his sword
against Catholics' causes him sore misgivings as he prepares to go
to sea at the Queen's command, and he derives great relief from
seeing that the ships he hopes to capture are Turkish, 'which will
prevent him from giving offence to any Catholic'. He rebuts the
inhuman suggestion of murdering the captives, pointing out that
they are 'Christian Catholics'. He leaves Isabela, not to do deeds

of valour, as in a conventional narrative of this type, but to kiss the feet of the Roman pontiff, confess his sins to the Chief Penitentiary and 'satisfy his conscience'. The 'Scottish maiden', too, is a Catholic. Clotaldo, a character of whom Cervantes evidently does not entirely approve,[1] gives Isabela the surely unnecessary caution against denouncing the family to the Queen as adherents of the old religion, since he has no desire to be a martyr.[2] While living at Court, the girl finds that the Queen respects her faith, though many attempts are made to 'divert her from her Catholic intent'. Because they fail, the robe-mistress advises the Queen to send her back to Spain, and, when her crime is discovered, her self-defence betrays her anti-Catholic fanaticism.

Both these characteristics seem to me attributable to Cervantes' desire to accentuate the 'foreignness' of his atmosphere. After all, the principal differences between English and Spaniards at that time were in speech and religion, differences in appearance and dress, both of which traits also receive notice, coming next in order. If he wished to stress the fact that he was talking about strangers in a strange land, such accentuation was the only way open to him.

For of local colour, in the ordinary sense of that phrase, the tale has, and could have, none. Cervantes knew even less about England than about gipsies. Consider, for example, the names of his characters. The hero is called Ricaredo; his father, Clotaldo; the 'Scottish maiden' is named Clisterna; the 'General' of the fleet whom Ricaredo succeeds is a Baron de Lansac; his page is called Guillarte; the Queen's lady is Madame Tansi. None of these forms except the first is even remotely English. Only the villainous Count might have passed muster in a crowd, for if the name Arnesto— not a name very suggestive of villainy—means anything English, it means Ernest. Of places, the story tells us nothing: in the English part of it there is no topographical description and hardly a single place-name. Cervantes must have felt relieved when he got Isabela and her parents back to Spain and hired them 'an important house opposite Santa Paula', in Seville.

---

[1] For, though a Catholic, he carries off a Catholic child against the express order of his Protestant commander, and 'no penalties or threats sufficed to make him obey'.

[2] Sr. Casalduero is perhaps (p. 98) a little severe on the 'weakness of the flesh' which inclines Clotaldo to renounce the 'bitter path' to martyrdom, and certainly on Ricaredo for harbouring the misgivings described above.

No doubt one of the principal attractions of the story to the author's contemporaries was that it professed to introduce them to England, that country of hearsay, with which, he tells them, there was at that time no communication—he was wrong here, by the way, for at the period of which he was writing the Spanish-English wars were over; but he cares little about anachronisms, for Queen Elizabeth continues to appear in the narrative several years after her death. As far as facts were concerned, he told them nothing, but today we think none the worse of him for that, for the really remarkable feature in his portraiture of a nation with which his own had for so long been at war is its generosity. In the very first lines of the story the Earl of Essex is represented as seeking for the stolen Isabela 'with great diligence, in order to restore her to her parents'. Having been careful to make his English hero a staunch Catholic, he goes out of his way to bestow upon him every mark of the very perfect gentle knight. Even his own men think him too lenient to the Spaniards in the ship: 'some held him as valiant, magnanimous and of a good understanding; others in their hearts judged him to be more of a Catholic than he ought'. Not content with landing them in Spain, he gives them 'abundance of provisions for more than a month' and 'four escudos each of Spanish gold', crowning his magnanimity, once more against the judgment of his men and his own judgment, by freeing the captive Turks.

Cervantes, then, was clearly anxious for an Anglo-Spanish understanding, and even more remarkable than his idealization of Ricaredo is his treatment of the personality and character of Queen Elizabeth. If it is noteworthy that a country for so long and until so recently Spain's enemy should have been portrayed with such objectivity, it is surely more remarkable still to find the author's maximum benevolence extended towards a ruler who to him must have been almost a personification of Protestantism. Yet such is the case. Elizabeth is of a 'haughty temper' and has a 'hard heart'—yes; when Ricaredo visits the Court on his return from the wars, onlookers quote against him the proverb 'Dádivas quebrantan peñas'—'gifts will shatter cliffs'—and add that the rich gifts which he has brought, chiefly of that valuable spice known as pepper, 'have softened the hard heart of our Queen'. But, apart from references to her reputation for severity, that is the only unsympathetic light thrown on her. From almost the beginning of the story to the end she broods over it like a fairy godmother. When she first sends for Isabela, 'the bosoms of all are

263

filled with anxiety, consternation and fear'. 'Alas!' says the Lady Catherine, Ricaredo's mother, 'what if the Queen gets to know that I have brought up the child to be a Catholic and infers thence that all of us in this house are Christians? For if she asks the girl what she has learned in the eight years since she became a prisoner, how can the poor child answer without condemning us?' But the Queen asks nothing of the sort, and, after commanding Isabela to speak to her in Spanish, goes on to pay her compliments ('even her name pleases me'[1]) and reproaches Clotaldo but lightly for having kept her in concealment. The religious issue arises only when the Mistress of the Robes begs the Queen to send Isabela back to Spain because of the staunchness with which she has resisted all the efforts made to proselytize her. To which Elizabeth replies:

'that she esteemed her all the more for being able to hold the faith which her parents had taught her, and as for sending her back to Spain she would not consider it, for her lovely presence and her many virtues and graces gave her great pleasure, and she would most certainly give her as wife to Ricaredo, if not on that same day, on the next, as she had promised him.'

After listening to such a testimonial as this, it was tactless of the Mistress of the Robes to excuse her attempt to murder Isabela on the ground that she would 'offer a sacrifice to Heaven by ridding the earth of a Catholic'.

The Queen's benevolence extends to Ricaredo, when he betrays his emotion at being parted from Isabela by her orders:

'Blush not to weep, nor think less of yourself at such a critical moment for having shown signs of your tender-heartedness, for it is one thing to fight with your enemies and another to take leave of one whom you love. Embrace Ricaredo, Isabela, and give him your blessing, for a man of his sensibility well deserves it.'

Such regard for sensibility seldom goes with haughtiness, and one quite regrets that the wedding had to take place in Seville, rather than in London, for one feels that Cervantes would have had no scruples in resuscitating the Virgin Queen to preside at it.

[1] Isabel(a) is the Spanish form of Elizabeth.

Cervantes Criticism Outside Spain

It will be obvious to all members of the Congress[1] that no adequate and comprehensive treatment of this subject is possible within the limits of a single paper, or, indeed, of a single book. Even if we omit, as I propose to do, Cervantes criticism in Portugal and in the nineteen American nations who speak the languages of the Peninsula, since these are so closely related to Spain as to be only in the geographical sense 'outside' it; even if we leave out of account the comparatively recent but very substantial and weighty contributions of investigators in the United States of America;[2] even if we omit mention of nineteenth-century Russia,[3] where Pushkin, Gogol, Turgenieff and Dostoievsky (especially the last) all testified to their admiration for the *Quijote*; even if we neglect the numerous books and articles on Cervantes by writers of what in a cultural sense we may, without giving offence, term the smaller nations, and confine ourselves to four European countries—France, Italy, Germany and England—we have still material for four large volumes. The author of *Don Quijote* has for centuries stimulated the critical faculties of Hispanists all over the world, and of many others whose only claim to be called Hispanists is the fact that they have drunk deeply of the wisdom and the art of one who is without question the greatest Spanish man of letters of all time.

---

[1] The Asamblea Cervantina de la Lengua Española, before which this paper was read on 17th April 1948. That it was written for a non-British public will be evident at many points in the text below. I refer to *Don Quijote* and to the 'Exemplary Novels' (*Novelas ejemplares*) by their Spanish titles throughout.

[2] See M. F. Heiser, 'Cervantes in the United States', in *Hispanic Review* (1947), XV, 409–35.

[3] Cf. L. B. Turkevitch, *Cervantes in Russia* (Princeton, 1949).

He challenges by his greatness—I mean, not so much by his immensity as by his transcendence:

> *Others abide our question, Thou art free.*
> *We ask and ask: thou smilest and art still*
> *Out-topping knowledge. . . .*

He attracts, at the same time, by his many-sidedness, which has led numerous critics to extract from him only, or principally, what they have themselves put into him, and by his strong human appeal, which has lured many into believing that they find simplicity in what is complicated in the highest degree.

These are indications, you may say, of the self-digged pits into which the critics have fallen rather than of the heights which they have attained. They are also indications, however, of the characteristics and idiosyncrasies of the critics themselves; and it is true to say that a systematic study of any branch of Cervantes criticism is likely to throw more light upon the critics than upon Cervantes. Nor is this type of enlightenment in the least to be despised. The study of the influence exerted by some great writer—Cervantes, Shakespeare, Goethe—upon some other individual, some epoch, some current of thought, is apt, at the present time, to be decried—chiefly because it is envisaged as adding something to our knowledge of the author whose influence is under discussion. How much more profitable, it is said, to read and assimilate the wisdom of Cervantes for oneself than to spend time resuscitating worthless books written by justly forgotten authors and giving them unmerited publicity because they plagiarized one so infinitely greater than themselves, not having the wit to write something of their own creation! To that very understandable contention many different answers have been given, but, if I may speak as one whose studies have often led him into those mazes of investigation which are concerned with literary influences, the answer which I find most satisfying is that, insignificant, perhaps sometimes despicable, as are these minor authors, the impact upon them of a mind so great as to be beyond their understanding, the attitude which they have taken towards a work whose range, whose depth, whose tragedy or whose pathos they have been incapable of appreciating, has illumined for me, not their own insignificant personalities so much as one corner of the age in which they lived. Any cultured Englishman would feel indignant that Voltaire could call Shakespeare a 'drunken savage', did he not immediately

266

reflect that the remark has long since recoiled upon its author: it tells the modern reader nothing whatever about Shakespeare but a very great deal about Voltaire. Again, the sensitive Englishman would resent the sacrilegious hands that were laid upon Shakespeare by Ducis—who, you will remember, re-wrote *Othello*, omitting from it Iago, and gave *Hamlet* a relatively happy ending—did he not, in so doing, also present an ironically and quite unintentionally devasting picture of the limitations of the eighteenth century.

Now many of the criticisms and appreciations of Cervantes— and especially of the *Quijote*—which have been made by foreigners have precisely that kind of value; and if I were to spend the hour which you have been good enough to allow me in attempting to cover the whole ground, I should not only have little more to offer than a catalogue of names and titles, but I should be mixing some genuine criticism with much that is a mere reflection of the writer's own prejudices and temperament. So surpassingly great is Cervantes that he is a universal touchstone—a mirror, if you like, into which the critic looks, believing it to be clear glass, and beholds his own reflection. 'In the *Quijote*', once wrote P. Bruno Ibeas, 'every reader sees what pleases him, according to his temperamental predisposition.'[1] Illustrations of that fact abound in every country and every century. Here, in seventeenth-century France, is the elegant materialistic philosopher Saint-Evremond, who somewhat shamefacedly avows that he reads the *Quijote* with pleasure, and cannot think how Cervantes was able to impart such interest to the story of a 'pauvre fou'. Here, in eighteenth-century England, is Tobias Smollett, author of several broad and farcically humorous novels in the picaresque vein,[2] who in the author of the *Quijote* thinks he sees a kindred spirit to his own, and, in the prefatory note to his translation of that book, resolves to 'maintain its ludicrous solemnity and self-importance'. A century later, Cervantes criticism reflects the course of the Romantic and of the post-Romantic movement, with all their exaggerations, in England, France and Germany. One of the latest, and most exaggerated, exponents of such criticism, Alexander James Duffield, believed

---

[1] *España y América* (1916), II, 193, cit. L. Pfandl, *Geschichte der spanischen Nationalliteratur in ihrer Blütezeit* (Freiburg im Breisgau, 1929), p. 289 (*Historia de la literatura nacional española en la Edad de Oro* (Barcelona, 1933), p. 321).

[2] Cf. pp. 245–6, above.

Spain in Cervantes' day to have been a country devoid of ideals, and saw Cervantes as the leader of a moral crusade.[1]

All this time interest in the *Quijote*, and to a lesser extent in Cervantes' other works, was rising. A current bibliography shows eleven English editions in the seventeenth century, 68 in the eighteenth and 176 in the nineteenth; and in France 27 editions in the seventeenth century, 69 in the eighteenth and 207 in the nineteenth. During the present century the vogue of Cervantes' immortal novel has been even greater, and at the same time far more attention than ever before has been bestowed upon the remaining works, with the result that Cervantes criticism has become wider, bolder and more subjective. At the time of the First World War, for example, a French critic called Scantrel, writing under the pseudonym André Suarès, published an extraordinary essay representing the story of Don Quijote as an allegory: '(Don Quichotte) se jette sur les moulins de la science et de la barbarie pour délivrer la Belgique torturée et la Serbie traînée par les cheveux, deux nobles sœurs au supplice. . . . Toboso est en France, aujourd'hui'.[2] No doubt Max-Hellmut Neumann's essay, also published in 1916, which I have not been able to see, entitled 'Cervantes y la guerra actual: consideraciones de un soldado alemán',[3] would tell a different story.

All that, of course, is fantasy, not criticism; but it is an exaggerated example of a tendency which has been increasingly prevalent since the beginning of the century, and in particular since the tercentenary celebrations of 1916. Thus, in 1929, the Russo-German, Joseph Bickermann, compares Cervantes with Goethe ('Den gleichen Weg gingen: der eine wie der andere führt seinen Helden zum Bankerott durch dialecktischen Prozess'), and both of them with Dostoievsky, the only other writer 'der mit gleicher, ja noch grösserer Eindringlichkeit die Nichtigkeit übermenschlicher Ansprüche seitens der sterblichen Menschen enthüllt'.[4] In the course of his main comparison, which I confess I do not find very convincing, Bickermann interpreted Cervantes' hero according to a formula which at that time was very common in Germany: he was a reprehensible example of the superman who brings about his own defeat by imposing his own arbitrary standards on society.

[1] Cf. p. 248, above.   [2] *Cervantes* (Paris, 1916), pp. 29–30.
[3] In *Homenaje a Cervantes* (Frankfurt-a-M., 1916), cit. *Die Neueren Sprachen*, XXV, 148 n.
[4] *Don Quijote und Faust* (Berlin, 1929), pp. 400, 401.

In view of the ideology prevailing in Soviet Russia, it will not be surprising to find that a Russian critic, Pavel Novitsky, sees in the characters of Don Quijote and Sancho Panza what he considers to be the tragic dualism of a bourgeois civilization hesitating between policies of spirituality and materialism, and not having the courage to make a choice.[1]

These are interpretations only one degree less fantastic than that of Suarès, but it is worth while to begin this address by calling attention to them, since they represent a tendency which has been colouring some of the more serious criticism to which I shall shortly refer. The pendulum of the political world, and even the pendulum of the literary world, have been swinging violently of late, and we find a strong subjective interest, amounting at times to passion, in the attempts made alternately to represent Cervantes as a conservative and as a revolutionary, to see him as typical, first of the Renaissance and then of the Baroque.

With these considerations in mind, I propose that we glance briefly at some representative contributions to the study of Cervantes in France, Germany, Italy and England.

[II]

In France, as in England, Cervantes had a considerable vogue from almost the beginning of the seventeenth century, and the history of that vogue, and, to some extent, of Cervantes criticism in France, has been studied of recent years by four authors, from four different countries: Esther J. Crooks, a professor from the United States, in *The Influence of Cervantes in France in the Seventeenth Century* (1931); Max-Hellmut Neumann, a young German, who died at the age of twenty-seven, and whose doctoral dissertation, *Cervantes in Frankreich*, published by Adalbert Hämel (1930), brings the same story down to 1910; Maurice Bardon, who in 1931 published his *Don Quichotte en France au 17ᵉ et au 18ᵉ siècles*; and an Englishman, George Hainsworth, who, in a much shorter study than either of these, examines the history in France of the *Novelas ejemplares*.

References to Cervantes' works by French writers begin soon after the publication of the *Galatea*—that is to say, before the end of the sixteenth century. The *Novelas ejemplares*, translations of

[1] *Cervantes and Don Quijote* (New York, 1936), cit. H. A. Hatzfeld, in *Hispania* (U.S.A.) 1947, XXX, 324.

which began as early as 1615, owe their early popularity to the
love of the exotic and the improbable which characterized the
early seventeenth century. *Don Quijote*, first translated by César
Oudin and François Rosset, in 1614, soon outdistanced these in
popularity, but principally on account of its striking incidents and
the force of its two main characters—it was not until much later
that any realization developed of the book's significance. Signs
of Cervantes' influence upon French poetry are few, but upon the
novel, many. Sorel, Du Verdier and Scarron have direct debts to
him. It was on the stage, however, that Cervantes had the greatest
influence. Pichou, about 1627, drew material for one of his plays
from *Don Quijote*, and Guérin de Bouscal used that work for no less
than three. Hardy takes three plots from the *Novelas ejemplares*,
which also influenced Guérin de Bouscal, Scudéry, Quinault,
Rotrou—the latter's adaptations being the best. The *Novelas*
which chiefly interested the French dramatists were the Romantic
ones, notably *La Gitanilla*, *Las Dos Doncellas* and *El Amante liberal*.
The influence upon the French stage of Cervantes' own plays is
almost nil.

For a long time the French had no conception of the depth, or
even of the true nature, of the character of Don Quijote. They took
the most superficial view of him, adapted it to the very unflattering
conception of the Spanish character which was current in seventeenth-century France, and represented him as a boaster, if not
also as a coward—almost always as a comic character. Sancho
Panza, as might be expected, is almost entirely comic. As the
seventeenth century advanced, imitations tended to decrease in
number, but to improve in quality.

The eighteenth century, as we should expect of the 'Age of
Enlightenment', was much less interested in Cervantes than the
seventeenth, but, as it was more critically inclined, such interest
as it did show was more intelligent. The attraction which Cervantes
had for Lesage, at the beginning of the century, is well known;
Marivaux, too, imitated him at this time. To Montesquieu *Don
Quijote* was the only good book which had come from Spain:
'le seul de leurs livres qui soit bon est celui qui a fait voir le ridicule
de tous les autres'.[1] Bernardin de Saint-Pierre understood both
Spain and Cervantes better and had some conception of what *Don
Quijote* meant; La Harpe, though typically impatient of the length
of the novel and of its author's indifference to what was known as

[1] *Lettres persanes*, 78.

the 'rigour of art', recognized its high quality: 'un bon (livre) . . . qui vivra'. '*Don Quijote*' was one of the answers given to the famous question 'What does one owe to Spain?' which Napoleon I's librarian, the Abbé Denina, made the text of his address to the Academy of Berlin, in which he asserted that France owed more to Golden Age literature in Spain than all other countries together owed to France. 'Tous les beaux esprits de France,' he said, 'n'ont jamais loué aucun ouvrage d'agrément autant que le *Don Quichotte.*'

The most remarkable tribute paid in French to the *Quijote* during the eighteenth century, however, was perhaps that contributed by a Dutch journalist, Just van Effen, to *Le Misanthrope*, a weekly review of his own. At last the conception of the true nature of the book is beginning to be suspected. It is one of the best works, he says, for the young, not only because it will amuse them, but for the formation of their judgment. Intellectuals will prize it both for its style and for its thought. It has much to teach philosophers. Its significance opens out before one as one grows older: indeed it is only the mature who can give it proper appreciation. Nothing more 'modern' had been written on *Don Quijote* in any language down to that date (1726).

During the pre-Romantic and Romantic periods, the popularity of *Don Quijote* in France began to increase with extreme rapidity. Cervantes and his master-work now invade poetry as well as the novel and the drama, and, as in every one of the countries under survey a typically Romantic conception of *Don Quijote* holds sway Chateaubriand, who described Cervantes' hero as 'the noblest, the bravest, the most lovable and [despite Saint-Evremond's dictum] the least mad (*le moins fou*) of mortals', not only exemplifies that conception, but also foreshadows the greater complexity of interpretation which the new century was to bring. In the French language it was probably the Genevan Sismondi, whose four-volume *De la Littérature du Midi de l'Europe* was published at Paris and Strasbourg in 1813, who first underlined the dualism in *Don Quijote* which criticism in succeeding decades was to throw into relief more and more. Though telling an amusing story, the book gave rise only to serious reflections. It was indeed a sad book, said Sismondi, as Byron was to say a few years later, and Sainte-Beuve later still: he even described it as the saddest book ever written. It illustrated the eternal contrast between the spirit of poetry and the spirit of prose. It presented a character admirable if regarded from the higher standpoint, laughable from a lower one. These are only a few typical points from Sismondi's exposition, but it will be seen how they harmonize with the Romantic love of antithesis, which helped to popularize this dualistic conception of Cervantes' art during the first half of the nineteenth century. It was attacked, together with the pessimistic attitude to Cervantes of Schopenhauer a few years later, by Prosper Mérimée, then a youth of twenty-three, who described it as ingenious and suggestive, but false to Cervantes. The *Quijote*, he asserted, was no satire on humanity: it was a gay and amusing story, full of 'constant good humour'—the work of 'a man content to live with society as he finds it'. Between the extreme positions of Sismondi and Mérimée stands Louis Viardot, who, while refusing to be led away by antithesis, and even seeing in Don Quijote and Sancho two brothers—'deux hommes devenus inséparables comme l'âme et le corps, s'expliquant, se complétant l'un par l'autre'—looks upon the book as having been born in the author's brain as a satire on chivalric romances but as having grown in that brain beyond recognition and become at last 'a book of practical philosophy . . . a gentle and judicious criticism of all humanity'.

And now come a host of critics, each with his own distinctive viewpoint, often influenced by some personal idiosyncrasy or literary affiliation. Puibusque returned to the theory of poetry versus prose and Charles Magnin repulsed it. Emile Littré marvelled at the psychological complexity of Cervantes' hero, which he considered the chief interest of the novel. Emile Montégut found symbolism in it, but refused to regard it as merely a conflict between two principles, such as the physical and the spiritual. It was the expression of Cervantes' own spirit, 'a remarkable and almost unnatural marriage between the heroic and the picaresque'. Sainte-Beuve, who in his 'Monday' articles had more than once occasion to intervene in these discussions, took, as one would expect, the objective line, attacking the Romantic position taken up by his adversary Victor Hugo, and warning critics that for some time they had been too apt to put themselves in Cervantes' place and to see tears mingled with his smiles. For himself, open the book where he might, he could detect no bitter satire at all.

Passing over a number of late-nineteenth-century critics, such as Emile and Philarète Chasles, Victor Fournel, Gustave Vapereau and Jacques Demogeot, we must pause for a moment, before coming to the most modern French criticism, at some characteristic

ideas expressed by two contemporaries at the turn of the century—
Alfred Morel-Fatio and Ernest Mérimée.

Both these belong to what one might term the *escuela simplista* of
Cervantine criticism, which, sometimes from reaction against
writers of excessive subtlety, and sometimes from a disinclination
to penetrate a mind of transcendent greatness, has had a surprising
number of adherents. Morel-Fatio, in his 'L'Espagne de Don
Quichotte' (1894),[1] finds in Cervantes' master-work weak reason-
ing and confused ideas combined with an amazing power of invention. Modern critics, he writes, have suffered from the disastrous
mania (*fâcheuse manie*) of interpreting him with excessive subtlety.
He was no precursor, no advanced thinker in matters of religion or
politics. He had not to practise self-restraint in order to avoid
certain delicate questions, which preoccupied some of his contemporaries—for he was not interested in these problems. When con-
fronted with 'grave social problems' which an 'indignant spirit'
(*esprit indépendant*) might have attacked resolutely, he treated them
like any other seventeenth-century Spaniard. Cervantes, concludes
the author, was *not* a 'universal genius', an 'exceptional being', or
even an *esprit fort*. What was he, then? Essentially a man of his
age, a highly skilled novelist (*très habile conteur*) and an *honnête
homme*.

Ernest Mérimée, in his History of Spanish literature, writes
not dissimilarly. *Persiles* 'manque de sens, de portée, de valeur
philosophique autant que d'intérêt. On ne sait vraiment ce que
l'auteur a prétendu faire.'[2] The *Quijote*, of course, is magnificent,
but also magnificently simple. We must not search it for esoteric
meanings or enigmas: it is 'simply an amusing and wonderfully
merry story: one can extract its marrow without cracking the
bone'.[3] And its author? Well, he is very Spanish: 'he expresses the
ideas, and even the prejudices, of the average Spaniard of his day
on religion, politics and morals, for in these respects he was in no
way superior to his contemporaries'.[4] His philosophy? Again how
simple! 'It pertains to no sect, no school, no dogma: it is simply
human.'[5] Some years after these judgments saw the light, a critic
in the United States, writing a book with the title *Is there a*

---

[1] Originally the Taylorian Lecture at Oxford for 1894. Reprinted in *Studies
in European Literature* (Oxford, 1900), pp. 149–208, and also in *Études sur l'Espagne*,
1ère série, 1895.

[2] *Précis d'histoire de la littérature espagnole* (Paris, n.d.), 2nd ed., p. 280.

[3] *Op. cit.*, p. 285.   [4] *Op. cit.*, p. 286.   [5] *Op. cit.*, p. 287.

Philosophy in the 'Quijote'?[1] decided that there was—but only 'a philosophy of faith in ideals, in the value of effort, in the triumph of justice, in the merit of sacrifice'. Writers who belong to the *escuela simplista* are surprisingly often in agreement.

But in spirit, if not in actual fact, this type of criticism is of the nineteenth century. Let us permit ourselves a brief digression before taking a glance at some criticism characteristic of the twentieth.

Since the two centenaries of 1905 and 1916 the main lines of Cervantes criticism have taken a fresh direction. Broadly speaking, it may be said that the seventeenth century regarded Cervantes in a merely superficial way—generally as the author of a single book whose hero was a madman, or a buffoon; that the eighteenth century varied between intelligent criticism and sheer falsification; and that the early nineteenth claimed him as its own, romanticizing and idealizing his great hero as 'un de ces fous qui naissent pour faire honte aux sages; un poète; un individu, défendant les droits de la personnalité humaine contre la masse ignorante et stupide; un héros tragique; un Mage' (I cite an almost contemporary French Cervantist: Paul Hazard).[2] But, as the nineteenth century proceeded, Cervantes criticism, rejecting Quintana's view that nothing new about him remained to be said,[3] went deeper than it had done previously and the general attitude of critics in 1900 was immeasurably superior to their attitude a hundred years before. While it is true that interpretations of *Don Quijote* were never more fantastic than in the latter half of the nineteenth century, it is also true that they had never previously been as numerous. And towards the end of the century an important lead was given to Cervantine studies—alike historical, linguistic, textual and interpretative—by Spain herself. It would be going beyond the scope of this address to do more than cite names revered by us all—Menéndez Pelayo, Rodríguez Marín, Bonilla y San Martín —which are associated with this resuscitation of investigatory zeal and enlargement of the critical field: others have followed, but to these is due our first tribute of remembrance.

---

[1] David Rubio, *¿Hay una filosofía en el Quijote?* (New York, 1924).

[2] 'Ce que les lettres françaises doivent à l'Espagne', in *Revue de littérature comparée* (1936), XVI, 11.

[3] 'Nada de nuevo al parecer hay que decir sobre Cervantes.' Cit. Aubrey F. G. Bell, 'The Character of Cervantes', in *Revue hispanique* (1930), LXXX, 653.

Several aspects of these new studies invite attention. The impressionist, symbolistic, almost mystical interpretations of *Don Quijote* which had been current for a century ceased, and a large part of Cervantine activity began to expend itself upon the establishment and elucidation of texts. Both historical and linguistic knowledge were called in for this work, which was pursued by men with the necessary scholarly preparation. Again, criticism, both textual and interpretative, was applied, not merely to *Don Quijote* and the *Novelas ejemplares*, as heretofore, but to the whole body of Cervantes' writing: it was felt useless to attempt a study of the part without the illumination cast by the whole. A third characteristic of these new studies was that, instead of being regarded as a world-phenomenon, Cervantes began to be regarded as a man of his country and his age—as a man of the Golden Age; as a contemporary of the Counter-Reformation; as a subject of Philip II; as a successor, in a strictly chronological sense, of Erasmus, and a harvester of the fruits of the Spanish Renaissance.

This digression, during which our eyes have been raised from France, to range over Europe, was necessary before we could go farther. For, when we pass from Morel-Fatio or Mérimée to Cassou or Bataillon, we are conscious of being almost in a fresh element. We are not in the air, but on the solid earth. We are studying a man in relation both to his country and age and to universal values. To Cassou, Cervantes is above all a man of the Renaissance. 'Le lecteur, qui garde dans sa mémoire la gamme des idées et des attitudes qu'a fait chanter la Renaissance, en retrouvera la résonance à travers toute l'œuvre de Cervantes.'[1] He sees Cervantes' work, to quote a contemporary critic, much as a man of the Renaissance saw the world after adjusting his mind from Ptolemaic ideas to Copernican—'as a poetic though tragic vision of the modern world created on the débris of the Middle Ages.'[2] Such a man—no ignoramus, as some have said, even if no erudite[3]—was among 'the advanced spirits of his age', and had, of necessity, either from 'moral scruples or political prudence', to conceal, from time to time, his real thoughts. This duality is only 'one of the numerous ambiguities, so complex and so subtle', which combine in the mind of Cervantes.[4] There is more than dualism here: there is continual oscillation, kaleidoscopic variety, a delicate

---

[1] *Cervantes* (Paris, 1936), p. 73.   [2] Hatzfeld, *op. cit.*, p. 323.
[3] *Cervantes*, pp. 61–2.
[4] Cervantes, *Nouvelles exemplaires*, tr. Cassou (Paris, 1928), I, 10.

balance between one type of opinion and another: 'avec Cervantes on est perpétuellement dans l'équivoque'.

Marcel Bataillon, who has been long known as a Hispanist of outstanding merit, and, with the publication in 1937 of his substantial volume on Erasmus and Spain, took his place in the first rank of critics, confirms and elaborates some of the findings of Américo Castro's well-known work *El Pensamiento de Cervantes* (1925) and corrects others. The idea that affinities existed between Erasmus and Cervantes had, of course, been adumbrated by Menéndez Pelayo, though, like so many other illuminating ideas which he was the first to enunciate, he left this for others to develop. Castro, while acknowledging his debt to Menéndez Pelayo, pointed out that he hardly coincided with him 'in more than words'. 'Cervantes' Erasmism', he remarked, 'meant much less to that great critic than it does to me; I would even venture to say that it meant something quite different.' 'To me Erasmus . . . represents a new religious conception, an ideology in harmony with humanistic ideas.'[1] Cervantes, Castro maintains, was in that sense an Erasmist, was more progressive than most of his contemporaries—notably in matters concerning religion, nationalism and the 'sentiment of honour'—and was forced to conceal his advanced ideas and to proclaim others in a way which amounted to hypocrisy. Bataillon, in a long article based upon Castro's book,[2] subscribes to Castro's conclusion, 'But for Erasmus Cervantes would not have been what he was', though he reaches that conclusion by other paths. He follows Castro far more critically and in greater detail than Cassou. Dissenting from him in various respects, notably as concerns Cervantes' alleged hypocrisy, he thinks his conception of Spanish Erasmism is too near to rationalism to be tenable: in general, he finds that to Castro the essentials of Erasmism consist in those aspects of it which appeal to him most. In his master-work, Bataillon enables us to trace the route along which he himself has travelled. Its final chapter summarizes his views on Cervantes' Erasmism. Cervantes may or may not have read Erasmus (Castro adduces some striking parallels which incline one to think that he had); in any case, however, Erasmus' influence upon him was not in the main direct, but came through the Spanish Erasmist movement which interposed itself between the periods of intellectual activity of the two great writers—Erasmus, it must be remem-

[1] *El Pensamiento de Cervantes* (Madrid, 1925), p. 263.
[2] *Revue de littérature comparée* (1928), VIII, 318–38.

bered, died eleven years before Cervantes was born—and in particular through his master Juan López de Hoyos. Far from leading him in the direction of a rationalism which denies the Christian faith, his Erasmism keeps him close to the great leaders of the Counter-Reformation. 'Ce n'est pas un incrédule qui cache sa secrète pensée derrière d'onctueuses protestations d'orthodoxie. C'est un croyant éclairé, pour qui tout dans la religion n'est pas sur le même plan, qui sourit de bien des choses auxquelles va la vénération populaire, et qui se permettrait d'en rire . . . si les exigences de la nouvelle orthodoxie tridentine ne l'obligeaient à une prudente réserve.'[1]

[III]

The greatest achievement of Germany in the field of Cervantine studies has been the important part which it played in the rediscovery of Cervantes at the beginning of the nineteenth century, and which has been expounded with typical French industry and skill by J.-J. A. Bertrand in his *Cervantes et le romantisme allemand* (1914) and more briefly by Max-Hellmut Neumann in an essay which, had he lived, he would no doubt have enlarged into a full-length study.[2]

It was one of the glories of German romanticism to have rediscovered, not only Cervantes, but many other great Spanish writers, and the discovery came with the greater force because, during the seventeenth and eighteenth centuries, Spain was almost unknown in Germany. Most of what knowledge of Spanish authors there was came through French translations. To that extent some interest was shown, during the seventeenth century, in realistic, and especially in picaresque, fiction, and, as in France, the *Quijote* (first translated, though only partially, in 1621) was considered mainly as an outstanding example of this: all Cervantes' other works were unknown. Some further knowledge about him came through English authors who had translated or imitated him; but it was not till late in the eighteenth century that Johann Andreas Dieze, who, in translating and editing Velázquez's *Orígenes de la poesía castellana*, in 1769, tried, in his own words, 'to open up for his compatriots a new and still unknown field of litera-

---

[1] *Erasme et l'Espagne* (Paris, 1937), pp. 827–8.
[2] 'Cervantes in Deutschland', in *Die Neueren Sprachen* (Marburg, 1917–18), XXV, 147–62, 193–213.

ture', set to work to interest them, not only in the *Quijote*, but in Cervantes' other works and in Mayáns' biography of their author. It was about this time that intelligent and cultured Germans (notably Link, Fischer and the Humboldts) began to travel in Spain, and much interest in the country developed. Cervantes now began to be translated directly from Spanish into German. Schiller knew Cervantes early and made frequent quotations from *Don Quijote*, which he thought of as a study in antithesis between idealism and reality. Goethe, too, was deeply impressed by the novel, the influence of which is shown in *Wilhelm Meister*.

Thus, although, at the end of the eighteenth century, Cervantes was far from being one of the best known of foreign writers in Germany, the way for his emergence as such was being prepared.

Of German Hispanists who contributed to Cervantine studies, one in this epoch is quite outstanding—both because he was a Classic by temperament and training and stood apart from the German Romantics, and also because his influence extended far beyond the bounds of Germany. This was the philosopher Friedrich Bouterwek (1766–1828), whose *Geschichte der spanischen Literatur* was first published at Göttingen in 1804. Essentially Bouterwek's aim in writing was to create and develop sympathy between Germany and Spain, and he was therefore particularly anxious to make and diffuse a just estimate of Spain's greatest writer. While he studied the *Galatea*, the *Novelas ejemplares*, the *Comedias* and *Persiles y Sigismunda*, Bouterwek had naturally most to say of the *Quijote*, the greatest novel ever written, by virtue of which its author belongs to the whole world. He sweeps aside the conceptions of the book which were current in his age, and which we have already examined, in favour of a profounder one. 'No greater mistake can be made than to consider the *Quijote* as merely a satire ridiculing the passion for reading romances of chivalry.' The knight of La Mancha is 'the immortal representative of all men of exalted imagination, who carry the noblest enthusiasm to a pitch of folly; because, with understandings in other respects sound, they are unable to resist the fascinating power of a self-deception, by which they are induced to regard themselves as beings of a superior order'. This conception, if not absolutely new, was sufficiently so to influence opinion in Germany, France and England. With it Bouterwek develops the dualistic aspect of the book: not only are the two chief characters, he says, essentially opposed to each other, but the entire theme may be considered as a conflict between

nature and reason on the one hand and the unnatural and unreasonable (*Unnatur* and *Unvernunft*) on the other.

Whatever Bouterwek's attitude to Romantic ideals, this conception has much in common with that of the Romantics, which
was first expounded by Friedrich Schlegel and soon afterwards by
his brother August Wilhelm. I have compared the gifts of the two
brothers in discussing elsewhere their judgments on Calderón.[1]
Here Friedrich was the pioneer, August Wilhelm the subtler critic;
the first indicated the directions to be followed, the second pursued
them. Both, like Bouterwek, studied Cervantes as a whole, though
his *comedias*, beside Calderón's, naturally seemed primitive and
immature. Tieck also passed from Cervantes to Calderón, and,
though he imitated and translated the *Quijote*, he regarded it more
imaginatively, and less critically, than his contemporaries. The
first four or five years of the nineteenth century mark the peak of
interest in Cervantes during the first Romantic period in Germany:
later, and to a most marked extent after 1820, attention turned to
Dante, Shakespeare and Calderón, who were the German Romantics' chief idols. But, none the less, Cervantes' influence continued.
The effect of the contribution of Schelling, who was led by the
Quijote to a symbolistic conception of the novel, was delayed by the
postponement of the publication of his criticism till 1859. But
meanwhile the current—if uncritical—interest in Cervantes was
carried on enthusiastically by Heine, who remarked, in 1837, that
'only a German can quite understand Don Quijote';[2] Grillparzer,
who was highly critical, attacked the views of the German Romantics which were upheld by Eichendorff, one of Cervantes' greatest
admirers in nineteenth-century Germany. The fecundity of the
Romantic tradition became evident during the latter half of that
century and the early years of the next. The dualistic conception
of the *Quijote* was upheld by Scherer (1851) and Rosenkranz
(1855): the book is an allegory of ideal versus real, and the vastest
allegory ever created. Bouterwek still had his adherents and Dohm
developed his ideas in the spirit of Schelling, while Tieck was followed by Friesen and J. L. Klein.

The value of the Cervantine criticism of the German Romantics
and post-Romantics lies less in the theories and conceptions that
it created and developed than in the spirit which animated them.
There was breadth in their work, both in that they were the first

[1] *History of the Romantic Movement in Spain* (Cambridge, 1940), I, 84-8.
[2] Cit. Neumann, *op. cit.*, XXV, 147.

group of critics outside Spain to cease regarding Cervantes as a man of a single book, and also in that their estimates of this book ranged widely over so many fields of thought. In adumbrating numerous lines of approach, in displaying Cervantes' immense power through numerous media, they inspired later critics, in many countries, who had more adequate preparation for their task; it is difficult to estimate the vast deal which our contemporary Cervantine criticism owes them. M. Bertrand's fervent tribute to them is scarcely an exaggeration: 'Their work', he says, 'lies at the root of all Cervantine criticism, both of the present and of the future. Thanks to them, the *Quijote* appears as an eternal spring of poetry, life and thought. It is because of their enthusiastic exegesis that that work has won for itself the noble authority of a *Faust* or a *Hamlet* and that Cervantes takes rank with the greatest writers of the entire world.'

It is not perhaps fanciful to relate this characteristically Romantic procedure with the attitude of the only contemporary German critic whom there is time to mention. Ludwig Pfandl, in his History of Spanish Literature in the Golden Age,[1] portrays Cervantes as in the main a man of the Renaissance, writing at the beginning of a Baroque age, and, in his *Entremeses* and *Novelas ejemplares*, paying tribute to the Baroque, 'before flying for refuge to the dreamy romanticism of his *Persiles*'. But the *Quijote*, which reflects its author more truly than does any other of his works, is not only not Baroque in its style, but is consciously anti-Baroque in its ideas and tendencies. The story of Don Quijote's initial adventures, no doubt, was conceived as a satire against chivalric romances, and as nothing more. But (says Pfandl) from the moment of his second sally, accompanied by the faithful Sancho, the author aims higher, and attacks the degeneracy of a Baroque age. The man of the Renaissance sees danger ahead in a world from which the spirit of the Renaissance is departing. The old *caballerosidad* has gone; in its place has come *picardía*.

But it is not so much in this view of Cervantes that Pfandl is in the tradition of the Schlegels and Schelling as in the view which he takes of the functions of Cervantes criticism, at any rate in relation to the *Quijote*. Not only does he repeat with approval the words in which P. Ibeas enunciates the subjective critic's favourite axiom, but he reinforces it with a quotation in his own language:

---

[1] *Geschichte, etc.*, German ed., pp. 289–92; Spanish ed., pp. 321–4; *et passim*.

. 'Wer ist Don Quixote? Wie jede grosse dichterische Figur: alles, was man aus ihm macht und noch machen wird.'[1]

Cervantes criticism, he asserts, with a perhaps unfortunate over-simplification, is divided into two opposed camps. Some critics—one would have thought very few—hold that 'the only motive that Cervantes had or could have had' in writing the *Quijote* was to engage in a literary battle against books of chivalry. On this view Pfandl pours heavy scorn, maintaining his solidarity with the other camp, which is of opinion 'that everyone, according to his personal viewpoint, can give to the novel a symbolic meaning of his own'. As I am attempting here to take an entirely objective position, I will not enter into a discussion of this principle, but merely record my agreement with Pfandl's view that 'the characteristic of great works of literature, of whatever epoch and nation, is precisely this ability to reveal one thing to one person and another to another, to compel all their readers to live them for themselves, and thus to create themselves anew, in a different way, with each reader'.[2] And having expressed my agreement with that dictum I will permit myself the single comment that it does not carry us very far.

[IV]

Returning to our survey, which takes us next to Italy, we find that almost all important Cervantes criticism there is quite recent. Cervantes, indeed, has made little impression on either creative or critical writers in Italy. Some forty years ago, Eugenio Mele collected what bibliographical indications he could of Cervantes' vogue and influence in Italy during the seventeenth century,[3] starting from 1622, the year in which Lorenzo Franciosini published the first translation of the *Quijote*, which was followed (1624) by the first edition of the *Viaje del Parnaso* to be published in Spanish outside Spain, the first Italian edition of the *Novelas ejemplares* in Spanish (1625) and the first Italian translation of the *Novelas*, that of Guglielmo Clavelli, and of *Persiles*, that of Francesco Ellio, both published in 1626. But, despite the early date of these works,

---

[1] A. Eloesser, *Der Spiegel, Jahrbuch des Propyläenverlags* 1924, cit., Pfandl, *op. cit.*, p. 289 (Spanish ed., p. 321).

[2] *Geschichte, etc.*, German ed., p. 290; Spanish ed., p. 322.

[3] 'Per la fortuna del Cervantes in Italia nel Seicento', in *Studi di filologia moderna* (Catania, 1909), II, 229–35. Cf. *Revista de Filología Española* (Madrid, 1919), VI, 364; (1921), VIII, 281–3.

the total results of Mele's investigations are described by their author himself as a 'miserable little handful,' and it must be admitted that, even with various later additions made by Benedetto Croce, Mele himself and others, it is a poor collection to come from the country of Ariosto.[1] During the whole of the seventeenth century no other Italian translator of the *Quijote* appeared. True, as early as 1678 there occurs (in Muscettola's *Epistole familiari*) the neologism *chisciotteggiare*, which suggests that the *Quijote* had penetrated more deeply into the Italian language, life and culture than a mere bibliography would indicate. Still, taken as a whole, the seventeenth-century evidence is negative. 'There is no question', declares Mele, 'of any genuine influence of Cervantes on the literature of our Seicento. . . . It cannot be said that he impressed himself upon the Italian spirit; the Seicento did not, and could not, understand him.'[2] Rosaria Flaccomio, who has studied the fortunes of *Don Quijote* in Italy in the seventeenth and eighteenth centuries[3], comes to a similar conclusion. The book, she says, 'had little success (*scarsa fortuna*) in Italy. . . . It left no profound traces on Italian literature, nor did it inspire any real work of art till . . . the end of the eighteenth century.'[4] As for Cervantes' other works, Paolo Savj-López declared rotundly, as recently as 1913, that 'in Italy they are almost wholly unknown'.[5] There are certain signs that, during the three centuries preceding the Cervantes tercentenary of 1916, the evolution of the views held in Italy on the *Quijote* was similar to that which took place in France, Germany and England. But nothing published before the tercentenary indicated that, after it was over, Cervantes criticism in Italy was going to rival that of any other country outside Spain.

Savj-López's *Cervantes*, published at Naples in 1913 and translated into Spanish four years later, is essentially a book for the general reader, beginning with a short biography and then considering in turn five aspects of Cervantes' genius, as expressed in the *Galatea*, the *Quijote*, the *Novelas ejemplares*, the *Comedias* and the *Persiles y Sigismunda*. In a book of this type, comparable with Hazard's study of the *Quijote* and Schevill's biography, one would

---

[1] Cf. 'Cervantes y Ariosto', in M. de Montoliu, *Historia de la literatura española* (Barcelona, 1930), pp. 864–8; 'Ariosto e Cervantes', in Casella, *op. cit.*, pp. 413–26.

[2] Mele, *op. cit.*, II, 248.

[3] *La Fortuna del Don Chisciotte in Italia nei secoli XVII e XVIII, etc.* (Palermo, n.d. [1928]).

[4] *Op. cit.*, p. 142.   [5] Cf. *Cervantes*, tr. Solalinde (Madrid, 1917), p. 41.

not expect to find a detailed discussion of any single problem or any great profundity of thought. But one might expect something subtler than Morel-Fatio's *honnête homme*. What one reads in Savj-López, however, is almost precisely the same thing: 'E insomma un buon suddito e un uomo dabbene, ma nulla di più.' His thought? He can hardly be said to have any. No lofty interpretation of the world is to be found in him, says Savj-López, no solid thought, whether political, religious or moral: he follows the faith of his elders, he respects established order and recognized truths—the throne, the altar. At most, he would like to see the things of this world going somewhat better, for the comfort of good people everywhere. In short, he is a worthy man and a good citizen, but no more. When he begins an argument, one realizes he has a solid, well-formed mind, sound ideas and plenty of mediocre conceptions and middle-class common sense. His spirit knows nothing of unquiet.[1]

Here and there, it is true, as in the passage where the critic discusses Menéndez Pelayo's views on Cervantes' attitude to the spirit of Classical antiquity,[2] there are indications of a subtler approach, but the quotation just made is fairly representative of Savj-López's general position. His Cervantes is an *honnête homme*, undistinguished for his thought either on art or on life—'he is no true philosopher as regards either art or life'[3]—a phenomenally spontaneous artist and a prolific creator of character, with intuitive gifts of a high order.[4]

Written very shortly after the publication of Savj-López's book, but published only in 1920, Giuseppe Toffanin's broad and substantial work *La Fine dell' Umanesimo* is essentially a study in comparative European literature—dealing with Humanism and the Counter-Reformation in Italy, Spain, France, Germany and England—and has only a single chapter of ten pages on Cervantes. But this chapter contains several features of particular interest. For one thing, it takes up very seriously the question of Italian influences on Cervantes, a subject which, as Savj-López had remarked, had previously hardly been examined at all.[5] These influences it connects largely with the years which Cervantes spent in Italy (1569–75)—the period of the appearance of the *poéticas* of Castelvetro and Piccolomini—and drawing suggestive parallels between Cervantes and Tasso. 'The first germ of the *Quijote*', he

[1] *Op. cit.*, p. 38. [2] *Op. cit.*, p. 248. [3] *Op. cit.*, p. 37.
[4] *Op. cit.*, pp. 37, 39. [5] *Op. cit.*, p. 212.

goes so far as to say, 'can be found in our literary polemics.'[1] Next, it appraises the book both as a triumphant satire on a certain form of literature and as a 'sublime satire on life'. It adopts a fresh view of the characters of Don Quijote and Sancho, the subtlety of which, as the twentieth century advances, is becoming more generally recognized. And finally it takes a somewhat extreme position on the relations of Cervantes to the Renaissance and the Counter-Reformation: 'The work is not one of the last fruits of the Renaissance—it is at the opposite pole from that: the fruit, unique and glorious, of the Counter-Reformation.'[2] The author does little more than enunciate this dictum: one would have welcomed a more reasoned treatment of the subject, which possibly, had the book been written in the following decade, it would have been given.

'It is born', says Toffanin of the *Quijote*, 'of sentiments of reaction': the phrase is repeated, four years later, with startling bluntness, by Cesare de Lollis in his arresting, provocative and widely attacked book, *Cervantes reazionario*. To Lollis, Cervantes belongs to the Counter-Reformation purely and simply: all his work suffers from not being impregnated with the most characteristic ideals of the Renaissance. This is the theory of an advocate, not of a judge, and would be as difficult to sustain, in the face of criticism, as the theory that Cervantes is inimical to the Counter-Reformation altogether. Castro, who attacks it violently, has no difficulty in exposing its weaknesses. It represents Cervantes as an untutored genius; a good fellow—'il buon uomo che tutti sanno'[3]—and nothing more; a man of 'slight education',[4] of small Latin and less Greek; a man who believed in astrology, witchcraft and the language of dreams; but above all a man whose sole learning came from his own observation of his fellows, a man who wrote a world-masterpiece, 'senza saper come e perchè'.[5] Again, the critic attacks Cervantes' psychology, and, in writing of *Persiles*, seems to think that, in this respect, even Mme de la Fayette, in *La Princesse de Clèves*, is his superior.[6] Possibly the best answers to this conten-

---

[1] Toffanin, *op. cit.*, p. 213. 'Questo scapigliato e freschissimo Don Chisciotte nascesse da un' ispirazione polemica che s' integrò con tutta la superba fantasmagoria cervantesiana, ma non disparve giammai.'

[2] *Op. cit.*, p. 416.

[3] Lollis, *op. cit.*, p. 186.

[4] Lollis, *op. cit.*, p. 140; A. Castro, *El Pensamiento de Cervantes*, p. 16.

[5] Lollis, *op. cit.*, p. 233 (cf. p. 184); Castro, p. 16.

[6] Lollis, *op. cit.*, pp. 152–3; Castro, p. 69.

tion, and to the whole thesis of the book, are to be found in the *Novelas ejemplares* and the *Quijote*. But, fantastic as much of the book may seem, its appearance was salutary, for it aroused interest, provoked healthy controversy and opened many new avenues of discussion. There was no danger that Cervantes would be thought of as a 'simple man' any more.

The last work which I shall choose as representative of modern Italian criticism is larger than the other three put together— *Cervantes: Il Chisciotte*, by Professor Mario Casella, of the University of Florence. The work, contained in two large volumes, totalling nearly nine hundred pages, was published in 1938 after being awarded the Bonsoms Prize in Barcelona, but, owing to the interruption of international communications by the World War, failed to receive the attention it merits. Its great length, together with its lack of an analytical table of contents and an index, may continue to impede its proper recognition.

From the very beginning of his study, Casella leads us to the opposite extreme from the *escuela simplista*. 'The *Quijote*', he says, bluntly, 'is an enigma';[1] and, finding none of the attempted solutions of this enigma satisfactory (he actively criticizes nearly all his chief predecessors), he propounds a philosophical explanation of considerable complexity. Brushing aside the 'ingenious acrobatics' of one critic and the sheer 'misunderstandings' of another, as easily as he brushes aside the idea that Cervantes wrote his work with the object of ridiculing the books of chivalry, he tells us that the 'central problem of the *Quijote*, the problem which after so many years have passed makes it a living work still, is that of art as an intellectual virtue, by means of which man directly controls his operations . . . according to the rational exigencies of the work to be done or the truth to be known'.[2] To put it more concretely, Don Quijote, who is 'pure poetry',[3] starts from an illusionary love of self, his illusions hiding the truth from him in such a way that he cannot see himself as he ought. But at the same time his idealism leads him to pursue the aims of charity and mercy, and his ideal world is more than a world of chivalry: it is a world ruled by ideals

[1] Casella, *op. cit.*, I, xviii.

[2] *Op. cit.*, II, 424–5: 'Il problema centrale del *Chisciotte*, ciò che lo fa vivo ancora dopo tanto tempo . . . è quello dell' arte come virtù intellettuale, mediante la quale l'uomo regola immediatamente le sue operazioni . . . sulle esigenze razionali dell' opera da farsi o della verità da conoscere.'

[3] *Op. cit.*, II, 418.

of the saintly and the Divine. 'Casella sees in Cervantes', as a critic has said, 'practically the last representative of the Middle Ages, a man who defends unshakeable truths against the mirage of a modern world, which seems successful only because, as Don Quijote complains, the personal valour of a daring knight is bound to succumb to the blind technical force of ambushed artillery.'[1] He seems sure of his thesis, but a good deal has yet to be said about his interpretation of the term 'Middle Ages' and its relation with the Renaissance, with the spirit of which Cervantes clearly had so much in common. It seems best, therefore, at this stage, not to attempt a judgment on this substantial contribution to Cervantine studies, which, we may hope, with the impetus of this quatercentenary reinforcing the opportunities for international contacts now slowly returning after the end of the World War, will advance greatly.

[v]

Great Britain can show hardly any Cervantists of the stature of the greatest of those already described. True, in the last century Henry Spencer Ashbee studied Cervantine literature and the iconography of *Don Quijote*, Norman MacColl translated the *Novelas ejemplares* and Butler Clarke wrote some fine pages on Cervantes' art. More recently the late Sir Henry Thomas has written on the chivalric novel,[2] William J. Entwistle has published a collection of Cervantine essays[3] and Aubrey F. G. Bell has added to numerous articles, of which the best known is 'The Character of Cervantes',[4] a quatercentenary biography. None the less, to the British reading public, Cervantism is synonymous with one name—that of James Fitzmaurice-Kelly.

It should, however, be said that, if we have occupied ourselves little in Great Britain with the ideas of Cervantes, we have been, from the beginning, in the forefront of his readers. 'No foreign nation', wrote Martín Fernández de Navarrete in his *Life of Cervantes* (1819), 'has equalled England in its appreciation of the merit of Cervantes and of his ingenious fable, the *Quijote*.' This just verdict is particularly applicable to translations. The first French translation of Cervantes' masterpiece appeared in 1614; the first German translation in 1621; the first Italian translation in 1622.

[1] H. A. Hatzfeld, *op. cit.*, XXX, 327.
[2] *Spanish and Portuguese Romances of Chivalry* (Cambridge, 1920).
[3] *Cervantes* (Oxford, 1940)·   [4] *Revue hispanique* (1930), LXXX, 653–717

But the first English translation, that of Thomas Shelton,[1] was written in 1607, and, after spending four years in a drawer, licensed in 1611 and published in 1612, two years before the French version of César Oudin. Since that early date there has been a continual succession of distinguished translators,[2] and fresh versions are appearing still. Nor is this all. For over three centuries 'English literature teems with significant allusions to the creations of Cervantes' genius, the greatest English novelists are among his disciples, and English poets, dramatists, scholars and critics, agreed upon nothing else, are unanimous and fervent in their admiration of him'.[3] It is probably not too much to say that the *Quijote* is embedded in our English literary tradition to an extent probably unsurpassed by any work not originally written in the English language, with the single exception of the Bible.

The admiration referred to above was not, of course, entirely uncritical; but, as the changing views produced by the centuries on the nature of Cervantes' art, and in particular on *Don Quijote*, were similar in England to those of the other countries which we have mentioned, I need not do more than refer to them. To Motteux, who was more at home with Rabelais, and to Smollett, who ought to have specialized in the picaresque, Cervantes was a cheerful buffoon; to Lockhart he is the 'calm and enlightened' creator of one of the most pathetic, if not tragic, characters of world-literature; to Byron, as to Sismondi, the *Quijote* is a sad book:

> *Of all tales 'tis the saddest—and more sad*
> *Because it makes us smile: his hero's right*
> *And still pursues the right . . .*
> *. . . 'tis his virtue makes him mad.*[4]

Duffield takes up Byron's idea of Don Quijote's pursuing the right (''gainst odds to fight, his guerdon') and turns Cervantes into a high-minded crusader, the leader of a moral revolution. Perhaps it is because these various views were urged in their day with so much vigour that later writers have reacted against them so strongly. But it is fair to say that the generations which understood least of Cervantes' inner meaning were the most assiduous in studying

---

[1] Cf. pp. 240–2, above.   [2] Cf. pp. 242–50, above.

[3] James Fitzmaurice-Kelly, in *Proceedings of the British Academy* (1905–6), p. 29.

[4] *Don Juan*, XIII, 9.

him. In 1738, for example, Tonson, a London publisher, issued Gregorio Mayáns' *Vida de Miguel de Cervantes Saavedra*—the first biography worthy of that name; and in 1777 John Bowle suggested to the Hispanophile Percy that the time was ripe for the publication of a fully annotated edition of the *Quijote* in Spanish—an edition which appeared in six volumes, in 1781, and was both praised and utilized by Pellicer and Clemencín.

I stress these modest contributions to Cervantine studies because they deserve to be set against the paucity of our production in profound and creative criticism. Even Fitzmaurice-Kelly was a biographer, an editor and a popularizer of Cervantes rather than an interpreter of him. It will be granted that he fulfilled all those first three functions admirably. As a biographer of Cervantes, for example, he is as secure of a place in history as is Rennert for his biography of Lope de Vega. Each, either in this respect or in that, will be superseded, but each represents a milestone of progress. Fitzmaurice-Kelly was also notable for the care with which he followed the progress both of biographical and of textual studies made by Cervantists in Spain and abroad. In 1920, for example, he published a survey of recent Cervantine studies which was admirable proof of the closeness of his contacts with foreign Cervantists even during the isolation of the years of the First World War.

But to our deeper understanding of Cervantes Fitzmaurice-Kelly made practically no contribution. He belongs to the reaction to which I have referred above—to the *escuela simplista* of Morel-Fatio and Savj-López. Let us now examine the very latest expression of his ideas, a book published posthumously by his widow.[1] Why, he asks, should we regard *Don Quijote* as anything more than what it essentially is—'a masterpiece of entertainment'?[2] It survives as 'a splendid synthesis in which the factors of romance and realism are blended to perfection, as a gorgeous pageant of society in Spain, and a masterly representation of life as life has been everywhere at all periods of historical time'.[3] It began, no doubt, as a satire on the books of chivalry, but 'unconsciously'—mark the word—Cervantes 'began to modify that intention. . . . Before he was aware of it'—again note the phrase—'he found himself committed to a far larger enterprise than he had thought of.'[4] So, then, 'let us take him as he was; as an artist better at practice than at

[1] *A New History of Spanish Literature* (Oxford, 1926).
[2] *Op. cit.*, p. 280.   [3] *Op. cit.*, p. 287.   [4] *Op. cit.*, p. 279.

theory; great in his natural faculties rather than in his acquired ones. . . . That is his character: naturalness.'[1] Yes, that is Cervantes: an entertainer who chanced to be a genius, a naturally observant man who had been blessed with a 'marvellously rich experience'.[2] Why make a mystery about him? Why turn into something complicated what is delightfully simple? Why search in his work for what you will only succeed in finding if you put it there?

One may speculate what Fitzmaurice-Kelly would have said of the work of Lollis, Castro or Bataillon had he lived to see it, but we can, if we wish, study the effect of one of these writers on another critic, who died only in 1950, Aubrey FitzGerald Bell. Here is a writer whose work on the Spanish Renaissance, and in particular on Fray Luis de León, is as much of a milestone as Fitzmaurice-Kelly's biographical work on Cervantes. His extreme sensitiveness to beauty has illumined not only this period, but many others, both in Spanish and in Portuguese literature, but at the same time his extreme idealism sometimes leads him into exaggeration. So, in his *Notes on the Spanish Renaissance*,[3] recently republished in Spanish as *El Pensamiento español*,[4] in his *Castilian Literature*,[5] and in such essays as 'The Character of Cervantes'[6] and 'Liberty in Sixteenth-century Spain',[7] he reacts as violently against Castro as does Castro against Lollis—or as Castro would have done had Lollis' book not appeared such a short time before his own.

Critics who take a downright position towards some particular issue are always apt to be judged—and unfairly judged—on that issue to the neglect of other aspects of what they have written. I think Hatzfeld does Bell less than justice when he charges him with 'minimizing the historical implications around Cervantes' to the point of 'almost denying the existence' of problems over which controversy has raged, and describes him as seeing 'only a well-balanced, unpolitical, harmless, smiling Cervantes', who, out of the idealistic thesis and the realistic antithesis, 'created a poetic synthesis of the eternal Castilian mind'. The criticism would have

---

[1] This quotation is translated from the author's *Historia de la literatura española* (written in Spanish), (Madrid, 1921), p. 211.

[2] *Proceedings of the British Academy* (1905–6), p. 15.

[3] *Revue hispanique* (1930), LXXX, 319–652.   [4] Zaragoza, Ebro, 1944.

[5] Oxford, 1938.   [6] Cf. p. 286, n. 4, above.

[7] *Bulletin of Spanish Studies* (1933), X, 164–79. This is largely a reply to Castro's 'Erasmo en tiempo de Cervantes', *Revista de Filología Española* (Madrid, 1931), XVIII, 329–89.

been more nearly exact had it been applied to Fitzmaurice-Kelly. Bell undoubtedly sees red when he sees Castro, and of the accusation of hypocrisy brought by the latter against Cervantes he is altogether intolerant. But the fact that he does not fence with the calm objectivity of Bataillon should not blind us to his awareness of many problems connected with Cervantes' character and milieu. If he sometimes idealizes the Counter-Reformation and the Inquisition, his rejection of a current and only too facile antithesis in asserting the continuity of the Renaissance in Spain and the Counter-Reformation is worthy of all respect. So is his portrayal of Cervantes as a late Renaissance writer: 'so individual, so Spanhis, so universal . . . the culminating height of the Spanish Renaissance'. Nor does Bell's judgment of Cervantes err, as has been suggested, through over-simplification. The author of the *Quijote*, he maintains, was a highly complicated personality, forced by circumstances into situations more complicated still. 'A real contradiction underlay his work.'[2] To this fact may be ascribed the accusations of hypocrisy which have been brought against him. At any rate, 'no one is likely now to doubt the extreme subtlety of Cervantes' mind'.[3] 'So great is Cervantes' subtlety, so deep and intricate his art, that we forget that Don Quijote is not real at all.' And this subtlety 'is evident also in . . . other characters', and goes far beyond them. For Cervantes 'used all the resources of his subtle inventive mind to probe far into all this unintelligible world and found in the depths of his own spirit a larger humanity beside which the subtleties of metaphysical wit and verbal ingenuity appear thin and artificial'.[4] On that suggestive conception of a 'larger humanity' we may fitly end this survey.

[1] *Revue hispanique*, LXXX, 588. [2] *Op. cit.*, LXXX, 594.
[3] *Op. cit.*, LXXX, 688. [4] *Castilian Literature*, pp. 156, 157.

PART V

A Man of God

A Man of God[1]

Of the many friendships which it has been my good fortune to make during more than thirty years of close contact with Spain, none is more memorable than that which I enjoyed with the one-time Prior of the Carthusian monastery of Miraflores, Dom Edmund Gurdon.

[I]

It began quite unexpectedly. Among the reviews sent me in 1924 by the publishers of my first book on the Spanish mystics was one of outstanding value. Previous reviewers had either known a great deal about Spanish and very little about mystical theology or a great deal about mystical theology and very little about Spanish. Here, at last, was one familiar with both. Asking to be put in touch with him, I was surprised, soon afterwards, to receive a letter from the Prior of Miraflores, inviting me to pay him a visit.

Miraflores, of course, I knew well, but I had never met the Prior or been told he was English: so, stopping for a night at Burgos on my next journey to Madrid, I made my way on the following morning across the river and up the steep hill dominating the surrounding country, where, in the fifteenth century, John II had built that great, gaily named Charterhouse on the site of a palace begun by his father. It was in the small and simple garden courtyard which leads into the vast church that I first met one of the most striking and most spiritually minded men that it has been my privilege to know.

[1] For some of the biographical details in this essay I am indebted to a sketch by Dom Michael Hanbury, O.S.B., entitled 'A Modern Carthusian', which ran serially through *Pax* for 1941–3. The passages in quotation marks are taken either from that sketch or from Dom Edmund's letters to me or to several other of his correspondents who have been kind enough to allow me to use them.

293

Dom Edmund was tall, and almost entirely bald, with finely cut features, a high forehead, deep-sunk, far-seeing eyes, and a humorous mouth, perhaps his greatest charm, which at intervals would shape itself into a peculiarly sunny smile. He spoke English so seldom that he had a pronounced though musical accent, and every now and then, in his long, conversational letters, he would use some colloquial phrase just differently enough from the way it is used in England to remind one that he had hardly lived in his own country since he was a boy.

When I found that he liked receiving visitors from England, I began to send friends and pupils who were staying in Burgos to see him. All came back with the same story. Full as he was of shrewd common sense and irrepressible humour, there was a spirituality about him, a combination of tranquillity and power, which made even a short time spent in his company unforgettable. Several times I sent him people who were in trouble. So far as I know, not one of these ever confided in him, but they all went away comforted.

Each summer, for several years, I brought a group of students from Santander over the hills to spend a day in Burgos. We invariably went up to Miraflores. The Prior would insist on showing us the church himself, dwelling upon the detail of the magnificent monuments to John II, his consort and their son Don Alonso, of the intricate carving of the choir-stalls and of the fine *retablo* of the high altar. From the church we went back into the courtyard, where the Prior would pose for our cameras against Colonia's statue of Saint Bruno, to whom, it was often remarked, he bore a notable resemblance. Finally, he would accompany us to our motor-coach and wave us good-bye. On the last of these visits, I remember, he stood on the step of the coach till it began to move; then, with a nimbleness unusual in a man of seventy, sprang lightly off, and remained there, a tall white figure with an arm extended high above his head, until we had turned the corner and disappeared.

That was the last time I saw him.

[II]

Arthur Leslie Gurdon was born on 7th April 1864 at Assington, in Suffolk, where his father, an Anglican clergyman, held a family living. Two years later, his parents were received into the

Church of Rome. His early life was not a happy or an easy one: his mother died when he was five; his father, a man of uncertain temper and almost morbid reserve, remarried; and he himself was tormented by hereditary asthma. His stepmother being French, the family left England and went to live in the south of France, taking with them the boy of nine who was only twice to return to his own country again.

His life in the Landes, where, after short stays at Biarritz and Cambo, they lived till he was eighteen, deeply impressed him. Indeed, it probably sowed in him the seeds of that love for solitude which helped to form his vocation. Years afterwards, for example, he wrote of the pine-forest near his house in the village of Anglet:

'I loved to go to roam in it, enjoying the solitude and the silence which you can find there to your heart's content. You can walk miles and miles in those pine-woods without meeting a single human being except in the season of the year when the woodmen are busy collecting the resin or cutting down trees. . . . And as for silence, the only sounds you hear are the twitter of birds, the murmur of the wind passing through the needle-foliage of the pines, and the distant roar of the breakers on the shore of the Bay of Biscay. I listened to all that and to the silence and plucked the tiny sweet-smelling pinks, the only flower to be found there.'

For flowers—'one of the most touching marks and proofs of God's love for us'—he had an affection which was only a particular example of his passion for Nature: 'I can remain for hours gazing on beautiful scenery', he once said, 'and I find beauty in nearly every sort of scenery.' He certainly had early experience of it in ample variety, for at eighteen he left the flats of the Landes for the heights of the Grande Chartreuse.

How this delicate boy, suffering the physical tortures and the psychological repercussions of chronic asthma, ever conceived, still less survived, a life of Carthusian austerity is hard to imagine. Though with his love for solitude were united remarkable gifts of concentration, he had hardly seen a monk when he became one, and his religious education had been but rudimentary. But one day, he records, when he was about fifteen, the call came to him:

'I left the house to go and saunter in a wood close by. On my way there, I stopped and looked across a meadow adjoining the wood, when all of a sudden, like a flash of lightning, there came to my mind the thought: "Supposing I became a monk?" It came like a bolt from the blue; nothing whatever had led up to it; it was completely unconnected with anything I had been thinking of or had been reading about. It made a great impression upon me . . . partly because it was so unaccountable.'

Three years later, on All Saints' Eve, 1882, Arthur Gurdon assumed the name of Edmund and the white habit of Saint Bruno, which he was to wear for nearly fifty-eight years.

'I took to my new life', he wrote, 'like a fish to water. I had found at last an atmosphere my soul could breathe in freely, a life that had a meaning in it, a life that was worth living, . . . a joy and a great one. I became as merry as a lark and as happy as the day was long.' The hard plank bed, the long fasts, the three-hour night office, the absence of any kind of heat in the church, chapter-house and refectory—these things, no doubt, were rigorous, especially in the snow-bound winters; yet, remarkable to relate, it was not the young monk that they killed, but his asthma. Martyr to it though he had been, it never gave him serious trouble again. Four or five slight attacks he had in four or five years, 'and after that nothing, nothing, nothing'.

'I have lived since then in various lands and in widely different climates, warm and cold, dry and damp, close to the sea and far from it, high above sea-level and low down on the plain, and not the slightest touch of asthma have I had anywhere.'

Taking his simple vows in 1883, and his solemn vows in 1887, the year before he received priest's orders, Dom Edmund remained in the mother-house for seven years. The lasting impression which it made on him he has described in many of his letters:

'The lofty mountains, the dizzy precipices, the deep ravines at the bottom of which run foaming torrents, the forests of grand old fir-trees and bushes that climb up the mountain-sides, the meadows that here and there fill the open spaces on the slopes, and in spring-time, as soon as the snow thaws, become a mass of the most lovely wild flowers—all form a picture, or rather a series of pictures, of unparalleled grandeur and beauty which must be seen and cannot be described. I remember particularly the lovely autumn hues of the forests: every shade and tint of red, yellow and brown on the beech-tree leaves mingling with the dark green of the foliage of the fir-trees and rising up all round the monastery amphitheatre-wise.'

In the year of his ordination he was sent to the English monastery of Parkminster—first as novice-master and then as sacristan—after which he spent eight more years in French houses of his Order, and, when in 1901 the monks were driven from France, migrated with his community to Italy. In this same year, however, the Spanish Charterhouse of Montalegre, near Barcelona, which had been partly destroyed in the riots of 1835, was reopened for Carthusians from France, and in October 1902 Dom Edmund was transferred there. It was the beginning of a period of thirty-two years in a country then completely strange to him but which he was to end by making his own.

The somewhat austere beauty of the surroundings of Montalegre, and still more its solitariness, which gave it complete freedom from visitors of the tourist type, delighted him. A natural linguist, he took to Spanish as few do who start learning it when nearly forty, and he learned to speak it almost without accent. The Catalans in whose country his house was set he found extremely attractive, though, to judge from conversations that I subsequently had with him, he never really understood their problems. He filled almost every office at Montalegre, and finally, in 1915, was appointed Prior. Curiously, but rather characteristically, he hardly mentioned this appointment to anyone—even to his nearest relatives. I have the copy of a letter, for example, in which he gives the information in a postscript. His correspondent has inquired the proper way to address him. 'In the Order,' he replies,

'In the Order I am generally known as Dom Edmund. My present outside friends who happen to know my surname call me Father Gurdon. Others call me the Prior of Montalegre. Pray for him.'

It was at Montalegre that Dom Edmund first got to know the Benedictine abbey of Montserrat, not only the jagged background of which, but the actual buildings, can, on a clear day, be discerned from the monastery. For years afterwards, when travelling to Italy, for the General Chapter of his Order, he would break his journey at Monistrol and trudge the four steep miles, with bag in hand, up to the abbey, say his Mass in the basilica, perform his private devotions and picnic in peaceful solitude on the mountainside before resuming his journey. It was a place, he wrote, 'where I loved to linger, in the body, and where my soul . . . will ever love to linger in thought and recollection'.

In 1920, after a short period in which he acted as Visitor to the monasteries of the French province, Dom Edmund was transferred to Miraflores, again as Prior. He went there with mixed feelings. The monks at Montalegre had all been French; at Miraflores they were Spanish; so he was bidding farewell to a people with whom he had spent almost the whole of his life.

The Miraflores church, incomparably finer than anything at Montalegre, attracted numerous tourists. The landscape, to one bred in the Landes and Dauphiné, was monotonous and dreary—Dom Edmund was never captivated by the magical charm of arid Castile. And if the intense cold of winter was no worse than at the Grande Chartreuse, the elderly Prior was three times the age of the youthful postulant. One of the most interesting things he told me about his experiences at Miraflores concerns the terrible state of neglect with which the vault beneath Siloe's alabaster tombs had been allowed to remain for over a century. He actually found it just as it had been left by Napoleon's soldiers when they pillaged the monastery in 1808.

'They thought the monks had hidden sacred vessels or other treasures in the vault, so they smashed the two coffins and threw away the bones they found inside, furious at finding nothing else. They also tore up the pavement of the vault and dug all about underneath hoping to come upon some treasures. The bones were afterwards collected by a lay-brother, but only a part of them could be found—that is, the skull of King John and some of his bones. These were carried back to the vault and merely laid in a heap on a bare stone and there they had remained ever since'.

One of his first tasks on his arrival was to have the vault repaired and the bones placed in a strong brass-bound cypress-wood chest made for the purpose. It is pleasant to reflect that Spain owes this act of piety to an Englishman.

For very English, as his visitors and correspondents know, Dom Edmund remained—surprisingly so when one bears in mind how, year in, year out, he saw practically nothing of his compatriots. I suppose the explanation lies partly in the strength of his personality and partly in the fact that, as a Carthusian, he mixed so little with his fellows that he never became assimilated either to the French or to the Spanish. It probably meant little to him, that, when the Second Republic passed the Law of Religious Confessions and Congregations, forbidding foreigners to be superiors of religious communities, he had to become naturalized as a Spaniard; certainly it affected him far less than the straits in which the Orders found themselves. 'The law,' he wrote,

'will strangle them by a series of prohibitions and vexations, unbearable impositions, which, if they are carried out to the letter will go far to make life next to impossible for them. It will certainly do so for teaching Orders, which will be reduced to absolute in-activity and powerlessness to pursue their vocation. There is more than enough, I won't say to make us despair, for that is not a word to be used by those who know God . . . but certainly to occupy our minds to the full and make our hearts heavy with sorrow.'

Rather to his surprise, he found himself, during the Republican years, becoming very markedly *persona grata* to an anti-clerical municipality. This was due to the understanding way in which he distributed the alms provided from the funds of the monastery. He had always been fond of giving, especially to children: at Montalegre he was well known as a purveyor of sweets to the poor children of a summer holiday camp held in the district, and at Miraflores the children of a similar colony welcomed his visits 'with screams of delight', knowing they invariably meant 'sweets or cakes' and occasionally 'concerts with a portable gramophone', including 'military and bull-fight marches, Aragonese jotas and other dances and popular songs'. Sometimes, too, he would go down to the Burgos prison and give his concerts there or provide meals for 'those poor fellows with no work set them to do, no occupation of any sort, so that the hours and days drag along heavily'. Another of his routine activities was the distribution of soup on great festi-vals outside the monastery door. The day on which I generally brought my students over was the Feast of the Assumption, and again and again I have watched the long trail of poor folk climbing up the steep hill from Burgos to receive their allowance of food from the Prior's own hands.

But the charity which won for Dom Edmund from a Republican City Council the honours of a Cruz de Beneficencia and a bronze tablet recording the city's gratitude was of quite another kind. Strongly though he felt and wrote about a government 'on the verge of bankruptcy', which, as he saw it, 'economically, socially and religiously', was 'leading the country to rack and ruin', he collaborated with the municipality not only in the selection of charitable institutions for help, without which at least one of them could not have remained solvent, but also in finding ways to check the alarming increase of unemployment. Burgos, at that time, was a poorer city than it is now; improvements and new buildings were sorely needed, but there was no money to pay for them. Much of that money was provided by Miraflores.

So, when on All Saints' Eve, 1933, Dom Edmund was about to celebrate the golden jubilee of his profession, he found that the city councillors, out of their sincere respect and warm regard for him, wanted to celebrate it too.

But it was not in this atmosphere of affectionate gratitude—'living terribly in the limelight' he called it—that Dom Edmund was to end his career. In April 1934, when he was just seventy, the General Chapter relieved him of his priorship and sent him as a simple monk to the famous Charterhouse of Pavia, in North Italy —a huge florid edifice, far more thronged with tourists than Miraflores had ever been, set in flat, dull, featureless country, unpleasantly warm in summer and unpleasantly damp all the year round. Dom Edmund's account of the place, written soon after his arrival, is worth quoting:

'Yes, this monastery is very sumptuous—one of the great wonders of Italy. . . . I knew that before coming here, and yet I had no idea of how very gorgeous the place really is; what I have seen surpasses immensely what I had imagined. In the church there is an inconceivable profusion of marbles and precious stones of every sort and hue, of marble statues and altar-frontals and medallions in high and low relief, oil-paintings and frescoes by well-known Italian masters, etc., etc., and the cloisters and other parts of the monastery have also been built on a splendid scale in accordance with the church. The whole place, both in size and in splendour of style, is just the opposite of what a Carthusian monastery should be. Indeed it ought not to be considered as a monastery at all, but rather as a museum, and that is precisely what the Italian Government considers it to be and nothing else. It was founded A.D. 1396, expressly for our Order, by John Galeazzo Visconti, Duke of Milan. While the building was going on, the Superiors of the Order, apprised of the magnificence of the style, were displeased, and the General Chapter one year remonstrated with the founder on the subject. He is reported to have answered: "I am building, not to please you, but to please myself, and I shall build as I like", and he went on with the work without heeding our complaint. When it was finished, the Order unhappily accepted the monastery. It was a mistake. I don't think the monks of my Order ought to have accepted such a place as this built in absolute defiance of all that monastic poverty requires.'

In the late nineteenth century, a poverty-stricken Italian government offered to sell the Carthusians their own building, which some years before one of its predecessors had taken from them. The General of the day refused the offer with proper scorn. But in 1931 an agreement was come to by which the Order leased part of the monastery for a period of twenty-nine years, the State keeping the rest so as to continue making money out of it through sightseers. The result was deplorable. Church, sacristies and parts of the cloisters were open to the public and it was impossible for the monks to keep the whole of their rule:

'On our way to and from the choir and other places we have very often to pass through groups of visitors of both sexes, and while we are singing office in choir we are frequently disturbed by the deafening noise they make in the nave and transept close to the choir. Sightseers of every description and country come here every year in their hundreds and thousands.

'Pray for us', he begged in November 1935; 'we are now thirteen choir-monks and four lay-brothers, completely lost in the vastness of this huge pile of buildings.'

But nevertheless, he had testified nine months earlier, 'my days here are flowing by very peacefully'.

'I am feeling more and more grateful to God for His having freed me from the heavy responsibility and manifold anxieties and worries which necessarily attend the discharge of an office like the Priorship. No employment of any sort has been given me here, so I am completely "au repos" and am most of the day shut up in my cell in utter solitude, all alone with God and my thoughts and my rich store of memories of the past. My books also keep me company. They are dear friends. . . . I read a good deal; I also pray a great deal, more, I think, than I have ever done before. I do also a certain amount of manual work, keeping my cell clean, tending my little garden, and sawing and chopping wood for the stove. Time never lags with me, nor has it ever done so. I have never in all my life known what ennui is. I find my days always too short. My life is indeed monotonous, but its monotony is only exterior, on the surface; my inward life, which is the soul's real life, is far from being monotonous; it is as variegated as a kaleidoscope. *Benedictus Deus in saecula!*'

It was in those tranquil surroundings, contrasting so tragically with the chaos of the Civil War which for two and a half years ravaged Spain and the subsequent thunder of the guns in France, that Dom Edmund spent his last six years. Despite his inward peacefulness, there is reason to believe that he felt his exile very keenly. Both Montalegre and Montserrat had been among the monasteries sacked in Spain and in each community there were monks who had been murdered. Dom Edmund also missed the robust personalities of his monks in Castile and the sound of the virile language of his adopted country. When I wrote, early in 1939, to tell him that I had started to translate the works of Saint Teresa, he was frankly delighted, and started to read her works all over again. 'She is one of my favourite saints', he wrote. 'I like so much her practical common sense and sound judgment. . . . She is to me a sympathetic saint, which all are not.'[1] Her Castilian, too—vivid, racy, elliptical, picturesque, dramatic—was exactly the Castilian he had been hearing all around him during his fourteen years in Burgos. 'What a peculiar and strong charm her style has!', he wrote to me. 'You relish it to the full as soon as you have got over the first difficulties of her phraseology.' Her works have 'delighted me more than ever'.

All his letters from Italy, I noticed, even in their more intimate form of subscription—'yours very affectionately'—tended to be more personal than those from Spain. The slow but steady though gradual approach of the World War saddened him. He never had any illusions about Munich: 'A sop has been given to the German wolf to keep him quiet for a bit. But afterwards?' 'And now the war has entered on a new phase', he wrote to me on 16th May 1940, 'and only God knows what we are heading for in Europe. May the Lord have mercy upon us'.

One further letter I received, after Italy's entry into the War, of necessity by a roundabout route, and then no more. In the spring of 1941 came a letter from the Prior of Pavia telling of his death. After he had said his Mass on the morning of the preceding

---

[1] This quotation, which could be reinforced by others, clearly disproves Dom Michael Hanbury's statement (*Pax* (Spring, 1943), p. 19) that Dom Edmund 'did not class her [Saint Teresa] among his favourites'.

8th October, the Father Vicar had called at his cell and found him unconscious. There was just time to anoint him before he slipped quietly away. Lover of simplicity as he always was, he would have wished nothing more than so simple a passing.

[III]

It is difficult to convey in words anything of the vivid impression which one retains of Dom Edmund's remarkable personality. He was neither an original writer nor a deep thinker, yet all he wrote was worth reading and all he said worth listening to. There was something about him which would have given distinction to the merest platitudes, and, had he said nothing at all, one would have gone away the better for his company. Going to see him bore a distinct similarity to going into retreat; one approached him receptively, said little oneself and left him the richer for having come. 'It was not anything he *said* that helped me, but what he is', wrote someone whom I had sent to see him at a time of deep distress. What I found in him myself was chiefly saintliness, which showed itself in small things as well as in great ones.

Take, for example, his attitude to culture, and in particular to literature. He had neither a highly educated taste nor a critical temperament. He knew what he liked—and disliked: 'I don't care for it a bit' is a phrase which frequently characterizes his references to poetry. He liked poetry; and, having had an excellent rote memory, had learned masses of it by heart in his boyhood. He had even written it a good deal, though few people knew that. But his favourite poet, in the English language, was Longfellow, with Adelaide Anne Procter ('I can't think why Q. excluded her from the *Oxford Book of English Verse*') a good second. I know no one else with such rudimentary tastes whom I could even bear to listen to on the subject. But I would draw out Dom Edmund, as one draws out a child, for the joy of savouring an enthusiasm born of piety.

Or take scholarship. He had not had a scholar's training, and was largely self-taught. But he had a scholar's instincts, which, as I see it, bear the most intimate relation to the attributes of saintliness. 'I have found some of the problems very tough ones', he wrote to me once about some textual difficulties in the works of Saint John of the Cross. 'I have had to ask the help of my Procurator, an intelligent Spanish monk, but he finds it no easier than

I do.... He guesses and surmises from the context what the meaning ought to be—a thing which I can do myself.' But he never did
do it himself. With a true scholar's perseverance and love of exactness, he would 'pore and pore'—to quote from his letters once
again—and he never abandoned a problem till he was satisfied
that his interpretation was at least tenable.

On a higher plane, the quality in him which most attracted one
—in so far as one can isolate individual qualities from the living
combination of them all—was his deep spirituality. His approach
to any question, even a trivial one, was the approach of the man of
God. In a famous phrase, he lived in the world as though there
were in it but God and his soul. His attitude, in particular, to
miracles and supernatural phenomena was identical with the
attitude of that most spiritual of saints, Saint John of the Cross.
I remember once discussing with him some lines of that saint
which, he said, touched a deep chord in his soul:

'He, then, that has supernatural gifts and graces ought to withdraw himself from desiring to practise them, and from joy in so
doing, nor ought he to care to exercise them; for God, who gives
Himself to such persons, by supernatural means, for the profit of
His Church and of its members, will move them likewise supernaturally in such a manner and at such time as He desires. . . .

'Those, then, who love to rejoice in these supernatural works
lose much in the matter of faith.'[1]

So unquestioning was his own faith that no supernatural experience could increase it; so keen was his sense of God's infinite
greatness that no miracle could intensify it. 'I wouldn't cross the
road to see one', he once said. The following incident, told by a
relative of Dom Edmund's and reproduced by Dom Michael
Hanbury, is most characteristic of him:

'He had been Prior of Miraflores for several years when it happened, and no member of the community had died during that
time. Then a choir monk died and, on the same day, two lay
brothers were sent out to dig his grave. Dom Edmund explained
to me that Carthusians are buried on the planks which have been
their bed, without a coffin, and that only a nameless wooden cross
is put on their graves, with the exception of the Generals of the
Order. You know how old Miraflores is, so there are a great many
monks buried in the cemetery. Dom Edmund was in his cell that

[1] Saint John of the Cross, *Ascent of Mount Carmel*, III, xxxi.

afternoon, when the two lay brothers arrived in a very excited state, and begged him to come to the cemetery at once. One of them had a spade in his hand, on which there were fresh blood-stains. Dom Edmund said his first thought was that there had been an accident of some kind. But when they could speak coherently they told him that they had dug down to a depth of about six feet, when one of their spades struck again something soft, and, when it was pulled out, had blood on it. Very much astonished, they put it down, and with their spades gradually uncovered the body of a young man. There was no sign of his habit, nor of any planks, but his tonsure was there, and blood was running from a wound in his arm. "He looked as if he was asleep." They had left him un-touched, and come to tell Dom Edmund so that he should see the miracle. "But I told them I wasn't going to the cemetery", said Dom Edmund. "Of course, I believed them, and I would have done so even if there had not been blood on the spade." "What *did* you do?" I asked, and I remember his answer quite clearly. "I said, there are many saints in the Carthusian Order. Cover him up again and give him a cross, so that he won't be disturbed any more."

The passages in Dom Edmund's letters most prized by his corre-spondents seem to have been those about suffering. No readers of these lines are likely to hold the belief, so common among the un-instructed, that men and women enter the cloister to live a shel-tered life in which suffering can have no part. But few would de-duce from the description I have given of him that suffering was Dom Edmund's close companion. 'I have suffered somewhat in my body,' he wrote, 'but immensely more in mind and heart—afflictions of many sorts, many of which had no remedy.' But, he added, 'I have never been a single day really unhappy—that is, discontented with my lot'. 'Never for a single moment have I . . . regretted having taken up the Cross.' 'One of the lessons I have learned in the cloister, and one which I value most, is that suffering need not necessarily impede happiness, but may even contribute to it and increase it.'

And the way to learn that lesson? He tells us that, too:

'Lose yourself in Him, lose yourself in the Saviour's loved Spouse, the Church. . . . By letting your thoughts dwell on the ever-lasting Goodness and Beauty, that picture will print itself on your soul.'

Finally, no account of Dom Edmund, however brief, can omit his views on holy poverty, the subject of some of his most impressive and forceful conversations and of some of his longest letters. 'If there is one thing the world dreads and abhors,' he would say, 'it is poverty. There are few who do not wish to be, and aim at being, as well-to-do as they can. When people in the world talk of "promotion", it is nearly always an improvement of their financial position that they are thinking of. And anyone who has the so-called misfortune to lose money is considered the unhappiest of men.' Poverty, he held, was not only a great leveller, but a great teacher. 'I cannot but encourage you', he wrote to a nun, 'to love poverty ardently, to love it in all its aspects, all its manifestations, to love it all the more in that nowadays it is very little loved, not only in the world but elsewhere also. What a splendid book could be written on God's and Christ's love and esteem for poverty and the poor!'

But the most characteristic part of his views on poverty concerned the religious Orders. The craze for being 'well off'—'la maladie de la pierre'—has invaded the cloister. 'Who is it', he asks, 'that said of these stately monasteries that one sees nowadays, "They are the ruins of the vow of poverty"?' He would quote with approval passages from Saint Teresa's *Way of Perfection* and *Foundations* which develop this theme.

'It seems very wrong, my daughters, that great houses should be built with the money of the poor; may God forbid that this should be done; let our houses be small and poor in every way. . . . As for a large, ornate convent, with a lot of buildings—God preserve us from that! Always remember that these things will all fall down on the Day of Judgment, and who knows how soon that will be?'[1]

'O God, how little have buildings and outward comforts to do with the inward life of the soul! For love of Him, I beg you, my sisters and fathers, never to be other than very modest in this matter of large and sumptuous houses. Let us bear in mind . . . those holy Fathers from whom we are descended, for we know it was the road of poverty and humility which they took that led them to the fruition of God.'[2]

'Those sentiments,' he wrote, with unwonted (and quite Teresan) emphasis, 'are mine entirely, entirely.'

The monastic life should be, as regards poverty, 'the life of

[1] Saint Teresa of Jesus, *Way of Perfection*, II.   [2] *Foundations*, XIV.

decent working folk, not the comfortable life of gentlepeople', and communities sufficiently endowed to assure the maintenance of that standard 'would do well to refuse all additions to their real estate whenever it is possible for them to do so'. On one occasion, when holding the office of prior, he had the opportunity of putting his opinions into practice. One of his monks, who came from a wealthy family, wanted to buy the community a property of considerable size adjoining the monastery. 'As we had no need whatever of it,' wrote the Prior, 'I would not listen to his proposal but point blank rejected it; I consented only to receive a sum of money to be expended in alms to the poor. That', he added, 'is my way of thinking and acting, in that respect, but I am aware that very few monks share my opinion. Poor Dame Poverty is decidedly out of favour nowadays in many places where she ought to be honoured and to hold full sway.'

It would be appalling to think of a man who wrote and acted thus spending his last days in the vast and sumptuous charterhouse of Pavia, were it not clear to those who read of him, and clearer still to those who knew him, that, far from impairing his interior life, contact with wealth and display could only enhance and refine his Christlike poverty of spirit.

Index

(Main references are given in heavy type)